Theatre History Studies

2017 VOLUME 36

Edited by
SARA FREEMAN

PUBLISHED BY THE MID-AMERICA THEATRE CONFERENCE
AND THE UNIVERSITY OF ALABAMA PRESS

Manufactured in the United States of America

Template Design: Todd Lape / Lape Designs
Production by Publications Unit, Department of English, Illinois State University
Production Director: Steve Halle
Production Intern: Abby Keim

Essays appearing in this journal are abstracted and indexed in
Historical Abstracts and America: History and Life

∞
The paper on which this book is printed meets the minimum requirements
of American National Standard for Information Sciences-Permanence of
Paper for Printed Library Materials, ANSI Z39.48-1984.

MEMBER
CELJ
Council of Editors of Learned Journals

Cover Art
"The hostile press and the consequences of crim. con., or, Shakspeare in danger." Robert Cruikshank, artist, published by J. Fairburn, Broadway, Ludgate Hill, London, 1825. Folger Shakespeare Library Collection

Cover Design
Todd Lape / Lape Designs

Please note: there was no issue published in 2013.

Theatre History Studies is an official journal of the Mid-America Theatre Conference, Inc. (MATC). The conference is dedicated to the growth and improvement of all forms of theatre throughout a twelve-state region that includes the states of Illinois, Iowa, Nebraska, Kansas, Missouri, Minnesota, North Dakota, South Dakota, and Wisconsin. Its purposes are to unite people and organizations within this region and elsewhere who have an interest in theatre and to promote the growth and development of all forms of theatre.

Theatre History Studies is devoted to research in all areas of theatre studies. Manuscripts should be prepared in conformity with the guidelines established in the *Chicago Manual of Style* and e-mailed to Sara Freeman at sfreeman@pugetsound.edu. Consulting editors read the manuscripts, a process that takes approximately four months. The journal does not normally accept studies of dramatic literature unless there is a focus on actual production and performance. Authors whose manuscripts are accepted must provide the editor with an electronic file, using Microsoft Word. Illustrations are welcomed and should conform with the instructions listed on the style guide on the website: http://matc.us/theatre-history-studies-4/theatre-history-studies-the-matc-journal.

This publication is issued annually by the Mid-America Theatre Conference and The University of Alabama Press.

Subscription rates for 2017 are $25 for individuals, $35 for institutions, and an additional $10 for foreign delivery. Subscription orders and changes of address should be directed to Allie Harper, The University of Alabama Press, Box 870380, Tuscaloosa, AL 35487; (205) 348-1564 phone; (205) 348-9201 fax.

Any single current-year issue or back issue is $34.95 each if ordered through the Chicago Distribution Center. (Please note: there was no issue published in 2013.)

Theatre History Studies is indexed in *Humanities Index, Humanities Abstracts, Book Review Index, MLA International Bibliography, International Bibliography of Theatre & Dance, Arts & Humanities Citation Index, IBZ International Bibliography of Periodical Literature*, and *IBR International Bibliography of Book Reviews*, the database of *International Index to the Performing Arts*. Full texts of essays appear in the databases of both *Humanities Abstracts Full Text* and *SIRS*. The journal has published its own index, *The Twenty Year Index, 1981–2000*. It is available for $10 for individuals and $15 for libraries from Sara Freeman, Associate Professor, Theatre Arts CMB 1084, University of Puget Sound, 1500 N. Warner St., Tacoma, WA 98416; (253) 879-2438.

CONTENTS

CONTENTS

CONTENTS

PART IV
BOOK REVIEWS

CONTENTS

ILLUSTRATIONS

Introduction

—SARA FREEMAN

Theatre History Studies is an annual journal. We print one issue per year, and we assemble it almost a year in advance. I write this introduction in the immediate aftermath of the 2016 US presidential election and I find it hard to project what commentary might be the most applicable in the fall of 2017. The scholarship in this issue resonates with several developments that dominate the global political sphere, such as upheaval in conservative and liberal social positions and tactics, ongoing debates about national identity, new contours of generational conflict, upsurges in student activism, and resistance to or embrace of change, in any format.

Laura Ferdinand Feldmeyer's documentation and analysis about a key line of dialogue in the play adaptation of *Peter Pan*—"to die will be an awfully big adventure"—unfolds J. M. Barrie's history of writing war propaganda during World War I and his change of heart about the project of war in relationship to the Western cultural imaginary about masculinity and adventure. Feldmeyer tracks how the line was included or excluded from performances of the play and the treatment of the line both onstage and off while investigating the great generational divide operative in both the experiences of the Great War and its aftermath. Attending to that divide transforms *Peter Pan* from a delightful, uplifting piece of theatre to an elegiac one. That unsettled, simultaneously childish and mournful status of *Peter Pan* is still reflected in contemporary theatre made in adaptational dialogue with Barrie's tale, including *Peter and the Starcatcher*, Sarah Ruhl's 2016 play *For Peter Pan on Her 70th Birthday*, and Sally Cookson's production of *Peter Pan* appearing at the Bristol Old Vic and the National Theatre in London across the end of 2016 and the beginning of 2017. It is still unclear, in the wake of a UK vote to "Brexit" the European Union and of the election of

Donald Trump to the US presidency, what masculinity means and if our societies are willing to grow up.

Feldmeyer begins her article by considering a 1922 address Barrie gave to students at St. Andrew's University about youth and age. La Donna Forsgren's Schanke Award-winning paper from the 2016 Mid-America Theatre Conference also takes college campuses as the loci of its analysis and makes a diachronic link between black student activism in the 1960s and the 2010s, especially as such activism used performative demonstrations at Northwestern in 1968 and the University of Missouri (Mizzou) in 2015. In doing so, Forsgren also recovers the history of Black Folks's Theatre at Northwestern University, which was formed as the artistic branch of For Members Only, the Northwestern black student union founded in the wake of 1968 campus protests. Forsgren connects Black Folks's Theatre to the Black Arts Movement, strengthening our theatre-historical sense of how the artistic branches of social movements participate to bring about institutional change.

Julie Jackson's article explicating the practices of "Chicago-style theatre" and what the phrase denotes about acting technique, approach to staging, or audience experience follows not only how theatre interacts with institutional change but also how insurgent theatres become institutions. Her history of the Chicago theatre as "not just rock 'n' roll" gives new depth of understanding to the style characteristic of the artist-operated ensemble theatres that define Chicago's scene. At once a close reading of press discourse about Chicago theatre, a personal history drawn from four decades of watching and making theatre in Chicago, and a cataloging of key companies in Chicago theatre beyond the highly mythologized Steppenwolf, Jackson's scholarship provides a sophisticated analysis of the dynamics of realism and artifice at work in Chicago theatre aesthetics.

Likewise, Gabrielle Houle wrestles with "style"—a combination of realism and artifice in performance techniques—while revealing the struggles with mask work experienced by twentieth-century commedia dell'arte star Marcello Moretti. Houle's masterful set of propositions about the challenges a mask presents a performer and her materialist attention to the role of mask-makers and mask-making techniques in helping performers reclaim the mask culminates with insight about the role of "nonhuman collaborators" in performance and the slow return to the historical practice of wearing masks for commedia after two centuries of being out of favor in performance. This essay turns on the recovery of a historical practice and its remaking in twentieth-century theatre in the service of vitalizing or freeing a different set of artistic energies.

David Donkor's article on theatre architecture in postindependence Ghana also records artists recovering a part of historical theatre practice: that of building a flexible performance space in the round (a "circular-complete house"). The first theatre building of Ghana's new national theatre movement, the Ghana Experimental Drama Studio, was inspired by communal housing complexes of the Akan people of Ghana and reflected the spatial concept *gyase*, which links human existence to ancestral attachments grounded in place. In his contextual history of that building, Donkor establishes pioneering postindependence theatremaker Efua Sutherland's choices about theatre architecture as part of a vividly debated Pan-Africanist conversation and the simultaneous project of building postcolonial national consciousness in Ghana.

Importantly, Donkor also explores Sutherland's playwriting for the Studio as part of his history of the space and his discussion of the role of national theatres. This thread of his article connects with the focus of this issue's special section, namely, histories of new writing for the theatre. As unfolded in the section introduction and the eight wide-ranging articles, the times and places where a particular confluence of focus on the creation of new plays or the encouragement of new artists to write for theatre pinpoint eras where theatre's role in a nation or culture is in active negotiation, whether because of changing demographics, new approaches to forms and styles, or experiments with modes of collaboration and spectatorship. This special section endeavors to do history about the creation of plays and probes the role of playwriting in theatre structures like companies or cultural economies, struggling with both writing and newness as functional and conceptual drivers of artistic production.

The studies in this issue predominantly excavate a particular style, space, controversy, or event. *Theatre History Studies* may be blessedly able to be microcosmic and documentary of theatre and performance: it is a journal in the field of theatre and performance studies where we are as historical as we want to be. But as the scholarship in this issue demonstrates, theatre is made in the world and for the world. And that world is frequently unstable, full of contradiction, and constantly remaking parts of its past. The work of theatre history therefore strives not only not to forget but also to create anew our understanding of both the past and the present.

Part I

STUDIES IN THEATRE HISTORY

Resisting Arlecchino's Mask

The Case of Marcello Moretti

—GABRIELLE HOULE

In 1951, Paduan sculptor and mask-maker Amleto Sartori delivered a commedia mask to the Piccolo Teatro of Milan.[1] As he ventured into the rehearsal hall, he saw an actor performing acrobatics with a very large rifle. It was Marcello Moretti (Venice 1910–Rome 1961), for whom he had made the mask and who was currently rehearsing the part of Arlecchino for a production of Goldoni's *L'amante militare*, directed by Giorgio Strehler.[2] Moretti tried the mask on during the rehearsal, but quickly lost his temper. Sartori remembers, "He was furious like a wild colt forced to wear the bridle for the first time," and adds that Moretti exclaimed, "'I cannot act with this thing on my nose, it hurts me, I cannot see' and he slammed the mask on the ground."[3] What started as a disagreement, however, turned into an enduring professional relationship between Sartori, Strehler, and Moretti that led them to successfully reimagine the commedia tradition after World War II.

Although Marcello Moretti played at least forty-four roles at the Piccolo Teatro of Milan, as well as many other roles for other theatre companies, he is best known for his interpretation of Arlecchino in Strehler's productions of *The Servant of Two Masters*.[4] Strehler staged ten different productions of that play at the Piccolo Teatro between 1947 and 1997.[5] By 1997, these stagings had been performed 2,394 times in 36 countries.[6] Over the years, and through unprecedented exposure in Italy and around the world, these productions revived scholars' interest in the performance history of the commedia dell'arte and arguably became the most influential models for artists to follow, emulate, learn from, and sometimes challenge. Marcello Moretti played the central character in the first three of Strehler's productions of *The Servant of Two Masters*, between 1947 and 1960.[7] His performance was seen hundreds of times, touring across Italy and in another twenty-six countries, on three continents, reaching thousands of spectators.[8] The international press hailed him as "the greatest Arlecchino of the 1900s," the "Italian Clown Prince," the "Italian Charlie Chaplin," and the "Universal Arlequin."[9] In *Tricks of the Trade*, Dario Fo crowned him "the father-figure of all Harlequins of the last half-century."[10] Luigi Ferrante even compared him to Antonio Sacchi, the famous Arlecchino-Truffaldino for whom Goldoni initially wrote *The Servant of Two Masters*.[11]

Arlecchino and his mask followed Moretti throughout his career. As Jacques Lecoq recalls: "Moretti was shy, and I often met him in a little restaurant behind the dome for lunch. He had his mask in his pocket, and from time to time he took it out to look at it, to touch it, he lived with it."[12] "The mask was for Moretti equivalent to the character," Guy Freixe claims, adding, "[It signified] its concrete presence. He knew that it was stronger than the actor, and able to outlive him."[13] By the end of his career, Moretti felt vulnerable without the mask and wondered what would happen to him when he would no longer be fit to play Arlecchino. Yet, he refused to wear a solid mask in Strehler's first staging of *The Servant of Two Masters* in 1947. Instead, he painted his face to reflect the image of the character, using dark, wax-based makeup. Only in 1952 did Moretti start wearing a solid mask in this production.[14]

The purpose of this article is not to explain how Moretti overcame his resistance to the mask and became one of the most influential Arlecchinos of the last century. Rather, it investigates why he refused to wear a mask in the first place.[15] This account of Moretti's experience will, I hope, fill a gap in the study of contemporary stagings of the commedia dell'arte by focusing on the performance practice of a single actor whose career has been overlooked in English-speaking scholarship, largely because it is often discussed only in relationship with the lives and works of other artists (such as Giorgio Strehler and Amleto Sartori) and because of a language barrier (Moretti gave few interviews, none of them in English, probably because he did not speak it). In 1962, the Piccolo Teatro of Milan issued a collection of essays celebrating Moretti, and in 2002–3 Silvia Cacco wrote a dissertation about him.[16] Both works are in Italian.[17]

This article is based on archival research at the Piccolo Teatro of Milan and at the Centro Maschere e Strutture Gestuali in Abano Terme. Documents consulted include but are not limited to theatre programs for different stagings of *The Servant of Two Masters* at the Piccolo Teatro, a video recording of Strehler's second staging of the play with Moretti in the title role, publications by Silvio D'Amico about masks, makeup, and the commedia dell'arte, and dissertations about Moretti and Ferruccio Soleri, Moretti's successor in the role of Arlecchino at the Piccolo Teatro. I also examined theatre reviews of *The Servant of Two Masters* published between 1947 and 1997 in Italian, French, English, Spanish, and German to get descriptions of what audiences saw onstage over the years. Most reviews published between 1947 and 1960 discussed Moretti's acting, those published in 1952 and after sometimes mentioned his mask, and all of them helped me understand how his performance was received. I also consulted publications about Moretti, Strehler, Amleto and Donato Sartori, the Piccolo Teatro's history, the commedia dell'arte during Goldoni's time, and masked work in Europe during the first half of the twentieth century. I synthesize this research in this article to provide context to Moretti's first theatrical experiences and to explain the practical, psychological, and historical reasons that prompted him to initially refuse to wear a solid mask. Finally, I did a series of interviews with theatre practitioners who worked with the Piccolo Teatro, with Giorgio Strehler, and in some cases with Marcello Moretti.[18] I chose to include long citations from the sources listed above because many have not been translated into English elsewhere. I did so not only to give a voice to the people whose stories this article examines and uses but also to provide material in English to theatre practitioners and historians interested in the topic. Unless otherwise indicated in the notes, most translations from French and Italian into English are mine.

Marcello Moretti: Background, Training, and Early Influences

Marcello Moretti was born in 1910 in Venice, to a working-class family.[19] Before finding a vocation in the theatre, Moretti tried several trades, from elevator operator to traveling salesman, and from postman to electrician.[20] Those who would become his colleagues and close friends in the theatre would never precisely know what initially sparked his interest in the performing arts. He was almost twenty-eight when he enrolled in the Accademia nazionale d'arte drammatica in Rome, the first state theatre school in Italy. This school offered a rigorous and comprehensive vocational training for actors and directors. Moretti was a student there from 1938 to 1940.[21]

The accademia was founded in 1936 by Silvio d'Amico, who remained its artistic director until 1954.[22] The school's primary objective, as Gian Giacomo Colli posits, was "to introduce the interpretative and organizational rigour that was already established in other parts of Europe."[23] Until the first part of the twentieth century, the Italian stage was ruled by the *capocomico* (the actor-manager of a theatre company). Günter Berghaus reports on this practice: "[The] center of attraction was never the play, but the star actor or actress. . . . It was not the actor who had to adapt to the role, but rather the role was adapted to the star. Texts were often changed beyond recognition."[24] Several actors (such as Eleonora Duse) were born into the profession, and while there were schools of declamation and acting in the peninsula, many professional players did not have any formal training. Instead, they learned their craft by trial and error in performance, through apprenticeships, and by emulating the techniques and style of other performers. Rehearsals were generally short, ranging from one to two weeks for a lead actor, depending on whether the role was comic or serious; commercial success was paramount to the survival of companies; and plays by foreign authors, especially French *pièces bien faites*, were highly ranked in their repertoire.[25] Troupes were, for the most part, nomadic enterprises—they often did not have a permanent home and needed to tour for a living.[26] "At the end of the nineteenth century," Marvin Carlson writes, "the greatest concern in the Italian theatre was the establishment of a permanent company or companies to give focus and stability to the Italian stage."[27] This concern remained central to Italy's theatre discourse during the first half of the twentieth century.

In 1919, Silvio D'Amico proposed to create a Teatro d'Arte (a theatre of art) modeled after foreign companies, such as the Comédie-Française. He laid out the necessary features of such a theatre in two articles dated September 27, 1919, and October 4, 1919, respectively. "Theatre of Art doesn't necessarily mean State Theatre," D'Amico specifies in the second article: "In a few words, theatre of art should have no purpose other than to *take the control of the stage away from actors, [and] bring them back to their role of interpreters*."[28] Under the new model, the management of theatre companies would no longer be left to actors. Instead, the administration would be delegated to an artistic director who would work with one or more *metteurs en scène*. These metteurs en scène would be responsible for choosing plays, assigning parts, directing actors, "outlin[ing] their tasks to set designers, costume makers and stagehands," and serving the playtext and the author's vision "religiously."[29] To exist and thrive, the theatre of art would have to be supported by the State. It would also require a new kind of actor and a new school to train them. This school, D'Amico recommended, should inculcate "respect of the text, [and] love of great poetry" to future actors.[30] Its curriculum would include voice and speech delivery, movement, dance, fencing, and music. It should also include history of theatre, history of costume, history of set design, art history, and courses in dramatic literature.[31] Such were the blueprints of the Accademia nazionale d'arte drammatica.

According to Raul Radice, who succeeded D'Amico as director of the accademia, Carlo Goldoni's work stood high in the school's curriculum; a cold reading of a scene by Goldoni was often part of the entry audition, his plays were studied in class and performed during public examinations in the first and second years, and staging full-length plays by Goldoni was not uncommon for students of directing.[32] While Goldoni's work was valued at the school, it seems that masked performance in the commedia tradition was not. At least, this is what the following comment by D'Amico suggests:

> It is perfectly true that the primitive actor, in order to "become someone else," appealed to the mask. This strategy is explained by recalling how, for many centuries, the setting of theatre performances was the outdoors, where for obvious reasons very registered features were needed. And our commedia dell'arte actors held on to the mask: not only because the commedia dell'arte originated in the open, but above all because the actor, wearing it, intended to become a stylized "character type," fixed once and for all.
>
> As it moved from outdoor to indoor settings, the theatre performance acquired an intimate aspect, for which the conventional, puppet-like immobility of the mask was no longer appropriate. This is how the actor's mimicry, until then expressed through the entire body, was preferentially directed to the face, which is forever the seat of the most elevated human expressions. Furthermore, with the transformation of the characters and of their personalities it became essential that the actors' faces change each time, and this made necessary the use of makeup: the modern tool par excellence, which in modern times has produced excellent results.[33]

While it was published almost a decade after Moretti's first encounter with D'Amico, and though the context in which it was published suggests that it had been written to promote either a makeup school or a makeup course associated with the accademia, the text quoted above implies that D'Amico found masks incompatible with modern acting techniques and production conditions. Moreover, D'Amico—who advocated for a theatre of authors, the respect of the text, and the director's authority over the star-actor—would have been suspicious of the histrionic connotations of the commedia masks and their association with "character types" and extempore creations. In all likelihood, the subtle and ever-changing expressions of the actor's face would have won over solid masks at the accademia.

Soon after his training, Moretti started working as an actor.[34] In 1944, he played Truffaldino in Alberto D'Aversa's staging of Goldoni's *Servant of Two Masters* at the accademia. Little has been written on this production, but according to Alberto Perrini, Moretti's performance in it broke away from "dated" interpretations of Goldoni and instead explored the idea of the "well-rounded" actor who could be "mime, acrobat, musician, dancer, [and] super-marionette" all at once.[35] The actor did not perform with a solid mask in this production. Instead, he painted a "glossy black mask" on his face.[36] This was not an isolated case on Italian stages at the time. During the first half of the twentieth century, Italian actors sometimes performed commedia characters with a solid mask, sometimes with a thick makeup imitating a mask, and sometimes without a mask at all. The reasons for this interpretative "flexibility" vary. In his 1699 *Treatise on Acting, from Memory and by Improvisation*, Andrea Perrucci explained how solid masks may be used for "buffoons and comic types."[37] These masks, he informed readers, are made of colored "cloth or papier-mâché, and wax," and, in the case of old men and magicians, are often complete with beards and wigs.[38] While useful to actors playing more than one character, Perrucci warned that masks should not be used for the parts of furies or demons when they contain long speeches "so as not to hamper the breathing nor the pronunciation."[39] Actors in these roles would instead paint their face with lead-based makeup.[40] While shedding light on mask-making practices and design in the late seventeenth century, Perrucci's treatise also confirms that some of the period's performers chose not to wear solid masks for fear of hindering vocal production.[41]

Much like Perrucci and his actors, early twentieth-century Italian performers may have found it more convenient to speak a text without a mask. Others may not have owned solid masks. Others still may not have known how to act without the use of facial expressions, and given the short rehearsal periods typical of Italian productions during the first half of the 1900s, neophytes probably had little time to fully investigate masked performance techniques and conventions. It is also possible that some actors, because they wished to be easily recognized by their audience, simply refused to cover their face regardless of the role they played. Finally, many actors adopted a realistic acting style in performance, including in plays influenced by the commedia tradition. For example, Cesco Baseggio (1897–1971) and Ermete Zacconi (1857–1948) were two actors known for their naturalistic interpretation of Goldoni's plays.[42] Another example is found in Emilio Zago (1852–1929), a celebrated Pantalone whose style was described as "natural" by his contemporaries.[43]

Already in 1750, Carlo Goldoni had proposed reforming the Italian theatre by bringing it closer to nature. He presented the key elements of his reform in his play-manifesto *Il teatro comico*. The main features of his reform were: (1) the adoption of a new, realistic, and yet highly codified gestural vocabulary by the actors; (2) the memorization and the respect of a fully written text by the performers; (3) the almost complete abandonment of generic material and improvised pieces; (4) the independence of the playwright from Aristotelian rules when they interfere with verisimilitude; (5) the democratization of the language spoken onstage to reflect what can be observed in nature; and (6) the abandonment of solid masks. Goldoni elaborates:

> A mask should always remain an obstacle to the actor's actions, either in joy or in sadness; when he acts in love, shy or amused, it is the same old leather that we see, and though he gesticulates and changes tone, the actor never expresses with his face, which is the window to the heart, the various passions that move his soul. . . . Today, we want an actor with a soul [i.e., psychological depth], and the soul under the mask is like fire under ashes.
>
> This is why I had planned to reform the masks [i.e., characters] of Italian comedies, and to replace farces by plays.[44]

For playwright Carlo Gozzi, Goldoni's contemporary and his main adversary on the Venetian stage, Goldoni's reform program did no less than "cut the throat of the innocent *Commedia dell'Arte*."[45] And indeed, many of that period's actors could not submit to Goldoni's new playmaking principles. This was the case of the Sacchi troupe, for whom Goldoni initially wrote *The Servant of Two Masters* and whose "inability to adapt to scripts which were daily becoming less and less suitable for improvisation, or even to act without mask,. . . had relegated them to the margins of Venice's intense theatrical life."[46] For Goldoni, however, who advocated for the abandonment of farcical theatricality and for creating the illusion of reality onstage, it was essential for commedia dell'arte actors to memorize fully written texts, commit to a new acting style, and perform bareface. Those performers in the nineteenth and twentieth centuries who were acting commedia characters in a realistic manner and without a mask were therefore continuing a practice that Goldoni had initiated more than a hundred years earlier.

Despite the general preference for realism on early-twentieth-century Italian stages, there is evidence that actors performed both with and without masks, sometimes alongside each other. Photographs of Renato Simoni's 1940 staging of Goldoni's *Donne curiose* provide excellent examples of such "visual mixture."[47] In Simoni's production, Otello Cazzola (Brighella) and Francesco Rissone (Arlecchino) wore dark solid masks, while Antonio Crast (Pantalone) performed with a painted face imitating a mask. Marcello Moretti played Lelio in that show; he performed bareface.

What we know of Moretti's training and early career suggests that he had not been encouraged to engage in long-term research into masked performance before joining the Piccolo Teatro. In fact, his experience at the accademia may have taught him to be suspicious of solid masks. His participation in Simoni's and D'Aversa's productions, paired with the past two centuries of commedia dell'arte history in performance, confirmed that wearing a solid mask was not, after all, paramount to playing commedia characters. Masks, Moretti convinced himself, could conveniently be replaced by thick makeup.

The Masks

The poor quality of the first masks used at the Piccolo Teatro was yet another cause of Moretti's refusal to wear a mask. These masks were made of superposed layers of gauze and papier mâché; they hurt the actors and melted onto their faces in performance.[48] As Strehler recounts: "The masks were 'infernal,' impractical, painful. The parts in relief soon penetrated in the flesh, visibility was relative and distorted. Worn as they were so close to the face, with a primitive elastic system, deprived of flexibility, the masks did not allow the eyelids to move. The eyelashes of the actor touched the edges [of the mask] and made the eyes weep eternal and secret tears. . . . When the masks were being used, the actors' sweat penetrated the cardboard and little by little dissolved the solidity of the mask. At the end of the show, we were holding in our hands a few black rags, dripping with sweat, that returned to a certain shape and solidity only on the following day."[49] Not only were they uncomfortable, these objects also increased the risk of injuries in performance. The set of Strehler's first staging of *The Servant of Two Masters* comprised a raised platform, limited at the back by a painted backdrop and framed on the sides by three-faced rotating panels. This design, imagined by Gianni Ratto, was loosely inspired by eighteenth-century decor; it alluded to the trestle stages that early modern commedia companies set up in streets, halls, and marketplaces for performance; and it resembled a *castelet* for puppet theatre, an image that was reinforced by the players' marionette-like acting style in the 1947 production.

Ratto's set was not only metatheatrical but also designed with speedy traverse in mind. The trestle stage was 7.6 meters wide by 5 meters deep; players could easily cross it in a few steps, giving the illusion of covering a great distance in no time.[50] At the end of the second act, when Arlecchino serves a meal to both his masters at the same time, Moretti had to cross the stage back and forth in a matter of seconds, with his hands full of plates and faux food. Acceleration to reach frantic speed at that moment was key to displaying the actor's athletic skills, raising the heartbeat of the spectators, and bringing the scene to a climax. Moretti may have been concerned with dropping props or falling off the stage both during that scene and at other moments in the production. Safety, Donato

Sartori suggested to me in an interview, likely became an argument Moretti used to convince Strehler that he should paint his face rather than wear a solid mask.[51]

Acting Techniques and Principles

A third reason that prompted Moretti to initially refuse to wear a mask was his ignorance of masked performance techniques and conventions.[52] This is not to suggest that there is a universal, uninterrupted set of acting principles with masks; there are so many ways to perform with a mask, and so many types of masks, that reducing masked performance practices to a handful of fixed notions would not reflect reality. Yet, as the face is covered and facial expressions hidden, the character needs to be expressed with the body and the voice in ways that are different from those associated with the realistic acting style familiar to Moretti.

"The mask is a mysterious, terrible, tool," Strehler explained in the early 1960s, "It has always given me a sense of dismay": "With the mask, we are at the threshold of theatre mystery; it reveals the demons, the fixed, immobile, and ecstatic faces at the roots of theatre. It is soon noticeable that the actor, when on stage, cannot touch the mask with an ordinary gesture (like putting a hand on his forehead, a finger on his eyes, or covering his face with his hands). Such a gesture becomes absurd, not human, and wrong. To recover expressiveness, the actor must make the same gesture with the hand, and not execute it on the mask in a realistic way."[53] Acting conventions with masks, such as the importance of not touching it realistically, were not yet known to Strehler and Moretti in 1947. Among the notions that have since been named and are now regularly practiced and taught in several European and North American acting schools are concepts pertaining to the "mask" and "counter-mask." "Mask," Jacques Lecoq teaches in *The Moving Body*, refers to the "broad outline" of a character as already expressed in the design of the mask.[54] As for "counter-mask," it refers to the "opposite of what the mask appears to suggest."[55] "For example," Lecoq observes, "a mask whose face seems to present 'cretin' will at first be performed as just that." He continues: "The character will be foolish, timid, clumsy. Next, we consider what if the character might be knowledgeable, clever, sure of himself, supremely intelligent? Here the actor is performing what we call the *counter-mask*, revealing a second character behind the same mask, lending it a depth which is much more interesting."[56]

Vocabulary to discuss masked performance notions and techniques differ from one performance tradition, institution, or performer to another. In the summer of 2000, Bruce Marrs, a mask-maker, actor, and former instructor at the Dell'Arte International School of Physical Theatre in Blue Lake, California, distributed an enlightening glossary to his students during a two-week mask-making and masked performance workshop.[57] Titled *Masks Concepts and Vocabulary*, this document identifies and explains a series of acting principles with masks that Marrs learned over the years both from experience and from teachers and peers, including Carlo Mazzone-Clementi, Joan Schirle, Arne Zaslove, Valeria Campo, and Ralph Hall.[58] Each of these artists, whether they are aware of it or not, have a first, second, or third degree of separation from the Piccolo Teatro of Milan, Giorgio Strehler, Amleto Sartori, and Marcello Moretti.[59]

In Marrs's glossary, Lecoq's notion of "mask" becomes "zero of the mask." As for the "counter-mask," Marrs called it "swing of the mask" in his teaching. But the notions explicitly taught at Dell'Arte at the turn of the twenty-first century went beyond "zero" and "swing," extending to something called "reveal," "lampshade," "resonance," and "report."[60] The "reveal" of the mask happens during or soon after the entrance of a masked character on stage and refers to the moment when "the audience gets to get a satisfactory first read of the mask."[61] A "reveal" may be performed subtly, in a split second of suspension, as though an instant photograph of the character was being taken. "Lampshade" refers to the liveliness, or rather lack thereof, of a solid mask in performance. Marrs writes, "The audience wants to believe," and adds, "That, and good craft allows the mask to be alive, to be magic."[62] "When it's not magic," Marrs learned from Ralph Hall, "the actor is walking around with a lampshade on his or her head. It's either magic or a lampshade. There's not much in between."[63] "Resonance" points to the connection between the mask and the body. It implies an extradaily state of alertness and a flow of energy from head to toe in performance. As Marrs explains: "The head is connected to the spine. The spine is connected to the hips, to the legs, to the feet, to gravity. The cause and effect of actions below the head must travel up to the mask. Think of a deer's head as it walks; caution in the feet, weight change, ends in a movement of the head: resonance."[64] Finally, the "report"—a notion Marrs remembers learning from Valeria Campo—refers to a look the masked character gives to the audience that communicates what it thinks at key moments during the performance.[65] These reports may be thought of as brief asides to the public that punctuate the action by establishing visual contact between masked characters and spectators. "The audience needs to know what the mask thinks," Marrs's glossary reads, also explaining, "every thing that happens; every sight, every discovery, every thought needs to be presentationally acted. It needs to be shown. . . . The mask must report to the audience."[66] The notion of "report," while not adopted by all performers, is nonetheless practiced by many actors today, including those who are currently performing in the latest staging of *The Servant of Two Masters* at the Piccolo Teatro of Milan.[67] The Italian players in this production, actor Giorgio Bongiovanni explained to me during an interview, learned it from each other in performance; they call the gesture of reporting to the audience a "colpo di maschera."[68] In actor Michele Bottini's contribution to the *Routledge Companion to Commedia dell'Arte*, the "report" of the mask, or "colpo di maschera," is translated as "mask-shot."[69]

Sets of techniques and conventions like those mentioned above are not universally practiced, are not called by the same names everywhere (when they have a name at all), and are not suitable for all productions. Nevertheless, they constitute a useful repertoire that had yet to be reinvented when Moretti first approached the mask. This is not to say that Strehler and Moretti did not consult with older actors to learn masked performance techniques; on the contrary, Odette Aslan indeed reveals that "in order to convince [Moretti to wear a mask in the first productions of *The Servant of Two Masters* at the Piccolo Teatro], Strehler brought him to Bologna to meet a very old actor, heir of generations and generations of Italian Arlecchinos, to gather information on performing with a mask. Unfortunately, it so happened that the elderly actor had only ever played with a bare face. Even in Italy, the tradition of performing with a mask had been forgotten."[70] Moretti's ignorance of masked performance techniques in 1947 and the necessity for him to discover them in a very short rehearsal period were certainly among the chief reasons for his initial refusal to wear a mask.[71] To them was added the sensory disorientation an actor may feel when covering his face with solid material.

Sensory Challenges and the Nonhuman Collaborator

"[Wearing] a mask," Dario Fo states in *Tricks of the Trade*, "can, in an actor, induce anxiety deriving not so much from the use itself as from the fact that the mask restricts both visual field and acoustic-vocal range."[72] He continues: "Your own voice seems to be singing at you, stunning you, ringing in your ears and, until you master it, you cannot control your breathing." Echoing Fo, Giorgio Bongiovanni describes his first experience with the mask: "When you put it on for the first time, there is a sensation of disappearance and confusion since all of a sudden you lose all your points of reference; you can't distinguish left from right, you see the world through a small hole, and thus you can only see in front of you and not to the sides."[73] The sensory disorientation here described by both

Fo and Bongiovanni may have contributed to the "personal drama of the actors who did not feel [like] themselves in the masks."[74] "By a psychological phenomenon," Strehler remembers from his early explorations with masks at the Piccolo Teatro, "the actor, with his face covered, did not have the right feeling about himself and his colleagues."[75] The players in 1947 found themselves obliged to work with the sensory disorientation and perceived loss of identity that the acoustic and visual limitations of the masks caused, much like earlier commedia dell'arte performers did.

"Seventeenth-century masks of Harlequin," Domenico Pietropaolo explains in *Scenario and Performance in Commedia dell'Arte*, "typically had very small eye holes, no larger than the irises of the actors wearing them, and naturally, could not fit snugly over the eyes, so that the openings, in addition to being very small, were at some distance from the pupil."[76] To perceive what was in front of them, performers wearing these kinds of masks would have had to execute small movements of the head, piecing the image together as if it were a puzzle. These movements would inevitably change the rhythms of the actor in performance, as well as alter her breathing, vocal production, and the quality of her movements, giving the character a nervous, animalesque, even puppet-like demeanor. While the actor may have an image of the character in mind, the design of the mask—including its quality, weight, and flexibility, its colors and shapes, and the size and location of its breathing holes, mouth, and eye openings—will lead the performance in directions the player may not have guessed. Many performers today develop their own approach to "reading" the features of the mask, and, in performance, translate those features in their voice, body, and rhythms.

According to Mace Perlman, an actor who studied and worked at the Piccolo Teatro and has devoted much of his career to the study of commedia dell'arte in practice, "the nose at the mask's center presents the fundamental relationship [the character] has with the world."[77] In his contribution to the *Routledge Companion to Commedia dell'Arte*, he analyzes the features of a leather mask of Capitano created by Renzo Antonello: "This mask is focused along his barrel of a nose, expressing a core of ever-energized invasive intention. . . . There is also a very noticeable twist to the nose, which speaks of the effort involved in pushing his agenda out into the world."[78] This interpretation of the design of this mask is undoubtedly informed by the characteristic features of the stock character throughout history, but also results from personal theories about extracting and translating information from one medium (the mask) to another (the body). Such a process of translation is exemplified by Wout van Tongeren's description of the work of Carlos García Estévez, an actor, director, and theatre educator who studied under both Jacques Lecoq and Donato Sartori: "Carlos García Estévez has a particular way of dealing with the formal aspects of commedia dell'arte, in which the mask is of elementary importance. One could say that Carlos 'draws' the figure and gestures of a character from the mask. This process begins by looking through its simple expressive features (snub nose, pronounced eyebrows, curled moustache, etc.) and discovering its structural or 'spatial' qualities. . . . To give a simple example: a mask that contains many strong, straight, outgoing lines will demand from the actor a way of moving and speaking that is equally strict and forceful. Even the temporal qualities, like the rhythm of a character's movements might be learned by the careful study of a mask."[79] Examining the mask carefully, of course, is not the end of the actor's process. Trying it on, and experiencing and adapting to its limitations and possibilities, is essential to discovering how the mask "works." As such, the relationship a masked performer has with his mask is, in many ways, analogous to that of a puppeteer and her marionette.

Bruno Latour explains that puppeteers "will rarely behave as having total control over their puppets." He adds: "They will say queer things like 'their marionettes suggest them to do things they will have never thought possible by themselves.' When a force manipulates another, it does not mean that it is a cause generating effects; it can also be an occasion for other things to start acting. The *hand* still hidden in the Latin etymology of the word 'manipulate' is a sure sign of full control *as well as a lack of it*. So who is pulling the strings? Well, the puppets do in addition to their puppeteers."[80] The mask, an inanimate object that brings its "own historical, cultural, and ideological baggage," will also shape the actor's work.[81] Much like puppeteers, masked performers are simultaneously in control of the mask and lack control over it. Commedia masks are associated not only with character types but also with individual performers, specific productions, stories, and ideals. The cultural baggage of a mask along with its design will inevitably shape the actor's physical and vocal production, the ways in which she relates to the performance space, and her perception of the fictional character she plays. The performer needs to work with the mask, not against it. Accepting the notion of working with a nonhuman collaborator and learning to do so successfully was certainly challenging to Moretti.

Collaborations, Discoveries, and Identity

The fear of disappearing behind the character was the final barrier to Moretti's initial acceptance of working with masks. He was indeed scared that

Arlecchino should become his second identity onstage. Little by little, however, Moretti finally acquiesced to wearing a mask, thanks to the help and guidance of Giorgio Strehler and Amleto Sartori, who, as noted in the introduction, created Moretti's Arlecchino mask for *L'amante militare*. After the actor rejected an early version of this mask during a rehearsal, Sartori designed lighter, more comfortable masks, some of them with large eye openings adapted to contemporary production conditions.[82] He proposed different designs for various Arlecchino masks, such as an "Arlecchino-cat" mask, an "Arlecchino-fox" mask, an "Arlecchino-bull" mask, and the mask of a primitive Zanni, all of which Moretti is believed to have worn at various points in his career.[83] According to Strehler, however, the first Arlecchino mask Moretti adopted was the "cat," because, the actor believed, it was "the most agile."[84] Over the next decade Moretti, Strehler, and Sartori developed, completed, and perfected each other's knowledge of masks, of masked performance techniques, and of the commedia dell'arte tradition. Sartori remembers: "Marcello made me notice that the eye openings, especially those on the primitive Zanni masks, had a very small diameter, and that if these eyes gave an interesting, animal look to the mask, they also removed, or reduced to a minimum, the ability to see. This [design] created the need to perform very rapid, successive movements [of the head], arranged in a sequence that goes roughly like this: take possession of the field of action visually; constantly look at one's own feet to assess [one's position] and to avoid any obstacle; perform the movement in a minimum amount of space and time. As a result of these actions, [the actor's] gait is jerky, [punctuated by] jumps, and highlighted by movements of the limbs and of the head that are almost mechanical."[85] As Moretti explored ways to use Sartori's mask in performance, he discovered techniques to use it effectively that would later be passed on to new generations of actors. "It was [Moretti]," Strehler claims, "who first discovered masked performance techniques for everyone." He continues: "He discovered that with the mask, the mouth becomes more important than on a bare face. As soon as you highlight it with a white line, the moving, lively mouth that comes out of the upper part of the face covered with a mask takes on incredible expressive value. On his own, he discovered a few inclinations of the head that I noted and this marked the starting point of a practice that I taught my actors, with patience, over time."[86]

For the public, Moretti's lively and skillful performance in *The Servant of Two Masters* excited admiration. For his close friends, his ability to work through his initial struggles with the mask, his continuous and eclectic research on commedia dell'arte, and his persistent efforts to bring Arlecchino's mask to life commanded respect.[87] For Sartori: "[Moretti] evokes some inexplicable faculty, by which a man, starting from the blank page of his own life, without mastering or knowing a tradition, succeeds, through mysterious ways, in reconnecting together the parts of this tradition and in becoming, himself, the symbol and pillar of a world that is partly forgotten, but eternal."[88] The man who was afraid of the mask and who entertained a bittersweet relationship with Arlecchino was eventually "freed" by it. Moretti, Strehler recalls, was a reserved, difficult, and peculiar actor with imperfect diction and limited range.[89] With the mask of Arlecchino, however, he let go of his inhibitions; the mask fulfilled a double purpose to "protect" the actor by hiding him and to "reveal" his full potential in performance. With the solid mask, Marcello Moretti achieved unimaginable size and inventiveness, as well as international fame. In time, the actor allowed himself to be "possessed" by the mask, until "one night," Strehler remembers, "Marcello, a modest man, secret and solitary," confessed feeling *naked* without it.[90]

As I hope this article demonstrated, Moretti's refusal to wear a mask in 1947 was not a spontaneous caprice. Rather, it speaks to what commedia dell'arte had become by that point and reveals the complexities (technical and psychological) involved in wearing a mask. Moretti's initial rejection of the mask and his decision to paint his face with thick makeup was coherent with the values he had learned at the Accademia nazionale d'arte drammatica. It was also in continuity with what he had previously seen (and done) onstage. And it was rooted in the last two hundred years (or so) of commedia dell'arte performance history, during which traditionally masked characters slowly started to lose their masks. By the late nineteenth century and early twentieth, roles could be performed with a mask, with a thick makeup imitating a mask, or realistically, without a mask at all. Moretti's story also sheds light on production practices during the early days of the Piccolo Teatro of Milan, including its short rehearsal periods and the inadequacy of its first masks. It is also a prelude to the historical collaboration between Strehler, Moretti, and Sartori. Had Moretti accepted to wear a mask from the start, the nature and outcome of that collaboration might have been different. After all, sculpting the now iconic Arlecchino-cat mask, with its large eye openings, likely was one of Sartori's answers to Moretti's complaint that he could not see with a mask on his face. Moretti's story also opens a window onto the more personal, little discussed fears actors may have when covering their face with a mask and working with this nonhuman collaborator for the first time. Finally it is a key event in the history of reimagining the commedia dell'arte in the twentieth century. While it is difficult to know precisely what acting techniques

Moretti pioneered, it is certain that his discoveries with the mask contributed to creating the vision many theatre practitioners have of masked performance in the commedia dell'arte today.

Notes

1. The material in this article took shape in my doctoral dissertation "Masks and Masked Performance in Giorgio Strehler's Vision of the Commedia dell'Arte" (University of Toronto, 2013). I would like to thank Julie Sutherland for helping me copyedit an early version of this article.

Amleto Sartori (1915–1962) was a sculptor and mask-maker from Padua. He is now often credited with the post–World War II "rediscovery" of mask-making techniques with leather. He created the leather masks for Strehler's second staging of *The Servant of Two Masters* in 1952 as well as for several other productions at the Piccolo Teatro of Milan. Throughout his career, he sculpted masks for other theatres, directors, actors, and educators, such as Jacques Lecoq, Jean-Louis Barrault, Eduardo de Filippo, Serge Pitoeff, Orazio Costa, Gianfranco De Bosio, and Carlo Mazzone-Clementi. Sartori's work is discussed in several publications in Italian (some of which has been translated into French). The majority of these publications was prepared and edited by his son, Donato Sartori, and by Paola Piizzi, close collaborator and wife of Donato. Donato Sartori published a chapter in the *Routledge Companion to Commedia dell'Arte* in English that traces his father's journey with masks (2015). A study of Amleto Sartori's creation process and an analysis of his "rediscovery" of mask-making techniques with leather are also included in *Masks and Masked Performance in Giorgio Strehler's Vision of the Commedia dell'Arte* (Houle, 2013). In this article, I sometimes use the term "mask-maker" when I discuss artists who create masks. I am aware, however, that many of these artists, mostly contemporary artists working in France and in Italy, including members of the Sartori family, prefer to be referred to as "sculptors" of masks.

2. Amleto Sartori, "Ricordi intorno a una maschera," in "Marcello Moretti," ed. Paolo Grassi, Giorgio Strehler, and Ruggero Jacobbi, special issue, *Quaderni del Piccolo Teatro* 4 (1962): 21. *L'amante militare* was first performed in 1751 by the Medebach company, with whom Goldoni collaborated extensively. It is this company that first performed Goldoni's play-manifesto *Il teatro comico*. Written in 1750, *Il teatro comico* presents the elements of Goldoni's reform of the theatre (see the "Marcello Moretti: Background, Training, and Influences" section in this article for a discussion of the key elements of this reform). It was also for members of the Medebach company that Goldoni wrote *La locandiera* in 1753, which is perhaps the first play to follow the principles laid out in *Il teatro comico*. Written and first performed between *Il teatro comico* and *La locandiera*, *L'amante militare* retains the fixed character types of the commedia dell'arte, the traditional relationships between these characters, and the four masked characters: two old men (Pantalone and Don Sancio) and two servants (Brighella and Arlecchino). The play also features the theme of "Arlecchino soldier," which is found in earlier commedia dell'arte scenarios (Zorzi, introduction, 9). And while the play is fully scripted, several scenes leave plenty of room for improvisation.

Ludovico Zorzi, introduction to *L'amante militare*, by Carlo Goldoni (Turin: Giulio Einaudi editore, 1982), 5–16.

3. Ibid.
4. "Marcello Moretti," ed. Paolo Grassi, Giorgio Strehler, and Ruggero Jacobbi, special issue, *Quaderni del Piccolo Teatro* 4 (1962).
5. Strehler's successive stagings of *The Servant of Two Masters* are often referred to as "his" *Arlecchino*. In 1947, Strehler changed the name of the central character from Truffaldino to Arlecchino. In 1948, he added "Arlecchino" to the title of the play. From then on, Strehler's productions of Goldoni's *The Servant of Two Masters* would be known around the world as *Arlecchino Servant of Two Masters*. This step and many others (e.g., including the insertion of original gags in the production; making changes to the dialogues; giving Brighella the stutter characteristic of Tartaglia; requesting his actors to perform at a frantic speed to avoid psychological realism; and using masks that dehumanized the characters and went back to commedia dell'arte before Goldoni's reform) sealed Strehler's authorship of the production. In this article, I choose to retain the original title Goldoni gave to the play.
6. Daniella Bologneti, "Arlecchino servitore di due padroni per la regia di Giorgio Strehler" (Diss. Università degli Studi di Napoli—Federico II, 2000), 176.
7. "Marcello Moretti," ed. Paolo Grassi, Giorgio Strehler, and Ruggero Jacobbi, special issue, *Quaderni del Piccolo Teatro* 4 (1962), 29–31. Aside from his participation in *The Servant of Two Masters*, Moretti performed as Arlecchino (or Truffaldino) in four other plays at the Piccolo Teatro, namely *Il corvo*, by Carlo Gozzi, and *L'amante militare*, *La vedova scaltra*, and *La putta onorata*, by Goldoni.
8. "Arlecchino servitore di due padroni di Carlo Goldoni: regia di Giorgio Strehler [programme notes]," *Piccolo Teatro di Milano* 2, no. 3 (1979): 56.
9. *Messagero Veneto*, March 30, 1983, accessed September 30, 2010, Archivio multimediale del Piccolo Teatro. J. M. R., "An Italian Clown Prince Comes to Stratford," *Leamington Courier*, February 13, 1959, accessed September 30, 2010, Archivio multimediale del Piccolo Teatro. Peggy Doyle, "Italian Stage Group Serves Fun Aplenty," *Boston Eve*, March 12, 1960, accessed September 30, 2010, Archivio multimediale del Piccolo Teatro. Jorge Palma, "Marcello Moretti, el arlequín universal," *Mundo uruguano*, July 8, 1954, accessed September 30, 2010, Archivio multimediale del Piccolo Teatro.
10. Dario Fo, *The Tricks of the Trade*, trans. Joe Farrell, ed. Stuart Hood (New York: Routledge, 1991), 26.
11. Luigi Ferrante, "Note per la storia di un personaggio," in "Marcello Moretti," ed. Paolo Grassi, Giorgio Strehler, and Ruggero Jacobbi, special issue, *Quaderni del Piccolo Teatro* 4 (1962): 15.
12. Lecoq quoted in Guy Freixe, *Les utopies du masque sur les scènes européennes du XXe siècle* (Montpellier: Éditions L'Entretemps, 2010), 292.
13. Guy Freixe, *Les utopies du masque*, 169.
14. Before wearing his first leather mask in *The Servant of Two Masters*, in 1952, Marcello Moretti performed with solid masks in at least two other productions at the Piccolo Teatro, both staged by Giorgio Strehler: *Il corvo* by Carlo Gozzi (which premiered in the 1948–49 theatre season) and *L'amante militare* by Carlo Goldoni (produced in 1951). Both plays were inspired by the commedia dell'arte; they retained the masked characters, storylines, and themes typical of this tradition. The mask Moretti wore in *Il corvo* was likely

made of papier mâché and gauze. There are no credits for the masks in this production; actors perhaps created them themselves. The mask Moretti wore in *L'amante militare*, on the other hand, was made by Amleto Sartori (see endnote 82 for a brief discussion of this mask); *1947–58 Piccolo Teatro* (Milan: Nicola Moneta Editore, 1958).

15. Giorgio Strehler, "In margine al diario," in "Marcello Moretti," ed. Paolo Grassi, Giorgio Strehler, and Ruggero Jacobbi, special issue, *Quaderni del Piccolo Teatro* 4 (1962). In "In margine al diario," Giorgio Strehler states several reasons for Moretti's initial refusal to wear a solid mask. This article has been quoted in numerous works (mostly written in French and in Italian) that discuss the Piccolo Teatro of Milan, Strehler's stagings of *The Servant of Two Masters*, Moretti's biography, and Strehler's contribution—along with contributions by Amleto Sartori, Gianfranco De Bosio, Dario Fo, and Jacques Lecoq—to reimagining the commedia dell'arte tradition in the twentieth century. Moretti's resistance to the mask, however, has not yet been comprehensively investigated.

16. "Marcello Moretti," ed. Paolo Grassi, Giorgio Strehler, and Ruggero Jacobbi, special issue, *Quaderni del Piccolo Teatro* 4 (1962); Silvia Cacco, "'Maschera" viva' L'Arlecchino di Marcello Moretti" (Diss., Università degli studi di Venezia Ca' Foscari, 2002–03).

17. Parts of the 1962 publication about Moretti have since been translated into other languages and appear in works about Strehler, about Sartori, or about masks and commedia dell'arte. There is no English translation of the entire publication.

18. I conducted interviews with actresses Narcisa Bonati, Giulia Lazzarini, and Andrea Jonasson-Strehler, with movement educator Marise Flach, with actors Ferruccio Soleri, Tommaso Minniti, Enrico Bonavera, and Giorgio Bongiovanni, and with lighting designer Claudio De Pace in Milan in 2009, when working on my doctoral dissertation. I interviewed Donato Sartori at the Centro Maschere e Strutture Gestuali in Abano Terme, also in 2009. They had all worked with the Piccolo Teatro at some point in their careers, and some of them were still working there at the time of the interviews. Bonati, Soleri, Lazzarini, Flach, and Sartori knew Moretti.

19. Ruggero Jacobbi, "Meditazione su un mito e su una biografia," in "Marcello Moretti," ed. Paolo Grassi, Giorgio Strehler, and Ruggero Jacobbi, special issue, *Quaderni del Piccolo Teatro* 4 (1962): 50.

20. Ibid., 51–52.

21. Cacco, "Maschera viva," 12.

22. "Chi siamo," Accademia nazionale d'arte drammatica Silvio D'Amico, accessed May 15, 2015, http://www.accademiasilviodamico.it/. According to the accademia's website, D'Amico converted the Regia Scuola di Recitazione "Eleonora Duse" (known as Scuola di "Declamazione e Gesto" from 1893 to 1921 and as the "Eleonora Duse" acting school from 1921 to 1934) into the Accademia nazionale d'arte drammatica in 1934. The founding year of the accademia, according to its website, is 1936, although 1934 and 1935 are sometimes cited by other sources as founding dates of the school.

23. Gian Giacomo Colli, "The Impossible Tempest: Giorgio Strehler or the Director as Interpreter" (PhD diss., University of Toronto, 2009), 37.

24. Gunter Berghaus, *Italian Futurist Theatre, 1909–1944* (Oxford: Clarendon Press, 1998), 14.

25. Berghaus, 24; Roberto Tessari, *Teatro italiano del Novecento: Fenomenologie e strutture, 1906–1976* (Florence: Casa editrice Le Lettere, ca. 1996).

26. Ibid., 54.

27. Marvin Carlson, *The Italian stage from Goldoni to D'Annunzio* (Jefferson, NC: McFarland, 1981), 201.
28. Silvio D'Amico, "Il dopoguerra del Teatro drammatico," in *'La vita del teatro: cronache, polemiche e note varie' Vol I 1914–1921 gli anni di guerra e della crisi* (Rome: Bulzoni editore, 1994), 282.
29. Ibid., 283.
30. Ibid., 285.
31. These courses were the ideal, not necessarily what the accademia ended up offering.
32. Raul Radice, "Vent-anni di regia goldoniana, dalla scuola al palcoscenico," in "Atti del Convegno internazionale di studi goldoniani, promosso dal comune di Venezia, dall'Istituto veneto di scienze, lettere ed arti, e dalla Fondazione Giorgio Cini Venezia, 28 settember–1 ottobre 1957," ed. Vittore Branca and Nicola Mangini, special issue, *Studi goldoniani* 1 (1960): 127–41. Raul Radice was the director of the accademia from 1955 to 1963. In "Vent'anni di regia goldoniana," he lists the plays by Goldoni that were staged by the Compagnia dell'Accademia (the company attached to the school) between 1944 and 1956.
33. Silvio D'Amico, "Scuola di trucco," *Teatro Scenario*, January 15, 1952, 11.
34. Please see Cacco's thesis on Marcello Moretti for a survey of productions he acted in during his early career.
35. Perrini quoted in Cacco, "Maschera viva," 47–48.
36. Jacobbi, "Meditazione," 54.
37. Andrea Perrucci, *A Treatise on Acting from Memory and by Improvisation (1699), Dell'arte rappresentativa, premeditata ed all'improviso*, ed. and trans. Francesco Cotticelli, Anne Goodrich Heck, and Thomas F. Heck (Lanham: Scarecrow Press, 2008), 150.
38. Ibid.
39. Ibid.
40. Ibid., 151.
41. There is evidence that commedia actors also used leather masks in performance. For example, the Bibliothèque du Musée de l'Opéra in Paris holds five leather masks and five wooden molds for making masks. Little, unfortunately, is known about these objects. It isn't clear who exactly wore them, when, and whether they were used in theatrical productions, in masquerade balls, or both. In an e-mail he sent to me in 2009, Pierre Vidal, from the Bibliothèque, specified that Maison Hallé, which has provided stage properties to the Opéra since the eighteenth century, donated the masks and the molds to the Musée. They were exhibited several times since the Exposition Théâtrale de l'Exposition Universelle of 1878, and a photograph of one of these masks can now be seen online on the Bibliothèque Nationale de France website (Vidal, e-mail). Images of these objects have also been published in *Masks: Faces of Culture* by John W. Nunley and Cara McCarty (New York: H. N. Abrams in association with the Saint Louis Art Museum, 1999); Pierre Vidal, e-mail message to author, March 29, 2009.
42. Giovanni Calendoli, *L'attore: Storia di un'arte* (Rome: Edizioni dell'Ateneo, 1959), 323, 328.
43. Paolo Bosisio, *Il teatro di Goldoni sulle scene italiane del Novecento* (Milan: Electa, 1993), 24. I agree with Paolo Bosisio that the use of the words "realistic" and "natural" in this context can be misleading. Bosisio specifies that when it is used to describe the acting style of Goldonian performers in the early 1900s, the word "natural" is often relative, dated, and likely points to a "codified enactment of spontaneity" (Bosisio, *Il teatro di Goldoni*,

60). The natural acting style of most early-twentieth-century Goldonian actors, Bosisio asserts, was influenced by a certain mannerism inherited from the nineteenth century.

44. Carlo Goldoni, *Mémoires / précédés d'une notice sur la comédie italienne au 16e siècle, et sur Goldoni par M. Moreau* (Genève: Slatkine reprints, 1968), 2:25.

45. Carlo Gozzi, *The Memoirs of Count Carlo Gozzi*, trans. John Addington Symonds (London: John C. Nimmo, 1890), 2:128.

46. Alberto Beniscelli, "Carlo Gozzi," in *A history of Italian Theatre*, ed. Joseph Farrell and Paolo Puppa (Cambridge: Cambridge University Press, 2006), 177.

47. These postcards are kept in the Biblioteca Livia Simoni, the Teatro alla Scala's archives. I consulted them in 2009. Renato Simoni (Verona 1875–Milan 1952) was a dramaturg, theatre critic, author, director, and avid collector of theatre artifacts. He developed and shared his vision of Goldoni's work through his writings and stagings and was considered a living resource for those who wished to learn about Goldoni and the commedia dell'arte tradition. He owned an eighteenth-century Arlecchino costume as well as first editions of rare theatre manuals, and he possessed a large but undetermined number of masks from different theatrical traditions that he later donated to the Teatro alla Scala. Simoni also gave to this theatre an impressive collection of forty thousand books, images, figurines, magazines, costumes, puppets, autographs, and manifestos. *1947–58 Piccolo Teatro* (Milan: Nicola Moneta Editore, 1958), 38; Enciclopedia dello spettacolo, s.v. "Renato Simoni."

48. In "In margine al diario," Strehler states, "We made [the first masks used at the Piccolo Teatro] ourselves, so to speak, with our hands, day by day" (Strehler, 59). It is not clear from this text who "we" refers to—the Piccolo Teatro actors, or design team, or both. It is certain, however, that the first masks used at the Piccolo Teatro were not made by people who had a firm grasp of mask-making techniques for the theatre.

49. Strehler, "In margine," 58.

50. Catherine Douël dell'Agnola, *Gli spettacoli goldoniani di Giorgio Strehler (1947–1991)* (Rome: Bulzoni Editore, 1992), 40.

51. Donato Sartori, personal interview, June 2009. Donato Sartori (1939–2016) was a sculptor and mask-maker from Padua. He continued the work of his father after Amleto Sartori's death in 1962 but also developed his own approach to masks and masking. In 1979, Donato Sartori, along with Paolo Trombetta and Paola Piizzi, founded the Centro Maschere e Strutture Gestuali, a laboratory space dedicated to the exploration and multidisciplinary study of masks and masking. At the Centro Maschere, Sartori taught local and international cohorts of students how to create masks using different materials, including paper and leather. He also produced large-scale performances called "mascheramenti urbani" (urban masking) that involved covering buildings, streets, and public squares with material resembling a spider web and inviting the crowd to interact with the installation. On December 30, 2004, the Sartori opened the Museo Internazionale della Maschera Amleto e Donato Sartori in Abano Terme, Italy. This museum was inaugurated in 2005 by Dario Fo and Franca Rame. *Amleto Sartori (1915–1962): Centenario della nascita: Itinerario tra le opere pubbliche e private nel territorio padovano*, ed. Donato Sartori, Sarah Sartori, Paola Piizzi, and Virginia Baradel (Padua: Comune di Padova and Centro Maschere e Strutture Gestuali, ca. 2016), 104.

52. Strehler, "In margine," 60.

53. Ibid., 59.

54. Jacques Lecoq, *The Moving Body: Teaching Creative Theatre*, trans. David Bradly (New York: Routledge, 2001), 52.
55. Ibid., 59.
56. Ibid.
57. I received a copy of this document in August 2000, when I participated in a mask-making and masked performance workshop at Dell'Arte.
58. Bruce Marrs, e-mail message to author, February 3, 2015.
59. Carlo Mazzone-Clementi studied theatre at the University of Padua under Gianfranco De Bosio, Amleto Sartori, and Jacques Lecoq. In 1951 Lecoq joined the Piccolo Teatro of Milan, where he taught mime for a year. There, Lecoq worked with Moretti on two plays: *L'amante militare* by Goldoni and *The Flying Doctor* by Molière. Lecoq was the movement coach for both plays. These plays were performed as a double bill at the Piccolo Teatro in 1951. Strehler directed the pieces, and Moretti played the central roles. After studying in Padua, Mazzone-Clementi worked with Dario Fo and Franca Rame at the Piccolo Teatro, where he undoubtedly interacted with Strehler and likely saw Moretti in performance, wearing the Arlecchino mask Amleto Sartori made for him around 1952. Sartori made masks for Mazzone-Clementi, who brought them on an American tour in 1958 and made them known on that side of the Atlantic. Both Joan Schirle and Arne Zaslove worked with Mazzone-Clementi in the United States, as did Ralph Hall, who also trained with Lecoq in Paris. As for Valeria Campo, she mentions in her online curriculum vitae having learned masked performance and commedia dell'arte from Marcello Bartoli. Bartoli began his career in 1967 by collaborating with various theatres, including the Piccolo Teatro of Milan. It was with this theatre, Bartoli's online biography reads, that "he toured internationally with Ferruccio Soleri, performing various shows of the Commedia dell'Arte in the roles of Zanni, Brighella, and Pantalone." Ferruccio Soleri was Marcello Moretti's understudy in the role of Arlecchino in 1960. He succeeded him as the Piccolo Teatro's Arlecchino in 1963 and has now played the role for more than fifty years. This is not to say that Mazzone-Clementi, Zaslove, Schirle, Campo, and Hall owe their knowledge of commedia and mask work to the Piccolo Teatro of Milan exclusively. But, given their first, second, or third degree of separation from that theatre, it is likely that they were influenced, at least to some extent, by the work of Strehler and Moretti. "Bio It [Valeria Campo's online CV]," CirComedy, accessed May 15, 2015, https://sites.google.com/site/circomedy/biografia-1; [Marcello Bartoli's online CV] Accademia dell'Arte, accessed May 15, 2015, http://www.dell-arte.org.
60. Bruce Marrs, "Masks Concepts and Vocabulary (Additional to Joan Schirle's "S" list/ Instructor Bruce Marrs)" (Course notes, Dell'Arte International School for Physical Theatre, Blue Lake, 2000).
61. Ibid.
62. Ibid.
63. Ibid.
64. Ibid.
65. Marrs, e-mail.
66. Marrs, "Masks Concepts."
67. I saw this staging in 2009 in Milan.

68. Giorgio Bongiovanni, personal interview, May 9, 2009. Bongiovanni plays Pantalone in the production.

69. Michele Bottini, "You must have heard of Harlequin . . . ," in *The Routledge Companion to Commedia dell'Arte*, ed. Judith Chaffee and Olly Crick (New York: Routledge, 2015), 55–61.

70. Odette Aslan, "L'Arlequin serviteur de deux maîtres," *Le masque: du rite au théâtre*, ed. Odette Aslan et al., 2nd ed. (Paris: CNRS Editions, 1999), 174.

71. The rehearsal period for the first production of *The Servant of Two Masters* at the Piccolo Teatro of Milan in 1947 was extremely short. As Strehler recounts: "[During the first theatre season at the Piccolo Teatro] we rehearsed the productions for only a few days, ten–fifteen rehearsals, as it was the custom then." Strehler quoted in Flavia Foradini "Introduction," in *Intorno a Goldoni: Spettacoli e scritti*, by Giorgio Strehler, ed. Flavia Foradini (Milan: Mursia, 2004), 57.

72. Fo, *Tricks*, 26.

73. Bongiovanni, interview.

74. Strehler, "In margine," 59.

75. Ibid.

76. Domenico Pietropaolo, "Scenario and Performance in the Commedia dell'Arte," in *The Performance Text*, ed. Domenico Pietropaolo (New York: Legas, 1999), 249.

77. Mace Perlman, "Reading and Interpreting the Capitano's Multiple Mask-Shapes," in *The Routledge Companion to Commedia dell'Arte*, ed. Judith Chaffee and Olly Crick (New York: Routledge, 2015), 84.

78. Ibid., 85–86.

79. Wout van Tongeren in Carlos García Estévez, "Mask Performance for a Contemporary Commedia dell'Arte," in *The Routledge Companion to Commedia dell'Arte* (New York: Routledge, 2015), 130.

80. Bruno Latour, *Reassembling the Social: An Introduction to Actor-Network-Theory* (Oxford: Oxford University Press, 2005), 59–60.

81. Andrew Sofer, *The Stage Life of Props* (Ann Arbor: University of Michigan Press, 2003), 17.

82. The mask Moretti wore in *L'amante militare* in 1951 and the first leather mask he wore in *The Servant of Two Masters* in 1952 had wide eye openings that allowed a contemporary actor with no previous training with masks to see more easily. It also allowed the audience to see the eyes of the actor better. In all likelihood, when the light from the electrical projectors illuminated the masks, it made Moretti's eyes shine, which no doubt gave additional expressiveness to the masks. The Arlecchino mask Sartori made for *L'amante militare* probably helped Moretti transition from wearing a thick makeup in *The Servant of Two Masters* in 1947 to adopting a leather mask in the 1952 staging of that play.

83. Strehler, "In margine," 60.

84. Moretti quoted in Strehler, "In margine," 60.

85. Sartori, "Intorno," 21.

86. Strehler, "In margine," 60.

87. Sartori, "Intorno," 24.

88. Ibid.

89. Strehler, "In margine," 60.

90. Ibid.

Making Space for Performance

Theatrical-Architectural Nationalism in Postindependence Ghana

—DAVID AFRIYIE DONKOR

On October 21, 1961, the Ghana Experimental Drama Studio, a theatre house, opened in the center of Accra, Ghana. Founder and design conceptualist of the Studio, Efua Theodora Sutherland, welcomed an invited audience comprising members of the international press, diplomats, University of Ghana faculty, market women, party officials, nuns, a local chief, and young women who, as historian Robert July describes, were "swathed in brilliant prints. . . . lightly turbaned, loaded with gold" and "anciently elegant in a manner that Europe would not dare."[1] As Sutherland completed her welcome speech, the growling of motorcycles and the wail of sirens emerged and ended with the sound of slamming car doors. Amid applause, guest of honor and president of Ghana Kwame Nkrumah strode into the Drama Studio with his retinue. In scheduled remarks, he spoke about his hope for the renaissance of the arts in Africa and his dream of Pan-African unity aided by the language of art. He pointed to Africa's long-standing reliance on outsiders for material and cultural growth and charged Africans to "look inwards" to "our own exertions. . . . endeavors" to "bring about the progress, unity, and strength of Africa."[2] Four years earlier, at Ghana's independence in 1957, Nkrumah had declared that Ghanaians were going to "create our own African Personality and identity." His 1961 remarks thus connected the Studio with the projection of a new postcolonial national cultural consciousness to the world.

In this essay I examine the architecture and dramaturgical work of the Ghana Experimental Drama Studio in the context of the Pan-African cultural nationalism of the early postindependence era in Ghana. Nationalism is at root belief in the idea (with its corresponding claims, attitudes, sentiments, behaviors, and/or projects) that an aggregate of individuals or communities has a common origin, history, or cultural ties so as to constitute a distinct people or "nation" with a congruent political-economic unit. Several theorists view nationalism as something that arises out of the historical processes and conditions of modernity, in tandem with the nation-state—the most significant political-economic unit in our modern world.[3] Efforts to forge a coherent national identity entail a good deal of cultural construction: active defining of the contours (social, cultural, economic, political) and constitution of that nation in the imagination of its people. So, it makes sense that after independence in 1957 Ghana—a turn-of-the-nineteenth-century geopolitical invention, scalded from the still-smoldering ashes of British colonialism—would be the ground of an intense Pan-African nationalist cultural construction. But, nationalist cultural projects have broad notions of identity that must inevitably confront the problem of multiple selves and worlds: individuals and communities have a complex cluster of interplaying identities that matter in any given context of cultural representation. What about the nation did the Ghana Experimental Drama Studio represent, and how did this representation fare amid competing ideas about nationalist art and/or cultural practice?

My question arises in view of a historical background in which the work of theatre and architecture in the construction of national cultural identity is relatively well documented. Less represented, although still present in the historical literature, are the theatrical and architectural nationalisms of the African countries that sought a new national consciousness in the wake of their independence from European powers during the mid-twentieth century. Yet, practically nonexistent is consideration of the theatre architecture of this postindependence (arguably postcolonial) era wherein theatrical *and* architectural nationalism met in the representation of African national culture and identity. This yet-to-be-properly-accounted-for African domain of theatrical-architectural nationalism is what I engage with in this essay. I begin with a biographical sketch of Efua Sutherland's life, focusing on the political environment in the period from her return to Ghana after studies abroad to when she started making plans for the Studio in 1960. I turn my attention then to the Studio itself, focusing on its design and the inspiration for that design. I then examine the status of the Studio as a national theatre by looking at the historical factors (those having to do with colonial hegemony, primarily) that prompted Ghana's national theatre movement of the 1950s and 1960s; the theatrical precedents of the theatre movement; and the connection among Nkrumah's ideology of the African

Personality, the movement, and Studio. I conclude with a broad sketch of the Studio's life after the political demise of its most powerful patron, Kwame Nkrumah. This concluding discussion highlights the contested character of the nation (including its heritage), especially in a politically turbulent history such as the one Ghana has had, and the problem this poses for the endurance of any firm idea of what constitutes a national theatre.

Before the Studio's Birth: Efua Sutherland and the Rise of the Ghana National Theatre

In 1950, more than a decade before the opening of the Ghana Experimental Drama Studio in Accra, Efua Theodora Morgue (later Sutherland) returned to the British Colony of the Gold Coast (later Ghana) after three years of specialized advanced teacher training in the United Kingdom, two years at Homerton College, Cambridge, followed by a year at the University of London. Sutherland's years and experience abroad only intensified her wish to work among students in her own country.[4] When she returned to the Gold Coast in 1950, the colony was more politically charged than when she had left in 1947. In 1948 simmering opposition to colonial rule rose to the surface in boycotts against the colonial administration's export trade regulations that favored large expatriate-run companies and displaced African merchants. African exservicemen marching to petition the governor with grievances about their postwar remuneration faced fire from a British officer and lost three of their company. After this, crowds gathered in the streets of Accra and vented their fury by destroying cars, looting goods, and burning shops. Authorities blamed the United Gold Coast Convention (UGCC), the new nationalist party that sought transfer of governmental authority to native hands in the shortest possible time, for the upheaval and arrested six of its leaders.

One of the arrested leaders was Kwame Nkrumah. Like Sutherland, he had done further studies abroad. However, he was recruited back to the colony in 1947 to work with the UGCC. By the time of Sutherland's return in 1950, Nkrumah, who was released from jail after the 1948 unrests, had subsequently broken from the UGCC to form his own Convention People's Party (CPP) and was already back in jail for trying to force the hand of the colonial administration with nonviolent demonstrations, strikes, boycotts, and civil disobedience for self-government. In 1951 Nkrumah's party won a general election on the future of the colony, forcing the authorities to re-release him from jail and appoint him to a sort of prime-ministerial role as the Leader of Government Business.

Meanwhile, Sutherland rejoined St. Monica's, the secondary school and teacher-training college staffed by Yorkshire-based Anglican Sisters of the Order of the Holy Paraclete (OHP). Although she grew up and had her early schooling in the seaboard city of Cape Coast, she had attended and then taught at St. Monica's before leaving for advanced studies in the United Kingdom. The Sisters' missionary zeal to improve the quality of life and education in nearby villages not only strengthened Sutherland's sense of vocation but also affected her writing—Kyerefaso, the setting of her short story "New Life at Kyerfaso" (later expanded into the play *Foriwa*), is based on an actual town in the vicinity of St. Monica's. In April 1951 she was posted to Accra to Achimota School and began—as James Gibbs put it—to "take her writing seriously."[5]

Poetry dominated Sutherland's early writing. Some of this early writing had a religious dimension that James Gibbs attributes to the deep impact of the OHP Sisters and Sutherland's interest in spirituality (at Homerton, her special subjects were divinity and education). Gibbs reads "The Dedication," for instance, as "a meditative poem" whose "biblical echoes and images contribute to the exploration of Christ's Sacrifice and allow her [Sutherland] to lead up to the somewhat metaphysical paradox of a blossoming cross."[6] However, there is a critical engagement in Efua Sutherland's representation of the Christian themes. As Robert Fraser observes, "The Dedication" is concerned with "the hypocrisy behind the church's call to patriotic violence in which the poet starts by asking awkward questions from the back row of the Sunday school."[7] "The Redeemed" has echoes of biblical Eden but inverts the result of Eve's encounter with the serpent. A serpent lies in wait for a woman. She walks along his path bearing a plantain load upon her head with beauty and pride. The serpent senses "the smell of the maiden Eve" on her. Raging "like forest fire" from the biblical curse, he wishes to destroy her. "Love I the flaming melody of your frame" he says, but threatens, "I must silence it . . . come I to crush you; break the mercury glint in you and leave you there by the debris of your plantain load, in the tangle of your emerald robe, spent, overcome." However, something about her frustrates his designs. The serpent's venom boils over and clots in the glare, and he recoils helplessly. The poem says the woman's "dark lips smiled, her dark eyes beamed delight, the copper neck swerved back with its load, and down the slope of the market she strode." Sutherland presents us with an African Eve who, for once, inverts the biblical narrative and gets the better of the serpent.[8]

Sutherland's vision of an African Eve is an imprint of that which would define much of her work: her desire for artistic expression in an African idiom. In fact, this impetus had been with her throughout her study abroad. Her lecturers at Homerton encouraged her in her wish to orient all her college work to Africa.

Those who worked with her at Homerton College observed that she conveyed, to some of the classes she taught, a vivid sense of what it was like to live in Africa. She had textual analysis of Shakespeare's plays but also a (presumably African) storytelling session in the English classes that she taught. Her subsequent specialization at the University of London in Vernacular Languages and Dramatic Studies indicates her orientation toward a local vernacular idiom of artistic representation.[9] Part of this desire came from her assessment there are important areas of traditional life to which she lacked proper exposure, because of her closeted background, namely, her upbringing in the anglophile city of Cape Coast and her relatively cloistered life at St Monica's. Sutherland's interest in art expressed with an African idiom was the result of not only her own sense of lack but also her concern, as a teacher, that children educated in the Gold Coast continued to suffer from this lack. As Robert W. July observes, "School texts, literary works, . . . school plays were all Western" and largely transmitted through oral means; "traditional ideas were seldom in print."[10] Her objection to the children's books in the colony pushed her to realize her dream that African children in the Gold Coast would have books that are attractively produced and that reflect local African experiences, just as she had seen available for children while she studied in the United Kingdom.

Soon, Sutherland was pursuing her interests in the corridors of power. In 1954, a year in which Kwame Nkrumah's party won another general election and grew his political influence, the prime minister began to imagine a national theatre movement for the soon-to-be-independent country. The historical record is silent on exactly from whom or where he got the idea. However it is very possible that Sutherland had some part in the prime minister's new attention to theatre. That year Sutherland married Bill Sutherland, a Pan-Africanist, pacifist, and employee of the African Minister of Finance, Komla Gbedemah. Therefore Sutherland's and Prime Minister Nkrumah's circles may have crossed at least after—and possibly before—1954. By 1955 Nkrumah inarguably knew about Efua Sutherland's literary-artistic interests. That year he appointed Sutherland and nine others to a committee charged with examining how best to develop a national theatre movement. The committee recommended that the emergent government take the initiative by setting up an arts council along the lines of the United Kingdom's—a statutory, publicly funded body to organize the arts and encourage their promotion. In June 1955 the government set up the Arts Council of the Gold Coast, but perhaps due to the high political tension between Nkrumah and the opposition National Liberation Movement the council saw little action before independence, in March 1957.[11] It was evident however that drama, one of Sutherland's specializations at the University of London, had become a major preoccupation of hers by this time. She returned to St. Monica's to direct a production of *Lady Precious Stream* by S. I. Hsiung. The dramaturgical experiment of Hsiung's play, subtitled "Old Chinese Play Done into English According to its Traditional Style," provided an Asian example that was relevant to her preoccupation with producing art in an African idiom.

By 1958 Sutherland was focused on African-centered dramaturgical experiments. She launched the Experimental Theatre Players to, in her words, "give Ghanaians another reason why people would want to write."[12] She more or less wanted to provide the opportunity to have one's written play performed by the players as the incentive for authorial pursuits. The desire to offer, as she put it, "something familiar" but also "new" to the Ghanaian people continued to be the hallmark of her and the group's work.[13] The goal was a theatre that did not shy away from non-African dramatic texts and forms but spoke, no matter what it drew from, in an idiom with which an African public could identify. The players' first experiment involved their development of short plays based on Anansesem. Anansesem is a time-honored storytelling tradition associated with Ghanaian folkloric spider-trickster Ananse. Just as the spider has a crafty, creative, and sometimes unnerving disposition toward evading predators and capturing prey, Ananse is likewise a crafty and deceptive figure full of comic delight and social significance. Anansesem denotes both stories about Ananse and a storytelling act itself. Musical and mimed interludes and audience participation punctuate the Anansesem performance. Sutherland considered Anansesem as "a marvelous source" and "exciting food for dramatists" when "recreated and contemporized."[14] Her direction of Hsiung's play *Lady Precious Stream* had allowed her to see great dramatic possibilities in the complete rejection of illusionist theatre. Finding this paralleled in Anansesem, she led her players to experiment with Ananse performance conventions onstage. From the European literary tradition they "borrowed the position of authorial authority implicit in producing a written script, and the convention of impersonation in which an actor takes on a specific role." And from the African tradition she took the lore and participatory performance conventions of the Akan oral tradition. The result of this experiment was a hybrid dramatic form that Efua Sutherland called Anansegoro (Ananse play).

As Sutherland's effort to encourage writing through theatre practice—specifically, through her work with the players—intensified, she found the need for a suitable home for its rehearsals and performances. An ideal home for Sutherland's Experimental Theatre Players, as she saw it, was one that would represent her group's work in a "palpable and tangible" way or, in her words, "stand as a symbol" for a "place where experiments in African drama are going on.'"[15] On the same theme, one recommendation the committee advising Nkrumah on the national theatre movement made to him in 1955 was to construct a national theatre house, the first such consideration in the country. The issue resurfaced after a lull in activity of the Arts Council between 1955 and 1957, when the promotion of national culture became a matter of parliamentary query in August 1958. Ghana's minister of education, who bore responsibility for this work, assured parliament of his government's cultural policy "to preserve and demonstrate the character and traditions of the people of Ghana." The minister indicated the government's plans not just for a national theatre movement but also to construct a national theatre building.[16] It is unclear whether the Studio, built shortly afterward with funding from the Arts Council (among other institutions) and inaugurated by Nkrumah himself, was just a building to house the African-centered work of Sutherland's players or whether it was viewed as *the* government's envisaged national theatre house. I shall return to that question but will first focus on describing the Drama Studio.

A Compound House: The Drama Studio and Its Inspiration in "Traditional" Architecture

Sutherland modeled the Studio after the architecture of an Akan dwelling, the traditional communal compound home. As Labelle Prussin has explained, these communal complexes comprised four (sets of) rooms, or *pato*, and thatch-roofed-over spaces, or *dampon*, arranged corner-to-corner around a quadrangular courtyard, or gyase (figure 1). The lower walls of these rooms were painted in a reddish-orange ocher color to three feet above the ground and the upper walls were washed waxen white. The complexes usually had a decorated entrance facade but no surface decoration for the external bounding walls. The emphasis and preoccupation was with elaborating the interior facades that faced the gyase, usually with mural carvings of an *adinkra* (a traditional icon used on building designs and jewelry, and as a favored symbol on cloth), which suggests that the critical component of space was a bounded internal courtyard. Cooking, washing, and other housework occurred in the gyase, which was kept clean with the daily application of red and white earth. Gyase provided the nomenclature for the institution of *gyase-hene*, head of the exchequer in the palace of the Asante, for it was in the courtyard that the king sat to receive and give gifts. As a reception area it was, naturally, also the site of entertainment. The *gyase* was also an architectural replica of a paradigm core unit of an Akan shrine house and so was also a scene of critical ritual in an Akan dwelling. An altar, *gyase-dua* (or gyase tree), also known as *nyame dua* (god's tree), consecrated every gyase. The gyase-dua was either an actual tree or a branch planted in the ground with a calabash or brass pan wedged in the forks of the branch for holding sacrificial offerings.[17]

Figure 1. The traditional Akan style of architecture. The buildings are arranged in the typical compound configuration with the courtyard and surrounding units. Artist's impression by David A. Donkor, 2017.

More than a literal space, gyase, which means "beneath the hearth," is also a spatial concept. Gyase embodies the idea that human existence (in the form of the individual, the family, the clan, or the entire political system) derives its validity from ancestral attachment and that such attachment comes about through the establishment of a place—a location in space—where, through ritual behaviors, one can manipulate and incorporate the natural environment into a conscious spatial frame.[18] An adinkra symbol called "Fihankra" (figure 2) represents this spatial concept. Fihankra translates as "a circular-complete house" in the Twi language of the Akan people of Ghana, but the symbol connotes not just circularity but also the "safety and security," and more, of a communal house.[19] A. Kayper-Mensah poetically interprets the icon as follows:

> One wall shells our homes:
> Tells the world we share
> One compound, pebbled yet safe;
> Living on a common ground of being;
> Living with, and not against;
> Praying at a common stool:
> Our experiences, our school![20]

The Fihankra symbol captures the bond and safety of community ("living with, and not against") that arises in the environment of shared prayers, shared learning, and shared space that the enclosed gyase provides. It, in that regard, visualizes the indigenous principles of architectural and spatial integrity that underlie the design of the Akan communal compound house.

Figure 2. The *Fihankra* symbol. Artist's reconstruction by David A. Donkor, 2016.

Inspired by the Akan communal complexes symbolized in Fihankra, Sutherland sought in the Drama Studio a similar integrity of spatial deployment arising from attentiveness to what she appreciated as "a wholesome [social and aesthetic] . . . community experience."[21] Sutherland modeled the Studio after the Akan communal complexes with a full awareness of their significance and signification. She recognized that there is a principle of "spatial integrity" that supports and promotes vibrant and fulfilling community life in the traditional dwellings. She reiterated the Akan idea of spatial-architectural integrity by stressing that architecture represents a careful, calculated, and sensitive enclosure of a space continuum for a community experience and, thus, constitutes an inviolable event that should not be taken capriciously. She acknowledged that space, enclosed, should harmonize naturally with the corresponding social activities to fit a community's needs. The courtyards (gyase) of the compounds are a focal point for a lot of creative activity in traditional Akan society: they are the locus of community where, she acknowledged, "everything that happens dramatically" in the life of the people, like "naming ceremonies and puberty rites," occurs.[22] She believed that a courtyard motif for the Drama Studio would establish intimacy between actor and audience—a true sense of African drama as shared or communal experience—and avoid total surrender to the European idea of distancing the audience from the actors."[23] More simply, she believed the architectural style would be familiar to audiences: it would offer them something into which they could walk "and feel at home."[24]

In 1959, with funding from the Arts Council of Ghana and from the Farfield, the Fund for Tomorrow, and the Rockefeller Foundations, Danish architectural firm of Geelack and Giles began construction of the Drama Studio, bringing Sutherland's architectural concept into physical being. Like Akan traditional dwellings, the Studio was an enclosed arena with "dazzling" whitewashed walls and a dark brown trim.[25] Its main entrance had an overhanging roof that was the color of the trim and incorporated into its design the motif of an Akan stool (with the typical semicircular seat). Two wooden sculptures of Akuaba (fertility dolls)—one male, one female—by the Ghanaian artist Oko Ampofo were hung on each side of the entrance. Geometrical designs, like the wall paintings of the Gurensi (a northern Ghana ethnic group) decked the inside of the stool-shaped entrance (figures 3 and 4). A raised platform with an overhanging roof stood opposite (like dampong of Akan complexes) and almost faced the stool-shaped entrance. Behind and on the flank of the platform, ancillary rooms (like the pato of Akan complexes) served as a scene shop, a green room, and other purposes. The outer walls of the building made an octagon and enclosed "a central acting area [equivalent to the gyase] indicated only by an octagonal performing area" that was raised an inch or two (figures 5, 6, 7, and 8).[26]

Figure 3. Outside the original Drama Studio showing the stool-shaped entrance, flanking Akuaba dolls, and Gurensi geometric designs. Source of the photo undetermined; probably taken around 1965.

Figure 4. Outside the replica Drama Studio, showing the stool-shaped entrance. The Akuaba dolls and Gurensi designs are now combined into the motif of a colorful mural. Photo by Joseph Frimpong, 2017.

Figure 5. Inside the replica Drama Studio showing the reverse side of the stool-shaped entrance. A couple of removable platforms provide one of the several staging spaces in this "flexible" theatre house. Photo by Joseph Frimpong, 2017.

Figure 6. Inside the replica Drama Studio showing more staging spaces, including the slightly raised octagonal central stage or "courtyard." Photo by Joseph Frimpong, 2017.

Figure 7. Inside the replica Drama Studio, presenting the opposite of the view shown in figure 5. The raised platform with an overhanging roof and the slightly raised octagonal central stage are visible in the image. Photo by Joseph Frimpong, 2017.

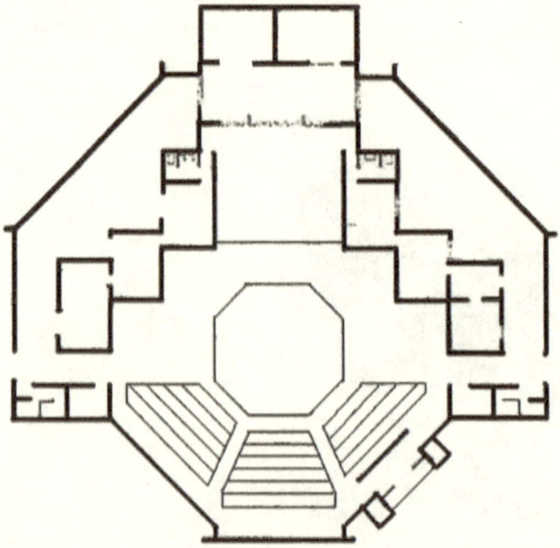

Figure 8. The floor plan of the original Drama Studio. Artist's reconstruction by David A. Donkor, 2008.

Upon its completion in 1960, the Drama Studio stood small and "unpretentious but handsome."[27] It shared Accra's urban space with numerous public buildings designed by European modernist architects. Many of these buildings were articulations of the International Style—a label put on modern architecture around 1930s to recognize its growing acceptance around the world.[28] The expatriate architects, specifying their dialect of the style as "Tropical Architecture," were a presence on the Accra landscape.[29] They filled an important gap: almost no local expertise existed for the scale of ongoing construction in the new nation.[30] But Nkrumah had other points of connection with them. Tenets of their style, like attention of design to local context, was consistent with Nkrumah's wish to "improve the standard of life in a tropical country" by promoting "concrete studies of the problems of the tropical world."[31] The architects echoed this emphasis on "functional-vernacular tradition" by championing the firsthand experience of African climatic, social, and cultural conditions to offer innovative interpretations of modernist design.[32] Max Fry and Jane Drew, for example, sought to harmonize "native" values and modern technology and to represent "collective and individual identity with local aesthetic and natural forms." They designed Accra's community center with a colonnaded courtyard, wooden door panels carved with scenes of fishing, chiefs with ceremonial umbrellas and staffs, a mosaic mural of traditionally dressed figures by local artist Kofi Antubam, and text in the local Ga language: "It is good that we live together in friendship and oneness."

Sutherland's Drama Studio, "traditional in inspiration yet modern in design," shared with the expatriate-designed modernist architecture of independence-era Accra an emphasis on the harmony of native values and modern technology. Fry and Drew had stated about their own work that it "is a collaboration with nature to establish a new order in which human beings may live in harmony with their surroundings," similar to Sutherland's conviction that enclosed space must harmonize with its corresponding social activities to express community needs and that dramaturgical inspiration must be drawn from the vibrant community life that the traditional architecture facilitates. However, we must be careful not to parallel the objectives of the Drama Studio's design and those of the expatriate-designed buildings too closely. Notwithstanding their shared belief in a harmony of native values and modern technology, and in a basic link between architecture and community, Sutherland's objective for the design of the Studio was fundamentally different from the independence-era expatriate architects' objectives for their buildings in the country. Most of the work of these expatriate architects in Ghana was part of the significant "transoceanic migration" of modern architecture.[33] Their recognition and advancement of the prestige of African society and culture was ultimately to legitimate modernism as a universal expression, whatever localized contours or contexts this expression had. Whereas the European expatriate architect sought to show the universality and multicultural translatability of modernism, Sutherland, in contrast, sought to affirm African society and culture by showing the translatability of African indigenous social-aesthetic values in a neoteric architectural form.

An African Personality: The Studio through a Historical/Ideological Frame

Was the Ghana Experimental Drama Studio, then, postindependent Ghana's first national theatre? Since at least the nineteenth century—some would say the eighteenth century—the idea has prevailed in Europe and elsewhere that theatre could make compelling images of the nation, that it could assemble before it an audience that we may consider as representative or microcosmic of the nation, and that that audience could in turn recognize itself onstage as constituent of the coherent nation.[34] In the wake of the French and American Revolutions, nationalist movements arose all across Europe, spreading ideas about democracy, citizenship, and national distinctiveness and provoking, sometimes also making, demands for self-determination. National theatres participated in the legitimation of nationalist aspirations as well as the construction of national identities. Sutherland's work upon her return to the Gold Coast happened in a context that demonstrated that as independence approached there was clearly talk in the colony, at the highest level of government, of the need for a national theatre. The ten-person committee (including Sutherland) that Nkrumah charged with starting a national theatre movement recommended not just that an arts council be formed to promote this movement but also that a national theatre building be constructed to house its work. And, as mentioned earlier, Nkrumah's minister of education reiterated his government's commitment not only to a national theatre movement but also to a national theatre building. In the end, there would not be a building in Ghana officially designated as a "national theatre" until 1992, but Nkrumah's presence and statements at the opening of the Studio suggests that he envisioned that it would house theatre work focused on developing the national consciousness.

National theatres promote representations of certain ideas about the nation, whether the representation is in resistance to or is underwritten by state authorities. Whether the Drama Studio was a "national theatre"—and if so, how—is thus a question about what kinds of nationalist representations the newly independent state sought through a national theatre movement. What ideas of Ghanaian national cultural identity did Nkrumah seek to construct? When the Arts Council formed because of the committee's reccomendations, its main intent was to consolidate and preserve Ghanaian national and cultural identity. The committee made the recommendation out of its concern for what it saw as "a threat to the traditional culture" of the country's people, arising from something referred to in local parlance as "colonial mentality."[35] As theatre theorist Ben Halm explains, colonial mentality is "psychological and ideological dependency" on the "seductive forms" and the "self-and-world representations of the colonizer." Literary scholar Kofi Agovi traces that dependency to a colonial cultural policy of direct and indirect patronage of private initiatives in the arts, designed to put Africans in a position of total allegiance to Western forms of representation. In the Gold Coast, the colonial authorities deployed performance practices and spaces for such purposes in two key sites, the European social clubs and the colonial schools.[36]

European social clubs were first set up to relieve the boredom of colonial administrators and expatriate staff, but they transformed into centers of European cultural excellence and behavior held up by the African elite as worthy of emulation. They modeled taste in European wear, ballroom dancing, theatre production, and "'civilized' social interaction between the races," with Europeans showering approval where expected standards had been met. In the schools, performances deployed to hegemonic ends included those of Empire Day celebrations in which students enacted allegiance to the British Crown in pageants and plays. By the 1930s colonial authorities had adopted an alternative approach with schools, as liberal voices in the British colonial service suggested that Africans should be allowed to respect their own traditions and customs and take pride in their past. This approach, conditioned by the theory of the separate development of the races, fit with the colonial strategy of indirect rule in which authorities promoted African cultural forms but only as part of a hierarchy in which European forms of expressive culture remained at the apex. Performance spaces privileged box (proscenium) sets common in European-style theatres over "traditional" African in-the-round staging. Basically, in both the schools and the clubs, African self and world representations remained subordinated to those of the colonizers.[37]

It is against this background that the committee advising Nkrumah on steps toward a national theatre movement indicated that there was a threat to the "traditional culture" of people of the Gold Coast and recommended the setting up of the Arts Council to "formulate and carry out a practical policy for the national theatre movement." The national theatre movement itself was envisioned to bring about a postindependence national theatre that would draw "its vitality and authenticity from roots firmly planted in the traditions of the people." Returning to one's roots, however, did not mean imprisoning one's self in the past. Thus, the movement was charged, equally, with "refashion[ing] indigenous Ghanaian traditions to suit the modern theatre through creative experimentation."[38] In seeking to fulfill this two-pronged mission, the national theatre movement found models in the work of African playwrights from the colonial period, such as Kobina Sekyi, F. K. Fiawoo, and J. B. Danquah. Sekyi's *Blinkards* (1915) scathingly lampooned African imitators of European ways of life, casting them as slavish, perverted bearers of "all the marks of a decadent pseudo-Western-civilization." Yet Sekyi's critique—judging by, at least, the literary-dramatic mode of its expression—was targeted at the uncritical mania of the mimicry and not at mere appropriation from Europe. F. K. Fiawoo described his *Fifth Landing Stage* (1937) as a message "from the forefathers" in the form of a "little book" for "the benefit . . . of all who desire to know something about the customs of our ancient [Anlo] people." The play, he added, retains one of "three unities," the unity of action, that Aristotle and his followers viewed "as fundamental principles of drama." Using a different dramatic model, Danquah's *Third Woman* (1943) is inspired by a story from the corpus of Akan Anansesem and F. de P. Castell's book *Prehistoric Man in Genesis*. It dramatizes the future leadership of the European-educated modern African évolué who, until that future's resolution of self-doubt, will remain out of his element with no satisfactory place in an African society. The play opposes Africa to Europe but views the conflict optimistically, suggesting that some things inherited from the West can contribute to the "world of harmony concord and peace" that the "third woman" symbolizes.[39]

Nkrumah's own concern with forging a coherent national culture/identity also prompted his vested interest in the national theatre movement during the 1950s. He was of the opinion that colonialism had stunted the development of the African Personality. Nkrumah borrowed the idea of African Personality from the St. Thomas–born Liberian Edward Blyden, a clergyman and professor who served in the Liberian government as secretary of state and ambassador. Blyden did not question race as a category. In other words, rather than seeing race as the social construct that it is, he accepted European theories that divided races by presuming that each has enduring and thus defining moral-cultural and intellectual characteristics.[40] But somehow, he took the theories to different conclusions. He believed that just as we see some variation of God's thought and beauty in every form of the universe, "so in each separate man, in each separate race, something of the absolute is incarnated."[41] He challenged conclusions of white superiority by arguing that no scale of achievement necessarily placed one "race" above another: "Races" were different but equal and complementary, and each had its own "personality" to contribute to human civilization; so while a given race may be less successful in some pursuits, it was likely more successful in others.[42] He validated civilization as it had developed in Africa apart from European influence, maintaining that Africans could pursue time-honored, time-tested ideas, outlooks, and customs, secure in the knowledge of their intrinsic merit as unique elements of African culture/genius that constituted Africa's distinctive positive contribution to the progress of humanity.

Blyden believed in the fundamental communality of African life, that Africans are distinctive in their values of cooperation and mutual aid, in contrast to the "harsh, individualist, competitive and combative" character of European society. Similarly, Nkrumah believed that "the personality and conscience of Africa" was rooted in communitarianism or, as he put it, "duty to support one another and make the happiness of others a condition for the happiness of oneself." He thus defined the African Personality in terms of nonexploitative, cooperative communalistic principles that presumably underlie indigenous African society.[43] Blyden argued that European education was designed not to bring out the genius of the African Personality but to present him as "a funny, inept creature," implant in him an "inferiority complex," and make him an "inadequate copy rather than equal" to the European. Nkrumah echoed this, writing: "We were trained to be inferior copies of Englishmen, caricatures to be laughed at with our pretensions to British bourgeois gentility . . . denied knowledge of our African past and informed we had no present . . . taught to regard our culture and traditions as barbarous and primitive."[44] Blyden "constructed a shield of cultural nationalism to repulse the assault of European cultural imperialism," maintaining that Africa could rise to its ordained heights only through its own cultural and educational institutions. Nkrumah similarly believed that although the alienation and abuses of colonization had suppressed the African Personality, Africa could "redeem its past glory . . . [and] renew its strength . . . in a new era of prosperity and power" by embracing this Personality.[45] Finally, Blyden, convinced a fully realized African Personality "would animate and govern independent Africa," called on Africans to merge into one "great, strong, populous and prospering state." Again, like Blyden, Nkrumah believed that a complete African Personality would be possible only in tandem with African unity; he wrote that to make possible the full expression of the African Personality, African people would have to nurture their culture *and* to politically unite.[46]

In was thus in Blyden's shadow that Nkrumah declared on the night of Ghana's independence that Ghanaians were going to create their own African

Personality. The African Personality, ethnomusicologist J. H. Kwabena Nketsia explained, was "at once liberating and creative, bringing into focus African alternatives to Western values and institutions." This was necessary to "combat the claim to the universality of Western culture" with "an African alternative that would assert a valid African civilization, both at home and abroad."[47] He feared that due to the enduring effects of colonialism, Africans were, even after independence, likely to continue to articulate their selves and their worlds in colonial terms, with a mindset that retained representations of the former colonial master. Political sovereignty was thus important but just a first stage of decolonization that would not result in full flowering of the African Personality. He envisioned a secondary decolonization, what Halm describes as a "cultural ontological revolution" of a sort on the symbolic realm.[48] This revolution was to effect the blossoming of the African Personality by raising the erstwhile colonial subject from prostration to the discourses and representations of the departed colonizer. Nkrumah's notion of African Personality was not an atavistic imprisonment in the traditional "past." He believed, for instance, that the economic goals of socialism were harmonious with those of traditional African principles. His quest for the African Personality was thus, as I have stated elsewhere, a determination to recast African society in its traditional forms, wedding what is valuable from the past to modern ideas while developing a new identity that was wider than ethnic and national affiliations. The Arts Council of Ghana to which he appointed Sutherland, the national theatre movement that the council was charged to organize, and the national theatre building proposed to house work of the theatre movement were all part of Nkrumah's project to shatter the colonial mentality and restore the African Personality.

Sutherland, in line with the idea of the African Personality and the vision for the national theatre movement, sought "to link modern theatre to the [indigenous] dramatic traditions of the country."[49] Her experimentation with plays based on the folkloric spider trickster Ananse was one example of this effort to speak to Ghanaians "in terms that were important to them."[50] Her construction of the Drama Studio allowed her the space to continue her effort through the national theatre movement to recuperate the African Personality. *Foriwa*, and *Edufa*—both plays she wrote and debuted at the Studio—dramatize a suppression of the African Personality and the possibilities for its full flowering. *Edufa* reworks Euripides's play *Alcestis* in an African idiom: insecure but prosperous Edufa obtains a charm to thwart a forecast of his death, a charm that works by making whoever declares the most love for him his death substitute.[51] When his wife becomes his substitute he tries, in vain, to reverse the charm. *Edufa* is the tragic drama of the self-confessed "emancipated" man whose emancipation takes the form of a destructive individualism that violates his community's values. *Foriwa* draws on folklore, ritual, and ceremony to dramatize "a dawn of consciousness" when the debilitative parochialism of the inhabitants of the fictional town Kyerefaso gives way to an inclusive, progressive, truly communal society. In it, Sutherland divests "tradition" from connotations of dormancy, narrow conservatism, and stale repetition and valorizes it as a site for reimagination, renewal, and transformation. Kyerefaso emerges as the model for the African Personality of the postindependent Ghanaian nation.[52] The design of the Drama Studio, where these plays were performed, had the expected features of a modest modern theatre but was spatially and architecturally cast to imbue it with the sacredness of an ancestral communal community space, making it a strong example of what historian Mitchell Schwarzer calls "architectural nationalism." The Drama Studio exemplified how the "design of a building . . . represents or advances ideas of the nation" and was equally a superb embodiment of the national theatre movement's mandate to draw vitality from indigenous traditions and refashion them in modernist experimentations.[53]

Of Monuments and Replicas: The Life (and Death?) of the Drama Studio after Nkrumah

Nkrumah's government did not officially declare the Drama Studio a national theatre. But, his presence at the Studio's opening, and his linking of it to the African Personality, indicates that he saw it as a liberating and creative alternative to Western values and institutions and an assertion of the validity of African civilization. Because the building and the work that went on within it was thoroughly concerned with representing and thereby promoting ideas about the nation—whether the representation was in resistance to or underwritten by the state authorities—and because it assiduously pursued the national theatre movement's vision of causing the nationalist cultural, countercolonial African Personality to blossom through a theatre that unsettled rigid boundaries between African tradition and African modernity, the Drama Studio was, in looks and deeds if not in name, very much a national theatre. However, as I noted at the beginning of this essay, most nationalist cultural projects have broad notions of identity that must inevitably confront the problem of multiple selves and worlds and the complex cluster of interplaying identities that we, as individuals and communities, entail in any given context of cultural representation. What this means is that the contours and constitution of the "national" rarely have a consensus in or across time. John Tomlinson speaks to this when he writes, "National identity is nearly always a vexed form of identification" and quotes Anthony Giddens's observation that feelings of national belonging are "rather more complex than a set of symbols and beliefs force-fed to a population."[54] The Drama Studio, as I now show in my concluding section, was born amid contentions in Ghana about what kind of theatre house should represent the nation. While it won out for a good part of the new nation's history, time and another iteration of the idea of the national brought interest in a gyase-type theatre-in-the-round to its end.

Principal theatre practitioners in Ghana during the 1950s and 1960s were not in agreement about framing the objectives of the national theatre movement in terms of the African Personality. Even those who were often disagreed about what kinds of theatre—or theatre architecture—represented the idea. Director-playwright Joe de Graft was quite resistant to what he saw as the overbearing ideological imperatives of the national theatre movement. He questioned the very idea of the African Personality, writing, "The idea of 'the African Personality' needs looking at very critically, especially if at the center of it is to be placed the African fossil, with all that constitutes his supposed 'traditional culture,' for the edification of curious scholars and easy-handed tourists."[55]

As a theatre practitioner, de Graft feared not simply the fossilization and exoticization of culture that could arise from an emphasis on traditional and indigenous cultural but also what that would do to the African dramatists who "are fundamentally individualist with a fierce pride in their individual effort, their unique ideas, their artistic integrity, and their achievement." De Graft saw such an artist saddled with a burdensome dilemma of satisfying his drive to a uniqueness of thought and expression while responding affirmatively to his African roots—to "return to attitudes and modes of creative thinking that are more in consonance with a folkish milieu that is probably fast ceasing to exist for him." We should not expect, de Graft warned, all artists to be "temperamentally capable of responding affirmatively to the call."[56]

De Graft opposed the part of the African Personality idea that suggested that the communal ethos is the underlying and unchanging true soul or essence of the African. He saw this as an essentialist cultural revivalism that could be uncreative. He did not want Ghanaian theatre and drama to be limited by having to be seen as African projects per se. One can deduce from his views that he divorced individualism from the debilitative and competitive colonial mentality and pathology that Blyden and Nkrumah assigned it and instead associated individualism with artistic integrity and personal achievement. What is more, de Graft did not regard a national theatre building to be a present priority, not just because "one needs not wait for theatre buildings before one engages in theatre" but also because, he said, it is "unwise to spend a lot of money on theatre buildings" when this money could be used "to a better advantage financing training programs for the performing arts and encouraging drama in schools." Still, he was not against a national theatre building under the following conditions: "if development of human skill and superior artistic product were central to the building scheme; if the plans were for several modestly designed community centers with flexible staging facilities [like the Drama Studio]," rather than "an imposing" building sited in a prestigious area of town where "few ordinary people ventured during nonworking hours of the day"; and if the "blueprints" of the building scheme were not overdetermined by "an ideological approach" to theatre.[57]

Morriseau Leroy—a Haitian émigré who joined the movement—jabbed at artists like de Graft, saying that they are blinded by what they call "artistic liberty" and "ideological neutrality" to "the reality of their ideological commitment to the opposing side of Africa's struggle for cultural emancipation."[58] Sutherland is reported to have called de Graft "a new colonialist," and ethnomusicologist Kwabena Nketsia recalls thinking that de Graft was not interested in African theatre.[59] The collaboration between Sutherland and de Graft (e.g., de Graft was the first director of the Drama Studio) shows that, the contention notwithstanding, there was more middle ground for their mutual endeavors in the movement. Still, there *was* contention over how much the work of the movement should be determined by the cultural nationalist idea of African Personality—a contention that had theatre-architectural implications.

Observers tend to agree that there was at least something of a flag in the vibrancy of the national theatre movement by the end of the 1960s. The "first deep reason" the national theatre movement "failed," Halm argues, is the "intractable problems" of its ideological concern with "appropriating romantic-racialist terms of African personalism and neo-African culturalism" and of attempting to "recuperate a nostalgic-atavistic pre-colonial self-and-world" and dismissing any alternative projects as somehow "ideologically indefensible."[60] For Asiedu Yirenkyi the national theatre movement was "a ghost movement from the start" that existed merely "in the dreams and rhetoric of its exponents." He charges that the days of the call for the African Personality "were not days of objectivity" but, rather, of high emotion and "cultural polarization"—a state of "national controversy"—that imposed artistic limitations. Emotional "slogans of cultural nationalism" so "bombarded" the theatre that sometimes "it was difficult to evaluate where political rhetoric ended and where cultural revival and arts began." This problem, he adds, "exercised the most crippling effects" on the artists who operated in the national theatre movement and posed a major impediment to the “free and natural development” of the theatre.[61] Halm and Yirenkyi suggest that a stunting effect on creativity in a movement overdetermined by an essentialist ideology—the very problem de Graft warned about—seemed to have been the undoing of the movement right from its start. What they note here seems to me to be the problem of nationalism itself, which, although it plays a powerful role in instilling a sense of national commitment and belonging, relies on essentialist, exclusionary notions of identity.

For Yirenkyi the Ghana Experimental Drama Studio was as emblematic of the failure as it was of the ideology. He charges that the Drama Studio “sacrificed art and creativity for a politics of nationalism” and that the building was “inspiring” from a “theoretical and nationalist point of view” but “made for bad theatre and a headache for a director.”[62] I would find Yirenkyi’s critique more compelling if he provided more details about what he means by “bad theater” and what constituted a “headache.” A theatre building is usually mostly good for the kind of theatre it is designed to occupy. And if history has anything to teach us, what is “bad” or “good” theatre has many times been in the eyes of the proverbial beholder. In any case, whether the national theatre movement was in fact a failure, there is no doubt that after February 28, 1966, when a military coup ousted Nkrumah from office, the movement lost the critical government support and state-level prominence and patronage that it had enjoyed. In 1968, the new military regime reconstituted the Arts Council by a decree. However, by 1969, some of the council’s departments were virtually dead.[63] The School of Performing Arts (SPA) at the University of Ghana, which Nkrumah challenged to develop “new forms of drama and creative writing . . . related to Ghanaian traditions and expressive of Ghanaian aspirations” (perhaps because of the intellectual freedom that protected it), became a de facto site of the national theatre movement.[64] Sutherland had joined the faculty of the SPA in 1963, and in 1972 she handed over the Studio to the university for use in training theatre artists, asking that its architectural presence on an important site in the capital be protected without compromise.[65]

While less the kind of de facto national theatre than it had been in the 1960s, the Studio under the SPA became something of a monument to the national theatre movement. In 1968 Sutherland started a new theatre group committed to the use of Akan, the most widely spoken local language in Ghana, and this represented a new phase of her theatre work. Although this group thrived briefly in the late 1960s, it had been, by the 1970s and especially by the 1980s, affected by the turbulence of political instability and economic inflation. Around the same time, the government of Flight Lieutenant J. J. Rawlings took power through another military coup, amid a pervasive venality that public corruption and a spate of political and economic instability had created in Ghana. Rawlings observed that, both materially and politically, the people of Ghana suffered from a kind of national malaise: a "loss of dignity . . . confidence and . . . moral fiber." He thus proclaimed "a battle for national survival," to renew Ghanaians' belief in their selves and in their capacity "to transform their societies" by "virtue of their own abilities and energies." A part of this battle was a national cultural revival to heal the malaise.[66]

Rawlings pledged to promote "all that is good and admirable" in Ghanaian culture, including the ability to "resolve problems using Ghanaian experiences and cultural background." He suggested that a properly promoted national culture program focused on Ghanaians' sense of identity and pride as members of a national community could instill personal discipline and inspire a commitment to work and social justice—all things that would address unemployment and inequality and stave off the depression and apathy that political and economic instability under previous regimes had wrought. He indicated his confidence in Ghanaians' creativity—"inborn talents" that "necessitates the creation of opportunities for self-expression"—as a quality that they could translate into their social and economic uplift.[67] He signaled the role that he saw for theatre in the cultural revival when he appointed Yirenkyi—a former student of Sutherland who, as I showed earlier, wrote as a critic and skeptic of the national theatre movement and the Drama Studio—to head his Ministry of Culture. Rawlings tasked Yirenkyi with instituting a cultural revival program to give "direction and guidance" to cultural workers and "the broad mass of the people."[68] Yirenkyi insisted that an "attempt to revive culture in Ghana" would "be meaningless" *without a proper edifice for the purpose*, but he left office in 1984 without any concrete plans.[69]

Yirenkyi's successor Mohammed ben Abdallah, also a dramatist and former student of Sutherland, took on the project with the result that in 1985 Rawlings signed a Co-operation Agreement for China's government to construct a National Theatre Complex. Rawlings's military government chose the site of the Drama Studio for the new National Theatre Complex. There was no public explanation for the Rawlings government's choice of this particular location for the new theatre to my knowledge, nor have I come across one. This silence makes for much speculation, but it is no speculation that Sutherland was not pleased at all with the planned demolition of the Drama Studio. Her displeasure made the government negotiate with the Chinese, who were to fund and build the new complex and to also build a replica of the Drama Studio "somewhere else." Sutherland found no comfort in such a replica and wrote a memo to the government, copied to the university, warning that if it went ahead with demolishing the Studio it would be signaling the "decisive conclusion of a 25-year period of research and creative work" in "the development of Ghana's . . . dramatic arts." She also asked that "the proposition of a substitute Drama Studio somewhere in Accra" be discarded and that "attention [be] given to research and experimental creative work around the country where rich lodes of our distinctive dramatic heritage abound."[70] In 1987 the University of Ghana completed a yearlong celebration of the Studio's twenty-fifth anniversary with an impressive and symbolic ceremony. That same year there was a government order for the demolition of the Studio—this concrete tangible legacy of the national theatre movement—to make way for a new National Theatre Complex on the same location.

In 1990 the Rawlings government tore down the Studio and, at the same time, rebuilt a replica at the University of Ghana campus and began constructing the National Theatre Complex. Sutherland refused to set foot in either the replica or the new complex for the rest of her life; she died in 1995.[71] The decision to demolish the Drama Studio and replace it with a new National Theatre Complex highlights the crucial distinctions between history and heritage in the role architecture plays as an embodiment of national identity and community. Identities are built, to some degree, on memories. Consequently, as Delanty and Jones observe, "the presence of the past," of history, in present-day architecture "cannot be denied."[72] However, a major change occurs when architecture is claimed as part of a nation's heritage as opposed to part of a nation's history. The former acknowledges "a debt": it implies that the architecture somehow contributes significantly and positively to the construction of present-day identity.[73] Yet, the question remains: Which memories are to be preserved? What is it about the past that makes present-day architecture worth keeping? Distinctions between history and heritage become blurred, and architecture becomes, as happened with the razing of the Drama Studio, "a major focal point for cultural tensions and even conflicts."[74] The building of a replica of the Studio did not placate what appears to be Sutherland's anguish that the Studio had been tagged simply as part of our national history and not, more importantly, as part of a national heritage. This, it seems, is what nationalisms—theatrical and architectural nationalisms included—are made of; the dominant ideas of national culture and identity are forged and maintained by force fields of power. When the tide of history changes, and different priorities and ideas occupy the purview of those force fields, what is here today may be gone tomorrow.

Notes

1. Robert W. July, *An African Voice* (Durham, NC: Duke University Press, 1987), 73.
2. Ibid., 74.
3. Benedict Anderson, *Imagined Communities: Reflections on the Origin and Spread of Nationalism* (London: Verso, 1983), 46–47; Anthony Giddens, *A Contemporary Critique of Historical Materialism, Volume One: Power, Property and the State* (London: Macmillan, 1981), 182–202; Ernest Gellner, *Nations and Nationalism* (Oxford: Blackwell, 1983), 35–43.
4. James Gibbs offers a very good account of Sutherland's transition experience abroad and her transition into teaching and theatre work upon her return. See *Nkyin-Kyin: Essays on the Ghanaian Theatre* (Amsterdam: Rodopi, 2009), 92–96.
5. Ibid., 96.
6. Ibid., 100.
7. Robert Fraser, *West African Poetry: A Critical History* (Cambridge: Cambridge University Press, 1986), 142.
8. Efua Sutherland, "The Redeemed," in *Messages: Poems from Ghana*, ed. Kofi Awoonor and G. Adalai-Morty (London: Heinemann, 1971), 159.
9. Gibbs, *Nkyin-Kyin*, 94–5.
10. July, *An African Voice*, 74.
11. Kwame Botwe-Asamoah, *Kwame Nkrumah's Politico-Cultural Thought and Policies: An African-Centered Paradigm for the Second Phase of the African Revolution* (New York: Routledge, 2005), 156–70.
12. Gibbs, *Nkyin-Kyin*, 98.
13. July, *An African Voice*, 76.
14. Efua Sutherland, "Venture into Theatre," *Okyeame* 1, no. 1 (1960): 48.
15. July, *An African Voice*, 76.
16. Botwe-Asamoah, *Kwame Nkrumah's Politico-Cultural Thought*, 159.
17. Labelle Prussin, "Traditional Asante Architecture," *African Arts* 13, no. 2 (1980): 58–62.
18. Ibid., 58.
19. H. N. A. Wellington, "Architecture, Spatial Development for Community," in *The Legacy of Efua Sutherland: Pan African Activism*, ed. Anne V. Adams and Esi Sutherland Addy (Banbury, UK: Ayebia Clarke, 2007), 179–85.
20. Albert Kayper Mensah, *Sankofa: Adinkra Poems* (Tema: Ghana Publishing Corporation, 1976), 17.
21. Wellington, "Architecture, Spatial Development," 185.
22. July, *An African Voice*, 76.
23. K. E. Agovi, "Towards an Authentic African Theatre," *Ufahumu* 19, nos. 2 and 3 (1991): 72.
24. July, *An African Voice*, 76.
25. Ibid., 73.
26. Patience Addo and James Gibbs, "Ghana," in *The World Encyclopedia of Contemporary Theatre*, Volume 3: *Africa*, ed. John Rubin (New York: Routledge, 1997), 145.
27. July, *An African Voice*, 73.
28. There were direct connections between some of the expatriate architects of these public buildings and European architectural giants. Harry Weese, designer of the American Embassy building, was a former student of Finnish architect Alvar Aalto. Maxwell Fry,

designer of the National Museum and Accra Community Center, worked with pioneering masters of modern architecture such as Le Corbusier and Walter Gropius.

29. Among them, James Cubitt designed the Accra Technical Institute, and Kenneth Scott designed a Barclays Bank branch building and several other office complexes, wards of the Korle Bu Teaching Hospital (the third largest hospital in Africa and the top referral center in Ghana), and the British Council Library.

30. A School of Architecture in Kumasi was opened in 1957 but did not really take off until the 1960s, so expatriates' expertise was a default choice for the architectural commissions of the era and for training an emergent cadre of local architects. See Le Roux, "Networks," 349.

31. Nkrumah cited in H. O. McWilliam and M. A. Kwamena-Poh, *The Development of Education in Ghana* (London: Longmans, 1978), 94.

32. Hannah Le Roux, "Architecture in Postcolonial Ghana and Nigeria," *Architectural History* 47 (2004): 369.

33. Rhodri Windsor-Liscombe, "Modernism in Late Imperial British West Africa: The Work of Maxwell Fry and James Drew, 1946–56," *Journal of the Society of Architectural Historians* 65, no. 2 (2006): 188.

34. Loren Kruger, *The National Stage: Theatre and Cultural Legitimation in England, France and America* (Chicago: University of Chicago Press, 1992), 3.

35. Botwe-Asamoah, *Kwame Nkrumah's Politico-Cultural Thought*, 158.

36. See Ben Halm, *Theatre and Ideology* (Selinsgrove: Susquehanna University Press, 1995), 178; and K. E. Agovi, "The Origin of Literary Theatre in Colonial Ghana, 1920–1957," *Research Review* 6, no. 1 (1990): 6–10.

37. Agovi, "The Origin," 6–10.

38. Ibid., 3.

39. See analysis of Fiawoo's play by Graham-White (*The Drama of Black Africa* [New York: Samuel French, 1974], 86) and of Danquah's by O. R. Dathorne (*The Black Mind: A History of African Literature* [Minneapolis: University of Minnesota Press, 1974], 402–3).

40. It is ironic that these were theories enunciated by colonizationists and upholders of slavery. These people were united by their belief in, among other things, the innate and permanent differences in the moral and metal endowments of races—for example, the Frenchman Count Arthur de Gobineau, whose *Essay on the Inequality of the Races* was regarded as the classical nineteenth-century statement on the subject, and the English School of Anthropology, led by James Hunt and Richard Burton—in the "unnatural" character of miscegenation, in the idea that racial homogeneity was necessary for successful nation building, and in the notion that mulattoes were immoral and weak (see Hollis R. Lynch, *Edward Wilmot Blyden: Pan-Negro Patriot 1832-1912* [London: Oxford University Press, 1967], 58–60). Today, it is almost superfluous to point out the indefensibility of these ideas. However, these men, and Blyden, held such ideas.

41. Edward Wilmot Blyden, *The African Problem and the Method of Its Solution* (Washington, DC: Gibson, 1890), 22–23.

42. Edward Wilmot Blyden, *African Life and Customs* (London: C. M. Phillips, 1908), 8–9; *African Times*, July 22, 1865.

43. See Lynch, *Edward Wilmot Blyden*, 61–62; and Kwame Nkrumah, *Consciencism* (New York: Monthly Review Press, 1964), 49–50, 74.

44. See Blyden, *Christianity, Islam and the Negro Race* (Edinburgh: Edinburgh University Press, 1967), 38; and Nkrumah, *Africa Must Unite* (London: Heinemann, 1963), 49.
45. See Robert July, *The Origins of Modern African Thought: Its Development in West Africa During the Nineteenth and Twentieth Centuries* (London: Faber and Faber, 1968), v; and Nkrumah, *Axioms of Kwame Nkrumah* (London: Panaf Books, 1967), 17.
46. See Jacob Drachler, *Black Homeland/Black Diaspora: Cross Currents of the African Relationship* (Port Washington, NY: 1975), 53–54; M. Frenkel, *Edward Blyden and African Nationalism*, 109; and Nkrumah, *Africa Must Unite*, 49.
47. Kwabena Nketsia, quoted in Robert July, *An African Voice*, 181.
48. Ben E. Halm recognizes the fetishizing of European cultural imports by using the term "magical-symbolic" for them in *Theatre and Ideology*, 178.
49. July, *The Origins of Modern African*, 75.
50. Ibid., 76.
51. Efua Sutherland, *Edufa* (London: Longmans, 1967).
52. For more detailed analyses of these two plays, see Lloyd Brown, "The African Woman as Writer," *Canadian Journal of African Studies* 9, no. 3 (1975): 497; Charles Angmor, *Contemporary Literature in Ghana: A Critical Evaluation* (Accra: Woeli, 1996), 201; G. Wilentz, *Binding Cultures: Black Women Writers in Africa and the Diaspora* (Bloomington: Indiana University Press, 1992), 25, 34–35.
53. Mitchell Schwarzer, "The Sources of Architectural Nationalism," in *Nationalism and Architecture*, ed. Darren Dean and Sarah Butler (New York: Routledge, 2016), 19.
54. John Tomlinson, *Cultural Imperialism* (Baltimore: Johns Hopkins University Press, 1991), 79. Tomlinson quotes Giddens, *A Contemporary Critique*, 192.
55. J. C. de Graft, "Dramatic Questions," in *Writers in East Africa*, ed. Andrew Gurr and Angus Calder (Nairobi: East African Publishing House, 1974), 55.
56. J. C. de Graft, "Roots in African Drama and Theatre," *African Literature Today* 8, no. 1, (1976): 32.
57. J. C. de Graft, "Drama Workshop 1963," *Okyeame* 2, no. 1 (1964) 48–50; de Graft, "Dramatic Questions," 64–65.
58. Felix Morriseau-Leroy, "African National Theatre," *Okyeame* 4, no. 1 (1968): 91.
59. J. W. Shipley, *Trickster Theater: The Poetics of Freedom in Urban Africa* (Bloomington: Indiana University Press, 2015), 61.
60. Halm, *Theatre and Ideology*, 185, 187, 193.
61. Asiedu Yirenkyi, "Kobina Sekyi: Founding Father of the Ghanaian Theatre," *The Legacy* 3, no. 2 (1977): 39–40.
62. Ibid., 46.
63. Jawa Apronti and Akyea Ofori, "Interview with Arts Council Staff," *Okyeame* 4, no. 2 (1969): 105.
64. Nkrumah, "African Genuis, Speech Delivered at the Opening of the Institute of African Studies on October 25, 1963," in *Handbook of the 30th Anniversary Celebration of the Institute of African Studies and the School of Performing Arts* (Legon: University of Ghana, 1993) 12–21.
65. See Wellington, "Architecture, Spatial Development," 184.
66. "Towards a Better Ghana," *Selected Speeches of Flt. Lt. J. J. Rawlings*, vol. 2 (Accra:

Information Services Department, 1983), 73; "Preserving Our Environment," *Selected Speeches*, 60; "Using Creative Potential to Improve Living Standards," *Selected Speeches*, 2:1.

67. "Using Creative Potential to Improve Living Standards," *Selected Speeches*, 2:1.

68. Ben Ephson, "Ghana's Cultural Revival," *West Africa* (July 1982): 1759.

69. Ibid.

70. Addo and Gibbs, "Ghana," 119.

71. Shipley, *Trickster Theater*, 98.

72. Gerard Delanty and Paul Jones, "European Identity and Architecture," *European Journal of Social Theory* 5, no. 4 (2002): 460.

73. Nigel Whiteley, "Modern Architecture, Heritage and Englishness," *Architectural History* 38 (1995): 222.

74. Delanty and Jones, *European Identity*, 460.

Preparing Boys for War

J. M. Barrie's *Peter Pan* Enlists in World War I's "Great Adventure"

—LAURA FERDINAND FELDMEYER

To die will be an awfully big adventure.
SIR JAMES BARRIE, *PETER PAN*

On May 3, 1922, renowned author and playwright Sir James Barrie stood fearful and silent before the students of the University of St. Andrews.[1] Three years earlier, he had been honored by the student body when they elected him rector of the university—a position given to men, and later women, of "great worth and fame" to serve on the University Court as a student advocate.[2] Elected in 1919 at the close of World War I, Barrie had delayed his inaugural address several years, delivering it at last near the end of his term as rector in his self-proclaimed "first and last public appearance."[3] Finally provoked by the audience to speak, Barrie delivered his famous speech "Courage," which personified "Youth" and "Age" as symbolic characters. In it he questioned Britain's engagement in World War I, accused Age of ignorantly glamorizing warfare, and urged the Youth to demand a say in the national matters that concerned them. Seeing himself as part of Age, which he also referred to as "the Old Men," Barrie confessed, "When war did come, we told Youth, who had to get us out of it, tall tales of what it really is and the clover beds it would lead to. We were not meaning to deceive, most of us were as honourable and as ignorant as the Youth themselves; but that does not acquit us of stupidity and jealousy, the two black spots in human nature which, more than love of money, are at the root of all evil."[4] Unknown to the audience (and unknown to the public until 1935), Barrie had participated in the War Propaganda Bureau (WPB), a secret government operation that turned to English writers for help.[5]

Although most of the papers of the WPB (also referred to as Wellington House) were lost or destroyed when the bureau shut down at the end of World War I, there is strong evidence that Barrie—along with other writers such as Rudyard Kipling, John Galsworthy, and Sir Arthur Conan Doyle—contributed to the bureau that organized "public statements of the strength of the British case and principles in the war by well-known men of letters."[6] However, as Jeffrey Reznick writes in *John Galsworthy and Disabled Soldiers of the Great War*, "many former WPB writers and other authors became deeply embittered about the Allied propaganda machine and their role in the creation of patriotic pamphlets, heroic fiction and 'front line' but glamorized reporting" long before the end of the war.[7] Remorseful of his involvement in creating and promoting the "tall tales" that equated war with a great adventure, Barrie sought to empower youth: "You have more in common with the youth of other lands than Youth and Age can ever have with each other. . . . Even the hostile countries sent out many a son very like ours, from the same sort of homes, the same sort of universities, with the same sort of hearts, who had as little to do as our Youth had with the origin of the great Adventure."[8] Barrie's use of the phrase "great adventure" would have undoubtedly recalled one of Peter's most famous lines ("To die will be an awfully big adventure") in the minds of the audience, as *Peter Pan*, in addition to being a popular play and novel, had become one of Britain's most pervasive propaganda tools during the war. As such, Peter's youthful declaration of bravery became an anthem of pro-war sentiment: a great adventure for "The Great War."

In the context of our contemporary culture—in which the phrases "boy crisis" and "crisis of masculinity" have entered our everyday vocabulary with publications such as the *Peter Pan*-referencing *Lost Boys: Why Our Sons Turn Violent and How We Can Save Them* (1999) by James Garbarino—histories that discuss the ways in which boys are taught to be men take on a new poignancy and immediacy. As the ways boys are raised and the definitions of masculinity come into question, an interrogation into the myths that shape notions of boyhood and masculinity is increasingly important. *Peter Pan* is a particularly apt heuristic device for understanding the changing conditioning of boys because it has endured and evolved for well over a century. With movie adaptations in 2003 and 2015, fictionalized Broadway and Hollywood biographies of J. M. Barrie (*Finding Neverland*), a Tony Award–winning prequel (*Peter and the*

Starcatcher), and countless other contemporary iterations such as the hit children's cartoon *Jake and the Never Land Pirates*, *Peter Pan* is as much a part of the cultural imagination as it ever was. And yet, the legacy of *Peter Pan*'s history with war and its use as British wartime propaganda has been almost entirely forgotten.

By returning to *Peter Pan* and interrogating its conceptions of boyhood and adventure in regard to its use as wartime propaganda, the ways in which young men are currently being conditioned may be better understood. Here I must give credit to Linda Robertson and her excellent essay "'To Die Will Be an Awfully Big Adventure': Peter Pan and World War I" (2009). Her work prompted me to delve further into the sentiment that pervaded England and America during World War I and, more specifically, into the connection between Barrie's relationship to the war and the script of *Peter Pan*. This article furthers Robertson's fine discussion by historicizing the role of *Peter Pan* in constructing boyhood and ideals of masculinity in the early twentieth century and beyond. Centering on Barrie's change of heart regarding the "adventure" of war and his attempt to reclaim his story amid its use as prowar propaganda, this study will reveal the cultural and political potency of a script too often dismissed as childish fantasy.

Charting the history of the line "To die will be an awfully big adventure" from its first use in the late 1890s until Barrie's death in 1937 reveals the ways in which *Peter Pan* both influenced and was influenced by the shifting cultural zeitgeist surrounding boyhood, masculinity, and war at the beginning of the twentieth century. Because Barrie did not publish the script of *Peter Pan* until 1928, twenty-four years after its premiere, his changing sentiment can be charted in his substantial revisions to the play, revisions that are preserved in his notebooks as well as in the extant rehearsal scripts from annual productions of the play at London's Duke of York's Theatre. Through a careful examination of the play's changing script, the treatment of the line "To die will be an awfully big adventure" both on and offstage, and other primary sources from Barrie's life and contemporaneous Western media, this article explores the effect of *Peter Pan*'s great adventure narrative on the Western cultural imagination and constructions of boyhood in the early twentieth century.

The Great Adventure

The great adventure myth was deeply ingrained in the Western cultural imagination at the turn of the nineteenth century. Popular adventure novels such as Robert Louis Stevenson's 1883 *Treasure Island*, Rudyard Kipling's 1894 *The*

Jungle Book, Stephen Crane's 1895 *The Red Badge of Courage*, and Jack London's 1903 *The Call of the Wild* had long captured the imaginations of British and American youth, who could now cultivate their own adventure skills through newly formed organizations such as the Indian Guides, YMCA, Explorer's Club, and Boy Scouts. Before the war, the appeal of the great adventure reached across the Atlantic and was embraced by both nations: the same adventure novels were read, the same adventure plays were watched (many plays, such as *Peter Pan*, had both London and New York debuts), and the same clubs were joined (the Boy Scouts, which began in Britain in 1904, held its first American meeting in 1906). Even President Theodore Roosevelt would epitomize the myth by dedicating his 1918 book *The Great Adventure: Present-Day Studies in American Nationalism* to "All who in this war have paid with their bodies for their souls' desire."[9] Here, again, adventure is equated with war, both noble and deadly.

It was not until after the war that the transatlantic nature of the great adventure myth began to erode. The two nations had very different wartime experiences as the casualties endured by each were grossly uneven; the United States sustained over 323,000 casualties while Britain endured more than three million, prompting this generation of young men to be known as "the Lost Generation."[10] Furthermore, the war fought at home strained the psyche of the British people, and the great adventure myth would start to be interpreted differently by the two countries as people reexamined whether or not death was really such an awfully big adventure.

In his book *The Great Adventure*, Michael C. C. Adams traces the genealogy of the myth of manhood, discussing how the sentiment of the late-nineteenth- and early-twentieth-century great adventure literature permeated British and American cultures and manifested itself in the journals and letters of soldiers, some real and some fictional. Because this myth was directed at and perpetuated through stories and organizations for young boys, it took on a connotation of innocence. Such a connotation, however, only worked (and continues to work) to make invisible the colonialist and hegemonic forces that are inextricably linked to "the great adventure."

The Victorian era, with its emphasis on the separation of the sexes, its rigidly defined gender roles, and its myth of manhood, preached athleticism, hardiness, and courage in stark contrast to the purported feminine traits associated with the cult of domesticity. At the time Barrie began developing *Peter Pan* in 1897, the Western idea of masculinity was undergoing a paradigm shift. As womanhood became clearly defined in relation to the cult of domesticity, the narratives that scripted the role of men in British society and in the Western world at large took shape in opposition to more "feminine" traits. Scholar Joanna

Bourke explains, "The womanly woman was gentle, domesticated and virginal: the manly man was athletic, stoical and courageous."[11] Out of this rhetoric rose an affinity for war as not only the true expression of manhood but also the only way to obtain it. Take, for example, an excerpt from American ambassador and former military general Horace Porter's 1888 "The Philosophy of Courage," in which he compares two boys: "Let one remain in a quiet city, playing the milksop . . . leading an unambitious namby-pamby life, surrounded by all the safeguards of civilization, while the other goes out on the frontier, runs his chance in encounters with wild animals, finds that to make his way he must take his life in his hand, and assert his rights, if necessary, with deadly weapons, and knows he will be drummed out of the community if he is once caught showing the white feather. In one particular trait of personal courage the frontiersman will undoubtedly become the superior of the lad who has remained at home."[12] Sentiments such as these further defined the domestic as feminine by kicking "superior" boys out of the house and denouncing those who would stay at home. The masculinity of a boy who does not partake in "adventure" (outfitting himself with the skills that would befit a soldier) is called into question, most notably through the homophobic slang term "namby-pamby" that equates lack of strength and courage with effeminate behavior. In 1959, psychologist Ruth Hartley theorized that boys learn to conform to rules of masculinity through repeated humiliations and reprimands—a theory that is still supported today.[13] Statements such as those made by Porter demonstrate the kind of rhetoric that shamed boys into conforming to narrowly defined gender roles.

In her book *Dismembering the Male: Men's Bodies, Britain, and the Great War*, Joanna Bourke begins to interrogate the construction of masculinity at the turn of the century, explaining that "men gained power within the public sphere, but they lost some of their domestic influence as they crowned women the 'angels of the home.'"[14] Masculinity, then, began to take shape in opposition to the role of women, which, by the 1870s, had taken on a rigid social structure as legislative reforms gave certain legal rights to married women and mothers.[15] As the role of women became more clearly defined in the British cultural imagination, both legally and ideologically, the role of men became less clear, as masculinity was constructed in opposition to a changing femininity. Thus, myths of masculinity and boyhood—especially adventure stories—were used as tools for understanding and constructing masculinity and boyhood, as the myths created a sense of community among men. Historian Michael Adams notes that in 1896 British Under Secretary for War and professional soldier George Wyndham, inculcated by this sentiment, wrote, "The terrible things in war are not always terrible; the nauseating things do not always sicken. On the contrary, it is even these which sometimes lift the soul to heights from which they become invisible. . . . Danger is a strong wine. The woman in love, the man in battle, may each say, for their moment, 'I was made perfect too.'"[16] Adams adds that for the kind of men that Wyndam describes (which, in his opinion, is all men in battle), war is the "ultimate expression of life, the equivalent of motherhood for women."[17]

Although there are many examples of the rhetoric that shaped the public discourse of masculinity, it can be difficult to determine the extent to which these ideals were embodied by the population. However, the history of *Peter Pan*, again, offers insight into the ways in which young boys internalized the tropes of masculinity that were espoused with such authority at the turn of the century. In his journals and in the preface to the published script of *Peter Pan*, Barrie reveals that it was not he who wrote some of his play's most famous words; rather, they were spoken for the first time by a young boy, George Llewelyn Davies, in the midst of an imaginary battle as he ran through London's Kensington Gardens: "To die will be an awfully big adventure!"

In 1897 (to give a brief and necessary history of the origins of *Peter Pan*), while walking his dog Porthos in Kensington Gardens, Barrie spotted the red hat of five-year-old George and began a game with him and his brothers Jack and baby Peter. Barrie and the boys met often in the park, where they would act out stories from their favorite adventure novels, playing pirates from Robert Louis Stevenson's *Treasure Island* and Indians from James Fenimore Cooper's *The Last of the Mohicans*. Over time Barrie developed a close (though sometimes strained) relationship with the Llewelyn Davies family—parents, Arthur and Sylvia, and two new brothers, Michael and Nico.

It was during one of their many games in Kensington Gardens that the character Peter Pan first appeared. Barrie and the brothers, whom Barrie referred to as "The Five," played with this idea for many years—taking turns playing Peter, making up characters, adding events, changing endings: *Peter Pan* was a game. In 1903, after the boys had been playing Peter for more than five years, Barrie began to write the manuscript for a play (temporarily called "A Fairy Play") that would eventually be titled *Peter Pan, or The Boy Who Wouldn't Grow Up*. The play, based on the games Barrie shared with the Llewelyn Davies brothers, premiered at London's Duke of York's Theatre on December 27, 1904, to instant success.

Peter Pan, a play whose warfare, ruggedness, and patriotism so squarely fit the ideal of Victorian manhood that it found immediate popularity in London, was transported across the Atlantic the following year. In the original review of the premiere, the *Times* gave a full report of the play, lingering over the moments of true patriotism with relish: "It is now time for the unhappy children to walk the plank—though two of them shall be spared to serve as cabin-boys if only they will cry 'Down with King Edward.' Proudly the dauntless boys reply with 'God save the King,' and 'Rule Britannia,' and so the dread plank is run out over the side."[18] Here, the myth of manhood is manifested in the notion of "dying well," a term that Michael Adams defines as dying nobly in battle.[19] In the scene referred to by the reviewer, Wendy says to the boys, "I feel that I have a message to you from your real mothers, and it is this: 'we hope our sons will die like English gentlemen.'"[20] To die well is the ultimate embodiment of masculinity, and as such the early twentieth-century idea of true masculinity is captured in the line "To die will be an awfully big adventure."

Wellington House

On September 2, 1914, less than a month after Britain declared war with Germany, Charles F. G. Masterman, head of the newly created Wartime Propaganda Bureau (WPB), held a secret meeting at the department offices at Wellington House.[21] In attendance were a large number of British writers who had been gathered to write in support of the British cause. "Seldom in recorded history," Peter Buitenhuis explains, "have a nation's writers so unreservedly rallied round a national cause."[22] Although most of the papers from the WPB were destroyed, evidence remains that these writers contributed by creating pamphlets, giving speeches, and writing news reports. Famous writers such as Arthur Conan Doyle, Rudyard Kipling, Arthur Machen, and Ian Hay all "created colourful fantasies in the form of novels and short stories which emphasized exploits of the Allies and the vileness of the Germans."[23] Among the writers summoned was Barrie, whose play *Peter Pan* had been annually revived in England and the United States since its premieres in 1904 and 1905, respectively. Barrie's work before the war, especially *Peter Pan*, was influential to the myth that sought to define manhood through enlistment into the "great adventure."

Writers were especially useful in creating propaganda for many reasons: for instance, since independent photographers were kept away from the front lines, and many militaries, including Britain's, forbid personal cameras, writers' accounts (instead of photographs) largely served to capture the experience of battle.[24] Most notably, however, was the new power of literature to sway public opinion. When war was declared in August 1914, the British government realized that this war would be different than all the ones that came before, because "late Victorian legislation had raised the general level of literacy and extended the franchise; consequently there were more voters in England to be persuaded of the rightness of the nation's cause, and they could be persuaded in writing. There were also potential soldiers to persuade, for this was to be a war fought by volunteers. And for the first time in English military history they would be *literate* volunteers."[25] C. F. G. Masterman's literary propaganda machine, then, sought to persuade English (and American) youth through a continuation of the great adventure myth they had already subscribed to by drawing upon popular stories and famous authors.

Although writing could educate civilians and potential soldiers and connect them to the soldiers away at war, in practice the writing generated by Wellington House "distanced and falsified the sordid reality of trench warfare."[26] However, the writers who gathered at Wellington House, as Barrie stated in his St. Andrews address, were not intending to deceive. Rather, they felt that they were fulfilling their patriotic duty. In a culture hostile to un-enlisted men (for instance, the public shaming practice of white feather–giving where of-age men not in uniform were presented with white feathers as symbols of cowardice), these authors—men too old to serve in the military—were happy to serve in any way they could. While Buitenhuis says there may have been economic incentives attached to writing for Wellington House (manuscripts were less in demand than before the war, and writers may have needed money), the "chief motivation that caused writers to be carried away by the tide of dedication and ardour that marked England's early war effort" was patriotic fervor.[27] Barrie carried this sentiment with him as he boarded the RMS *Lusitania* in late September 1914 on a trip to the United States meant to garner American support for the British war effort, as much of the WPB effort was directed at the United States.[28]

Despite his creative writings that upheld and perpetuated the great adventure myth that was now being deployed politically, Barrie did not see himself as a political man. Although Barrie began his career as a journalist, "he was never a reader of newspapers, and going into politics meant for him saying to a friend, 'Tell me what is going on in politics, and I'll stop you as soon as I think I have got my article.'"[29] Despite his purported lack of interest in politics, Barrie boarded the *Lusitania* a few weeks after the September meeting at Wellington House for an unofficial visit to the United States to promote American military involvement. The keystone of Barrie's visit was a meeting with Theodore Roosevelt, who was an active supporter of the war, having contributed to the manhood mythmaking (in a testament to the cross-cultural nature of this sentiment) when he penned *The Great Adventure*, and who would send his own sons to Europe as soldiers long before the United States entered the war.[30]

In 1938, journalist Peter Monro Jack discussed Barrie's journalism, saying Barrie "did not know what he was talking about. He had a sense of it, and that was all; but his sense went over, and his sentiment and sensibility did the rest."[31] Was it, then, Barrie's sense of the great adventure that sent him across the Atlantic to promote the war? Were it not for the events that occurred while Barrie was aboard the *Lusitania*, one might draw the conclusion that Barrie's mission was for love of country. "Barrie decided that he should go to America and drum up support for the Allies. Having said to a friend 'we must all try to do something,' he persuaded Gilmour and Mason to go with him. In utmost secrecy about their rather amorphous mission they set off aboard the *Lusitania*. Before they had arrived in the United States word had gotten out, and the clandestine ambassadors were met by letters from the Consul-General and the British Ambassador begging Barrie to call off his mission,' in case it should offend the Americans and embarrass the British government."[32] But Barrie did not call off his mission and instead forged on despite the wishes of his country and despite his aversion to the media. Arriving in New York, Barrie was met by his friend and business partner Charles Frohman. Frohman, the original producer of *Peter Pan* and one of the most successful theatrical producers in the United States and Britain, was a close friend of Barrie: "It was Frohman who introduced Barrie to the American theatre, and it was to Frohman that the shy author fled when besieged by reporters. All his life he had staved off interviewers, but in September 1914, when arriving in New York on the ill-fated Lusitania, he had to submit to this ordeal and did so gracefully."[33] Barrie's visit appeared to be for business only, as the *New York Times* wrote, "Except for a visit to Colonel Roosevelt at Oyster Bay, and his business conferences, Barrie succeeded in living an almost hermit-like life in the very heart of New York City."[34] Here, one cannot help but wonder why the self-professed apolitical Barrie would, against the will of his government, suffer through a siege of reporters to garner support for a war he was too old to fight. Surely sentiment alone would not lead Barrie across the Atlantic. In defiance of his government, evidence suggests it was not solely love of country but love of "The Five" that prompted Barrie's American visit.

Following the death of Sylvia Llewelyn Davies in 1910, Barrie became the guardian of the five Llewelyn Davies boys (George, Jack, Peter, Michael, and Nico) with whom he had created *Peter Pan*. Barrie biographer Lisa Chaney explains: "On 5th August [1914] Peter [Llewelyn Davies] arrived at Auch Lodge from London bringing a letter from the Adjutant of the Cambridge OTC, which said that it was the duty of all undergraduates to offer themselves for service. . . . He and George traveled down to London, leaving Barrie and [their nurse] Mary Hodgson with the two younger boys in Scotland. By early

September George and Peter had been enlisted in the army as junior officers, while Jack was already mobilised as a sub-lieutenant in the navy."[35] Three of Barrie's beloved wards and many of his friends were heading off to war, and he was going to get as much support for them as possible. So when the apolitical Barrie was called to Wellington House on September 2, 1914, he answered the call. Although it meant an uncomfortable public life for the private Barrie, joining in the Wellington House propaganda gave him the justification and the credentials to travel to America to meet with Theodore Roosevelt and to garner support for his country, but more importantly, for his boys. Despite the efforts of Barrie and the Wellington House, however, the United States would not enter war until the spring of 1917—two years after Barrie would have come to view the war much differently.

1915

On May 7, 1915, the British ocean liner RMS *Lusitania* was torpedoed and sunk by a German U-Boat, killing more than a thousand civilian passengers and eventually prompting the United States to enter the war. Among the 128 American passengers killed was Barrie's friend Charles Frohman. Producer of Barrie's plays, including *Peter Pan*, Frohman had visited the United States at Barrie's request to assist in the staging of his new play, *Rosy Rapture*.[36] Although Frohman was returning to London on business to look after his new productions, Barrie felt responsible for the timing of his travel.[37] According to the actress Rita Jolivet, Frohman's friend, who survived the attack, Frohman's last words paraphrased the famous words Peter Pan spoke as he awaited death in the scene Marooner's Rock: "To die will be an awfully big adventure."[38] Linda Robertson, in her article on the subject of *Peter Pan* and World War I, describes Frohman's last moments aboard the *Lusitania*: "As the first of two powerful green waves overwhelmed the four people clinging to each other, the man who holds our immediate attention [Frohman] said, 'Why fear death? It is the greatest adventure in life.'"[39] Frohman's last words were a tribute to the play he loved ("From the moment he read the play, he had been enchanted with it, sometimes stopping his friends in the street to act out bits of the play before it was produced"), and they were also evocative of the sentiment of the early twentieth century—a sentiment that equated adventure with war, and death with masculinity.[40]

May 7, the day Charles Frohman was drowned in the sinking of the *Lusitania*, marked a distinct shift in Barrie's attitude toward the war that had already killed many of his loved ones. Isaac F. Marcossan, Charles Frohman's biographer, in a *New York Times* interview spoke of Barrie's reaction to the losses he experienced in 1915, saying, "I found him much saddened. . . . Barrie is not writing much—in fact, none of the great English authors are producing much work these days. They, like all the rest of England, are roused to the tremendous meaning and significance of the great struggle. It has bitten into their very souls."[41] Barrie, in a letter to Marcossan, wrote, "I have been a week in bed and am not sure when I shall be right again, not that it much matters (for if we are not fighting we are mere cumberers of the ground)."[42]

The war had started going badly for Britain at the beginning of 1915: "The killing started very fast, and on a large scale. . . . In the first three months of war, almost the entire original British army was wiped out."[43] A sense of trepidation came over Barrie: "Although at the beginning Barrie had written to a friend that he believed 'our young men . . . are to be as right as rain,' three months into the war, when there had already been appalling loss of life, he was more apprehensive. He wrote frequently that he was longing to see George and Peter, and by mid-November a note of desperation had crept into his letters."[44]

But the toll of war was unavoidable, and on March 7, Guy du Maurier—the brother of Sylvia Llewelyn Davies and Gerald du Maurier and the actor who originated the role of Mr. Darling and Captain Hook—was killed in battle. On March 15, George Llewelyn Davies, the boy Barrie credits with first saying "To die will be an awfully big adventure," and "the boy for whom [Barrie] wrote 'Peter Pan'—the original, indeed, of 'Peter Pan'— . . . died in battle. This was the little boy who, through the kindly intervention of Charles Frohman, saw a special performance of 'Peter Pan' in his bedroom, because he was ill when the play had its first London performance."[45] Upon receiving news of George's death in 1915, Barrie yelled, "Ah-h-h! They'll all go, Mary—Jack, Peter, Michael—even little Nico—This dreadful war will get them all in the end."[46] Coinciding with Barrie's grief came a poignant change to the production script of *Peter Pan*, as the famous line "To die will be an awfully big adventure" was removed and would remain so for the duration of the war.[47]

Despite the terrible carnage of the war, British media was laden with falsified or inaccurate reporting that upheld the idea of the ever-victorious Britain, and Barrie, who knew the loss of the war firsthand, did not contribute to the Wellington House propaganda in 1915. However, Barrie's *Peter Pan*—especially the line from the Marooner's Rock scene, "To die will be an awfully big adventure"—had already been entered into the cultural imagination of the day and was being used as a rallying cry. Barrie must have felt conflicted as his words were being used to draw soldiers into a war he no longer supported, a war that had killed the boy who first uttered those words.

In November 1915, at the same time the Marooner's Rock scene was cut from all performances in Europe, "To die will be an awfully big adventure" was used again and again to characterize the deaths of Barrie's loved ones; "DEATH TO FROHMAN A GREAT ADVENTURE," read one headline.[48] When the *New York Times* published a tribute to Charles Frohman, not only Barrie's famous line but also images from *Peter Pan* were used to dramatize the last moments of Barrie's friend on the sinking *Lusitania*, saying Frohman "died not in bitterness, but as the protagonist in a great tragedy. In the face of death. . . . he dramatized himself and his last big scene as deliberately and as objectively as if it were the tragic, closing act of any one of the many plays he had directed for the stage at home and abroad. The moment was too magnificent as drama to be obscured by panic or futile temper. Instantly Frohman translated an incredible catastrophe into a thrilling dramatic scene, with himself as the star and the Germans as so many pirates. He saw himself in the predicament of another who had been fought by pirates and left marooned on a rock at sea."[49] Characterizing Frohman's death as a scene from *Peter Pan* (in an effort to romanticize a deadly and increasingly unpopular war), this newspaper story shows how thoroughly Barrie's story had become a propaganda tool to lure boys into enlisting, and "into this pit of death and deception came the United States, in the spring of 1917."[50] Historian Howard Zinn writes about the American perception of the war: "There is no persuasive evidence that the public wanted war. The government had to work hard to create its consensus. That there was no spontaneous urge to fight is suggested by the strong measures taken: a draft of young men [only 73,000 volunteered before the draft], an elaborate propaganda campaign throughout the country, and harsh punishment for those who refused to get in line."[51] Charles Frohman's dramatic (or dramatized) death upon the *Lusitania* became a popular parable to sway public opinion in favor of the war, creating a mythology that combined the deaths of innocent civilians with the beloved fairytale that had pervaded Western culture for more than a decade—a fairytale many of those enlisting would have grown up with. However, this parable was a boon for a propaganda machine that had the task of "rewriting" the sinking of the *Lusitania* to serve its cause. Howard Zinn explains, "The United States claimed the *Lusitania* carried an innocent cargo, and therefore the torpedoing was a monstrous German atrocity. Actually, the *Lusitania* was heavily armed: it carried 1,248 cases of 3-inch shells, 4,927 boxes of cartridges (1,000 rounds in each box), and 2,000 more cases of small-arms ammunition. Her manifests were falsified to hide this fact, and the British and American governments lied about the cargo."[52]

Thus, the *Lusitania* became a tool to bolster support for the war in America and draw in soldiers under false pretenses. Barrie would not have been aware of this falsification, but he was beginning to feel a strong sense that the soldiers were being misled by propaganda, propaganda to which he felt he had contributed. Although he spoke out against it, his words had already been entered into the cultural imagination that reified the myth of manhood and were no longer under his control. In much the same way that Peter becomes detached from his shadow, which in turn takes on a life of its own, Barrie became detached from his creation and was desperate to get it back.

Courage

Long after Barrie had stopped contributing to Wellington House propaganda, Peter was used as an icon to glamorize war. An article titled "The Young Airman: Winning His Wings," which appeared late in the war in the *Times*, on September 27, 1918, created an innocent depiction of war by using *Peter Pan* imagery: "We [the British] have vague ideas that boys become pilots as easily as Michael and Wendy Darling found out from Peter Pan how to fly to the Never-Never Land. The Peter Pans of the Air Service include drill sergeants, men familiar with each of the thousand parts of a 12-cyclinder engine, gunnery experts, and specialists in topography, as well as the flight instructors, who eventually teach the cadets how to loop and spin and roll in space."[53] Referred to as "The Peter Pans" of the Air Service, the image of Peter helped to soften the image of war—subsuming the dangerous realities of warfare into the friendly childhood fantasy of flying to Neverland.

Even after war ended in 1918, Barrie was still deeply troubled by the war and his involvement in the Wellington House propaganda. He felt a great divide between the generations in Britain and focused on developing the agency of British youth. In one of the notebooks he kept at the end of the war, mixed in with notes for *Peter Pan*, thoughts about his rectorial address at St. Andrews, and self-reflections, Barrie (referring to himself in the third person) wrote, "Great thing to form own opinion, don't accept hearsay. . . . Question authority. Question accepted views, values, reputations. Don't be afraid to be among the rebels. . . . Speak scornfully of the Victorian age. Of Edwardian age. Of last year. Of old-fashioned writers like Barrie, who accept old-fangled ideas.'"[54] When Barrie delivered his rectorial address at St. Andrews in 1922, he had become increasingly disturbed by the way war decisions were made *for* youth and actively sought to cultivate a more self-determining and critical youth that would challenge those decision-makers. He is openly self-deprecating in his speech, as he viewed himself as one of those decision makers, a contributor to the great adventure narrative propagandized by a government agency whose members were too old for military service.[55] The concept of the Old Men as the makers of the war and enemies of the young had many origins, but one was certainly that meeting at Wellington House in September 1914, when those middle-aged and old writers gathered to support a war in which they would not fight.[56]

Barrie warned the students of St. Andrews against this as he urged them to take action; "I want you take up this position—that Youth have for too long left exclusively in our hands the decisions in national matters that are more vital to them than to us. Things about the next war, for instance, and why the last one ever had a beginning. That the time has arrived for Youth to demand a partnership. That to gain courage is what you come to St. Andrews for."[57] Here Barrie attempts to rewrite the narrative of the great adventure, as he suggests the students will find courage not through warfare on the fields of battle but in the classroom. In the following years, Barrie would attempt to rewrite this myth by rewriting and publishing—for the first time—the script to *Peter Pan*. Written in the mindset that prompted him to "speak scornfully" of "old-fashioned writers like Barrie, who accept old-fangled ideas," Barrie, surprisingly, includes the Marooner's Rock scene and its most famous line in the final version of *Peter Pan*. In light of Barrie's remorse about spreading "tall tales" of heroic glory through the myth of the great adventure, why would Barrie include this fraught line in the published script? To understand this inclusion, the line must be considered within the context of the new additions to the script and the way in which Barrie ensured a particular legacy for his play.

It was not until 1928 that the script of *Peter Pan, Or the Boy Who Wouldn't Grow Up* was published. Along with the script came a new dedication and an additional final scene titled "When Wendy Grew Up: An Afterthought." Barrie dedicated his script "To The Five"—meaning the five Llewelyn Davies boys with whom he created *Peter Pan* while playing in Kensington Gardens. Only three of the boys were living when this dedication went to print (George had been killed in battle, and Michael had drowned a few years later while at school).[58] In the dedication, Barrie talks of the distance he feels within his relationship to the boys and to the script: "I talk of dedicating the play to you, but how can I prove it is mine? How ought I to act if some other hand, who could also have made a copy, thinks it worthwhile to contest the cold rights? Cold they are to me now as that laughter of yours in which Peter came into being long before he was caught and written down. There is Peter still, but to me he lies sunk in the gay Black Lake."[59]

The afterthought, originally written in 1909 and intended, according to Barrie, to only be performed once, had made its way permanently into the published script. Although the final scene of *Peter Pan* had seen many incarnations and revisions, from Wendy remaining in Neverland to Mrs. Darling visiting her children on the island by way of a magic carpet, Barrie definitively chose the afterthought to end the play, as he included it in the long-awaited publication. In this scene, Peter returns to the Darlings' nursery to find Wendy grown and unable to fly; she says: "I can't come with you, Peter—because I'm no longer young and innocent."[60] Why did Barrie choose to end the play in this way? There are several factors, including the death of the Llewelyn Davies's mother, Sylvia, and Barrie's disconnect with the boys who once loved him, that influence his decision. But it is Barrie's experience with the war, and its nearly thirty-seven million casualties (in the script, Hook describes "a holocaust of children"), that is most reflective of Wendy's lost youth, a youth that Barrie would strive to protect through his public life. Most notably, Barrie bequeathed the rights to *Peter Pan* to the Great Ormond Street Hospital Children's Charity in his will, eternally protecting the youth he so cherished.

At the time of Barrie's death in 1937, public sentiment had changed, too, calling Peter's line from the Marooner's Rock "terrible" in Barrie's obituary, and in 1938, on the verge of World War II, the *New York Times* published a review of Barrie's biography, saying, "Though it ends with the awful sentence: 'To die will be an awfully big adventure,' it manages by its own simplicity to survive that false naïveté."[61] In 1938, as Europe once again was headed to war, the cultural narrative of the great adventure had changed. Having experienced the harsh and unexpected realities of World War I, the once anthemic "To die will be an awfully big adventure" had lost its heroism. And yet, Barrie included it in his script.

Barrie's 1922 St. Andrew's rectorial address gives insight into the reasoning behind this inclusion. Speaking for the lost soldiers, Barrie says, "They [the soldiers] want to know if you have learned from what befell them; if you have, they will be braced in the feeling that they did not die in vain. Some of them think they did. They won't take our word for it that they didn't. You are their living image. . . . To us they have passed away; but are you who stepped into their heritage only yesterday, whose books are scarcely cold to their hands, you will still hear their cries being blown across the link—are you already relegating them to the shades?"[62] Barrie did not want the soldiers to be forgotten, and he did not want to perpetuate the idea that they died in vain. Tinged by his remorse, he felt a responsibility to protect youth of the past, present, and future. By including the heroic anthem of a lost generation of young men, Barrie sought to immortalize them. By speaking to the students of St. Andrews, Barrie hoped to empower and protect them. Finally, by donating the rights of *Peter Pan* to the Great Ormond Street Hospital Children's Charity, Barrie made sure *Peter Pan* would benefit youth in perpetuity. With this, he included a stage direction that captures Barrie's hope for the future: as Peter flies away from the nursery window back to Neverland, he thinks, "To *live* would be an awfully big adventure."[63]

Notes

1. "Rector Installation Speeches: Welcome by the Principal & Vice-Chancellor," http://www.st-andrews.ac.uk/news/archive/2015/title,254695,en.php, accessed January 5, 2016.
2. "History of the Rector," http://www.yourunion.net/voice/rectorelection/history/, accessed January 5, 2016.
3. "Youth and Its Destiny," *Times*, May 4, 1922, 13, accessed January 5, 2016, http://find.galegroup.com.proxy.lib.miamioh.edu/ttda/infomark.do?&source=gale&prodId=TTDA&userGroupName=muohio_main&tabID=T003&docPage=article&searchType=AdvancedSearchForm&docId=CS218436260&type=multipage&contentSet=LTO&version=1.0,.
4. Ibid.
5. Peter Buitenhuis, *The Great War of Words: British, American, and Canadian Propaganda and Fiction, 1914–1933* (Vancouver: University of British Columbia Press, 1987), 14–15.
6. Samuel Hynes, *A War Imagined: The First World War and English Culture* (New York: Atheneum, 1991), 26.
7. Jeffrey Reznick, *John Galsworthy and Disabled Soldiers of the Great War* (Manchester: Manchester University Press, 2009), 11.
8. "Youth and Its Destiny," 13.
9. Theodore Roosevelt, *The Great Adventure: Present-Day Studies in American Nationalism* (New York: Charles Scribner's Sons, 1918), vi.
10. John Graham Royde-Smith, "Armed Forces Mobilized and Casualties in World War I," *Britannica Academic*, s.v. "World War I," accessed May 11, 2017, http://academic.eb.com.turing.library.northwestern.edu/levels/collegiate/article/World-War-I/110198.
11. Bourke, Joanna. *Dismembering the Male: Men's Bodies, Britain, and the Great War* (Chicago: University of Chicago Press, 1996), 13.
12. Horace Porter, "The Philosophy of Courage," *Century Magazine*, June 1888, 253, http://babel.hathitrust.org/cgi/pt?id=chi.18110888;view=1up;seq=267.
13. David S. Shepard and Frederic E. Rabinowitz, "The Power of Shame in Men Who Are Depressed: Implications for Counselors," *Journal of Counseling and Development* 91 (American Counseling Association, 2013): 452.
14. Bourke, *Dismembering the Male*, 12.
15. Ibid.
16. Michael C. C. Adams, *The Great Adventure: Male Desire and the Coming of World War I* (Bloomington: Indiana University Press, 1990), 25, 48.
17. Ibid.
18. "Duke of York's Theatre," *Times*, December 28, 1915, accessed January 11, 2016, 4, http://find.galegroup.com.proxy.lib.miamioh.edu/ttda/infomark.do?&source=gale&prodId=TTDA&user.
19. Adams, *The Great Adventure*, 87–88.

20. James Barrie, *Peter Pan and Other Plays*, ed. Peter Hollindale (Oxford: Oxford University Press, 1995), 140.
21. Hynes, *War Imagined*, 26.
22. Buitenhuis, *The Great War of Words*, xvi.
23. Ibid.
24. Craig Allen, "Photographers on the Front Lines of the Great War," *New York Times* (New York, NY), Jun. 30, 2014, https://lens.blogs.nytimes.com/2014/06/30/photos-world-war-i-images-museums-battle-great-war/.
25. Hynes, *A War Imagined*, 28.
26. Buitenhuis, *The Great War of Words*, xvii.
27. Ibid., 7.
28. Ibid., 279.
29. Peter Monro Jack, "Barrie: Journalist and Genius," *New York Times*, March 13, 1938, accessed March 6, 2012, 87, http://search.proquest.com/docview/102682656?accountid=12434.
30. Linda Robertson, "'To Die Will Be an Awfully Big Adventure': Peter Pan and World War I," in *Second Star to the Right* (New Brunswick: Rutgers University Press, 2009), 60.
31. Jack, "Barrie: Journalist and Genius," 87.
32. Lisa Chaney, *Hide-and-Seek with Angels: A Life of J. M. Barrie* (London: Hutchinson, 2005), 304.
33. "Barrie Too Complex a Figure to be Catalouged by His Critics," *New York Times*, June 20, 1937, accessed March 12, 2012, http://search.proquest.com/docview/102067693?accountid=12434.
34. Joyce Kilmer, "Barrie, Saddened by War, Writes Little Now," *New York Times*, November 12, 1916, accessed March 12, 2012, SM11, http://search.proquest.com/docview/97828419?accountid=12434.
35. Chaney, *Hide-and-Seek with Angels*, 304.
36. James Barrie, Maria Tatar, and Arthur Rackham, *The Annotated Peter Pan* (New York: W. W. Norton, 2011), civ.
37. "Frohman Off for London," *New York Times*, May 1, 1915, accessed January 5, 2016, http://search.proquest.com/docview/97793528?accountid=12434.
38. The Marooner's Rock scene is also known as the "Mermaid's Lagoon" scene.
39. Robertson, "'To Die Will Be an Awfully Big Adventure,'" 50.
40. Ibid., 57.
41. Kilmer, "Barrie, Saddened by War . . . ," SM11.
42. Ibid.
43. Howard Zinn, *A People's History of the United States* (New York: Harper & Row, 1980), 360.
44. Chaney, *Hide-and-Seek with Angels*, 305.
45. Kilmer, "Barrie, Saddened by War. . . ," SM11.
46. Barrie, *The Annotated Peter Pan*, cii.
47. Chaney, *Hide-and-Seek with Angels*, 307.
48. "Death to Frohman a Great Adventure," *New York Times*, May 11, 1915, accessed January 5, 2016, http://search.proquest.com/docview/97705366?accountid=12434.
49. John D. Williams, "Some Stories of Charles Frohman," *New York Times*, November 21, 1915, accessed January 5, 2016, X8, http://search.proquest.com/docview/97754572?accountid=12434.
50. Zinn, *A People's History of the United States*, 361.

51. Ibid., 364.
52. Ibid., 362.
53. "The Young Airman: Winning His Wings," *Times*, September 27, 1918, accessed January 11, 2016, 4, http://find.galegroup.com.proxy.lib.miamioh.edu/ttda/infomark.do?&source=gale&prodId=TTDA&userGroupName=muohio_main&tabID=T003&docPage=article&searchType=AdvancedSearchForm&docId=CS68225851&type=multipage&contentSet=LTO&version=1.0.
54. Chaney, *Hide-and-Seek with Angels*, 339.
55. Ibid., 339.
56. Hynes, *A War Imagined*, 26.
57. "Youth and Its Destiny," 13.
58. It is unclear whether Michael had died at the time the dedication was written. One of Barrie's primary biographers, Andrew Birkin, believes Michael had probably died before Barrie penned the dedication. James Barrie's older brother, David, had also been drowned in an accident when Barrie was six years old. David is widely accepted as one of the inspirations for the character Peter Pan.
59. Barrie, *Peter Pan and Other Plays*, 77.
60. Ibid., 162.
61. Jack, "Barrie: Journalist and Genius."
62. "Youth and Its Destiny," 13.
63. Barrie, *Peter Pan and Other Plays*, 153. Emphasis added.

Not Just Rock 'n' Roll

Chicago Theatre, 1984–1990

—JULIE JACKSON

The notion of a Chicago-style theatre first began to appear in the press around 1984. In that year, the *New York Times* published a lengthy feature article under the headline "Chicago Theater Comes Into Its Own." Author Pat Colander began by noting that for more than three decades the track record for Chicago transfers to New York had been abysmal. She writes, "Theater companies came to life and were as quickly dissolved. Artists left for one coast or another and never looked back. Chicago's most successful productions collapsed upon arrival in New York City."[1] In the early 1980s, word of an emerging theatre scene in Chicago had begun to attract attention on the East Coast, but the odds of a successful transfer to New York remained slim at best. Nonetheless, in October 1982 Chicago's Steppenwolf ensemble decided to transfer their revival of Sam Shepard's *True West* to the Cherry Lane Theatre in New York City. The move was highly controversial within the company. A risky out-of-town production would deplete the ensemble and potentially disrupt the company's move to a newly renovated 211-seat facility on Halsted Street, the former home of David Mamet's St. Nicholas Theater. But after prolonged and heated discussions among ensemble members, it was agreed that only John Malkovich and Gary Sinise would travel with the production and the company would keep a low profile about the Chicago connection.[2] In 2005 *Newsday* critic Linda Winer recalled that, in early 1983, "nowhere in the program or the bios did it say these are people from Chicago, that this is from a company called Steppenwolf. And I realized that there had been so many shows imported from Chicago that had failed, that it was actually saying that being from Chicago was a liability."[3] Expectations among the company were not high—Malkovich later claimed he packed his bag only for a weekend. But the production ran for 762 performances, finally closing in August 1984, and the intense, head-butting performances of Malkovich and Sinise proved to be a turning point for the Steppenwolf and for Chicago theatre. In her article, Colander concluded that the city's "continuity of theatrical history has produced a recognizable Chicago style," and she links that style to an "emotionally raw, sometimes violent, mode of play for which many [Chicago-based theatres] have been acclaimed." In a 1997 article "The Real Roots of Rock 'n' Roll Acting," *Chicago Tribune* lead critic Richard Christiansen recalled, "The kind of manic energy that Sinise and Malkovich put to work, kicking and biting each other as two warring brothers, blew away Manhattan critics and audiences alike."[4] And so it began.

Good, bad, or indifferent, enough of the theatre produced in Chicago by Chicagoans around 1984 shared sufficient aesthetic values and formal aspects in performance—some more so, some less—to constitute what Ross Wetzesteon, a longtime editor of the *Village Voice* and a founder of the Obie Awards for off-Broadway (and off-off-Broadway) theatre, described in 1985 as "the most talked-about innovation in acting technique since the heyday of the Actor's Studio."[5] The Chicago style was born of the imposed intimacy of the makeshift storefront venues where Chicago actors, directors, and designers learned their craft, the financial and artistic structure that empowered the city's artist-run ensemble companies, and the energy, conceptual minimalism, and individual audacity of improvisational theatre. The result was a new and different kind of experience in the theatre. However, the catchy sound bites ("rock 'n' roll," "gonzo theatre," "raw naturalism") and stroppy abstractions ("gritty," "gutsy," "unpolished") of contemporary press coverage positioned much of the innovative work that emerged from Chicago during this period as atypical or marginal. Consider: the Organic Theater's wacky sci-fi serial *Warp!* (1971) by Stuart Gordon and Lenny Kleinfeld and the company's intimate, ensemble-devised *Bleacher Bums* (1971) and *E/R* (1984)[6]; the intense but strangely uninflected dialogue of David Mamet's early work at St. Nicholas; the electrifying theatricality of Remains Theatre's haunting adaptation of Melville's *Moby Dick* (1983), directed by guest artist Steven Rumbelow; the stunning street theatre of Red Moon's 1990 adaptation of the same book featuring the capture, butcher, and consumption of a life-size whale constructed of barrel staves and wire; the distilled passion and intense onstage presence of the Steppenwolf women in John Murrell's *Waiting for the Parade* (1981) and Craig Lucas's *Reckless* (1990); the poetic minimalism and shrewd detail of Kevin Rigdon's scenic and lighting design; Northlight Theatre's lyrical chamber musical based on

Nelson Algren's *City on the Make* (1984); the Cubist playground of Frank Galati's "She Always Said, 'Pablo . . . '" (1987); and Mary Zimmerman and Lookingglass Theatre's episodic tales of long-ago-and-far-away magic, love, and forgiveness, *The Arabian Nights* (1988). Only a few of these examples of Chicago theatre can be characterized as raw or gritty, none were unpolished, and several abandoned the conventions of naturalism all together. Nonetheless, each of these productions represent the Chicago style at its best.

Chicago theatre had a different lineage from the prevailing realism associated with New York's venerable training center the Actor's Studio and descended from separate stock than the dominant avant-garde. Chicago was not ahead of its time. It was very much of its time, perhaps more so than any other American theatre center of the period. In the mid-1980s, the city and its theatremakers were rightly perceived as ground zero for the next generation of significant innovation in American theatre. The key to theorizing this innovation and the shared values, practices, and defining qualities of Chicago theatre between 1984 and 1990 lies in the significant body of work that is marginalized or excluded by the reified terms of critical discourse. For the most part, the terms and outlook of this discourse were better suited to the criticism of mid-century psychological realism than to the theatre style that emerged in Chicago in the last decades of the century. To prevent the achievements and innovations of this style from being written off as a serendipitous confluence of innate talent or the praiseworthy achievement of a few Tony Award-winning regional theatres, the terms of this discourse need to be revisited in light of actual performance and a growing body of twenty-first-century performance theory and research.

I have tried to include representative samples of little known as well as well-documented performances, but firsthand experience was a determining factor in my selection of examples. I have seen all the productions and performances described in this article at least once, many of them multiple times in a variety of venues. I completed an MFA in design at the School of the Art Institute of Chicago's Goodman School of Drama in two years, but like my Chicago colleagues, I learned the craft of theatremaking in Chicago's intimate theatres between 1978 and 1995. During that time, I attended, designed, or assisted on more than forty productions and rehearsals per year. My theatre attendance was not motivated by taste but by the availability of free tickets, the invitation of colleagues and producers, or a desire to check out the work of potential collaborators, friends, and competitors. Many of the artists quoted in this article are friends and artistic colleagues. Undocumented quotations are recalled from informal conversations that span more than three decades. Many of them are ongoing.

"Chicago-Style" Theatre

In the 1984–85 season Chicago's Goodman Theatre transferred world premieres of David Mamet's *Glengarry Glen Ross* to New York's Golden Theatre and David Rabe's *Hurlyburly* to the Ethel Barrymore. Both productions were critically acclaimed and profitable. In that same season the Second City Review played an open-ended run at the Village Gate and the Steppenwolf Ensemble took productions of C. P. Taylor's *And A Nightingale Sang* to the Lincoln Center and Lyle Kessler's *Orphans* to the Westside Arts Theatre, and coproduced their "definitive" Chicago revival of Langford Wilson's first full-length play, *Balm in Gilead* with Circle Rep.[7] *Balm in Gilead* ran from May 31, 1984, to January 6, 1985. The Goodman production of *Glengarry* won the 1984 Pulitzer Prize for Drama, the New York Drama Critic's Circle award for Best Play, a Tony for Chicago actor Joe Mantegna, and Tony nominations for Best Play (Chicago playwright David Mamet) and Best Direction of a Play (Goodman artistic director Gregory Mosher). Steppenwolf Theatre was awarded the 1985 Tony for Regional Theatre Excellence. As Colander announced in 1984, "The curse of the Second City label . . . finally suffocated under the sheer weight of Chicago's theatrical presence in New York."[8]

The triumphs in New York were impressive, but by the summer of 1985 Chicago theatre no longer needed a New York endorsement to attract national and international attention. In that year alone, Norman Lear turned the Organic Theater's long-running ensemble piece *E/R* into a sitcom for CBS with recurring roles for Chicago actors Shuko Akune and Bruce Young. Stuart Gordon, the Organic's founder, relocated to Los Angeles to begin filming the cult classic *Re-Animator*, based on an original adaptation of a H. P. Lovecraft story developed for television by Gordon with Chicago colleagues Dennis Paoli and Bill Norris.[9] Louisiana State University commissioned Frank Galati to write and direct a lavish musical adaptation of John Kennedy Toole's picaresque bestseller *A Confederacy of Dunces*. Robert Falls's Wisdom Bridge production of *In the Belly of the Beast: Letters from Prison*, a ninety-minute tour de force performed by William Peterson, transferred to a larger Chicago venue for an extended run before touring London, Glasgow, and Washington, DC. In 1984 Peter Sellars, artistic director of the Kennedy Center's ambitious but short-lived American National Theater (1984–1986), brought four Chicago productions to the Center's Terrace Theater, including *In the Belly of the Beast*; the Wisdom Bridge production of *Kabuki Medea*, staged by Shozo Shato with Chicago actors Barbara Robertson and Dean Fortunato; the Steppenwolf ensemble production of Lynn Siefert's *Coyote Ugly*, directed by company member John Malkovich; and the

Steppenwolf's brutal and explicit production of David Rabe's *Streamers*, directed by company member Terry Kinney. "This," said Sellars of the Steppenwolf performance at the Kennedy Center, "is what we need to bring this place alive."[10]

Robert Falls has been artistic director of Chicago's prestigious Goodman Theatre for more than thirty years. But in 1984 he was a charismatic young Chicago director who lived in a cold-water walkup. Nonetheless, his reputation had already reached well beyond the city limits. He described the Chicago style to Colander as "crude, rough, energetic." "There's this tradition in Chicago," he continued, "of performance which does not have polish."[11] Without a doubt, the storefront theatres that proliferated in Chicago lacked the high gloss of a heavily financed Broadway blockbuster, but at its best—and Falls's work was among the best—Chicago theatre was intelligent, intensely focused, and highly crafted. William Petersen gave one of the most compelling and physically demanding performances of the era under Falls's direction in the 1983 Wisdom Bridge production of *In the Belly of the Beast: Letters from Prison*. Peter Sellers brought the production to the Kennedy Center's American National Theater in Washington, DC, and in an opening night address declared, "What we saw tonight from Bill Petersen . . . was not just an overwhelmingly committed and courageous evening of theatre. . . . We also saw impeccable technique, sheer Laurence Olivier technique.'"[12] He continued, "Every expression is exactly calculated and is perfectly deployed. That's not just somebody going on stage and spilling their guts."[13]

Not all artists and critics agreed that new ground was being broken in Chicago. Many preferred to credit the city's theatrical community with reinvigorating well-established theatrical conventions. In his 2001 memoir, *A Theater of Our Own*, Christiansen traces the development of Chicago's professional theatre community from the turn of the nineteenth century. However, the titular "theater of our own" emerges as a fertile point of origin and a serendipitous convergence of raw talent at a certain time and place rather than an innovation in theatrical style. At the 1986 meeting of the American Theatre Critics Association, Ted Mann, cofounder and artistic director of Circle in the Square (a "self-proclaimed regional theatre on Broadway") agreed that Chicago's unique history, political landscape, and economic conditions had combined to create a fertile and challenging artistic environment. However, Mann asserted, "There is no Chicago style."[14] Chicago actor John Malkovich and Goodman artistic director Gregory Mosher participated on the same panel and neither challenged Mann's statement, but both artists pointed out that theatre was made differently in Chicago: "The only problem with theatre in New York," said Malkovich, "is real estate."[15] The process and attitude toward making theatre in a particular time and place do not necessarily result in a new or different kind of theatre. Even so, wherever Chicago actors and productions traveled in the mid-1980s, from New York and Los Angles to London and Australia, the comments of critics, patrons, and artists suggested that a broad spectrum of Chicago-based productions shared a defining, if ineffable, pool of qualities and characteristics that constituted a theatrical style specific to Chicago.

Many Chicago theatre artists were uncomfortable with the rock 'n' roll theatre tag. Terry Kinney, a founding member of the Steppenwolf ensemble, objected, "If there's anything in a band that analogous to our acting, it's that we know each other so well. If you make a switch in tempo or key in a garage band, you can handle it if you've played together a lot, even if you're amateurish."[16] In 1988, *New York Times* critic Benedict Nightingale reported that many members of the Steppenwolf company "feel that they wouldn't be so simply categorized if the phrasemakers had seen the gentler, subtler work they haven't transferred to New York." "But," he continued, "they can't altogether disown the comparison."[17] The comparison of Chicago-style theatre with loud and sometimes violent or crude contemporary music is valid but not sufficient. Sheldon Patinkin, "a giant of Chicago comedy and theatre,"[18] mentored, advised, directed, and collaborated with thousands of individual theatre students, artists, fledgling theatre companies, and established institutions, including The Second City, a company he helped found, and the Steppenwolf Ensemble, where he was an artistic associate for more than three decades. Patinkin was a lifelong defender and advocate of what he identified as a Chicago style. He claimed to "see" this style when John Malkovich urinated downstage ("on the audience" was probably hyperbolic) in director Robert Falls's gritty production of Sam Shepard's *Curse of the Starving Class* (1979). But he also perceived a stylistic continuity in the lyricism of the Steppenwolf *Glass Menagerie* (1979), the wit and passion of director Michael Maggio's *Travesties* (1980), the postmodern maze of Robert Falls's *Mother Courage* (1981), and the spectacular storytelling of Frank Galati's eloquent *Grapes of Wrath* (1988). Patinkin consistently identified three basic elements of Chicago-style theatre: ensemble, risk, and improvisation.

Connections between ensemble theatre and improv run deep in Chicago's history. In 1969 Reverend Jim Shifflet, a Presbyterian minister, was on a mission "to let all the flowers of the arts bloom." He left the church to found the Body Politic, a community arts center on Lincoln Avenue that quickly "became a home for a swarm of visual and performing arts projects, patronized by a large, enthusiastic young audience."[19] Shifflet was inspired by Viola Spolin's nonauthoritative theatre games, introduced to Chicago through the early improvisational work of Spolin's son, Paul Sills, at the South Side Compass Theatre and carried over to the Second City (a spin-off from the Compass) as well as through Sills's own Story Theatre. Shifflet was delighted and moved by the spontaneity of the Second City performers and the remarkable warmth and lively exchange between the players and their audience, particularly when they fielded audience suggestions for situation improvs at late-night performances. "It was simple to see they weren't just dealing with games or theatre," he told reporter Linda Winer in a 1972 interview, "but with a basic communication between them and the audience."[20] The games and improvisations Shifflet admired were designed to build a vibrant and direct connection between the stage and the audience. The performance spaces of his improvised bare-bones performance center, the Body Politic, encouraged and supported audience-oriented performance that was directed outward, toward the audience, in a lively and enlivening exchange than assimilated the energy and spontaneity of improvisation into dramatic storytelling.

In an interview published in *The Director's Voice* (1993), Robert Falls observed, "There were two great and simultaneous influences on American theatre and American acting in the 1950s. One was the Actors Studio in New York, which is the one everybody knows about, and the other was the Second City in Chicago."[21] Saint Nicholas, Victory Gardens, Steppenwolf, Wisdom Bridge, Body Politic, "All of them," observed Falls, "had roots in the Second City." In 1984 Colander traced the genealogy of Chicago theatre to the Playwright's Theatre, a professional repertory company "heavily influenced by the ideas of [Paul] Sills's mother, the teacher Viola Spolin, and her use of improvisational games to solve theater problems."[22] Ross Wetzsteon argues that Chicago's long tradition of improvisation was formative in the development of the city's theatrical style. In 1984 he noted, correctly, that many of the younger theatremakers in Chicago regarded Second City as "a fossilized tourist trap." But Wetzsteon points out that Second City was a profound influence on the style of acting that emerged in Chicago. That influence, Wetzsteon argues, "lies less in its nurturing of comic talent than in its development of an acting style. In fact, the two major legacies of Second City—improvisation and ensemble—form the very basis of the Chicago style currently altering the contours of American theatre. . . . Groups like Steppenwolf didn't grow up in a cultural vacuum—like it or not, Second City was in the very air they breathed."[23] Improv theatre was also in the air that the city's theatre and entertainment patrons breathed. By 1984 Second City had offered the city good entertainment value at a minimal entry fee and cover charge for more than a quarter of a century. Chicago theatre patrons were conditioned to accept and even demand something more lively, immediate, and engaging than a sophisticated reproduction of everyday life. The compelling characters and structured storytelling of midcentury realism were still in demand, but the unapologetic theatricality and jaunty artifice of improvisation acclimatized the Chicago audience to a decidedly presentational and audience-oriented style of performance.

Second City developed a specific sketch-based form of improvisation that is very close to traditional theatre. Unlike long-form improvisation, which is devised in the presence of an audience, the Second City ensemble works together over a period of weeks or months to create carefully crafted scenes with a strong sense of character, situation, and message or theme. The catalyst of these scenes is a weekly late-night postshow session in which short scenes are improvised on the spot based on suggestions shouted out by the audience. The most promising of these "embryos" are taken into rehearsal to be polished and developed and then organized into a loosely themed review that runs for six weeks or longer. Outside the weekly improv secessions, which are popular and raucous, the dramatic script is more or less set. However, the performance script, that is, the physical choices made by actors in the moment of performance, is reactive, spontaneous, and directed outward, toward the audience in cabaret style. Actors are required to develop a keen awareness of each other and of moment-to-moment shifts in the audience.

Jeanne Leep explains, "Sketch-based improvisation becomes the most mainstream of the improvisational forms of performance, as it is most akin to a traditional theatrical experience." But, she continues, "because the most basic principles of improvisation are the same regardless of the form . . . the players of improvisation are not locked into one format, and bring with them, as they move from one theatre to the next, the ideas and ways of thinking that further the form."[24] From year to year and month to month Chicago actors, designers, musicians, artistic directors, writers, at least one busboy—David Mamet—and one classics scholar—University of Chicago professor and Court Theatre artistic director Nicholas Ruddell—attended performances, circulated in and out of comedy classes, or joined the company to develop one or more revues, consciously or unconsciously disseminating a Second City ethos throughout the city. The Second City technique is a highly structured game that culminates in a scripted review. Chicago ensemble acting begins with a dramatic or written text, but it depends on structured and unstructured improvisation to develop a unique and highly physical performance text. As actor Terry Kinney told Colander, "Sam Shepard calls for a lot of invention between actors. . . . The basis of doing him well is being able to play off each other, the ability to tap into wild behavior, with improvisation of overlapping dialogue."[25]

Improvisation is a game with rules but no script. Dramatic theatre has a script but no rules. However, the rules of improv clearly influenced the development of theatrical performance in Chicago. The first and primary rule of improvisation, "say yes, never say no," directs the actor to agree with whatever is introduced into the scene rather than negate, override, or ignore it. To accept requires the actor to suppress ego-driven intention in favor of a heightened awareness and receptivity in the moment of performance. The second rule, "say yes and . . . " disallows passive or neutral acceptance onstage. The shared goal in ensemble improvisation is to keep the momentum of the scene alive by always adding something new, something of one's own. For Chicago's ensemble actors as well as improv performers, acceptance meant taking whatever came your way as an opportunity. Guest artist Laurie Metcalf played a glamorous star of stage and screen in the Columbia College production of the 1938 screwball comedy *The Man Who Came to Dinner* by George Kaufman and Moss Hart. It was an unusual role for Metcalf; she was pleased by but unaccustomed to the slinky backless evening gown and high heels she was fitted for, and she took a few minutes to "work" the dress in front of the mirror. During rehearsal for an important second act reversal in which her character realizes that she has been outmaneuvered and betrayed, Metcalf found herself far upstage right with a barricade of fusty furniture between herself and the audience. It was a weak stage position, but on cue, she turned her back to the auditorium, spread her arms out against the upstage wall and clawed her way along the flowered wallpaper until she reached an unblocked position center. In performance, the muscles of her exposed back rippled in a series of spasms as tension flowed down her spine and expelled at the coccyx with a small butt bump. Having reached the open center position, she lifted her shoulders in a deep inhale, smoothed the satin at her hips, lifted her chin, and turned out. When she faced the audience she was upstage center, composed, dazzling, and clearly set on fanatical revenge. In a few stage moments, Metcalf went from privileged complacence to venomous determination—Carole Lombard to Cruella de Vil—and did so from an unfavorable stage position with her back to the audience. Director Sheldon Patinkin called the performance a master class in back acting. Metcalf's choice appeared to be intuitive, but her intuition was to "say yes" to the position she was given and add a palpable shift in tone and tension before handing the scene over to her scene partner. Without missing a beat, she turned the obstacle of a weak stage position into an opportunity and an unfamiliar costume into an asset. Such choices are not unusual for a savvy actor, but the nimbleness and invention with which Chicago actors could "say yes, and . . . " created the strong impression of spontaneity, immediacy, and invention associated with the Chicago style.

Rule three of improv is "Make statements." Statements open a scene up to greater possibility than questions or challenges do. If Metcalf had responded to the news of betrayal with shocked silence or a double take, as if to say, "You can't mean it!" the scene would have gone flat. Her response, a bold statement of single-minded revenge, gave her scene partners something concrete and exciting to work with. The fourth rule, "There are no mistakes, only opportunities," fueled Chicago ensemble performance as well as improv. When a loose flyer fell out of a magazine Tim Kazurinsky was working with in a Second City scene, he and his scene partner Mary Gross spontaneously turned the "mistake" into an original comic sketch. In a period production of *The Tempest* directed by Bob Falls at the outdoor Illinois Shakespeare Festival at Illinois State University, the director and actors decided that when low-flying planes passed overhead, which happened with disconcerting regularity, Prospero's crew would stop the action to follow the plane's flight in rapt wonderment. Sometimes no planes passed overhead. Sometimes a plane circled and sometimes several planes passed during the show but not at the same moment. One of the high points of the production was watching the actors improvise their way back into a dramatic or comic scene. A mistake, an unanticipated distraction, or an unplanned intrusion can be off-putting in rehearsal or performance. It can also enliven rehearsal and energize a scene unfolding onstage.

The director, teacher, actor, and improv guru Del Close is a legendary figure in Chicago and in the world of unscripted comedy. ImprovOlympic Theater, now called iO, was founded in 1981 by Close and Charna Halpern. This group specializes in competitive long-form improvisation and, like Second City, has developed a respected and highly attended training program. Close was with Second City from 1971 to 1981. In *The Second City Unscripted*, a collection of Mike Thomas's interviews with Second City alumni, Thomas describes Close as a man with a "searing intellect and rebellious nature" who was as compelling as he was problematic.[26] Close was an innovator and leader in the world of short- and long-form improv, but he was also an accomplished stage and screen actor. Author/actor/director Harold Ramis worked with Close at Second City and considered him to be a mentor and teacher. Ramis recalled, "Del always wanted to revolutionize the theatre."[27] His "whole crusade at Second City and after was to keep people in the moment. Del believed that the Second City games—he actually said this once—[are] just like life. Life is improvisation. We're constantly discovering our character, we're constantly discovering everyone else's character and we're in situations that are constantly evolving and changing."[28] Close may have been more successful in his crusade than he realized. Naturalism, spontaneity, restless invention, and in-your-face presence were qualities for which

Chicago-style theatre became famous. The Eleven Commandments Close formulated for improvisation are reflected in Chicago's distinctive ensemble style of performance.

1. You are all supporting actors.
2. Always check your impulses.
3. Never enter a scene unless you are NEEDED.
4. Save your fellow actor, don't worry about the piece.
5. Your prime responsibility is to support.
6. Work at the top of your brains at all times.
7. Never underestimate or condescend to your audience.
8. No jokes (unless it is tipped in front that it is a joke).
9. Trust . . . trust your fellow actors to support you; trust them to come through if you lay something heavy on them; trust yourself.
10. Avoid judging what is going down except in terms of whether it needs help (either by entering or cutting), what can best follow, or how you can support it imaginatively if your support is called for.
11. LISTEN.

A comprehensive analysis of Del Close's legacy to Chicago theatre is beyond the scope of this study. However, it is worth noting that Close's "commandments" resonate in each of the qualities of the Chicago style discussed in the following section. An unpretentious and energized intimacy in performance; intense focus on each other; penetrating intelligence; a disregard for illusionism and the clutter of realist verisimilitude; a profound respect for and engagement with the audience; individual empowerment; and a mutual trust that authorizes exhilarating risk and invention in the moment of performance. In the 1980s, Chicago improv and Chicago-style theatre clearly followed similar trajectories.

Close's Eleven Commandments reflect a profound and practical understanding of artistic collaboration, and collaboration was the engine that propelled Chicago ensemble theatre production in the 1980s. Cooperation is a protocol that allows artists to work together to achieve an identified goal or end product without getting in each other's way. Collaboration is quite different in that it requires participants to share in the process of knowledge creation. Collaboration is an unpredictable synthesis of information, talents, ideas, and perspectives to create something quite different than what each artist could have created or expected to create on his or her own. Collaboration, in spirit and in practice, is perhaps the Second City's and Del Close's most important legacy to Chicago-style theatre.

The "Chicago Style"

Press coverage in those seminal years was effusive and copious. In 2002 critic-turned-scholar Scott Fosdick considered the vital role of press criticism in the development of the "Chicago style." Fosdick's research and analysis of reportage in Chicago from 1975 to 1985, published in the *Newspaper Research Journal*, is comprehensive. In this study, he "probes the influence of daily newspaper reviewers on a theatre in which things went phenomenally right: Theatre companies sprouted and flourished, artists emerged and found a national success and a style of theatre coalesced."[29] Fosdick links the notion of a specific Chicago style to press coverage: "Commentators in Chicago, New York and elsewhere wrote of a style of theatre that distinguished the work of Chicago artists. The *Chicago style*, as it was sometimes called, was never given a completely consistent definition; most who used the term, however, referred to a physically demonstrative form of acting that found its fullest expression in highly naturalistic plays performed in intimate venues."[30] In his research Fosdick discovered a "perfect correlation . . . between the long held aesthetic preferences of [*Chicago Tribune* critic] Richard Christiansen and the Chicago Style."[31] Christiansen had a marked preference for "raw, humane, passionate naturalism," whereas he tended to censure "postmodern avant-garde work that highlights and comments on its own theatricality—an approach that is inherently anti-naturalistic, didactic and even, in a way, self-consciously pretentious, in that it articulates the pretense of art. As such, the dominant avant-garde is at direct odds with Christiansen's underlying aesthetic."[32] Fosdick concludes that "the kind of theatre Christiansen liked flourished and flourished so completely it became known as the Chicago Style."[33] It is clear that Richard Christiansen was a decisive and positive voice in shaping the terms of public discourse about Chicago theatre. But Fosdick goes further and credits him with a determining influence on theatrical production during this era. Not only did the kind of theatre Christiansen like flourish, writes Fosdick, but "the kinds of theatre [he] did not like dwindled."[34] Throughout his long and illustrious career Christiansen demonstrated a reliable predilection for humanist text-based drama over what theorist Hans-Thies Lehmann identifies as a postdramatic "drift" toward an audience-oriented aesthetic that is inherently antinaturalistic and frankly theatrical.[35] And yet, far from dwindling, highly theatrical, audience-oriented performance that played fast and loose with the conventions of realism and climatic structure thrived in Chicago. The Organic, Travel Light, and Free Street Theaters, Remains, Novel Ventures, Next Theatre, the NeoFuturists, the Practical Theatre Company, Lookingglass, Robert Breen's Chamber Theatre, Living Newspaper at

Northwestern University, and, most notably, the sketch comedy group Second City and its predecessors, the Compass Players and Playwrights Theatre Club, were self-consciously, often gleefully, theatrical and predominantly antinaturalistic. Each of these companies thrived in Chicago and many achieved national recognition and influence. Clearly, the kind of naturalism Christiansen favored was only one of several currents or tributaries in mainstream Chicago-style theatre during the last third of the twentieth century.

Fosdick parses out the salient characteristics of the Chicago style as it was drawn by Christiansen and his peers between 1975 and 1986: (1) "artists concentrated not on ideas or intellectual matters, but on the emotional life of the characters," (2) "emotions are displayed in their natural state, uncooked by acting that is overly refined, delicate or nuanced," and (3) naturalism, acting intended "to engender sympathy for the character portrayed," reigned. Each of Fosdick's points is telling and astute, but even if consideration is limited to the short list of production companies mentioned above—a complete list could fill many pages—it is clear that Chicago-style theatre was not all rock 'n' roll.

"Artists Concentrated Not on Ideas or Intellectual Matters, But on the Emotional Life of the Characters"

A theatre of "ideas or intellectual matters" is generally associated with performance that decries or challenges social, political, cultural, or aesthetic norms and appeals to an intellectual elite or gives voice to a disenfranchised minority. However, the theatrical tradition in Chicago is deeply rooted in an affirmation of the city's working- and middle-class audience rather than any political, cultural, or aesthetic agenda. In 1889 Jane Addams established the Hull House, a groundbreaking community center and kindergarten. Shortly after opening the center, she added a theatre program that served that community well into the twentieth century. She noticed that her young clients were engaged by theatre, but what excited them, writes Richard Christiansen "was not complex or exalted. It was burlesque and vaudeville and melodrama. . . . But it got to these young people as no amount of preaching would, and Addams, smart person and devout social worker that she was, knew that theatre, even of this variety, was a liberating force for them."[36] Jim Shifflet reclaimed Addams's vision in the twentieth century when he established the Body Politic in the belief that "a community without the arts is not worth having."[37] In 1972 he explained to arts reporter Linda Winer that he left the church because the upper-working-class members of his urban congregation "don't need their heads hammered. They need a way to enjoy their lives. These people feel so goddam guilty. It's pathetic—they've got to be told it's all right to enjoy."[38] Shifflet and those who came after him disassociated their client-oriented theatre practice from the intellectualism of the dominant avant-garde as well as the crass commercialism of mainstream entertainment.

This is not to say that Chicago theatre had no politics or ideas and was without commercial aspiration. However, binary distinctions that mattered greatly in New York—art verses commerce, intellect verses emotion, relevance verses entertainment—were of little concern in the Windy City. "More than New York," critic Frank Rich wrote about Chicago theatre in 1983, "Chicago is a practical, utilitarian place; it is, or at least once was, the city that 'works.' And the population's tough, unsentimental grip on reality has always been mirrored in the city's buildings, political life, literature and journalism."[39] Rich identified a similar attitude in the city's emerging theatre scene. Ross Wetzsteon noted, "Chicago has always been the preeminent American working-class city. Chicago actors see themselves less as artists or careerists (the two poles in New York) than as craftsmen working at their jobs."[40] Theatre was conceived in Chicago by tough, unsentimental realists as an irreverent, lively, immediate, and exuberant event intended to generate enough interest and income to make a living for its makers, and, failing that, enough to pull another show together.

Jackie Taylor has demonstrated the practical idealism of Chicago theatremakers since she founded the Black Ensemble Theater in 1976. She was twenty-five years old at the time. In 1984 the company produced *Muddy Waters: The Hoochie-Coochie Man*, the first of a long series of hugely popular jukebox musicals about inspirational black figures. Taylor's musical productions have sustained the company. They are unapologetically formulaic and immensely entertaining. They have provided an acting platform for thousands of actors of color and attracted a mixed-race audience for more than a quarter of a century. In 2011 she opened the 50,000-square-foot Black Ensemble Theater Cultural Center in Uptown, one of the most economically and ethnically diverse neighborhoods in Chicago. "Ask Jackie Taylor the mission of her . . . Black Ensemble Theater and she answers, 'To eradicate racism through theatre.' Ask her what makes a good play, and she replies, 'It has to make money.'"[41] Entertainment untethered from idea, thought, or social commitment would achieve neither goal, but Taylor never envisioned the stage as a soapbox or bully pulpit. The sound and rhythms of the music and the physical presence of compelling and dynamic artists of color: for Taylor, that is the message.

Taylor was one of a great many Chicago-based artists that director/actor/author Frank Galati spoke for and about in his keynote speech for the League of Chicago Theatres' seventh annual retreat, in 1987. His topic was art, activism, and, surprisingly, the obligation to fail. He told his audience, "It is in our purpose as theatre artists, that we fail. Or, perhaps, I should say, we 'woo' failure, we dance with failure, we get into our beds with failure. If we do not feel its nagging presence, we are not artists, we are merchants. . . . Our task is not just to 'expose' ourselves—the artist as flasher—but to INHABIT the world, to be of it, to reflect it, to ponder it and even . . . to take care of it, to keep it (the world and its community of humans) safe from harm."[42] Galati defined the artist as an activator rather than an activist. He continued, "And though we may again fail to ACTIVATE, we, obviously, will never stop trying . . . through comedy and satire and irony and tragedy . . . making every effort to shake the audience AWAKE, to arrest them, to detain them in the present moment, fully alive . . . and (conscious that they are WATCHING actors) they may themselves be ready to act." The "idea" of Chicago-style theatre was to deploy the energy of the actor/audience relationship to create a heightened emotional state capable of stimulating thought, ideas, and interpretation, even action, in the audience. Galati reassured his audience that theatremakers "may not be able to stop a war, but we may be able to make people a little less war-like." Likewise, Taylor remains undaunted by the near certainty that she will fail to eradicate racism in her city. But like many of her Chicago peers in the 1980s, she does not prioritize the ideas or intellectual content of the written text over the shared event of performance. In Chicago, success at the box office often depended on the energy of the actor/audience relationship, but when a production failed to deliver—and many did—patrons often returned to the theatre in hope of finding the fleeting but compelling sense of heightened awareness and community that Addams, Shifflet, Taylor, and Galati valued.

The emotional life of the character has been a linchpin in American acting and actor training programs for nearly a century, and it certainly mattered in Chicago. However, the psychological realism associated with the Actor's Studio and brilliant teachers like Constantine Stanislavsky and Sanford Meisner directs the actor's energies inward, whereas in Chicago's storefront theatres the actor's energy was directed outward, permeating and appropriating the spectator's space. In Stanislavsky-based training, particularly as extrapolated by the Method, the actor's focus is directed toward the interior life and personal history of her character. In order to develop a fully conceived, albeit fictive, character onstage, she calls on emotional memories that parallel those of her character. Sanford Meisner sought to divert the actor from overthinking, bringing her back to her emotional and instinctive impulses. His famous adage, to "live truthfully under the imaginary circumstances," encourages actors to play off each other in the moment of performance, thus supporting an ensemble ethos.

However, both techniques work toward an impression of authenticity contingent on the actor's willful suspension of disbelief. As the title of Charles McGaw's classic mid-century acting textbook asserts, in psychological realism *Acting is Believing*. But acting in Chicago wasn't primarily believing. It was doing. The high energy and potent physicality of the Chicago ensemble actor was not sustained by individual introspection, elaborate backstories, or a willful erasure of the theatre environment. Across a wide range of production styles and aesthetic variations, Chicago actors were inclined to work first and foremost toward a monumental summoning of energy to the authentic moment of performance and to direct that energy outward, toward the audience.

Christiansen recalled how the young Steppenwolf actors prepared for Israel Horovitz's *The Indian Wants the Bronx* in 1976. Gary Sinise and Terry Kinney dressed up as "urban goons and prowled the manicured streets of Highland Park, looking tough," no doubt intending to develop material for character development but at the same time watching the reactions of their unsuspecting audience with hawk-like intensity. At each performance, "they ran around the outside of the theatre screaming and carrying on. . . . Then, on a signal from the stage manager, they raced down from the top of the hill roaring . . . and rocketed onto the stage."[43] Their entrance amounted to a physical assault on the stage and the audience. More than two decades later, during a postshow talkback I attended, a longtime Steppenwolf patron recalled that moment. "You felt like they were going to grab you by the throat. It was amazing and scary. And really, *really* exciting."[44] The overwhelming energy of that explosive entrance displaced the spectator's inclination for empathy with the characters' emotional life in favor of a direct and immediate engagement with the action onstage. Director Michael Maggio called it an "OMG-I-can't-believe-that-just-happened" moment. The youthful Steppenwolf actors excelled at such moments, but the example is consistent with the Chicago actor's focus on the physical and external manifestation of an internal state and its effect in and on the audience. In the Travel Light Theater's barroom productions of plays by Sam Shepard, Harold Pinter, and John Guare at the Ruth Page Auditorium, where Barbara Gaines's fledging Chicago Shakespeare Theater made its mark; in the invasive staging of the Steppenwolf's *Balm in Gilead* by Langford Wilson (1984); in the basement of the Wellington Avenue Church, where Frank Galati and friends staged a chamber theatre adaptation of Nathanael West's expressionist black comedy *Miss Lonelyhearts* (1973); and in almost every Remains Theater production, the focus on an intense experience in the theatre forestalled the lurking voyeurism of fourth-wall illusionism.

Barbara Robertson, a quintessential Chicago actress/singer/dancer of tremendous range, has more than fourteen Joseph Jefferson Award nominations and is the recipient of eight "Jeffs" in multiple categories.[45] She is equally at home in the musical *Wicked* and Edward Albee's *Who's Afraid of Virginia Woolf.* Robertson received her first nomination for Best Actress in a Principal Role as Medea in Shozo Sato's 1983 Wisdom Bridge production of *Kabuki Medea*. Sato, at that time an instructor of art and design at the University of Illinois at Urbana-Champaign, synthesizes the highly stylized movement and voice technique of traditional Kabuki with classic Western drama. Demanding and proscribed nonrealistic voice modulations, gestures, and codified movement indicate gender, age, and emotional states. Body parts—shoulders, chin, nose—are broken down to portray specific character types. Sato explains, "You don't have to feel the character. This is technique."[46] Philadelphia *Inquirer* staff writer Stephen Salisbury points out that in Sato's work, "There is no question that Kabuki provides a densely textured, otherworldly theatrical experience; there is nothing 'naturalistic' or 'realistic' about it."[47] Although highly stylized, Kabuki was conceived as popular entertainment intended to occasion a compelling theatre experience rather than deliver the shock of recognition in a psychological or intellectual insight. Perhaps because of Kabuki's inherent emphasis on the theatrical experience, Robertson was unfazed by the highly physical expression and intense, focused energy required in the moment of Kabuki performance. "Here," says Sato, "every muscle you're using almost all the time. Even when you're not speaking, you're holding an elaborate pose. When you walk, everything is so athletic and difficult." Robertson's growling and contorted Medea packed the house. *Chicago Sun Times* reviewer Jae-Ha Kim wrote, "Sato's direction is true to Kabuki austerity. But where men portray all the parts in traditional Kabuki, the starring role belongs to Barbara E. Robertson. As the lovelorn Medea, Robertson dominates the stage with her coy mannerisms and strong convictions. Hers is a voice that is hushed at one moment, thunderous at another."[48] The powerful and highly charged audience response to the production challenged the conventional notion that aesthetic distance—a conscious awareness of the theatre and its environs—fails to engage the emotions and inner life of the spectator.

The lack of realist illusionism and pretense in Kabuki technique was freeing for the actress. "When there's no imitation of reality," she reflected, "performance can be truer. I think imitation takes us away from the moment."[49] Robertson felt that the simplicity, specificity of expression, and presentational style of this and other Chicago productions she worked on allowed the audience greater rather than lesser latitude to participate emotionally. However, rather than the vicarious engagement of an outsider's empathy for another's suffering or triumph, as in realist theatre, the audience's engagement was personal, intimate, and immediate. "Sometimes," she explained, "a realistic approach doesn't allow this." Robertson won that year's Joseph Jefferson Award for an Actress in a Principal Role (Equity production) over nominees Amy Morton (*Life and Limb*), Melva Williams (*Raisin in the Sun*), Rebecca Cole (*Lunching*), and Rondi Reed (*Fool for Love*). Each actor gave a compelling performance in a highly emotional and often gritty drama, but Robertson's passionate and frankly theatrical performance of Medea provided a powerful and immediate experience for the Chicago audience.

Designer Kevin Rigdon explained how this audience-oriented agenda drove his designs for the Steppenwolf's successive performance spaces. "You start from the audience. What is the relationship between the actor and the audience? How can you create a space where an actor can have a dialogue with the audience? That," he explained about his design for the company's first purpose-built 515-seat theatre on Halsted Street, "is what drove the apron into the auditorium, the wrap of the balcony and the shallowness of the audience. Two thirds of the audience is in the front third of the space, close to the stage. And the middle row is eye to eye with the actor on the stage." Rigdon was not unconcerned with wing space, acoustics, sight lines, or auditorium capacity, but his primary objective in designing a performance space for the Steppenwolf actors was to support the flow of kinetic energy between the stage and the audience.

For all their considerable differences, Robert Falls's 1981 treatment of Bertolt Brecht's epic antiwar text *Mother Courage and Her Children* and director Frank Galati's broadly farcical *Division Street* (1983) both demonstrate the buoyant affirmation and audience orientation of the Chicago style. Neither production was without pathos and both had an intellectual underpinning, but both productions were memorable primarily as celebrations of human imagination, exuberant vitality, and an unrepentant theatricality that fully acknowledged the presence of an audience in the intimate space of a makeshift theatre. The plot of *Division Street* was little more than a pretext for playwright Steven Tesich's manic theatrical rant. Galati succeeded precisely because he allowed himself, his cast, and the play's author to "over do," that is, to overflow the confines of logic, character, story, and nature. Actress Saralynne Critterden played a Polish-born, heavily accented African American landlady named Bruchinski, more or less the "straight man" in the piece, and Galati's longtime associates John Morhlein, Barbara Robertson, Ruth Landis, and B. J. Jones had free rein to invent outrageous accents and "bits" of physical humor. In the finale, a gigantic American flag unfurled as the cast lent their voices to a lusty recorded version of "America (My Country 'Tis of Thee)," encouraging an audience sing-along.

In his production of *Mother Courage and Her Children*, Falls cast Galati as a seventeenth-century accordion-playing cook in modern dress and had him sing for his supper with a microphone and under a spotlight. Second City actress Audrie Neenan mugged and held her ground in classic sketch comedy fashion. Designer Michael Merritt created an entirely different theatrical world for each scene—gritty at one moment, whimsical or threatening the next, and for the final scene, an undecorated stage floor illuminated by an unfocused and unforgiving light that spilled into the audience. Courage's daughter, Katrina, a deaf mute and the play's last vestige of human compassion, was played by Steppenwolf actor Glenne Headly. In the play's final scene, Katrina risks her life by attempting to warn villagers of imminent attack from an advancing army. Headly climbed onto Courage's rolling commissary, a wagon now stripped bare of goods and rigging. She waved frantically, jumped up and down, and stamped her foot in frustration at the attentive but detached audience. As indicated in the script, a small drum hung around her neck. She stood atop the wagon with legs splayed and glared directly at the audience as she pounded on the drum with every sinew of her pale, bony body—thump . . . Thump . . . THUMP! At an earsplitting boom, the sound of a gun the size of a small cannon, her body jerked back and she tumbled, arms flailing in what appeared to be a harrowing free fall. Sonja Lansener, who played Mother Courage, called out in anguish. Then, to the same beat as the now silent drum, Lansener slowly and methodically stripped Headly's body naked and rolled it to the stage floor. She piled the clothing, shoes, and drum into the empty wagon and without a backward glance, hauled it off to the same slow beat, leaving Headly's naked body sprawled awkwardly on the empty stage. Until that scene, the production had been inventive, playful, and intellectually engaging. But at the moment of least aesthetic distance, that is, the moment when the physical reality of stage and actor were most aggressively present to the audience, the production took on its greatest emotional power. The audience was agog at the audacity of what was actually happening right in front of them. In that moment, the actor's action and that of her character merged, not as the poignant illusion of a desperate but fictive protest against a long-ago-far-away injustice, but as a powerful warning delivered to an audience in present time with physical daring and absolute commitment.

In Chicago's storefront theatres, the audience was unquestionably in a theatre, and more often than not, the theatre was an exciting place to be because at the end of the day, the emotional life of the audience trumped the emotional life of the character.

"Emotions Are Displayed in Their Natural State, Uncooked by Acting That Is Overly Refined, Delicate or Nuanced"

At its best, Chicago theatre was never precious, over decorated, or cluttered, but the perception that "emotions were displayed in their natural state, uncooked" was born of a ruthless and often intellectual stripping away of extraneous or pretentious detail rather than a lack of refinement or nuance. This aesthetic choice amounted to an innovative and often thrilling form of theatrical essentialism. Designer Kevin Rigdon described how in the early years of the Steppenwolf Company, scenic elements, actions, and emotions were stripped to the bone, rendered "raw" by long, intense discussions and demanding rehearsals. He recounted a telling compliment: "I worked with Peter Hall at the National Theatre [in London]. One day, Peter stopped me to say how much he enjoyed working with me, he felt that that I 'got' it. He said, 'Your work is like a sauce reduction. You take all these ingredients and reduce and reduce until you have a single spoonful of theatre, an intense experience when you put it in your mouth.' That," continued Rigdon, "was what our work was like, what we learned in those early days with the company." Far from being "undercooked," the process Rigdon described required the constant and painstaking attention of master chefs. Robertson felt the same way about her work on *Kabuki Medea*. "Every thought," she explained, "had to be expressed in minimalist movement and specific vocalization. The challenge was to make it organic." The result of meticulously austere work made organic, whether the effect was raw or stylized, naturalistic or theatrical, extraordinarily poignant or thrillingly melodramatic, was experienced by the audience as immediate and close to the bone. Rigdon agreed that this minimalist aesthetic worked against calculated refinement. He recalled, "There was a roughness, a rawness to what we did, not messy or sloppy, but never pitch perfect and very immediate."

If the acting was rigorously stripped down to raw bone, so was design. Perfection in production values was never an option in those early years, but the aesthetic that emerged from choices made of necessity became a hallmark of Chicago production design. In 1975 designer Michael Merritt scrounged city dumpsters to construct a stunning, no-budget collage/environment for the premiere of David Mamet's *American Buffalo*. In his high-budget design for the 1984 Broadway premiere of *Glengarry Glen Ross*, the fly-by-night world of Mamet's sleazy real estate deals was more felt than seen. Act 1 is a series of conversations without reference to a specific time or place, but Merritt used strong horizontal lines, rigid geometric shapes, and a palette of intense reds and black to create a powerful sense of enigmatic menace and betrayal in the shallow banquet of a Chinese restaurant. In act 2, erratic converging lines and a carefully choreographed hodgepodge of battered office furniture in nondescript colors evoked a deeply disturbing sense of entrapment in a vast and untethered space. The absence of decor in each scene was unsettling. There was no sign of food service or consumption in act 1 and only minimal evidence of business being conducted in the office in act 2. Not a single item or element in Merritt's design was included solely for the sake of verisimilitude or realist illusionism. He created a frankly theatrical and experiential space with minimal reference to mundane reality.

"Back then," Rigdon explained, "we weren't interested in windows and doors. The closer the actor gets to an item, the more real it needs to be. If you didn't touch it, you didn't need it." In the cramped and makeshift performance spaces of the Steppenwolf's early homes, Rigdon gave the actors what they most wanted and needed—a barebones production style that indexed the company's powerful actor/audience dynamic. In the Chicago production of *Orphans* (1984), the entrance door of the apartment—important for symbolic as well as physical reasons—bounced against the doorjamb when it slammed and exposed shabby masking when it was pulled open. Rather than distracting from the performance, the lack of visual pretense underscored and enhanced the actor's unchallenged authority over the production. When Frank Galati joined the company as a director, he brought a new visual literacy to the Steppenwolf without curtailing the actors' sovereignty over performance. For Galati's 1987 production of Wallace Shawn's *Aunt Dan and Lemon*, Rigdon designed a shimmering environment of reflective panels that underscored the director's theme of personal responsibility. "Theatregoers," wrote *Sun Times* critic Glenna Syse, "see themselves mirrored in distortion and the characters have their own eerie luminosity that poisons the deceptive sincerity of their speech."[50] Theatre patrons watched themselves watching actor Martha Lavey quietly and methodically reveal the monster within a "frail young woman, who 'honestly' admires the thoroughness of the Nazi killing machinery."[51] Like Rigdon's setting, her performance was unencumbered by distracting detail and gratuitous information. The play begins and ends with her character addressing the audience directly. In her final speech, Lavey was rational, spontaneous, and completely at ease as she spoke to the audience. Her delivery was perfectly pitched to the banality of evil as she explained, "In polite society, people don't discuss it, but the fact is that it's enjoyable—it's enjoyable—to make plans for killing, and it's enjoyable to learn about killing that is done by other people, and it's enjoyable to think about killing, and it's enjoyable to read about killing, and it's even enjoyable actually to kill, although when we ourselves are actually killing, an element of unpleasantness always comes in."[52] Of killing, Lemon concludes, "We have to admit that, after we've watched it for all that time—well, we don't really actually care anymore." Her final words were bone-chilling and surprisingly sensuous, a single spoonful of theatre intense on the palate.

Naturalism, Acting Intended "to Engender Sympathy for the Character Portrayed"

The term "naturalism" appears with regularity in press coverage of Chicago actors and acting. Significantly, the terms "realistic" and "realism" rarely if ever appeared in reviews of Chicago performance in this period. The distinction between naturalism and realism is telling. The philosophical underpinning of twentieth-century realism holds the idea of the stage as an enclosed environment rather than the acting platform of Renaissance, Restoration, and eighteenth -century performance. On the realist stage, the theatre event is a reflection of reality conceived as an autonomous if ephemeral aesthetic object. Naturalism works toward a blurring of distinctions between art and life. Successful or not, the naturalistic actor of the twentieth century as well as the nineteenth century endeavors to "live" onstage rather than maintain the carefully constructed and controlled artifice of realist drama. However, the slice-of-life naturalism of Zola, Hauptman, Gorky, and their nineteenth-century colleagues was excessively detailed and essentially voyeuristic. In Maxim Gorky's *The Lower Depths* an alien and degraded reality was put on "show" for a privileged elite in the meticulous reproduction of a flophouse complete with rotting garbage and filth-encrusted clothing. Not so the naturalism of twentieth-century Chicago. Acting within a conventional scripted drama, Chicago actors created an impression of natural and spontaneous behavior so powerful it commanded the theatrical space as an acting platform, thus belying the basic conceit of twentieth-century realism. In the London *Times*, Holly Hill described Chicago actors as "brooding, explosive—going right to the edge of the cliff of disbelief and hanging over by their nails but never slipping off."[53] The edge Hill speaks of is that point where actor and character, real and fake, reality and illusion exist simultaneously, rendering the imaginary "fourth wall" of theatrical illusion porous and unreliable. Lehmann argues, "Naturalism can be found in theatre forms where, at first glance, nothing more is being offered than a more or less entertaining reproduction of everyday life."[54] But the naturalism that characterized Chicago-style theatre lies somewhere in the superimposed margins of illusion and reality, absence and presence, character and actor.

The notion of presence saturates a theatrical style described as "visceral," "immediate," and "in your face." But the religious and mystical undertones of "presence," with a lingering connection to the Catholic doctrine of "real presence" in the host, were too impenetrable and esoteric to gain much purchase with working actors and designers in Chicago during the 1980s. However, twenty-first-century research and performance theory has done much to redeem presence as a useful critical tool and a teachable quality. In his 2007 study of charismatic celebrity, *It*, Joseph Roach wrestles with the compelling but mysterious qualities of charismatic celebrity, those extraordinary people with "it." He acknowledges the essential paradox of acting and describes theatrical performance in general as "the simultaneous experience of mutually exclusive possibilities—truth and illusion, presence and absence, face and mask."[55] This experience lies at "the edge of the cliff of disbelief," where Hill places the Chicago actors she observed. However, Roach continues, "with the intensity of focus beyond the reach of normal people, those with It can project these and other anomalies at will." The actors who emerged in Chicago in this era were normal people who matured in ensemble companies that were decidedly anticelebrity, that is, anti-It. Those who have achieved fame and fortune in television or film are far too mercurial and private to have achieved more than a modest form of celebrity. In her 2008 book-length study, *Stage Presence*, Jane R. Goodall offers a more useful definition of presence as "a coalescence of energy, mystery, and discipline."[56] Energy and discipline certainly characterize the Chicago style. Still, Goodall leaves the mystery of innate "talent" and its link to presence uncontested.

The conception of "presence" most closely aligned with the theatrical achievements in Chicago during this era is articulated by voice and acting coach Patsy Rodenburg. Rodenburg has built a significant career on the conviction that presence is a teachable and necessary skill rather than a mysterious and innate magnetism, attraction, or radiance. To teach this skill, she identifies three circles of energy related to presence. "First Circle," she explains, "is energy that falls back into you. . . . It is absolutely to yourself and of the past." Third Circle is "generalized energy that is pushed out. . . . It's very loud, very controlling." The Second Circle is "an exchange of energy," a condition of absolute presence demanded of the actor.[57] The text introduction to her 2010 TED talk summarizes the nature of Second Circle presence in ways that a Chicago theatre artist or patron might recognize. "There's often an inflexible screen between us human beings and the performances we're shoehorned into every day, and we need to tear it out—establishing a space [Rodenburg] calls 'the Second Circle': a state of mind and body where confident, relaxed control allows us [to] establish intimacy and human connection where and when we want it."[58] Rodenburg didn't invent what she calls the Second Circle. She observed it onstage and off, studied its operations and physical attributes, and now teaches others how to achieve and use it. The actors most closely associated with the Chicago style were not trained by Rodenburg, but they were exceptionally adept at establishing the intimacy and human connection of the Second Circle in performance.

At its most intense, the visceral in-your-face performance style of Chicago actors provoked a more immediate and direct engagement with the audience than a conventional "sympathy for the character portrayed." With *In the Belly of the Beast: Letters from Prison*, William Petersen gave a gut-wrenching performance as the convicted murderer and self-taught essayist Jack Abbot. The script was taken directly from letters Abbot wrote to Norman Mailer from prison; they were published by Mailer under the same title.[59] Petersen prepared for the role by enduring twenty hours of self-imposed isolation and a punishing physical regimen. The work paid off: *London Times* reviewer Irving Wardle described Peterson's performance as "a revelation of human nature" played "at white heat and point blank range." He concluded, it is "one of the most important performances we're ever going to see in our lifetime."[60] Hap Erstein wrote in the *Washington Times*, "It's quite simply the most painful and moving theatrical experience you are likely to have all year."[61] *Chicago Tribune* entertainment writer Sid Smith listed "Petersen's courageous catalogue of visceral theatrics" in his portrayal of an erudite and articulate murderer who "raged against the injustices of prison life only to relive with muted wonder the moments spent carving out another man's insides." "But," Smith continues, "beyond the electrifying external technique is the indescribable way, from the very first moment when he storms onstage and fixes the audience with a defiant gaze, that Petersen demands his hearing. It seems to stem from everything from his sly, intermittent eye contact to his bone-chilling commitment to the role. In any event, no matter what intellectual distance or glib analytical trick you employ, it's hard to doubt that Abbott is there, and that we, the audience, are on trial."[62] As Smith says, the sociopath portrayed by Petersen was unbearably, excruciatingly present in the theatre. "For a lot of people," said director Robert Falls, "Bill Petersen is Jack Henry Abbott; there's no separation."[63] No separation because the flesh and blood actor Peterson and the character Abbott were equally and simultaneously present to the audience. Peterson delivered a series of long solo passages, usually alone onstage, that were neither traditional monologue (i.e., extended dialogue) nor soliloquy (i.e., externalized thought). The stage was his platform and the audience was clearly his intended auditor. He looked his listeners in the eye, intimidating, charming, menacing, and shocking them individually and collectively at every turn. He went "right to the edge of the cliff of disbelief" and hung on by his nails, never quite slipping off but never withdrawing from the precarious and paradoxical edge where actor, character, and audience exist together and separately at the same time.

I saw this production several times in a variety of venues and each time I was caught off guard by its ability to turn the tables on me. Petersen's portrayal of a charismatic, possibly brilliant, and undeniably murderous sociopath brought the horrifying possibility of the spectators' own chilling indifference dangerously close to the surface. Exactly as Smith described, I was not there to judge but to be judged. It was not a message play, a lecture, or a melodramatic plea for concern or sympathy. It was a call to self-awareness. Jack Kroll, cultural writer for *Newsweek*, declared, "It's one of those rare pieces that add to your awareness of life in your culture and your society."[64] There was no denouement, no poignant eleventh-hour confession, no plea for forgivingness or possibility for redemption, and, in my view, no attempt to "engender sympathy for the character portrayed." *Washington Post* staff writer David Richards described the performance as "a raw, abrasive production that hurls itself at an audience, jabs at its conscience and challenges its equanimity."[65] It was an experience not unlike a roller-coaster ride, and when it stopped I was aware, if only for a queasy moment, that we may all be sociopaths at heart and if so, no less accountable, abused, and doomed than the terrifying creature before us.

Significantly, Richards tempered his praise by faulting the Chicago production for a failure to probe the inner life of the character. "Falls and Petersen have a tendency to go for slam-bang urgency at the expense of Abbott's inner disquiet." But in this production, the inner disquiet of the audience took precedence over that of the character. *New York Times* critic Frank Rich was not a fan for similar reasons. He acknowledged the talent, energy, and skill of the performance but wrote, "Unfortunately, the 90-minute script remains a mound of unintegrated material. It adds few facts and no insights to the existing Abbott dossier, and it usually sidesteps the New York literary world's curious role in the criminal's post-parole recidivism."[66] Both the tone and the critical terms of Rich's review look backward, toward an era when dramatic literature and its elements—message, metaphor, empathy, and enlightenment—were essential to great theatre. In the same article he asserts that Chicago theatre could fulfill its burgeoning potential only by producing "its own indigenous drama" with authors like Chicago-born Lorraine Hansberry and David Mamet, who "flesh out and transcend the bare bones of naturalism with metaphor and psychological depth." Metaphor and psychological depth are literary terms and not particularly helpful in understanding the mechanics of performance in Chicago's storefront theatres. Whatever the individual spectator took away from a performance, Chicago-style theatre was conceived deliberately or instinctively as a personal and deeply felt experience in real time. For a great many theatre patrons, Peterson delivered such an experience in *The Belly of the Beast*.

The 1983 Steppenwolf production of *Orphans* by Lyle Kessler, directed by Gary Sinise, featured ensemble members Kevin Anderson, Terry Kinney, and John Mahoney. At one point, the script called for Mahoney to goad Kinney and Anderson into reenacting a scene on a bus by exchanging roles and imagining various outcomes—a classic improv theatre game. Mel Gussow wrote in the *New York Times*, "While Mr. Kinney's fury forces him into paths of hysteria, the once-timid Mr. Anderson suddenly becomes emboldened, relishing his role as a large, intimidating black man."[67] As the characters shed their mundane, albeit fictive, personalities to assume a "false" theatrical identity, the actors unleashed a terrible energy and latent violence that was bigger, more alive, and more confrontational than the masks of everyday life and realistic representation. Gussow noted the immediacy and improvisational feel for which the company was increasingly famous: "Watching that scene . . . one is aware of a definitive Steppenwolf style of performance, a style that is earthy, kinetic and instinctive. . . . It is the opposite of what is commonly regarded as the essence of British acting in what the English refer to as 'cup and saucer drama,' those 19th-century plays in which china is delicately tinkled in a salon. In the Steppenwolf plays, the crockery is cracked—as in a Julian Schnabel assemblage. Someone has been bashing it around the room."[68] Exhilarating as bashing crockery may be, without content or purpose the residue is little more than a vague cathartic afterglow and a room full of smashed saucers. There was content and argument in this scene, but it was kinesthetic rather than linguistic. The actors took the stage as an acting platform, leaving conventional verisimilitude in their stage dust as they revealed personality to be unstable and identity dangerously malleable. The transformation scene was an unsettling sleight of hand that announced itself as a trick performed by actors for an audience simultaneously within the aesthetic world of the stage fiction and the actual world of the stage platform. It is difficult to imagine an empathic connection to these violent and chimerical characters, but it was impossible to look away or disengage, because in the moment of performance the individuals onstage, unstable and violent as they were, seemed to be more alive, more real, than those of us in the audience.

Making Theatre Chicago-Style

In the fall of 1987 AT&T ran a full page in the *Chicago Tribune* and sponsored a prominent billboard on a major highway with the banner heading: "AT&T

SALUTES CHICAGO THEATRE BECAUSE, AS THE SONG SAYS, 'THEY DO THINGS THEY DON'T DO ON BROADWAY.'" In the seminal years of the 1980s, theatre was indeed made differently in Chicago than on Broadway. First, enduring formal and informal ensemble relationships were formed by young artists with little or no professional experience. The members of a vigorous and relatively untutored ensemble who worked together for months or years were able to experiment and challenge each other in ways a highly trained actor-for-hire could not. Second, ensemble company business and artistic leadership were managed in part or entirely by the artist members. Members of the ensemble were empowered to participate in the selection of scripts, directors, designers, and managers. Casting and scheduling were often decided in collaboration with part or all of the core company. Finally, emerging not-for-profit ensemble groups were generally self-supporting and not wholly, or in some cases, even partially dependent on corporate funding, board contributions, or private investors. These factors coalesced in the city to promote a culture of theatrical daring and achievement.

In 1984 Bernard Sahlins, cofounder of Second City and a passionate supporter of Chicago theatre, declared, "Chicago is the risk capital of the world."[69] Longtime Organic company member and Tony Award recipient Joe Mantegna agreed, "Chicago lets you fail without killing you. . . . Failure is not a terminal disease in Chicago. You learn more from your mistakes than you do from your successes." The city's reputation for risk-taking can be linked to the ensemble structure of Chicago production companies. Steppenwolf ensemble member and acting artistic director Randy Arney explained, "We can take risks we'd never otherwise take because we're in our own theatre with people we love. And risk is a large reason for our success." Martha Lavey, the company's artistic director from 1995 to 2015, addressed the issue of risk-taking in the American Theatre Wing's "Working in the Theatre" video series. "You have to take risks," she said with a small shrug. "What does that actually mean? That you go at things full throttle and not all of it works. I don't think of things we have done as mistakes. . . . Ok. We learned from that, we'll do something else."[70] Lavey passed away in April 2017 to great shared mourning in Chicago's theatre community. Her shrug in this video suggests that she considered risk to be implicit in making theatre, or at least in the way theatre was made in her theatre. If so, what was at risk and why did the risks taken in Chicago's small ensemble theatres achieve such a notable level of success? If a ready answer to this question were available, risk would be a sure thing rather than a gamble. Nonetheless, any theory or supposition about daring and risk must take into consideration the artistic and financial structure of Chicago's ensemble theatre community.

Ensemble theatre is an approach "that aims for a unified effect achieved by all members of a cast working together on behalf of the play, rather than emphasizing individual performances."[71] Ensemble work is not unique to Chicago. The Group and Guild theatres of the 1930s, Bertolt Brecht's influential Berliner Ensemble, even Broadway megamusicals like *Hair* and the box-office sensation *A Chorus Line* are examples of vibrant ensemble acting and theatre. However, in no other urban center of the twentieth century did ensemble theatre dominate the environment as it did in Chicago and in no other city were there so many self-governing resident companies. In 1985 critic Mel Gussow noted that "in this country . . . actors are generally regarded as hired hands, signed on for the duration of a project and seldom having a say in artistic decisions. . . . The idea of actors heading a company has not yet permeated the mainstream of American theatre, with one notable exception—the Steppenwolf Theatre of Chicago." Gussow, a New Yorker, was apparently unaware of the extent and range of artist-run ensembles in Chicago. Dinglefest, Pegasus Players, Mary-Arrchie, Remains, Organic, Free Street Theater, Chicago Actor's Project, Bailiwick, St. Nicholas, the Harper, Black Ensemble Theater, Practical Theater Company, Lifeline, Novel Ventures, Absolute Theatre, and Actor's Cooperative are only a sample of more than two hundred artist-operated ensemble companies that operated in the city between 1980 and 1990. Not all actors, directors, and designers were members of an officially constituted ensemble, but the attitude and work ethic of Chicago's artist-operated ensemble theatres permeated the theatre community.

Many of these companies have endured into the twenty-first century. Some lived from moment to moment, dispersing and reforming in varying configurations for a few seasons in borrowed or short-term rental spaces. A few became famous (Steppenwolf, Lookingglass, Neo-Futurists) while others dissolved as key members left for lucrative film, television, or Broadway contracts (Remains, Organic). But nearly all were formed by a group of friends who wanted to make theatre together and to make it often. Mission statements and company profiles evolved as the ensemble developed a unique identity through trial and a great deal of error. The Steppenwolf ensemble is one of the most famous and enduring of many Chicago companies that started as a loosely organized collective of artists with a shared history, aspiration, and commitment. In 1983 Terry Kinney reflected, "I think what has held us together is a shared vision of what acting could and should be, which was years and years of training together. . . . We wanted to make theatre an actor's event."[72] Ensemble acting is largely identified by the actors' ability to listen and react to each other in complex relationships. This quality was developed to an exceptionally high degree in Chicago, because for the most part, ensemble members learned their trade "on their feet," by listening to each other in rehearsal and in performance, often in the presence of an audience. With minimal production budgets, limited seating capacity, and a weekends-only performance schedule, rehearsal time was limited or interspersed with performance. Actors were compelled to work out problems and develop stage business during the run of the show, often in the moment of performance. Chicago's relatively untutored ensemble actors were empowered by the support of their peers and authorized by each other to play even their most daring choices with authority, as Lavey said, to play "full throttle." In theatre as in music, a wrong note played timidly is a wrong note. A wrong note played with authority is an interpretation. By the mid-1980s, the Chicago audience and press had licensed risk and audacity by defining "failure" as a failure of will, commitment, or energy rather than a failure to maintain established convention, traditional standards, authorial intention, or a director's vision.

"Ensemble Member" is an official title granted by invitation from an established company of artists who identify the group as their artistic home but remain free agents. No actor has a single "line of business" or specialization. Members are featured onstage in a wide variety of major and supporting roles and negotiate to create opportunities to direct or design that would not be offered to them in a more traditional hiring process. When an appropriate company member is not available for a required role, nonmembers are cast by audition or invitation. Directors and designers may come from within the company or be hired in, often establishing a continuing relationship with the ensemble. Company members may be precast or casting may be done in collaboration with a resident or guest director. The administrative structure of companies that formed in the 1980s or earlier varied. Some had a permanent artistic director, often a founding member, while others rotated administrative positions. But no matter how the theatre was constituted, the artist-run ensemble companies granted a significant measure of ownership and responsibility to individual members. "We were willing to postpone or sacrifice fame and fortune," Sinise told *Bomb* magazine in 1999, "for what we got in exchange—control over our work and decision-making power over what we wanted to do. We could decide to work on a Tennessee Williams or Harold Pinter play, and we wouldn't have to audition for it."[73]

Besides the formally constituted ensemble companies, informal ad hoc ensembles formed and reformed around freelance directors like Frank Galati and Michael Maggio, artistic directors Robert Falls (Wisdom Bridge) and Dennis Zachek (Victory Gardens), and author/director David Mamet (St. Nicholas Theater). Not all Chicago ensembles were formed by or around actors. In his first year as artistic director of the Goodman Theatre, Robert Falls established an ensemble of associate directors who collaborated on a themed subscription season that showcased each unique talent. This group began with directors Frank Galati and Michael Maggio and has evolved into a diverse collective of national theatre artists who have reshaped the theatre's artistic identity.[74] The Playwrights Ensemble at Victory Gardens continues to be a vital force in the city today.[75] Like the acting ensembles, the interests and commitments of individual ensemble members and the theatre company as a whole maintain a mutually supportive relationship. Those companies that survived have done so by continually drawing new and diverse abilities, interests, and talents into the ensemble.

Each group developed its own work process. Consequently, working outside one's artistic home could be problematic. This was particularly true of the Steppenwolf Theatre, where the niceties of backstage decorum were often ignored, including the unspoken rule that actors do not criticize or give acting notes to each other. The company was known for a constant, edgy critique exchanged among themselves. Designer Kevin Rigdon noted that "with ownership comes rights, the right to disagree and the right to excel."[76] Gary Sinise valued the positive energy of what outsiders might see as unproductive combativeness. "I can do work here I couldn't do anywhere else because we've a history together. You can . . . head bash and it can be misread as a creative assault. But [founding member] Terry Kinney and I can have enormous conflicts, and we know what we're really doing; we know we're forcing each other to dig deep and not settle for something easy."[77] This sort of active critique did not end with rehearsals. If a company member felt that a scene had grown stale by repetition, it was not uncommon for an actor to throw a "monkey wrench" into a scene in progress—land a stage punch in place of a slap, insert an unrehearsed movement or improvised reaction—actions so off-putting that in a more conventional theatre setting sanctions could be leveled against the instigator. "It's the way we interact during performances," explained company member John Mahoney. "Sometimes we cover up weakness, sometimes we goose each other if we're off, sometimes we break the pattern." The company has mellowed over the years, but core members of the ensemble continue to maintain a remarkable candor among themselves. "This is no place," said ensemble member Rondi Reed during *Valparaiso* rehearsals (1999), "for sensitive souls or tender feelings. That's not us. If you've got something to say, you say it."

In the early years of the company this sort of unconventional behavior did not allow an easy transition for Steppenwolf actors who accepted theatre roles outside the ensemble and were often perceived as arrogant, ungenerous, volatile, or stand-offish. Megan Mullally, best known as Karen in the sitcom *Will*

& Grace, started her career in Chicago while still an undergraduate at Northwestern University. In a 2003 interview she recalled, "They were a clique. But that's what made them cool, ya know? I mean the kind of theatre they were doing was insane and electric."[78] However, whenever ensemble members of this or any closely knit Chicago company were cast outside the group, they brought the full-out commitment and individual daring that characterized ensemble work. Many of the original members of the Steppenwolf and Lookingglass Companies have established careers in film and television but still consider the ensemble to be their artistic home. A few seldom or never accept roles with other theatre companies. Nonetheless, both of these ensemble companies helped shape and were shaped by the city's growing theatre community, and by 1984, the attitude and work ethic of Chicago's artist-operated ensemble theatres permeated the community.

D. W. Moffett, a highly successful character actor in film and television as well as stage, started his career as a founding member of Chicago's award-winning Remains Theatre. Remains was a true ensemble in that individual members collaborated in multiple administrative and artistic roles to create original and often unconventional work collectively. The internal structure of Remains was similar to that of the Steppenwolf, but their selection of material was more unconventional and significantly less commercial. Moffett credited a great deal of his success to his work at Remains. "An ensemble forces you to collaborate," he told a reporter in 1985, "to develop an imagination that transcends your own ego."[79] Music philosopher Stephen Davies describes a similar ethos in ensemble music. "When successfully engaging in music as a group, we do not merely share a great experience; we also promote our sense of belonging together, our belief in our capacity for effective collective action, and our joint commitment to ideals that go beyond our private wellbeing."[80] The ensemble artists who chose to make Chicago their home had healthy egos and did not hesitate to demonstrate self-interest. But along with their Chicago critics and patrons, they believed in the artistic muscle of collective action.

Actors who were intensely present to each other in Chicago's intimate venues were perceived as fiercely present ("in your face"), unpretentious ("earthy"), and alive ("visceral") or, when real sweat and spittle spewed off the actor's laboring body, "crude," "unpolished," and "raw." To achieve these qualities, Chicago actors went "right to the edge of the cliff of disbelief," engaging the audience in ways that put their ability to reclaim the fictions of character and story at risk. When the psychological proximity of performer and spectator is intensified and the physical distance between them diminished, performance can become a shared experience and a shared energy rather than a one-way transmission of meaning.[81] For all their aesthetic differences, the productions and performances described in this article were conceived deliberately or instinctively to activate a direct engagement with the real-time action onstage and a shared experience in the theatre. The artists who made this work did not prioritize the linguistic or intellectual content of the dramatic text but deployed the energy of the actor/audience relationship to create content, meaning, and emotion. Consequently, the emotional life of the flesh-and-blood audience trumped verisimilitude and the emotional life of the fictive characters. Designers, directors, and actors crafted an aesthetic essentialism conceived to clear the stage of any element that did not support and enhance the exchange of energy between stage and auditorium. Chicago-style theatre can be characterized by a monumental summoning of energy and commitment to the stage. In the most successful productions, this energy generated a heightened emotional state that provoked ideas, uncertainties, and intellectual engagement in enough theatre patrons to gain national and international acclaim. As Frank Galati declared in his speech to the League of Chicago Theatres, the best of Chicago-style theatre was intended "to shake the audience AWAKE, to arrest them, to detain them in the present moment, fully alive."

In 2000, the Nederlander Organization established Broadway in Chicago, an extremely profitable production company that brings "Broadway" shows to Loop theatres. No additional explanation is needed to clarify audience expectations; there is not and never will be a sister company called "Chicago on Broadway." Unlike the city's signature hotdog (celery salt, tomato slice, and piccalilli required) and gooey inch-thick pizza, Chicago theatre is a moving target, consistently vibrant, perpetually evolving, and increasingly eclectic. Even in the 1980s, the individual attributes of the Chicago style were not unique to the city, and by the twenty-first century, the style had been assimilated into the international theatre community. Today, theatre patrons are as likely to encounter ensemble-driven, frankly theatrical, audience-oriented storytelling on Broadway (*The Curious Incident of the Dog in the Night; Natasha, Pierre, and the Great Comet of 1812*) and London (*Harry Potter and the Cursed Child*) as at the Steppenwolf, and just as likely to encounter realist illusionism and brilliant acting in the style and tradition of psychological realism on the Steppenwolf stage (*Between Riverside and Crazy*) as in an American classic directed by Frank Galati (*Twelve Angry Men*; *The Little Foxes*).

Nonetheless, the fierce, independent spirit of the Chicago style still thrives in the richest as well as the poorest of the city's institutions. In January 2017, *Chicago Reader* critic Justin Hayford reviewed a production of Racine's 1677 French neoclassical tragedy, *Phèdre,* staged at the Trap Door ensemble's "cramped, sepulchral, amenity-free cubbyhole, where the shoestring company has been mounting intractable, inscrutable plays for 22 years."[82] The production may not have been, as Hayford claims, "the greatest Chicago theatre success in the last quarter century," but it was Chicago-style theatre at its best, still challenging "conventional understandings of what theater is, how it operates, and why it matters." The setting was minimal—a rough-hewn wooden slab and a few suspended ropes—the storytelling straightforward, the ensemble intense and integrated, and the staging frankly theatrical with "intermittent doubling of characters, [and] barking choral laughter." The production offered compelling evidence that if, as Hayford asserts, "theater's primary value lies in its communal investigation of our cultural truths—exposing our social existence as it is, rather than as moneyed interests would have us believe—then ours is the rare theater scene that truly matters."

Notes

1. Pat Colander, "Chicago Theater Comes into Its Own," *New York Times*, May 27, 1984, Late City Final Edition ed., sec. 2, accessed January 10, 2016, http://www.nytimes.com/1984/05/27/arts/chicago-theater-comes-into-its-own.html?pagewanted=all.
2. Scott Elliot, "Interview with Gary Sinise," *Bomb Magazine*, January 1999, accessed July 8, 2016, http://bombmagazine.org/article/2193/gary-sinise.
3. "Working in The Theatre: Steppenwolf Theatre Company," Directed by Margarita Jimeno, (New York: CUNY TV, 2015), video, accessed July 8, 2016, https://www.youtube.com/watch?v=D60SoZKDHQc.https://www.youtube.com/watch?v=6mjPLWroMNg.
4. Richard Christiansen, "Revealing the Real Roots of the City's 'Rock 'N' Roll Acting,'" *Chicago Tribune*, May 18, 1987, accessed February 13, 2016, http://articles.chicagotribune.com/1997-05-18/news/9705180214_1_chicago-style-chicago-style-theater.
5. Wetzsteon, "Can an Electric Theater Style Revive New York?" *New York*, December 16, 1985, 50, accessed July 8, 2016, https://books.google.com/books?id=8skBAAAAMBAJ&pg=PA52&lpg=PA52&dq=when+did+the+steppenwolf+production+of+true+wes t+open+in+nyc&source=bl&ots=b1Fe4XHBIy&sig=p3woFCCtJ1Z73QECh1hVhsV9-Ow&hl=en&sa=X&ei=ylUtVef9M5LVoATXnIHYBQ&ved=0CCYQ6AEwAjgK#v=onepage&q=when%20did%20the%20steppenwolf%20production%20of%20true%20west%20open%20in%20nyc&f=false.
6. "The city's longest-running hit, 'E/R Emergency Room,' is a literal slice of gritty urban life—a documentary look at 'the human parade' in a North Side community hospital's emergency clinic. Attributed to eight authors, the play was based on research conducted in hospitals by the members of the Organic Theater Company (whose similar portrait of Chicago Cubs fans, 'Bleacher Bums,' was seen in New York a few seasons back)." Frank Rich, "Critic's Notebook; Chicago Has Blossomed into a Theater Center," *New York Times*, October 13, 1983, accessed July 8, 2016, http://www.nytimes.com/1983/10/13/theater/critic-s-notebook-chicago-has-blossomed-into-a-theater-center.html.

7. John Beaufort, "Definitive Revival of Lanford Wilson's First Full-length Play; *Balm in Gilead*," *Christian Science Monitor*, June 18, 1984, accessed July 8, 2016, http://www.csmonitor.com/1984/0618/061805.html.
8. Colander, "Chicago Theater Comes into Its Own."
9. *Re-Animator* was released by Empire Pictures in 1985 and is now considered a horror-comedy cult classic.
10. Richard Christiansen, "'Beast' Makes Its Mark on London," *Chicago Tribune*, May 24, 1985, accessed July 11, 2016, http://articles.chicagotribune.com/1985-05-24/news/8502020244_1_theater-critic-beast-gate-theater.
11. Colander, "Chicago Theater Comes into Its Own."
12. Sid Smith, "'Belly of The Beast,' 'Coyote' Electrify D.C.," *Chicago Tribune*, June 17, 1985, accessed April 4, 2016, http://articles.chicagotribune.com/1985-06-17/features/8502080454_1_coyote-free-theater-chicago-theater.
13. Andrew Webb, "'In The Belly of The Beast' Searing Tale Of Prison Survival," *Sun Sentinel* (Palm Beach), June 7, 1985, accessed December 10, 1995, http://articles.sun-sentinel.com/1985-06-07/features/8501230033_1_prison-inmate-abbott-artistic-director.
14. Christopher Rawson, "Regional Theater to the Rescue," *Pittsburgh Post-Gazette*, January 21, 1986, accessed May 1, 2016, https://news.google.com/newspapers?id=BLRRAAAAIBAJ&sjid=Qm4DAAAAIBAJ&pg=7223,4782907.
15. Ibid.
16. Samuel G. Friedman, "Steppenwolf Theater's 10-Year Climb to Success," *New York Times*, July 15, 1985, accessed July 8, 2016, http://www.nytimes.com/1985/07/15/theater/steppenwolf-theater-s-10-year-climb-to-success.html.
17. Benedict Nightingale, "Steppenwolf Plays Together, Stays Together," *New York Times*, October 23, 1988, accessed July 8, 2016, http://www.nytimes.com/1988/10/23/theater/theater-steppenwolf-plays-together-stays-together.html?pagewanted=all.
18. Chris Jones, "Sheldon Patinkin, a Giant of Chicago Comedy and Theater, Dies at 79," *Chicago Tribune*, September 21, 2014, accessed July 8, 2016, http://www.chicagotribune.com/entertainment/theater/chi-sheldon-patinkin-dies-20140921-column.html.
19. Ibid.
20. Linda Winer, "Body Politics' Friendly Giant and a Miracle on Lincoln Av," *Chicago Tribune*, August 27, 1972, M7 sec.
21. Arthur Barlow, *The Director's Voice: Twenty-One Interviews* (New York: Theatre Communications Group, 1999, 93.
22. Colander, "Chicago Theater Comes into Its Own."
23. Wetzsteon, "Can an Electric Theater Style Revive New York?" 56.
24. Jeanne Leep, *Theatrical Improvisation: Short Form, Long Form, and Sketch-based Improv* (New York: Palgrave Macmillan, 2008), 113.
25. Colander.
26. Mike Thomas, *The Second City Unscripted: Revolution and Revelation at the World-Famous Comedy Theater* (New York: Villard, 2009), 54.
27. Ibid., 57.
28. Ibid., 56.
29. Scott B. Fosdick, "Newspaper Critic Shapes Chicago Style of Theater," 114, *Newspaper*

Research Journal 23, no. 2/3 (April 2002): 118, accessed July 8, 2016, http://scholarworks.sjsu.edu/cgi/viewcontent.cgi?article=1006&context=journ_masscomm_pub.

30. Ibid.
31. Ibid.
32. Ibid., 125.
33. Ibid., 118.
34. Ibid.
35. Chicago and Chicago-style theatre do not fall within Lehmann's concept of postdramatic performance. The story structure and "mental signification" of realist theatre, that is, the thought, theme, or message of classic dramatic literature, never wholly disappeared. However, as Lehmann points out, "If one reduces the distance between performers and spectators to such an extent that the physical and physiological proximity (breath, sweat, panting, movement of the musculature, cramp, gaze) masks the mental signification, then a space of a tense centripetal dynamic develops, in which theatre becomes a moment of shared energies instead of transmitted signs." Hans-Thies Lehmann, *Postdramatic Theatre* (London: Routledge, 2006), 150.
36. Richard Christiansen, *A Theater of Our Own: A History and a Memoir of 1,001 Nights in Chicago* (Evanston, IL: Northwestern University Press, 2004), 47.
37. Ibid., 151.
38. Linda Winer, "Body Politic's Friendly Giant and a Miracle on Lincoln Av," *Chicago Tribune*, August 20, 1972, M7.
39. Frank Rich, "Critic's Notebook; Chicago Has Blossomed into a Theater Center," *New York Times*, October 13, 1983, accessed July 8, 2016, http://www.nytimes.com/1983/10/13/theater/critic-s-notebook-chicago-has-blossomed-into-a-theater-center.html.
40. Ibid.
41. Gina Bazer, "Chicagoans of the Year 2011: Jackie Taylor," *Chicago Magazine*, January 4, 2012, January 2012, accessed July 8, 2016, http://www.chicagomag.com/Chicago-Magazine/January-2012/Chicagoans-of-the-Year-2011-Jackie-Taylor-Black-Ensemble-Theater/.
42. All punctuation, capitalization, and ellipses appear in the handwritten manuscript from which Galati spoke. Frank Galati, Convocation Speech League of Chicago Theatres Retreat, 1987, MS, Frank Galati Private Archive, Chicago.
43. Christiansen, *A Theater of Our Own*, 221.
44. Postshow talkback, Steppenwolf production of *One Flew Over the Cuckoo's Nest* staring Gary Sinise, attended by the author, April 17, 2000.
45. The Joseph Jefferson Awards, known as the "Jeffs," are the Chicago equivalent to New York's Tony Awards. "The Jeff Awards has been honoring outstanding theatre artists annually since it was established in 1968. With approximately 50 members representing a wide variety of backgrounds in theatre, the Jeff Awards is committed to celebrating the vitality of Chicago area theatre by recognizing excellence through its recommendations, awards, and honors," accessed July 8, 2016, http://www.jeffawards.org/home/index.cfm.
46. Shozo Sato, "Kabuki Actor's Technique | Japanese Culture," PBS LearningMedia, accessed July 08, 2016, http://www.pbslearningmedia.org/resource/jacult.arts.drama.technique/japanese-culture-kabuki-actors-technique/.
47. Stephen Salisbury, "Theatre That Is Born of the East and West 'American Kabuki,' Which

Will Be Presented Here, Blends Two Cultures," *Philadelphia Inquirer*, September 21, 1986, accessed July 8, 2016, http://articles.philly.com/.

48. Jae-Ha Kim, "Greek Classic Gets Japanese Twist in 'Kabuki Medea.'" *Chicago Sun-Times*, October 20, 1993, accessed July 8, 2016, http://www.jaehakim.com/entertainment-reviews/stage-reviews/greek-classic-gets-japanese-twist-in-kabuki-medea/.
49. Barbara Robertson, "Kabuki Medea" telephone interview by author, May 6, 2016.
50. Glenna Syse, "'George,' 'Aunt Dan" Better Here than in New York," *Chicago Sun-Times*, June 28, 1987, accessed 2016, http://www.highbeam.com/doc/1P2-3833018.html?refid=easy_hf.
51. Richard Christiansen, "'Aunt Dan and Lemon' A Magnificent Play," *Chicago Tribune*, June 15, 1987, accessed July 8, 2016, http://articles.chicagotribune.com/1987-06-15/news/8702140035_1_aunt-dan-lemon-shawn.
52. Wallace Shawn, *Aunt Dan and Lemon: Acting Edition* (New York: Dramatists Play Service, 1986).
53. Holly Hill, "Theatre in the United States: 'Steppenwolfen' Take New York by Storm," July 8, 1985, *London Times*.
54. Lehmann, *Postdramatic Theatre*, 117.
55. Joseph R. Roach, *It* (Ann Arbor: University of Michigan Press, 2007), 19.
56. Jane R. Goodall, *Stage Presence* (London: Routledge, 2008), 19.
57. Patsy Rodenburg, "Patsy Rodenburg: The Second Circle" (lecture, Michael Howard Studio, NYC), October 9, 2008, accessed July 12, 2016, https://www.youtube.com/watch?v=Ub27yeXKUTY.
58. "Patsy Rodenburg," TED: Ideas worth spreading, accessed July 08, 2016, https://www.ted.com/speakers/patsy_rodenburg.
59. Falls's script was based on an earlier script written by Adrian Hall. "Falls staged the play at Chicago's Wisdom Bridge Theatre on 29 September 1983. The critics praised the production, which ran for five months and later played in Glasgow, London, and the Kennedy Center in Washington, D.C. Falls acknowledged that he had used Hall's play as the basis for his script, but included new material. Although no credit was given to Hall and no royalties were paid to Trinity [Theatre], Falls explained that he 'thought Adrian Hall was getting royalties through Seymour Morgenstern.'" Mary Ellen Wright, "Adrian Hall's Adaptations of In the Belly of the Beast," *NEBULA: A Journal of Multidisciplinary Scholarship* 3, no. 4 (January 2007): accessed July 8, 2016, http://nobleworld.biz/images/Wright.pdf.
60. Quoted by Richard Christiansen, "'Beast' Makes Its Mark on London," *Chicago Tribune*, May 24, 1985, accessed July 11, 2016, http://articles.chicagotribune.com/1985-05-24/news/8502020244_1_theater-critic-beast-gate-theater.
61. Sid Smith, "'Belly Of The Beast,' 'Coyote' Electrify D.C.," *Chicago Tribune*, June 17, 1985, accessed April 4, 2016, http://articles.chicagotribune.com/1985-06-17/features/8502080454_1_coyote-free-theater-chicago-theater.
62. Ibid.
63. Andrew Webb, "'In The Belly of The Beast' Searing Tale Of Prison Survival," *Sun Sentinal* (Palm Beach), June 7, 1985, accessed December 10, 1995, http://articles.sun-sentinel.com/1985-06-07/features/8501230033_1_prison-inmate-abbott-artistic-director.
64. Quoted in Smith, "'Beast,' 'Coyote' Electrify D.C.," 1985.
65. David Richards, "Theater Cry From the Heart ANT Imports a Powerful 'Beast,'" *Washington*

Post, June 17, 1985, accessed July 10, 2016, https://www.washingtonpost.com/archive/lifestyle/1985/06/17/theater-cry-from-the-heart-ant-imports-a-powerful-beast/c1fc0b94-6b9c-4ebc-8d48-12b471cf5174/?utm_term=.f11101975af4.

66. Frank Rich, "Critic's Notebook; Chicago Has Blossomed into a Theater Center," *New York Times*, October 13, 1983, accessed July 8, 2016, http://www.nytimes.com/1983/10/13/theater/critic-s-notebook-chicago-has-blossomed-into-a-theater-center.html.
67. Mel Gussow, "Stage View: 'Orphans' Is a Study in the Steppenwold [*sic*] Style," *New York Times*, May 16, 1985, accessed July 9, 2016, http://www.nytimes.com/1985/05/19/theater/stage-view-orphans-is-a-study-in-the-steppenwold-style.html?pagewanted=all.
68. Ibid.
69. Colander.
70. Margarita Jimeno, dir., "Working in the Theatre: Steppenwolf Theatre Company," February 5, 2015, accessed July 8, 2016, https://www.youtube.com/watch?v=D6oSoZKDHQc.
71. "Ensemble Theater: A Chicago Tradition," Chicago Public Schools Department of Arts Education, accessed July 08, 2016, http://chicagoguide.cpsarts.org/chicago-pages/theater/ensemble.
72. Colander.
73. Scott Elliot, "Interview with Gary Sinise," *Bomb*, January 1999, accessed July 8, 2016, http://bombmagazine.org/article/2193/gary-sinise.
74. Accessed July 9, http://www.goodmantheatre.org/Artists-Archive/collective/.
75. Accessed July 9, http://victorygardens.org/about/playwrights/.
76. Kevin Rigdon, "Kevin Rigdon, Designer," telephone interview by author, February 12, 2015.
77. Colander.
78. Nina Metz, "Mullally's Roots Run Deep in Chicago 'Will & Grace' Star Got Start at Local Theaters," *Chicago Tribune*, November 16, 2003, accessed July 9, 2016, http://articles.chicagotribune.com/2003-11-16/news/0311160440_1_supreme-music-program-northwestern-white-slavery.
79. Sid Smith, "Success May Not Spoil D.w. [*sic*] Moffett, But What About Remains Theatre?," *Chicago Tribune*, June 30, 1985, accessed July 9, 2016, http://articles.chicagotribune.com/1985-06-30/entertainment/8502120159_1_moffett-steppenwolf-fatal-vision.
80. Stephen Davies, *Musical Understandings: And Other Essays on the Philosophy of Music* (Oxford: Oxford University Press, 2011), 86.
81. "If one reduces the distance between performers and spectators to such an extent that the physical and physiological proximity (breath, sweat, panting, movement of the musculature, cramp, gaze) masks the mental signification, then a space of a tense centripetal dynamic develops, in which theatre becomes a moment of shared energies instead of transmitted signs." Hans-Thies Lehmann, *Postdramatic Theatre* (London: Routledge, 2006), 150.
82. Justin Hayford, "Is Trap Door Chicago's greatest theater success of the last quarter century?" *Chicago Reader*, January 11, 2017, accessed March 5, 2017, http://m.chicagoreader.com/chicago/is-tiny-trap-door-chicagos-greatest-theater-success-over-the-last-quarter-century/Content?oid=25001111.

Part II

Histories of New Writing for Theatre

New Writing and Theatre History

Introduction to the Special Section

—SARA FREEMAN

The essays in this special section arrived in response to a call to consider new writing for the theatre, a call asking about when there have been particular densities of new play production, specific initiatives for new types of writing to be developed, or major shifts in the styles of theatre writing. The call for submission reflected a desire to extend current Anglo American discussions of new play production and the role of new writing in theatre economies by potentially *going back further* when looking at examples of the role of new writing in theatre, *looking elsewhere in world geography* for examples of period or initiatives marked by a desire for new plays to be written for theatre, or *developing closer case studies* about contemporary examples of new writing initiatives. British and American scholarship about primarily the twentieth century, outlined below, convincingly suggests that it might be fertile to give such moments attention in their individuality but also in their connections. The idea for this section came from wondering what can be seen when looking across instances where the role of the writer, the procedures of producing theatres, the dynamics of language, and the theorization of dramatic structures contend with different models of and desires for newness—for new writing, new plays, new audiences, or a new theatre. The category of newness in theatre exerts a perpetual draw for artists and audiences alike, while what characterizes the new is always contextual, always culturally conditioned, always changing, making it a very fruitful category for theatre historical analysis. Being mindful of Thomas Postlewait's caution about buying into paradigms of aesthetic revolution or historical rupture too heavily has provoked patient considerations and reconsiderations of writers or writer's theatres in this section, as well as some new articulations of moments when new plays or new modes of writing formed.[1] These are histories of new writing that are interested in continuity as much as they are in rupture.

Still, these histories recognize that the draw of producing new writing for theatres has both inspirational and aspirational trajectories, demonstrating the siren call of the new as a concept. Inspirationally, the production of new plays gets positioned as a manifestation of one of theatre's highest callings—that is, to be in a lively and current dialogue with its immediate audience. A strong new writing scene also sends signals about the artistic health and vitality of theatre, because it indicates that theatre artists are thinking about the future as much as the past and that there are opportunities for and interest in people's voices and developments in the form. Aspirationally, it can put a theatre on the map. It can impart a reputation for discovering new writers who come to be regarded as among the greats or for producing new plays that define a period or command attention and box office in ever-widening circles. These types of trajectories can be documented, explicated, and historicized, whether in case studies or in synchronic and diachronic overviews of events related to the encouragement and production of new writing for the theatre. This introduction provides one possible pathway through Anglo American histories of new writing as a preface to the articles in the section, which do the work of unpacking specific moments or projects in detail.

In both scholarly and journalistic writing about the last hundred years of British theatre, there is a strong strain of analysis about the role of new writers and programs in encouraging new writing for the English, Scottish, Irish, and Welsh theatres. This analysis often evokes the observation that the coronation of Elizabeth II, in 1953, ushered in a new Elizabethan age and that the late twentieth century is marked by an upsurge of new play production that is deeply stirring to national conversation and propelled by the vital presence of young, compelling playwrights at a density not seen since Shakespeare's time.[2] The body of analysis became more self-consciously historical in the first two decades of the twenty-first century as conferences, government reports, and Arts and Humanities Research Council (AHRC) projects received funding to support archival work and to gather data. Notable among these initiatives are two reports published in 2000, one from Peter Boyden Associates on the roles and functions of English regional producing theatres and the other titled *The Next Stage*, an Arts Council England statement on a "national Arts policy for Theatre in England." Additionally, the 2009 British Theatre Consortium's report "Writ

Large: New Writing on the English Stage, 2003–2009" provided a holistic assessment of support and attitudes toward new plays from surveys and interviews. Together these three reports sit alongside the AHRC project "Giving Voice to the Nation: The Arts Council of Great Britain and the development of Theatre and Performance in Britain 1945–1995," which culminated in a 2013 conference at the University of Reading called "Turning the Page: Creating New Writing, 1945–2013" as major documentary and analytical efforts to discuss new writing for the theatre.

Historiographical analysis of treatments of the role of new writing in British theatre is also emerging post-2010. Jacqueline Bolton's detailed 2012 article "Capitalizing (on) New Writing: New Play Development in the 1990s" sets out a nuanced materialist reading of different strands of philosophy driving the assumptions and procedures of the British new writing sector since the 1990s.[3] In Rosemary K. Bank and Michal Kobialka's *Theatre/Performance Historiography: Space, Time, Matter* (2015), Yael Zarhy-Levo's chapter on Aleks Sierz's publications about British new writing theatres since the 1990s does important work on the narrative strategies used when British scholars discuss new writing for the theatre.[4] Zarhy-Levo reflects on Sierz in particular because dating from his 2001 publication of *In Yer Face Theatre: New Theatre in the 90s*, which gave a more lasting name to the upsurge in production of potent plays by young "Neo-Jacobean" writers during that decade, his voice has been topic-defining.[5] Sierz does not write so much as a historian as he does as an arts critic and cultural commentator, a partisan, and a gadfly. He acknowledges he writes in a personal and polemical mode. But he helps set out territory for what "new writing" means for British theatre both aesthetically and as a sector of the arts economy. In later publications, he does not turn to heavy emphasis on archival materials or specific historical methodologies to drive his analysis, but his discussions of the present become more reflective about the patterns he is naming and more explicit about delineating forms within British theatre production.

When Sierz published *Rewriting the Nation: British Theatre Today* (2011), he differentiated what he calls "New Writing Pure" from "organisations whose primary focus is on ensemble acting, physical theatre, devised work, live art, multi-media experiments, site-specific ventures, street theatre, theatre-in-education, one-off one-person shows, circus, or whose main objective is community work, work with children, young people, prisoners or puppets." This distinction addresses the now well recorded sense of fissure in the late twentieth century between new plays and new works for theatre ("performance") driven by experimentalist approaches to body, visuality, ensemble, and language that resist mapping by authorship or text. Sierz defines "new writing pure" as being "often difficult, sometimes intractable, but it usually has something urgent to say about Britain today," in a way that challenges both form and content. Moreover, says Sierz, it is work that "stages a struggle around the question, what kind of England do we want? Or, for that matter, what kind of Britain?"[6]

In this frame, "new writing pure" is scripted theatre with a strong bias toward state of the nation plays: the legacy of literary and art theatre movements. The heritage of the independent theatre movement and the creation of art theatres that moved through Europe in the late nineteenth and early twentieth centuries and had taken hold in the United States by the 1910s is a strong antecedent for most Anglo American new play theatres or initiatives to encourage new writers (or new types of writing) for the stage since the 1880s. Anna Irene Miller's *The Independent Theatre in Europe: 1887 to the Present*, published in 1931, for instance, focuses on the dramatic revival ushered in by the founding of free and independent theatres, little theatres, repertory theatres, and art theatres. Miller argues both sides of her equation, positing both that innovative writing brought new theatres into existence and that the goals of new theatres encouraged new writing. Her conclusion argues the importance of experimental, artist-driven new writing theatres in their own right but also forcefully declares that the "greatest gift of the free theatre to the commercial houses has been plays and playwrights."[7] What her history does, and Sierz does the same, is revealingly describe the way that theatre artists often work out of an alternative, reforming, or rebellious urge when making new writing, while at the same time acknowledging how the project of encouraging new writing for theatre becomes a mainstreaming proposition that depends on institutional apparatus and not just aesthetic innovation.

As Todd London writes in the pages of this special section, there are both social and artistic reasons for interest in new drama, reasons in both areas having to do with reform, innovation, and what he calls the production of wonder. Both in the United States and in the United Kingdom, new writing theatres and initiatives to encourage new play production are understood to be related to the goals of the independent theatre movement, that is, to establishing a meaning-driven mode of theatre production participating actively in civic life, its values based on aesthetic and cultural achievement (and London's *wonder*) rather than box office receipts. Pushes for new writing for theatre are also related to drives to establish national theatres, whether a centralized national theatre (Lincoln Center, the Kennedy Center, the National Theatre) or cultural centers across a national geography providing direct access to theatre commenting on or propelling important civic and artistic trends (the Federal Theatre Projects, regional theatre movements on both sides of the Atlantic, the Ford Foundation grants, alternative touring companies). Finally, new writing programs reflect interest in youthful revival and radical critique through the development of new voices and new modes of wonder. A persistent twinning of alternative and mainstream ethos, of disruptive and establishing urges toward institutions, and of both populist and anticommercial desires for audiences marks the histories of new writing in the United States and the United Kingdom.

Indeed, in post–World War II US theatre, arts journalism and publications for artistic organizations discuss new play development programs with some regularity, notably when focused on dramaturgy and the role of literary management, because those are the places where the management of the simultaneously alternative and mainstream nature of new writing theatre collides. Articles in *TDR* and *Theatre Topics* by Douglas Anderson, Rick DesRochers, and David Eshelman provide scholarly documentation and analysis about the project of producing new plays, focusing on the material systems and ideological formations that support the pathways for those newly written plays.[8] The reflection and lament of playwrights about the shape of careers within American theatre since the 1970s also provide sources about new writing theatres in the United States, as seen in Roberta Levitow's representative and summative piece from 2002 in an *American Theatre* magazine special section on "The Future of New Work."[9] With those sources now joined now by Todd London, Ben Pesner, and Zannie Giraud Voss's *Outrageous Fortune: The Life and Times of the New American Play* (2009), a major book following up on the results of a pioneering survey of playwrights and artistic staff and explicating financial and ideological aspects of new play production, a space for scholarship about new plays as a category has taken shape in US theatre. London's contribution to this special section reflects on the boom in new American playwriting from the 1960s to 2016. Because of his simultaneously insider/outsider status as an arts critic, artistic director of a playwright advocacy organization, and academic who is consistently engaged with supporting, analyzing, and documenting the work of playwrights and the role of new writing in US theatre, London's observations provide a fitting coda to the studies in this section, as discussed below.

As an example of the types of histories that can emerge from documentation of the work of new play theatres and analysis of their role in the theatre scene and larger culture, Jeffrey Ullom's institutional history of the Humana Festival of New American Plays at the Actors Theatre of Louisville (ATL) exhibits exemplary breadth and depth. Ullom's book identifies an institutional sequence of discovery, surprising success, and formation of national reputation, resulting in a refiguring of relationships to commercial theatre in Humana's first twenty years. He argues that the festival then experiences two phases of significant changes and struggles about questions of the festival's relevance.[10] Ullom describes founding artistic director Jon Jory as shifting the focus of the festival from product to process in the late 1980s, even while facing an increasing corporatizing of theatre structures that affected the arts in the whole country. Ullom notes that those combined forces resulted in a streak of formulaic plays in the mid-1990s. Commissioning writers, and consciously encouraging the work of gay and lesbian, African American, and Latino playwrights while supporting "exploration through experimentation with form," drove the festival forward in the late 1990s and the turn of the century, even while the festival "endured many shakeups" and made "changes to stay in the limelight."[11] Ullom considers the form and content of new American plays encouraged by the festival as well as the structures that support their production at ATL. His history of ATL as a playwright's theatre is also a history of the phases the US new play sector has moved through since the 1960s.

It may be that recently published scholarship from the United Kingdom tends to focus on new writing theatres since the 1990s because the immediate postwar decades through the 1980s were already such objects of attention and mythology, with histories about the self-defined writer's theatre of the English Stage Company at the Royal Court Theatre and of first- and second-generation alternative groups regularly published and debated. In the United States, there is less argument that a new phase for theatre writing began in the 1990s and less focus on how new plays form an economic motor in the theatre scene. Forces of decentralization across enormous geographic distances in the United States mean that any sense of a coherent new writing sector is less about industry and economy, as found in UK framings, and more about philosophies, missions, or sets of conversations connecting across disparate conditions. Overall, there is consonance across Anglo American histories of new writing, though my reading suggests that while the histories tell similar stories about the phases of new writing theatres, their comparative timelines for when those phases take place are separated by decades of gap.

Anglo American histories of new writing track the role of new play production in and through theatre institutions and narrate four phases since the beginning of the twentieth century. First, there is an incipient phase wherein, for a variety of practical and aesthetic reasons, existing institutional theatres oppose or are indifferent to calls fomenting new writing, making the pursuit of new play production a fully alternative commitment except for specific types of West End or Broadway commercial propositions. Next, comes a seeding phase, wherein interest in new writing is seen as requiring dedicated focus, so some institutions begin to define their missions around new plays and others develop festival or second-stage programs for producing new plays or adjunct programs to encourage new writing. A third, expanding phase comes when almost every type of theatre institution across the board wants to be seen developing and producing new work (academic programs become focused on new works; even classical theatre companies start to have new writing programs!), but institutions are troubled by how to gracefully handle the impact of new writing processes on their production hierarchies and logistics. A consolidating phase showcases institutions starting to get marginally better at supporting new writing, even as theatre economics mean that risks associated with producing new plays are never fully ameliorated.

In the United Kingdom, that incipient phase took place from the end of the nineteenth century until World War II, while the seeding phase moved into gear fully in the postwar years due to the Royal Court and the alternative theatre movement. By the late 1970s, signs of the expansion of new writing programs were underway, with all sorts of institutions commissioning playwrights and exploring how to activate new writing, though those efforts were redirected and partially blighted in the 1980s by Thatcherist funding policies at the Arts Council—and writers produced scathing commentaries on that topic. Part of the upsurge of the UK new writing theatres in the 1990s was that institutions started to get better at managing new writing; the effects of that better management were in full effect by the first decades of twenty-first century, which led Bob Hedley and Harriet Powers to write an admiring *American Theatre* magazine article in 2012 comparing new play development "over there" to what they describe as a troubled US new play scene.[12] Meanwhile, the US incipient phase around new writing theatres began before World War I but lasted into the postwar decades of the 1950s and 1960s. By the 1970s, the United States saw the most concentrated seeding of mission-focused new writing theatres and programs. By the late 1990s and through the turn of the twentieth century, it became almost universal for theatres to want to support new work, while writers themselves commented consistently on being "developed to death" and on the bad fit between types of institutional structures and the needs of new plays. This is part of the situation recorded by *Outrageous Fortune*. In the second decade of the twenty-first century, though nothing is perfect, American theatres are starting to get better at handling new work, as detailed in commentary by Hedley and Power and London in articles published after *Outrageous Fortune*.[13]

Both Sierz and London also offer timeline patterns for thinking about the last century of new writing. Sierz identifies boom and bust cycles for support of new writing alternating by decade ('50s boom, '60s bust, '70s boom, '80s bust), but then differentiates how the boom since the 1990s has played out. He describes the 1990s as a "Newtonian reaction" to the state of new writing in the 1980s; in the 1990s new writing energies that had been blocked were freed and a strong new aesthetic formed. But then the freedom accelerated. Sierz posits that the 2000s were a "quantum decade" for new writing, with everything happening all over the place at the same time. He writes that British theatre resembled "a nuclear reactor: inside, everything is bouncing off the walls; common sense flies out the window; paradox rules." Outside, those conditions meant that instead of the "flowering of a style, what you had was a flowering of various sensibilities, a whole variety of voices."[14] Sierz's imagery positions the twenty-first century as both boom and bust. It doesn't produce a unified aesthetic, which is a type of failure in his eyes, but it is still capable of generating excitement and energy.

London wrote about the "states of American playwriting" in 2001. London's historical field in this piece goes back to Eugene O'Neill and narrates through contemporary work, outlining five states of attitude and action in the creation of new plays. State one London calls "The Great American Playwright is Dead; Long Live the American Playwright," and it concerns the decentralization of new play production since O'Neill's time. State two is "America as Many Americas," in which he notes the upsurge of artists from diverse identities writing plays and thinks about the influence of playwrights teaching other playwrights. State three receives the label "Dramatic Form as the Search for Form," a title that names London's sense that since the 1980s US playwrights haven't been writing to fit a form or reject a form but to find a form. London calls state four "Theater Everywhere and Not a Lot of Ink" and uses this section to grapple with the split between what actors are used to doing and what writers wanted them to do in the late twentieth century. State five is where London wonders "Might America Be a Figment of America's Imagination," and he argues that the turn-of-the-twenty-first-century state of new plays reflects a profusion of efforts to dream a unified America that does not yet exist. London's states provide a not exclusively linear timeline that meditates on how the history of new writing in American theatre doesn't move in a mode of direct progress or cycles of boom and bust (new plays triumph! new plays fail!) so much as it accretes and circles as it spreads.

Fifteen years after London's piece on the states of American playwriting, and five years after Sierz's 2011 book, many American commentators declared a high tide for the US new play scene and most British arts criticism isn't sure what the next big thing will be among UK new writing theatres. Overall, Anglo American commentaries are strong on enthusiasm for specific waves of new plays, while more comprehensive histories of new writing for the theatre are still testing models. Yet there is momentum to discussions of new writing for the theatre. Giving the 2015 LMDA Conference keynote speech, Tim Sanford, artistic director of Playwrights Horizons, opened by declaring "We are in a Golden Age of Playwriting."[15] The October 2016 issue of *American Theatre* magazine focuses several pieces on the state of new plays in America, anticipating major new productions and reflecting on playwriting trends. The issue's editorial comment by critic Helen Shaw trumpets the idea that the second decade of the twenty-first century marks a triumphal moment for "the American play" and quotes *LA Times* theatre critic Charles McNulty as saying: "This is the most vital period in American playwriting that I've seen. The prospect of a new play by Annie Baker, Samuel D. Hunter, Tarell Alvin McCraney fills me with inordinate excitement."[16] Meanwhile, the most anticipated new play on British stages in 2016 might have been John Tiffany and Jack Thomas's collaboration with J. K. Rowling to create a new entry in the Harry Potter universe. *Harry Potter and the Cursed Child* is a new play and new story, not a theatrical adaptation of an existing Potter narrative, which suggests that new writing for the theatre still coalesces in a way not entirely explained by simple brand extension.

Deepenings of scholarship about new writing and new plays are also underway in theoretical modes that address dramatic structure as well. In their treatment of contemporary theatre, Liz Tomlin and Dushka Radosavljevic are productively reevaluating the perceived divide between text-based, author-driven new writing theatres, on the one hand, and devised, ensemble-based, physically driven work that purports to be nontextual, on the other.[17] They are recuperating writing as an aspect of contemporary performance, opening up notions of authorship, reevaluating claims of newness, and challenging Hans Thies-Lehmann's theory about dramatic and postdramatic forms. These thinkers provide major revisions to the frames for discussing new plays as aesthetic objects and for theorizing the role of writing in the theatre. This special section makes its contribution to histories of new writing in a different way. It deepens the history of new writing by opening up different cases of when and why particular theatres might invest in new repertoire, demonstrating how artists use new forms to allow themselves different options in their careers, investigating the different models of success used to measure new plays, probing elitist and populist dimensions of creating new works, teasing out the delicate process by which the old is made new, and documenting how new plays expand the personnel of theatres and integrate new arrivals into both nations and signifying systems.

To that end, the eight essays gathered here are organized in rough chronological order, moving from eighteenth-century France to contemporary Scotland and America. The reach of the case studies into the past does not go as far back as it could and should; nor, with the exception of the Théâtre Italien and a discussion of Chekhov, does the special section succeed in looking at examples outside English-speaking theatre. This is consistent with the general limitations of scholarship in the field of theatre studies currently, and it means that perhaps the section's main accomplishment is to demarcate some of what might be done if more theatre scholars take up these questions about newness, forms, and the intersection of playwrights, institutions, and audiences in new writing theatres worldwide. At their best, however, these explorations of new writing in the theatre provide histories that are sensitive to debates about language and dramatic structure, that access primary and secondary records about collaboration and institutional processes, and that deftly situate newness within the relevant cultural and political contexts.

The section begins with a piece on the bilingual plays created for the Théâtre Italien in Paris in the early eighteenth century. Matthew McMahan's vivid, performance-sensitive contextualization of two macaronic plays commissioned by the Nouveau Théâtre Italien in 1718 takes into account the politics of the French language at the time, the cultural ambassadorship performed by Luigi Riccoboni, the expectations of French audiences, and the performance conventions with which the Italian performers were most comfortable. This powerful piece of scholarship establishes the transnational dimensions of Riccoboni's company and the way immigration and cross-cultural exchange shapes the need for new writing in theatre. The second essay, by Shannon Epplett, picks up in the mid-nineteenth century and tracks the writing collaborations of Thomas Robertson and Henry J. Byron. Epplett positions the dramatic forms Robertson and Byron employed across productive commercial careers in London theatre as indicative of major changes in new writing for theatre, even before the Ibsenism that inspired Shaw and the independent theatre movement. One of Epplett's smart strategies in this essay is to explicate the intersection of Robertson and Byron's writing with the goals held by the actress Marie Wilton, who was later the wife of Squire Bancroft and famous under that surname, to break free of performing first-boy roles and light entertainments and establish herself as a serious actress. Epplett's piece moves back the timeline on the stirrings of theatrical realism in England, vindicates Wilton's theatre management as an independent woman, explores the relationship of new writing to the nascent position of director, and documents collaboration as a key component in advancing new plays through institutions.

The third essay to treat a subject that has its roots in pre-twentieth-century theatre, Sarah Wyman's piece on Anton Chekhov's *Three Sisters*, makes a different type of argument, revisiting Chekhov's formal and narrative strategies and historicizing his innovations in writing as not the consolidation of theatrical realism but rather a manifestation of proto-poststructuralist aesthetics and epistemologies. In Wyman's rereading of *Three Sisters*, what is new for theatre about Chekhov's writing gets a different treatment, one that might productively engage with the historicized and historical rereadings of Stanislavsky's acting system that have been underway in theatre studies as well.

As a hinge in the middle of this section, there are two articles on the Oregon Shakespeare Fesitval's *Play on!* project to "translate" the canon of Shakespeare plays into contemporary language. This hinge links Elizabethan texts to important debates about the relationship of old writing and new writing in contemporary theatre through OSF's commissioning program. Formally launched in 2015, OSF's program is both a new-play initiative in contemporary theatre and, in its way, an attempt at a type of time-travel engagement with Shakespeare's plays as new writing for the sixteenth century. As with McMahan's work, language as the stuff of writing matters a great deal in these essays by Lezlie Cross, Martine Kei Green-Rogers, and Alex N. Vermillion. Cross's essay does particularly daring work challenging the fear of "losing Shakespeare" that motivates critiques of the *Play on!* project with a thorough historical overview of previous periods of "Shakesfear" about changing approaches to Shakespeare, from 1668 through each century to the present. Cross's bravery in facing her own Shakesfear allows her to historicize concerns about audience, the sacredness of Shakespeare, and the dynamic between literary elitism and theatrical production while situating the OSF commissions as a major outreach to diverse artists and in support of diversifying audiences. It is a bold and exciting argument. Green-Rogers and Vermillion demonstrate some of the processes at work in the *Play on!* project by documenting the work on Tim Solver's new version of *Two Noble Kinsmen* that took place at the University of Utah in 2015 and 2016. Theirs is a dramaturgical argument about the creative frisson between old plays and new writing for the theatre. Like Cross, Green-Rogers and Vermillion probe what it means for contemporary audiences to apprehend language in performance and query what is insoluble about a piece of writing for theatre, new or old.

The next essay in the section returns to an institution that stands at the center of British histories of new writing: the Royal Court Theatre. As mentioned above, the Royal Court's role as a writer's theatre remains a key aspect of the new writing sector in the United Kingdom. Nicholas Holden performs an extremely useful fine-tuning of the company's legacy by revisiting the dynamics of its 1958 first writers' group in light of an interview he conducted with former Court artistic director Bill Gaskill the year before Gaskill's death, in 2016. Gaskill's comments allow Holden to extend new analysis to the young writer's programs developed at the Court from the late 1960s onward and to advance a new argument about the types of success created by the Court's writer's programs, as opposed to the type of success mythologized in some of its histories. Also working in a UK context, Deana Nichols's analysis of the A Play, a Pie and a Pint series in Glasgow does the adept work of showing how a recent example of a program for producing new plays is both its own innovation and part of an alternative tradition dedicated to connecting with populist audiences as the goal of new writing theatre. Nichols argues alongside A Play, a Pie and a Pint series founder David MacLennan that the series, among the many models for new play development available in contemporary theatre, dispels the idea that there is not an appetite among audiences for new plays, and she investigates the content and the conditions that fruitfully connect with audiences.

The section wraps up with a report from the field by Todd London, who, having finished *Outrageous Fortune*, transitioned out of his leadership of New Dramatists and became the head of the University of Washington School of Drama in 2013. London's importance as a commentator on and advocate for new plays in the United States makes his contribution in this section a true grace note on the topic of new writing in the theatre. What appears here is a version of a public talk he gave in February 2016 at the UW School of Drama Performing Arts Lectures, a set of talks delivered on the theme of "Revisiting the Newness of New Drama." London's piece is a personal history and a type of institutional history of theatre in academic settings, but mostly it is an aesthetic history about stories, investigating modes of formal experimentation and how they emerge, spread, and find their foothold as new writers find their place in theatres. London mentions many writers but saves his closest analysis for five recent plays: Suzan-Lori Parks's *Father Comes Home from the Wars*, Taylor Mac's *Hir*, Carlos Murillo's *The Javier Plays*, Sybil Kempson's *From the Pig Pile*, and Branden Jacobs-Jenkins's *An Octoroon*. London reveals that his cross-country move from New York to Seattle has taught him that "everything I thought I knew about contemporary playwriting was partial" and that theatre is local and geography matters. His is a history of new writing for the theatre focused on story and on the people telling the story. London closes with the assertion that "what's new is that which is made new," which suggests there is a great deal more to be discovered when theatres commit to new writing and when theatre historians attentively document and historicize what's been written anew.

Notes

1. Thomas Postlewait, *The Cambridge Introduction to Theatre Historiography* (Cambridge: Cambridge University Press, 2009).
2. See, for instance, Michael Billington, *State of the Nation: British Theatre Since 1945* (London: Faber and Faber, 2007), and Richard Boon and Philip Roberts, "General Preface," *Modern British Playwriting, the 1990s: Voices, Documents, New Interpretations* (London: Bloomsbury Methuen, 2012), vii.
3. Jacqueline Bolton, "Capitalizing (on) New Writing: New Play Development in the 1990s," *Studies in Theatre and Performance* 32, no. 2 (2012): 209–25.
4. Yael Zarhy-Levo, "The Evolving Process of an Historical View: Aleks Sierz and British Theatre of the 1990s," in *Theatre/Performance Historiography: Space, Time, Matter*, ed. Rosemarie K. Bank and Michal Kobialka (London and New York: Palgrave Macmillan, 2015), 55–76.
5. Aleks Sierz: *In-Yer-Face Theatre: British Drama Today* (London: Faber and Faber, 2001).
6. Aleks Sierz, *Rewriting the Nation: British Theatre Today* (London: Bloomsbury Methuen, 2011), 4–5.
7. Anna Irene Miller, *The Independent Theatre in Europe: 1887 to the Present* (New York: Ray Long & Richard R. Smith, 1931), 380–83.
8. Douglas Anderson, "The Dream Machine: Thirty Years of New Play Development in America," *TDR* 32, no. 3 (Autumn 1988): 55–84; Rick DesRochers, "Where Do New Plays Come From?" *TDR* 52, no. 4 (Winter 2008): 7–12; David J. Eshelman, "The Art of the New Play Reading: Legitimacy and the New Play Showcase," *Theatre Topics* 21, no. 1 (March 2011): 75–84.
9. Roberta Levitow, "The Totemic World," *American Theatre* 19, no. 9 (November 2002): 24–26.
10. Jeffrey Ullom, *The Humana Festival: The History of New Plays at Actors Theatre Louisville* (Carbondale: Southern Illinois University Press, 2008), 45, 163.
11. Ibid., 45, 106–7.
12. Robert Hedley and Harriet Power, "Over There: Do New Plays Have a Better Shot in Britain than in the U.S.?" *American Theatre* 29, no. 12 (December 2012): 30–33, 79–81.
13. Hedley and Power note that in the United States major institutions have stepped up their productions of new plays since *Outrageous Fortune*, naming Arena Stage American Voices New Play Institute, Signature Reading 5, and Berkeley Rep Ground Floor, among others. London's 2014 address to the Mellon National Playwright Residency Program, reprinted on Howlround, reflected on post–Outrageous Fortune developments, and the nature of history, http://howlround.com/a-short-personal-history-of-a-beautiful-slippery-phrase.
14. Sierz, *Rewriting the Nation*, 26.
15. Sara Freeman, personal notes from Tim Sanford Keynote Address, LMDA 2015 Conference, New York City, Columbia University. I attended this conference and presented as part of the Hot Topics panels, discussing what LMDA's archive shows about the conference's history of discussing new play development in American theatre.
16. Helen Shaw, "The State of the Play: A Critic Addresses the Theatre Nation," *American Theatre*, October 2016, http://www.americantheatre.org/2016/09/21/the-state-of-the-play-a-critic-addresses-the-theatre-nation/.

17. Dushka Radosavljevic, *Theatre-Making: Interplay Between Text and Performance in the 21st Century* (London: Palgrave Macmillan, 2013). And see both Liz Tomlin, *Acts and Apparitions: Discourses of the Real in Performance Theory* (Manchester: Manchester University Press, 2013), and her forward "Dramatic Developments," in Vicky Angelaki's edited collection *Contemporary British Theatre: Breaking New Ground* (London: Palgrave Macmillan, 2013), viii–xxvi.

New Plays in New Tongues

Bilingualism and Immigration at the New Italian Theatre in France

—MATTHEW MCMAHAN

When the Regent Philippe d'Orléans invited Modenese actor Luigi Riccoboni to reinstitute the Comédie-Italienne in 1716, almost twenty years had passed since an Italian troupe had played in Paris. The new Italian troupe (aka the Nouveau Théâtre Italien) was led by Riccoboni, who had established himself as one of the more reputable actors in northern Italy at the time.[1] However, Riccoboni soon discovered that language was a significant barrier in Paris. The audience had not heard Italian on the French stage for nearly twenty years and, therefore, could scarcely understand the dialogue. In an effort to combat this problem, Riccoboni sought the collaboration of several French dramatists, such as Jacques Autreau and Louis Fuzelier, who wrote French dialogue on behalf of the Nouveau Théâtre Italien. Because not every actor could speak French well, the dramatists wrote multilingual plays that allowed for the Italians' varying linguistic talents. The resulting Franco-Italian plays offered the Italian troupe a new type of writing that not only experimented with language but also exploited the transitional and linguistic compromises that took place in the Italians' early years in France.

The multilingual aspect of the Nouveau Théâtre Italien was of great importance to its evolution in France. Some of the plays it performed were in Italian, others were in French, and some featured both languages simultaneously. The latter belongs to a literary category known as macaronics, defined as any text, word, or speech act that mixes two or more languages. In her book *Printers without Borders: Translation and Textuality in the Renaissance* (2015), Anne Coldiron defines macaronic texts as contact zones that offer the historian "shorthand expressions of wider cultural conflict."[2] Apropos the Nouveau Théâtre Italien, the macaronic plays deal directly with the theme of cultural conflict by depicting Italian characters in the very act of assimilation. The plays do not characterize the conflict as oppositional; rather, they convey a reciprocal relationship between the French and Italian languages. Conflict arises through the characters' desires to speak in the other's tongue.

The Italian troupe used the bilingual comedies to poke fun at its own limitations, exploit the comic tension of a French-Italian interchange onstage, and characterize itself as a company in translation. This essay addresses two of the Nouveau Théâtre Italien's earliest macaronic works that experiment with the performative nature of language and its correlation and import on immigrant and national identity: *Le Naufrage au Port-à-l'Anglais* (*Shipwreck at the Port-à-l'Anglais*, 1718), by Jacques Autreau, and *L'Amour, maître de langue* (*Love, the Language Instructor*, 1718), by Louis Fuzelier. I focus on these works because they were the troupe's first collaborations with French dramatists and, as such, are new writings in the repertoire of the Comédie-Italienne, new plays emblematic of the transitional and linguistic compromise that took place in the Italians' early years.

The two plays share a deliberate attempt to incorporate the performers' status as immigrants in France into the dramatic landscape of the play. On the one hand, performing macaronic plays was a contrivance for an Italian troupe ill-versed in the French language; on the other, the performers cleverly used the macaronic plays to comment on the very act of border-crossing and cultural translation that they performed. For this troupe of immigrant performers, language was merely one boundary that had to be crossed to develop a meaningful relationship with their audience: other, much deeper cultural rifts (such as taste, style, stereotypes, and prejudice) threatened the success of Riccoboni's troupe. By staging macaronic plays in their repertoire, the Italians made their process of acculturation a matter of public concern. They placed their bodies center stage and presented their foibles and their compromises, their tactics and their failings, as part of the dramatic landscape of their plays.

Cultural Stakes and National Integrity

For Riccoboni, the adoption of macaronic plays was more than a mere expedient to compensate for the inadequacies of his actors. In addition to producing, writing, and directing for the Nouveau Théâtre Italien, he assumed a unique function as director of the Comédie-Italienne: that of cultural ambassador. His mission was as much cultural as it was theatrical, and the issues of language became significant to his theoretical writings, his prologues, and his repertoire. What was at stake for Riccoboni was the translation of comedy across national lines. In regard to convention, France operated as the nexus of theatrical production and ideas in Europe. All nations and all theatres operated either in accordance with or in contrast to it. In his *Dissertation sur la tragédie moderne* (*Dissertation on Modern Tragedy*), attached to the latter portion of his *Histoire du théâtre italien* (*History of Italian Theatre*, 1728), Riccoboni deliberates on the state of tragedy in his day, but particularly, the state of French drama. Early in his treatise, Riccoboni argues that, "until now, we can say French tragedy stands alone in the theatre." So, he concludes, "It is not surprising that, in treating modern tragedy, I am obliged to speak of French tragedy more than any others."[3] In the preface to *Histoire du théâtre italien*, Riccoboni explains why he wrote a history of the Italian theatre in French: "The French language, which is known throughout Europe, puts the French in a position where they have no need of learning English, German, Spanish, or Italian, being sure that the French are read and understood by all other nations. The foreigners are obligated to speak French poorly and to write in it even worse to make themselves known to this nation . . . because the works which leave France have authority among foreigners."[4] The Italian theatre, on the other hand, had reached a state of degeneration, in Riccoboni's mind. He begrudged the fact that *commedia all'improvviso*, improvised comedy, had become representative of Italian theatre all across Europe. In his *Réflexions historiques et critiques sur les differens theatres de l'Europe* (*Historical and Critical Reflections on the Different Theatres of Europe*, 1738), he blamed the portability of the form for its proliferation: "Throughout Europe, where the Italian language is unfamiliar, and yet where the performance of Italian actors is sought after and applauded, the actors only perform common improvisation [*l'impromptu ordinaire*]. They are known by this form in all of Germany and particularly in France; and this is what has caused the French authors . . . to believe that the Italian theatre only consists of these sorts of buffooneries."[5] Riccoboni tried to reform the reputation of the Italian theatre by distancing himself from "common improvisation" and the buffooneries by performing scripted comedies, tragicomedies, and tragedies. He claimed, "I flattered myself to be able to show a very different Italian comedy from the one that had been seen elsewhere in France."[6] His attempts to combat both prejudices through the presentation of a neoclassical tragedy in Italian, Scipione Maffei's *Merope* (1714), faced critics such as the Abbé Desfontaines, who complained that Italian actors, "accustomed to a bourgeois and insipid discourse," were incapable of evoking the beautiful, elevated, and spiritual language that tragedy required.[7] In the opinion of Desfontaines, the Italian theatre had failed to elevate their language through the prominence of great dramatic poetry as the French had done. It was a "lower" language, coarser and more appropriate to farce.

Consequently, the adoption of French language plays at the Nouveau Théâtre Italien had important implications regarding the broader domain of Riccoboni's goals in Paris. As actor, writer, and producer for the troupe, he believed the reputation of the Italian theatre and its actors depended on the success of his projects. He sought to edify the Parisian public on the beauty of the Italian language. Riccoboni also hoped to revitalize Italy's importance as a contributor of *literary* theatre in Europe, and he tried to do both on French soil. But Riccoboni's mission faced one unremitting irony: to achieve his goals, to sustain a financially viable theatre in Paris, his Italian actors had to speak French. The macaronic plays thus offer an emblem of the aspirations, tensions, uncomfortable transitions, and necessary compromises facing an immigrant theatre in a new land.

The Politics of the French Language

Macaronic plays almost inescapably evoke sociopolitical tension by commingling multiple languages on one stage. Helena Buffery posits that a multilingual stage might "be viewed as a form of translational landscape, in which the words of others are represented, adapted, or strategically expropriated."[8] Whether they are conscious of it or not, dramatists of macaronic plays almost inescapably portray a language according to its social politics. One need not look long for examples. Shakespeare's *Henry V* (ca. 1599), for instance, weaves in French for dramatic purposes, depicting how "effeminate French language must yield to virile English."[9] Just as English King Henry conquers the French with the strength of his army, he subjugates the French Princess Katherine through his prowess with the French language. As Marvin Carlson notes, a nation's pride and loyalty are often at stake whenever an alien language is depicted onstage.[10] In the example of *Henry V*, the audience witnessed the subjugation of the French characters through the charming symbol of Henry. In this way, bilingual plays tend to exhibit two dynamic qualities: they illuminate an imagined hierarchy between the languages as they also construct, perpetuate, and reinforce the politics of a language's social identity.

What was the political relationship between the French and Italian languages during Riccoboni's tenure? In the sixteenth and seventeenth centuries, Italian dialects (Tuscano, in particular) held a privileged status in the French court, given the presence of two queens from the powerful Florentine House of Medici: Caterina de Medici, who served from 1547 to 1559, and Maria de Medici, who became regent just days after her coronation in 1610 after the assassination of her husband, Henry IV.[11] She ruled until her son, Louis XIII, took power in 1617. Italian influence continued with the institution of Cardinal Jules Raymond Mazarin as the chief minister of France in 1642. After Louis XIII died in 1643, Cardinal Mazarin practically served as de facto ruler alongside Queen Anne until his death in 1661, when Louis XIV effectively assumed power.

Over the course of the century the Italian language lost its privileged place in the court. Louis XIII's heavy reliance on his chief minister, Cardinal Richelieu, led to the establishment of the Académie-Française in 1635. Charged with regulating and purifying the French language, the Académie-Française also sought to elevate its status as the most powerful language in Europe. In his *Dictionnaire universel* (*Universal Dictionary*, 1690), Antoine Furetière described French as "the master and sovereign of living languages."[12] Similarly, in the *Le Dictionnaire de l'Académie françoise* (*The Dictionary of the French Academy*, 1694), the Académie framed its goals as ideological as they were imperial. In a letter to Louis XIV, printed in the first edition of *Le Dictionnaire*, the authors expressed their desire that "no other language will have any advantage over ours. . . . The superiority of your power has already made [French] the dominant language of the most beautiful part of the world."[13] The Académie continued to articulate that its work was made necessary by the king's military conquests, establishing French all over Europe; it had a duty to elevate the language so that its beauty may equal its prowess and become "the language of peace wherever it is known."[14] Nearly a century later, an essay by Antoine de Rivarol, *Discourse sur l'universalité de langue française* (*Discourse on the Universality of the French Language*, 1783), written for a competition organized by the Berlin Academy (not the Académie-Française), testified "the widespread view held at the time that French was the universal language."[15] In a relatively short amount of time, the Académie had advanced its influence across the European landscape.

In her book on the genesis and promulgation of French fashion, Joan DeJean claims that the French "national personality was the product of the type of elaborate and deliberate image making" aspiring to evoke "graceful elegance and tasteful opulence" in all regards.[16] French dramatists played no small role in this cultural mission. The plays of Molière and Racine helped spread the notion of a "pure" French language throughout Europe (some like the Venetian dramatist Carlo Goldoni learned French to read Molière in the original).[17] The Abbé Dubos boasts about the "vogue of the French language," which, for the past sixty years, had given it prominence in courts all around Europe, "corrupting" English, German, Dutch, and Italian with French phrases and expressions. He credits "the writings of the great men of our nation" for "promoting our language to the destiny of Greek and Latin" as a "learned language."[18] The perceived heritage of the French language characterized its literature and its theatre, the Comédie-Française, as an exemplar of its national legacy.

The Nouveau Théâtre Italien's bilingual plays are informed by the Académie's linguistic aspirations. Not only were the Italian actors constricted to what was considered an inferior genre (as opposed to the tragedy and high comedy of the Comédie-Française), but their language was ideologically correlated with that genre. As Riccoboni himself stated, Italian simply lacked the centrality or pervasiveness of French (especially in France), and its international image had become closely tied to *commedia all'improvviso*.[19] A "unitary language constitutes the theoretical expression of the historical processes of linguistic unification and centralization," but comic genres, like *commedia all'improvviso*, embodied a diversity of languages. An audience watching a commedia performance might have heard dialects such as Tuscano, Bergamask, Neopolitan, and Venetian in the course of a single performance.[20] In early modern Europe, mixed-language performances met with a disapproving eye. They were marked as "low" and undeserving of literary merit. In her study of Ruzante and Goldoni, Linda Carrol posits that dialect works "were always considered as being outside the mainstream of literacy development. No matter what the topic or the quality of an author or composition, he or it would frequently be lumped with authors from other regions with other interests under the general rubric of 'dialect works' or 'minor works.'"[21] Authors like Ruzante, Carrol argues, used dialect work deliberately as an affront to patrician standards of literature (even though his plays were performed for a noble elite).

Riccoboni's goals differed from those of Ruzante, as he pursued another approach. He mixed French into his company's plays to entice a French audience wishing for plays of a higher literary appeal. However, as a genre of mixed languages commedia stood in contrast, as the French understood it, to the purity and eloquence of French dramatic poetry. The intermixing of Italian with French dialogue muddied the poetic waters. Although Riccoboni hoped to use the macaronic plays as a way to transition to a more reputable French repertoire, in the process of so doing, he simultaneously contributed to his company's status as a disreputable theatre. Cleverly, the macaronic plays of the Nouveau Théâtre Italien accounted for the paradox. Especially since the plays were written by French dramatists, they did not seek to challenge the authority of the French language; rather, they celebrated it as the language of love, grace, and allure, just as they exalted it as one the Italian actors hoped to adopt. They cast the French dialogue as a metaphoric tool that helped lift the plays from the dross of the Italian tongue.

Incorporating French at the Comédie-Italienne

Riccoboni's troupe had motivation beyond the artistic. A repertoire of plays spoken entirely in Italian simply failed to draw a steady Francophone audience. According to the brief historical account printed with the 1733 edition of the *Nouveau Théâtre Italien*, the initial appeal of the troupe in Paris wore off at a striking pace: "Those attracted by the actors' *jeu* [play acting] and by novelty, and those who did not understand Italian, little by little ceased to attend the theatre, which was no longer frequented except by foreigners and a few amateurs of the language. Because the few number of attendees failed to provide enough for the expenses and necessary costs, the actors thought about returning to their home country."[22] Faced with a diminishing audience, the Italians heard repeated calls to incorporate French scenes and French plays, even though the troupe itself did not feel capable of doing so. The middling dramatist and self-appointed critic of the Nouveau Théâtre Italien, Nicolas Boindin, labeled himself as an influential voice in the matter. He insisted throughout his essays on the troupe that the Italians should collaborate with French dramatists in order to compete with the other theatres in Paris.[23] He also speculated, prior to the addition of the French actor of Italian ancestry, Pierre-François Biancolelli, *dit* Dominique fils, that the fairground celebrity could sprinkle some French into the repertory, which would offer those "who don't know Italian a little more basis for understanding [the plays]" and would help "attract far more people, especially women who gradually abandon this theatre."[24]

The Italians were frank about the gendered nature of the issue. In Fuzelier's prologue *La Mode* (1718), performed at the Comédie-Italienne before *L'Amour, maître de langue* (1718), Trivelin argues that he and his ilk needed to "think about ways to attract ladies to our performances."[25] They visit La Mode (Fashion) personified, who tells them that if they want to see ladies of quality attend the Comédie-Italienne, they must speak French first: "The ladies do not understand you without an interpreter, and they are not in the humor of having fun merely through the report of others. Try to mix in some lively French scenes, seasoned even with a bit of your Italian *jeu*. This is how to attract the ladies to your plays; a performance is poorly decorated when the most beautiful half of society does not glisten there."[26] Particularly in regard to her last point, Scapin agrees: "Madame la Mode is right: when I see only masculine auditors in our theatre, I fear the world is at an end."[27] While Scapin worried for the end of days for purely procreative reasons, Riccoboni and his troupe felt concern about the lack of their theatrical progeny without women in attendance at the Comédie-Italienne. Incidentally, the ladies in the audience were the most active in seeking out translations of the Italians' works. Reporting on the success of *Arlequin bouffon du cour* (*Arlequin the Court Buffoon*, 1716) at the Comédie-Italienne, Antoine d'Origny attests to the proliferation of translations in the *loges* of the Hôtel de Bourgogne: "This work resulted in an inexpressible pleasure: extracts of the play were printed for the convenience of the ladies. They exhibited the greatest desire to learn Italian. All those who taught the language were in demand. It was fashionable to have one of these teachers in the boxes in order to translate the play."[28] The language barrier actually excited the attention of the *dames*, at first. The exoticness of the language created an allure, but the attraction, as Fuzelier's prologue suggests, eventually wore off.

Feeling the need to appeal to the ladies in the *loges* and the critics in print, the Italians recruited French dramatists to add to their repertoire. But circumstances required them to do so before they were fluent. Many of their actors could not speak French well at all. According to Boindin, those who could did so with varying accents. He provides this disparaging account:

> Among them, Flaminia and Silvia speak the best French; as for Violette, it has been said she does not know a single word yet and that French will not be familiar to her any time soon. Lélio speaks with a Swiss accent. Mario makes himself understood only after stumbling with considerable effort. Pantalon keeps to his Venetian tongue, and avoids trouble by doing so, which, by all appearances, would be as tiresome for him as it would be for the public. The Doctor could speak French the best if he applied himself. Scapin, they say, makes a singular study but without much in the way of progress. Meanwhile, he gradually appears to forget his own language, to the extent that before six months are out, he won't know how to speak one or the other, and would to God Scaramouche fall to the same disadvantage. In regard to Arlequin, he should keep to his Bergamask dialect, until he has rendered himself intelligible in ours. It is astonishing that since he has been in Paris, he has not yet learned to speak French.[29]

The Italian actors were stuck in a quandary. Financial needs pressured them to perform French plays in order to attract larger audiences, but they still struggled to learn the language—even after two years of being in Paris.

The Italians were not the only ones who struggled with the language barrier. Their audience too had difficulty with the transnational exchange, sometimes to comic results. The audience and the actors' inability to understand one another contributed to the theatrical event. The Parisians' individual skills with Italian, as Boindin writes, informed the response of the audience. Amused, he says, those who did not understand Italian tended to laugh loudest of all. Then, "they ask why they have laughed; after they have learned [what was said], they laugh a second time, but more judiciously."[30] A second type of audience member, who knows a little Italian, could be seen demonstrating that knowledge through a "mad and vain ostentation" by loudly and indiscriminately throwing around Italian phrases they had just learned.[31] A third party in the audience annoyed Boindin because, when they laughed, they "showed discontentment over having laughed."[32] The sheer variety of audience responses was informed by their disparate knowledge of and attitude toward the Italian language. Maurice Lever believes the Italian language, "far from constituting an obstacle . . . contributed to [the troupe's] success" because the audience delighted in the translational exercise.[33] That may be so in the troupe's first few years, but over time Riccoboni and his colleagues sought to bridge the gap with more French-language plays.

The troupe's willingness to bend to the demand resulted in new avenues of dramatic creation. Ola Forsans marks the incorporation of plays from Autreau and Fuzelier in 1718 as "a decisively new period in the history of the New Théâtre Italien, one that 'Frenchifies' the programming more and more. From the season 1718–19 to the season 1721–22, we see the establishment of what we now call the 'foundation' of the new repertoire."[34] From the collaboration with French dramatists, the troupe itself sought to become *Italiens francisés* or frenchified Italians. However, Forsans's identification of the 1718–19 season as the one that Frenchifies the troupe underestimates the tremendous difficulty the troupe had performing French dramas early on. The transition was anything but fluid. The troupe performed Italian plays *all'improvviso* throughout Riccoboni's tenure. Additionally, the troupe was hardly capable of Frenchifying the repertoire in 1718. A thorough adoption of plays written entirely in French took years to achieve. Thanks to the ingenuity of two French dramatists, Autreau and Fuzelier, the Italians incorporated their inadequacies into their plays. The dramatists employed the troupe's very inability to speak French well as an opportunity to ignite dramatic conflict. In the plays, amorous intentions are confounded by language barriers. The results are several macaronic texts whose linguistic and dramatic qualities were informed directly by the immigrant actors who first embodied them.

Tempering Expectations: Autreau's Dramatic Prologue

Even though the Nouveau Théâtre Italian was not entirely equipped to perform French plays, the French dramatists created flexible scripts to account for this fact, making room for both improvisation and Italian dialogue. The mixture of improvisation had the same effect as the interposal of multiple languages in the plays; it reduced their literary merit. Yet, it also provided an avenue for the dramatists to create tension between the actor's various linguistic talents. With improvised Italian juxtaposed with scripted French, the dramatists further emphasized the distinction, cultural and linguistic, between the two languages. What is more, the dramatists took advantage of the distinction between the French and Italian speakers and underscored bilingualism as a narrative device.

Jacques Autreau's *Le Naufrage au Port-à-l'Anglais* verbalizes this tactic primarily through the dramatic prologue of the play. Four actors—Silvia, Flaminia, Trafiquet (a *courtier du Parnasse* and so-called author of the play), and Arlequin—openly discuss their trepidations over performing a play in French for the first time.[35] Xavier Courville's biography of Riccoboni writes off the prologue as a "fitting and charming divertissement to justify the accents of all the actors," but it achieves far more than that.[36] This prologue is historically significant not simply because it introduced the first French language play performed by the Nouveau Théâtre Italien; it confirms the very attitudes and stereotypes held by the French. At the beginning of the prologue, Flaminia confronts Silvia and asks her why she appears so nervous. Silvia replies that she has never performed a play in French before. The very prospect makes her tremble. Flaminia responds, "Why tremble? What we are going to perform is not difficult. It is a small, light play . . . in which we present characters very similar to ourselves, that is, newly disembarked Italians. The faults in our pronunciation will do us honor even. The audience will believe we make these mistakes on purpose."[37] With a touch of irony (Flaminia knows the audience can hear her), her statement points to the strategy behind Autreau's play. The Italians incorporated their own foibles into the dramatic landscape of the play as a means to bolster the authenticity of their performance.

In addition, Autreau attempted to mitigate audience expectations. The prologue characterizes the play as an *amuse-bouche* meant to wet the palate and entice far more capable dramatists. When Trafiquet, representing the French in the audience, climbs on stage, he states as much. He compares the French theatre to a grand feast and notes that the French are stuffed. They get most of their substance from the Comédie-Française and come to the Italian stage for the sweetness of a light dessert, digested as a delicate treat "not meant to upset the stomach and purely for amusement."[38] While depicting his play as a mere bagatelle or trifle, Autreau also framed it as a means to test the Italian stage for better things to come. Trafiquet continues to reassure the Italian actresses that earning the approval of their Parisian audience should be an easy affair. "Do you feel we ask much of you?" he asks. "Make yourselves understood, say nothing too dull or trite, vary your scenes, entertain with spectacle, *divertissements* set to music, and especially with Arlequin in his *jeu*, until he knows how to speak French."[39] Meant to assuage the Italians' fears, these statements also reinforce the limited respect and expectations of the Italian stage. The Comédie-Italienne was not a place for serious drama but a house of merry entertainment where little was at stake.

By airing this opinion out loud in the prologue, Autreau and the Italians verbalized the very quagmire of their position. The French believed the Italian theatre was of less substance than the French theatre, home only to *divertissements* and *lazzi*. Yet, it was because of the absence of French language drama that the Italians had to make recourse to such devices. The layers of this problem folded onto themselves. The Italians could not attract good French authors because of their reputation, but they could not escape from presenting piffle without quality plays written in a language their audience could understand. This prologue offered *Le Naufrage au Port-à-l'Anglais* as a compromise and a first step in a long journey over controlling public opinion and taste. The prologue in tandem with the play itself draws parallels between the actors and the characters they play. Just as Flaminia and Silvia worry about performing a play in French for the first time, the characters fret over courting Frenchmen for the same reasons. The women hope the French will find their foibles endearing; similarly, their characters in *Le Naufrage au Port-à-l'Anglais* are endearing because of their cultural temerity. In such a way, the prologue and the play react, reflect, and comment on one another.

Given the financial success of the play, Autreau's tactics clearly struck a chord. The Nouveau Théâtre Italien's calculated risk paid dividends. According to the troupe's registers, *Le Naufrage au Port-à-l'Anglais* ran no fewer than nine times in the course of the 1718–19 season, earning 886 livres at its debut and taking an additional 5,203 livres in the months of April and May alone.[40] The Marquis d'Argenson complained that the play was filled with "caprices, a plot without action, dissonances, banter, foreigners, disconnected scenes, burlesques, *lazzi*, obscenities, no character, no manners, both in Italian and French."[41] But these very qualities likely led to the play's success. Fast paced, filled with the qualities that the Parisian audience liked about previous Italian troupes in France, and exhibiting a love story in a language they could understand, the play offered the French the balanced *mélange* of French and Italian styles they craved. Most importantly, the periodical *Le Mercure de France* believed the play opened the doors of the Hôtel de Bourgogne for French playwrights: "Without a doubt, [Autreau] will soon be followed by rivals . . . and these *messieurs* can no longer excuse themselves based on the difficulty the Italian troupe has in reciting French scenes. The proof that has just been made by Flaminia and Silvia is an argument all too persuasive *not* to enlist them in this cause."[42] The talent of the actors, particularly that of the two leading ladies, proved the Italians could ably switch codes between French and Italian, exhibiting a flexibility that would soon become a hallmark of their theatre.

Immigrants in Love

The success of *Le Naufrage au Port-à-l'Anglais* inspired another dramatist to furnish the Italians with plays written in both French and Italian: Louis Fuzelier, one of the most prolific dramatists in eighteenth-century France. He wrote 237 plays, including the libretto for Rameau's *Les Indes galantes* (The Amorous Indes, 1735), and worked for every major theatrical venue in Paris, including the fairground theatres, the Comédie-Italienne, the Opéra, and the Comédie-Française. Pierre Larousse's *Grand dictionnaire* (1866–77) describes him as "better known for his fecundity than his talent," adding "a *faiseur* in all senses of the word."[43] *Faiseur* means an operator or deal-maker, but in this instance, the term carries a strong connotation of "hack writer."[44] Regardless of this reputation in his own time, Fuzelier was instrumental to the Nouveau Théâtre Italien's success in Paris. He collaborated with the Italians throughout Riccoboni's tenure, penning several plays, parodies, and satires.

Unlike Autreau's dramatic writings, which anticipated the sentimental comedies of Marivaux, Fuzelier's plays accentuated low comic devices common to the farces and *opéra-comiques* of the fairground. David Trott describes Fuzelier's collaboration with Riccoboni as a "clash of styles," noting the ironic transposition of styles between an Italian actor who sought to remove himself from the commedia dell'arte tradition and a French dramatist who embraced street performance as his modus operandi: "The clash of styles which took place between Fuzelier and Riccoboni was therefore not as simple as the mere incompatibility of Parisian and 'Italian' (i.e., commedia) theatre. It was rather a clash between an Italian who, in one sense, betrayed commedia dell'arte, to become, in the words of Patrice Pavis, 'more French than the French,' and a Frenchman who was unwilling or unable to espouse a view of theatre as anything other than live—and therefore ceaselessly changing—performance."[45] When Fuzelier wrote *L'Amour, maître de langue* in both French and Italian, he tried to cater to the Italian actors' linguistic strengths. But, as Trott indicates, Fuzelier's tastes did no favors for Riccoboni's artistic aspirations. Fuzelier's play aligns more closely with the Parisian fairground than it does with Riccoboni's reformist ideals.

In *L'Amour, maître de langue*, Fuzelier presents language as an initial barrier between the lovers, which eventually becomes the driving force of the plot. Translated as either *Love, Language Instructor or Tongue-Master Love*, the title's clever play on the words *maître* (master, instructor) and *langue* (language, tongue) alludes to the erotic potential of courting a foreigner. The story commences when the Marquise de Floras, a provincial French lady, and the Italian Lélio, the Marquis de Rosetti, meet in the border town of Strasbourg, France. Because they do not know how to speak to one another, they exchange only longing glances. The two are separated shortly thereafter. Fuzelier's play starts several months later in the port town of Toulon, where each has made a resolution to seek out the other. The French heroine's attempt to learn Italian in hopes of one day reencountering the object of her affection is mirrored by Lélio, who similarly tries to learn French. The comic device of the play is that neither knows the other is in Toulon, and the play's action simply delays their inevitable encounter. They finally meet one another again and express their love in their respective learned languages.

Both have hired servants to help them in their cause. As the Marquise learns Italian, she employs the Italian Scaramouche to compliment her French servant, Zerbine. Similarly, Lélio has enlisted the bilingual Trivelin (played by the Franco-Italian Dominique fils), a self-proclaimed *Italien francisé*, to compliment his Italian valet Arlequin. Trivelin knows both French and Italian, which makes him a particularly powerful ally, yet he acts like a *fourbe intrigant*, or clever rascal, a scheming, manipulative, and self-interested type of servant. He often uses his mastery over language to contradict orders and embarrass those around him. The Marquise's servant Zerbine is similar in this regard. Both want to keep their masters in Toulon as long as possible because they have their eye on their own objects of affection. While Trivelin loves Zerbine, she loves Arlequin (a fact that eludes Trivelin until much, much later). As with their masters, the object of affection is someone from another land and who speaks another language. Both *amants* are immigrants in love. And, like their masters, the lovers are brought closer by learning how to speak to one another. They bridge the cultural divide by familiarizing themselves with the language of their beloved.

Of the thirty-five scenes in the play, nineteen are in French, six are in Italian, and ten are in a mixture of the two. Unlike Autreau's play, which separates language according to the class of the characters' *emplois* (the lovers speak French, whereas the servants speak Italian), Fuzelier's *L'Amour, maître de langue* maintains a level of verisimilitude and divides the languages according to the characters' countries of origin. As Arlequin and Scaramouche speak only Italian, Zerbine and Trivelin speak French. Lélio is the exception to the rule. Although he is an Italian, he speaks French throughout the play. But his French is driven by his desire to learn the language better. Language functions as a means to divide the characters into two camps: (1) the French group, who are connected to the Marquise, and (2) the Italian one, connected to Lélio. The languages spoken in each scene are dependent on which group is present, while bilingual scenes take place when there is a conflation of the two.

The love triangle between Trivelin, Zerbine, and Arlequin not only burlesques the bilingual courtship of their masters but also embodies precisely the conflicts that their masters fear. Language barriers forestall amorous intentions. While Trivelin loves Zerbine, she actually loves Arlequin. Because Zerbine and Arlequin do not speak the same language, they must rely on Trivelin as a translator. Unfortunately, neither Arlequin nor Zerbine realize that Trivelin is Arlequin's rival. As the *fourbe intragant*, Trivelin uses the opportunity to make a fool out of Arlequin and to manipulate the situation in his favor. He deliberately mistranslates for the two. First, he agrees to speak on behalf of Arlequin, even though he really speaks for himself:

TRIVELIN, *in Italian, aside to Arlequin*: I am going to speak to her for you and press her more strongly.
ARLEQUIN, *in Italian*: I am indebted to you!
TRIVELIN, *in Italian*: I speak to her, I swear to you, as if it were for myself.
ARLEQUIN, *in Italian*: You are the best of friends.
TRIVELIN, *in French to Zerbine*: What, with your passionate eyes, you are cruel and rebuff the tender sighs of Trivelin?
ARLEQUIN, *in Italian to Trivelin*: I think you are speaking about yourself.
TRIVELIN, *in Italian, aside to Arlequin*: Yes, I said that she could trust Trivelin, that he knows better than yourself the love that he professes.
ARLEQUIN, *in Italian*: Oh what a good friend I have in Trivelin![46]

Too simple-minded and ignorant of French, Arlequin does not realize that Trivelin betrays him before his very eyes. Even though Trivelin compliments Zerbine, she rebuffs his advances. Since Arlequin believes Trivelin speaks on his behalf, Arlequin takes Zerbine's dismissive tone personally. In response to this rejection, Arlequin cries out, "The ingrate! The inhuman who does not love Arlequin!" The display of emotion only elicits Zerbine's sympathies, confusing

Arlequin: "Trivelin, you told me that she hated me. But she looks at me with eyes like those of a cat meowing for my favor." Clearly, where words have failed, longing glances and tender gestures have prevailed. Trivelin, who finds himself undone, cries, "Damn, this goes poorly for me. When two lovers don't speak the same language, they communicate through gestures."[47] The same could be said of the Italian troupe and their French audience. When words did not suffice, their gestures were sure to entertain.

When the lovers, Lélio and the Marquise, finally meet, they are shocked by the opportunity that chance has given them. Even though she was bound for Italy, and Lélio Marseilles, they have crossed paths once again in the port town of Toulon:

LÉLIO: Madame, you are going to Italy?
LA MARQUISE, *in Italian*: And you, *monsieur*, you came back to France?
LÉLIO: It seemed to me, Madame, that you didn't know Italian in Strasbourg.
LA MARQUISE, *in Italian*: It seemed to me, *monsieur*, that you didn't know French.
ZERBINE: It seems to me that you both have learned these two languages from the same teacher.[48]

Their first words together are spoken in a foreign tongue, but both Lélio and the Marquise adopt the language of their beloved. While Lélio speaks French, the Marquise speaks Italian. They have crossed their respective lexical borders and now speak to one another from the other side. Just as love has united them in Toulon, it has also united them in language.

The two are able to share their amorous affections with one another in their respective languages. Lélio, speaking French (after having repeated this line to himself in a low voice), recounts to the Marquise, "I have made this confession to you in a language which is strange to me. I owe my familiarity only to love. I don't know if I made a good student; I only know that it made me a very faithful lover."[49] When the Marquise tries to respond, she loses the facility to express herself. Zerbine encourages her to speak French so the two can finally express their sentiments clearly to one another. The Marquise articulates what amounts to be the principal theme of the play: "Can different languages prevent identical sentiments from being intelligible? No, the heart speaks and hears all: love travels the world without an interpreter."[50] In Fuzelier's play, the distance created by language is one repeatedly surmounted by love alone. *Amor viucit lingue*. Love will conquer the tongue. Fuzelier depicts love as a universal force that supersedes all dialectical and cultural distinctions. It is an optimistic message that touches upon the Nouveau Théâtre Italien's long-term success in Paris. While facility in language was important, the Italians could communicate the sentiment of their plays by other means. What's more, Fuzelier's play implies that the mutual affection between the Italians and their Parisian audience would ensure their longevity in France, even amid a daunting language gap.

L'Amour, maître de langue did not experience the same success as *Le Naufrage au Port-à-l'Anglais*. The play was revived about once a year, usually to sparse audiences. On June 2, 1721, it earned only 126 livres. On November 19 of the same year, it drew only eighty-two people, for a total of 109 livres. And on October 28, 1722, it was paired with *Arlequin soldat au camp de Porché-Fontaine* (Arlequin, Soldier in the Camp of Porchéfontaine) earning around 395 livres. Boindin personally hated it. He said the play was "drowned in bad *lazzi*" and "larded with French."[51] He believed it deserved to be performed at the fairground and not at the Comédie-Italienne. How far Boindin's opinion of the play was informed by Fuzelier's reputation as an author of opéra-comique is speculative. But it seems Boindin was hopeful that the Nouveau Théâtre Italien would soon divorce itself of such spectacles. Even if the bilingual plays helped the Italian troupe establish itself in France, its status as "low" drama perpetuated the Comédie-Italienne's image as a house of farce.

Conclusion

In his history of the Italian theatre in France, *Histoire anecdotique et raisonnée du théâtre italien* (*Anecdotal and Reasoned History of the Italian Theatre*, 1769), Jean Augustine Julien Desboulmiers claims that the Italian actors successfully overcame the challenges of immigration. He declares, "The Nouveau Théâtre Italien, whose plays were first as foreign as the language they spoke, seems to have been naturalized by the depictions it has made of *our* manners . . . and especially by its devotion to fix the public's attention."[52] These early bilingual works, according to Desboulmiers, worked to acclimatize the Italian troupe. Transforming first the style of their works and then the language they spoke, the Italian actors bridged the gap between their plays and their audience, rendering the actors *Italiens francisés*.

Addressing the audience on behalf of her husband, Riccoboni, in 1725, nearly ten years after the troupe's arrival, actress Elena Balletti boasted of the troupe's cultural malleability: "The Italian theatre is susceptible to an infinite variety. It accommodates all: tragedy, comedy, today purely in Italian, tomorrow in the French taste, sometimes in Spanish, sometimes English; finally, it is a canvas on which a painter can employ all sorts of colors and shapes. What amusement for the public!"[53] Balletti's address points to her colleagues' virtuosity as border crossers par excellence. Their flexibility, battle tested, characterized them as the most malleable of all actors in Paris. Although the distance between the French audience and the Italian actors initially posed one of the Italians' major challenges, their ability to bridge such a gap eventually became a claim of their greatest strength. Their proficiency in switching languages, genres, and cultures not only evoked the troupe's immigrant identity but also exhibited a doubled national identity: once Italian, now *also* French.

Immigration is an obvious, yet overlooked, aspect of the Nouveau Théâtre Italien. The challenges the Italians faced and the artistic decisions they made were influenced strongly by their status as outsiders. Research on immigrant performers and immigrant theatres are prominent in theatre studies today, but few look beyond the twentieth century for examples. In her introduction to *Italian Culture in Northern Europe in the Eighteenth Century* (1999), Shearer West identifies a lack of scholarly attention on the eighteenth-century Italians who "moved across cultural and national boundaries, and the consequent infiltration of Italian cultural ideas and influences into northern courts and cities."[54] She urges historians to explore the "wider implications of Italian immigration, especially given that cultural interchange was a two-way process."[55] The Nouveau Théâtre Italien and its macaronic plays offer an example of such a transcultural enterprise, and the field of theatre history could be enriched by further exploration of transnational companies like Riccoboni's prior to the age of globalization, demonstrating how bilingualism, mobility, and cross-cultural exchange have shaped the theatre (and how the theatre has shaped immigration) throughout time.

Notes

1. For further information on Riccoboni and the Nouveau Théâtre Italien, Xavier de Courville's biography is the standard-bearer on scholarship on Riccoboni's career as actor, dramatist, and theorist. See *Luigi Riccoboni dit Lélio: chef de troupe en Italie (1676–1715)* (Paris: Université de Paris, 1967). More recently, Ola Forsans provides "an organized synthesis of the common characteristics identified in the fabrication of the plays" of the Nouveau Théâtre Italien in *Le Théâtre de Lélio: Étude du répertoire du Nouveau Théâtre Italien de 1716 à 1729* (Oxford: SVEC, 2006), 7. Sarah Di Bella provides a thorough examination of some of Riccoboni's key treatises. She outlines the notion of experience in theatrical theory and how Riccoboni's role as a practitioner informed his writings in *L'Expérience théâtrale dans l'œuvre théorique de Luigi Riccoboni* (Paris: Honoré Champion Éditeur,

2009). In this text, Bella also offers one of the most recent and complete translations of Riccoboni's acting treatise, *Dell'Arte Rappresentativa* (1728), out of Italian.

In English, there are very few works that consider the Nouveau Théâtre Italien at length. The first and most important contribution is from Clarence D. Brenner, whose *The Théâtre Italien: Its Repertory, 1716–1793* (1961) provides a meticulous listing of the troupe's repertory and its earnings. His prefatory essay provides a historical survey of the troupe, but his concerns are primarily economic and entrepreneurial. Joining Brenner, Maria Park Bobroff limits her dissertation out of Duke University to a study of the Nouveau Théâtre Italien's literary contribution to the field of French drama. She seeks to provide the "first attempt at gauging this troupe's literary impact on French theatrical history." See Maria Park Bobroff, "Acts of Seduction: French Theater and the Nouveau Théâtre Italien, 1718–1729" (PhD diss., Duke University, 2003).

2. A. E. B. Coldiron, *Printers without Borders: Translation and Textuality in the Renaissance* (Cambridge: Cambridge University Press, 2015), 33.

3. Luigi Riccoboni, "Dissertation sur la tragédie moderne," in *Histoire du théâtre italien* (Paris: Cailleau, 1730), 251. Translations, unless otherwise noted, are mine.

4. Ibid., vii.

5. Riccoboni, *Réflexions historiques et critiques sur les différens théâtres de l'Europe* (Paris: Guérin, 1738), 34.

6. Riccoboni, "Preface," in *Nouveau Théâtre Italien ou Recueil general de toutes les pieces représentées par les comediens de S.A.R. Monsiegneur le Duc d'Orleans, Regent du Royaume* (Paris: Antoine-Urbain Coustelier, 1717), 1:6.

7. Pierre François Guyot Desfontaines, *Lettre d'un comédien français au sujet de l'Histoire du Théâtre Italien écrite par M. Riccoboni, dit Lélio* (Paris: Pissot, 1728), 31–32.

8. Helena Buffery, "Negotiating the Translation Zone: Invisible Borders and Other Landscapes on the Contemporary 'Heteroglossic' Stage," in *Translation Studies* 6, no. 2 (2013): 156.

9. David Steinsaltz, "The Politics of French Language in Shakespeare's History Plays," *Studies in English Literature, 1500–1900* 42, no. 2 (Spring 2002): 326.

10. Carlson, *Speaking in Tongues: Language at Play in the Theatre* (Ann Arbor: University of Michigan Press, 2006), 25.

11. The Medicis were a banking family of enormous influence and wealth. In addition to two French queens, the Medici family consisted of four Popes (Leo X, Clement VII, Pius IV, and Leo XI) and ruled the Grand Duchy of Tuscany until 1737.

12. Antoine Furetière, *Dictionnaire universal, contenant généralement tous les mots françois* (Paris: La Haye, 1690), s.v. "usage."

13. See "Epistre au Roi," in *Le dictionnaire de l'Académie françoise* (Paris: Poignard, 1694), 1iii.

14. Ibid.

15. Robin Adamson, *The Defence of French: A Language in Crisis?* (Clevedon, UK: Multilingual Matters, 2007), 7. Adamson's first chapter provides a terse summary of the establishment of the Pléiade, a group of poets committed to elevating the literary status of French, to the establishment of the Académie-Française, the publication of the first dictionaries, and the establishment of French's prestige throughout Europe in the eighteenth century.

16. Joan DeJean, *The Essence of Style: How the French Invented High Fashion, Fine Food, Chic Styles, Sophistication, and Glamour* (New York: Free Press, 2005), 5–6.

17. Carlo Goldoni, *Memoirs of Goldoni*, trans. John Black (London: Hunt and Clarke, 1828), 1:188.

18. Jean-Baptiste Dubos, *Réflexions critiques sur la poésie et sur la peinture* (Paris: Neaulme, 1732), 2:467.
19. Riccoboni, *Réflexions historiques et critiques*, 34.
20. Mikhail Bakhtin, *The Dialogic Imagination*, trans. Caryl Emerson and Michael Holquist (Austin: University of Texas Press, 1981), 270. For more on the multiple use of language in commedia dell'arte, see Kenneth and Laura Richards, *The Commedia dell'Arte* (Oxford: Basil Blackwell, 1990), and Gianrenzo P. Clivio, "The Languages of the commedia dell'arte," in *The Science of Buffoonery: Theory and History of the Commedia dell'Arte*, ed. Domenico Pietropaolo (Toronto: Dovehouse Editions, 1989).
21. Linda Carol, *Language and Dialect in Ruzante and Goldoni* (Ravenna: Longo Editore, 1980), 10, 120.
22. "Mémoire pour servir à l'histoire," in *Le Nouveau Théâtre Italien*, 1:xviii–xix. The Brothers Parfaict point out that the Italians never had any intention of going back to Italy but instead were petitioning to ply their trade in England for a short time. They were ultimately denied permission from the Regent to do so. This incident is dramatized in the play *La Désolation des deux comédies*. See Parfaict, *Dictionnaire des théâtres de Paris* (Paris: Rozet, 1767), 1:292.
23. Four in all, Boindin's letters about the Comédie-Italienne are addressed to a friend in the provinces. See Nicolas Boindin, "Troisième Lettre," in *Lettres historiques à M. D*** sur la Nouvelle Comédie Italienne* (Paris: Prault, 1719), 5.
24. Boindin, "Seconde lettre," 15.
25. Later, the play was included as part of an *ambigu-comique* alongside *La Méridienne* (1718) and *Le Mai* (1718). Louis Fuzelier, *La Mode*, in Loïc Chahine, "Deux auteurs français à la Comédie-Italienne: Louis Fuzelier et Marc-Antoine Le Grand (1718–1721)" (PhD diss., Université de Nantes, 2010), 199. For Fuzelier's plays *La Mode* and *L'Amour, maître de langue*, I cite directly from the transcription provided by Chahine.
26. Fuzelier, *La Mode*, 211.
27. Ibid., 211.
28. Antoine d'Origny, *Annales du théâtre italien* (Paris: Duchesne, 1788), 1:29–30.
29. Boindin, "Quatrième lettre," 8–9.
30. Boindin, "Première lettre," 25.
31. Ibid., 26.
32. Ibid.
33. Maurice Lever, *Théâtre et Lumières: Les spectacles de Paris au XVIIIe siècle* (Paris: Fayard, 2001), 161.
34. Forsans, *Le Théâtre de Lélio*, 60.
35. For the sake of the article, I focus only on the prologue. For an excellent and well-researched study of the full play, see Richard Waller, "Jacques Autreau's *Le Naufrage au Port-à-l'Anglais* and the Nouveau Théâtre Italien," in *En marge du classicisme: Essays on the French Theatre from the Renaissance to the Enlightenment*, ed. Alan Howe and Richard Waller (Liverpool: Liverpool University Press, 1987).
36. Courville, *Luigi Riccoboni dit Lélio*, 2:123.
37. Jacques Autreau, *Le Naufrage au Port-à-l'Anglais*, in Jacques Truchet, *Théâtre du XVIIIe siècle* (Paris: Gallimard, 1972), 341.
38. Autreau, *Le Naufrage au Port-à-l'Anglais*, 343.
39. Ibid.

40. Clarence D. Brenner, *The Theatre Italien, Its Repertory, 1716–1793* (Berkeley: University of California Press, 1961), 53–54.

41. Clearly D'Argenson responds to a reading of the play and not a performance. See René Louis de Voyer de Paulmy, marquis d'Argenson, *Notices sur les œuvres de théâtre*, ed. Henri Lagrave (Geneve: Institut et Musee Voltaire, 1966), 2:699.

42. *Le Mercure*, mai 1718, 105. My emphasis.

43. Pierre Larousse, "Fuzelier," in *Grand dictionnaire univers du XIXe siècle* (Paris: Administration du grand Dictionnaire universel, 1866–77), 13:898.

44. Charles Dill, *Monstrous Opera: Rameau and the Tragic Tradition* (Princeton: Princeton University Press, 1998), 25.

45. David Trott, "A Clash of Styles: Louis Fuzelier and the 'New Italian Comedy,'" in *The Science of Buffoonery: Theory and History of the Commedia dell'Arte*, ed. Domenico Pietropaolo (Toronto: Dovehouse Editions, 1989), 103.

46. Fuzelier, *L'Amour, maître de langue*, 170.

47. Ibid., 171.

48. Ibid., 181.

49. Ibid., 182.

50. Ibid., 183.

51. Boindin, "Quatrième lettre," 42–44.

52. Jean Auguste Julien Desboulmiers, *Histoire anecdotique et raisonnée du théâtre italien, depuis son rétablissement en France jusqu'à l'année 1769* (Paris: Lacombe, 1769), ii. My emphasis.

53. *Le Mercure*, April 1725, 828.

54. Shearer West, "Introduction: Visual Culture, Performance Culture and the Italian Diaspora in the Long Eighteenth Century," in *Italian Culture in Northern Europe in the Eighteenth Century*, ed. Shearer West (Cambridge: Cambridge University Press, 1999), 2.

55. Ibid., 3.

The Waterloo Summer of the Prince of Wales's Theatre

New Writing, Old Friends, and Early Realism in the Victorian Theatre

—SHANNON EPPLETT

Prologue

In her joint autobiography with her husband, Squire Bancroft, *Mr. and Mrs. Bancroft: On and Off the Stage*, actress and theatrical manager Marie Bancroft (*née* Wilton), writes that following the 1866 season, her Prince of Wales's company obtained an engagement in Liverpool: "Before starting, we were told that there was a sort of epidemic at Liverpool; so several of us decided to live at Waterloo, a pretty seaside place a few miles off, where the train could take us every night after the performance was over. We occupied several villas facing the sea, and formed quite a little colony of our own, including Mr. Robertson (who came down for the purpose of finishing and producing his new comedy, *Ours*), Mr. and Mrs. Byron, Mr. and Mrs. Hare, my sister Augusta, myself, and Mr. Bancroft. We spent a delightful six weeks there."[1] "Mr. Bancroft" was the actor Squire Bancroft, who would soon become Wilton's husband and partner in the theatre company. For the sake of clarity, Marie will be referred to as "Wilton," although she was known professionally as Marie Bancroft after their marriage in 1867.

While Mr. Bancroft, Wilton's sister Augusta, Mr. and Mrs. Hare, and Mrs. Byron were no doubt lovely people, they are walk-on players in this opening scene: Wilton herself, Mr. Byron, and Mr. Robertson are the leading players. "Mr. Robertson" was the playwright T. W. Robertson; his play *Society* had been a long-running hit for the fledgling Prince of Wales's company in the previous season. "Mr. Byron" was Henry J. Byron, a successful playwright well-known for his comedic burlesques and Wilton's then-current management partner. The nostalgic picture of seaside bliss that Wilton paints in her autobiography masks the tempest underway in the three interlocking relationships. There is a significant body of scholarship on Robertson and Wilton, but what is often overlooked is the role of Byron as a catalyst, and the interrelatedness of the three relationships: the friendship of Byron and Robertson, the business partnership of Byron and Wilton, and the artistic collaboration of Wilton and Robertson. Together, Robertson and Wilton would change the face of Victorian theatre in pursuit of a new type of verisimilitude; theatre history often treats Ibsen as the motive force of modern realism, when in truth, Robertson and Wilton were moving the Victorian stage away from melodrama and toward realism two decades before *A Doll's House* played in London. If not for Byron, Robertson and Wilton never would have met, and Robertson might not have persisted as a playwright. Wilton made use of the talents of both men in her quest to shift her public image from "burlesque boy" to leading lady. In theatre history, it is often easy to lose sight of the human relationships that underlie the work that is created: Theatre is created by people in relationship to one another, and these relationships impact the work that is produced, for good and ill. Out of the interlocking alliances between Byron, Robertson, and Wilton, came a new way of writing a new kind of play. This article explores the interrelationships of three Victorian theatre artists, the work they created, and the impact they had on the popular theatre of their time.

To return to our summer at the seaside, Wilton writes that the Liverpool assizes (a circuit court that heard the most serious criminal and civil cases) were in session that summer. Wilton and other company members were friends with many of the barristers, who, like the acting company, were in town for the short term:

> Our legal friends came down to Waterloo once every week, and the evenings were dedicated to entertainments improvised by ourselves. We had several mock trials in which Mr. Hare[2] was always condemned to the ignominious position of representing the criminal in the dock. It was interesting to hear the clever speeches, all about nothing, delivered by these rising young barristers. I was sometimes the Judge, and gave imitations of the various gentlemen I had seen on the Bench. My robe was a pink wrapper, and my wig made of cotton-wool. On one occasion, for

> variety, we got up a mock opera, in which I was the prima donna, Mr. Gilbert[3] the lover, Mr. Hare his rival, with large cloak, broad-brimmed hat, and knives and daggers all over him; Mr. McConnell was the prima donna's father, whom he made a deaf old man, so that we were obliged to shout all our recitatives at him through an improvised ear-trumpet. The opera was sung throughout in Italian gibberish, and was a most amusing bit of foolery.
> Our audiences were small but appreciative, for they included both Mr. Byron and Mr. Robertson; I never saw them laugh so much in my life. We were all young then, and the fun, perhaps, appeared greater than it would now, but it was a happy time.[4]

There was a great deal of subtext beneath the surface of this "happy time." Wilton's gauzy memories of the improvised theatricals played at the seaside conveniently brings the three leading players together in a single setting, yet their individual stories unfold mostly in duets: Robertson and Byron's long-standing friendship, Byron and Wilton's shaky business partnership, and Robertson and Wilton's simpatico as artistic collaborators. The final pairing—between Robertson and Wilton—resulted in a new type of work that approached a then-unseen level of theatrical realism and evolved into a new method of working: the auteur director. If not for the previous two duets, however, the final one would not have been possible. This scene on the beach at Waterloo would mark a point of fracture and coalescence among our three leads—Byron, Robertson, and Wilton—that would determine the direction of the rest of their lives, and by extension the direction of Victorian theatre for years to come.

Act I: Exposition

The story begins in 1849. That year, Tom Robertson moved to London to begin his theatrical career. In his biography about his father, Robertson's son indicates that Robertson and Byron first met at Flesher's, "a well-known dramatic agent," and that "a friendship commenced which ripened into affection and esteem, lasting in a brotherly fashion all their lives. They acted together in provincial stock companies, and in these 'palmy days' hatched many a scheme to make 'both ends friendly.'"[5] Considering their differences in background, experience, and temperament, they made an unlikely but memorable pair.

Thomas William Robertson was born in 1829, the fourth generation of a provincial acting family. Robertson's family toured the "Lincoln Circuit"—eight towns in the East Midlands. He made his stage debut at age five, in a benefit performance of *Rob Roy*, playing Hamish.[6] Robertson later described his theatrical childhood as having been "nursed on rose pink and cradled in properties."[7] He attended school from age seven and worked in the family business on school breaks; however, his formal education ended at age fifteen due to the family's financial condition. With twenty-two children[8] and dependent on the stage for an income, the Robertson family always struggled, but with the rise of the railroads, the provincial circuit system and their way of life was dying.[9] Robertson decided to strike out on his own in his late teens. Savin indicates that Robertson made the rounds of London theatres seeking work, "but managers were unimpressed by his Green Room pedigree. The fact of the matter is that Tom was not a spectacular actor."[10] Robertson returned home to his family. His acting abilities are the focus of some scholarly debate; based on reviews and contemporary opinion, he seems to have been competent but was never an audience favorite. After another bid for independence, this time an unsuccessful adventure working at a boarding school in Holland, Robertson again returned to his family, just in time for the demise of the Lincoln Circuit in 1849. At this point, Robertson again sought work in London as an actor and playwright.[11]

By contrast, Henry James Byron's childhood was as privileged as Robertson's was colorful and financially precarious. He was born in Manchester in 1834, the eldest son of the British Consul to Haiti and a distant cousin of the poet Lord Byron. He attended school in Essex and later St. Peter's Collegiate School in London. Byron rejected a naval career, which his family wanted him to pursue, in favor of medicine, but he soon abandoned it for life as an actor.[12] Between 1853 and 1858, Byron is known to have acted in provincial companies in Colchester, Oldham, and Rochester, and he seems to have arrived in London at some point during this period.[13] Byron's theatrical ambitions can perhaps best be interpreted as a rejection of his upper-class background.

Two particular anecdotes concerning Byron and Robertson's early days as struggling actors seem to present their relationship in microcosm. These stories appear in the first biography about Robertson, written by his son, T. W. S. Robertson, and published in 1889. They are repeated nearly verbatim in an 1891 biography by T. Edgar Pemberton, as well as in books by Wilton, her husband, Squire Bancroft, theatre critic Clement Scott, and Robertson's sister, the actress Dame Madge Kendal. Both Byron and Robertson were popular figures within their theatrical milieu, as the multiple retellings of the same stories attest. The first concerns Robertson and Byron as struggling actors attempting to produce their own work by renting a room in London's Gallery of Illustration: "Once, during a long vacation, they were in London together and mournfully wondering what was to happen next. There was a room in the Gallery of Illustration 'to let.' Now Byron and Robertson had written and played an entertainment with 'varying success' (always varying). It was so constructed that while Byron was on the stage in the first part, Robertson was the money-taker, and during Robertson's performance, and prior to their appearance in a duologue, which wound up the bill of fare, Byron took his place in the pay-box, a proceeding he stated 'to be wholly unnecessary, for reasons quite obvious.'"[14] With borrowed money, they rented the room and paid for advertising. For their efforts, they attracted a single audience member, who turned out to have come into the room expecting to see a troupe of Chinese acrobats, who were performing elsewhere in the building. Between collecting the sole patron's money and starting the show, Robertson used some of the box office funds to purchase a beer to calm Byron's nerves. As Robertson handed Byron the beer, Pemberton records the following exchange:

> "Have the critics arrived?" asked Byron in an anxious voice.
> "No," replied Robertson; "but, then, they are always late."
> "Are they?" asked Byron dubiously.
> "Of course they are," was the answer. "Come, you had better commence and get it over."
> "Tom," said Byron, with the spirit of prophesy upon him, "I think this is going to be a failure."
> To this, Robertson deigned no reply, and returned to his pay-box.[15]
> Byron's opening monologue was titled "The Origin of Man."
> "In the beginning there was only one man—" here Byron paused.
> "Yes," said the "front seat," "and I'm the damned fool," and the man hurried out to Robertson and demanded his money back, saying he had come to see "The Chinese." Robertson assured the infuriated one that Byron was a Chinaman, but to no purpose, and finally had to return one shilling and eightpence, having spent fourpence of the two shillings in stout for Byron.[16]

The other often-repeated anecdote about the two is that they once became so desperate that they attempted to escape their poverty by enlisting in the Horse Guards. Byron was accepted, but "Robertson failed to pass the medical exam; and, stoutly declining to accept the shilling without his friend for a comrade, Byron abandoned his intention, and the two went back to fight their weary war against editors and theatrical managers."[17]

No dates are associated with either story; instead, the incidents are said to have occurred during the two men's early days in London, in the 1850s. The value of these tales lies in their illustration of the nature and character of their subjects, rather than as documentary history. In the first, Robertson is the more confident and experienced of the two, while Byron is anxious and uncertain. Robertson reassures his friend that everything will be fine, knowing full well that Byron's suspicions are correct and the performance is already a disaster.

Robertson presents perseverance in the face of adversity, while the more mercurial Byron is ready to give up. In the enlistment story, we see that Byron is loyal to his friend and would rather face the continued uncertainty of life in the theatre with Robertson than in the military without him. Robertson's combination of determination and cynicism born from a life in the theatre and Byron's mixture of *naïveté*, professional caution, and friendly devotion inform their relationship and subsequent interactions throughout their lives. Robertson also seems to serve as a mentor to Byron at this point in their lives; having grown up in a theatrical family, Robertson knew the ins and outs of the stage, which could not have but impressed the younger and less stage-savvy Byron. By doing so, Robertson earned the loyalty of a man who would never fail to help his friend if it was in his power to do so, as was subsequently demonstrated by the enlistment story.

To create a context for their relationship, and for the plays they would each write, it is necessary to understand the theatrical and literary world in which they lived. Often, history books tend to describe English theatre in the late nineteenth century as being at "a low ebb."[18] The London theatre was growing in economic terms but stagnating artistically. Shakespeare was still performed, but plays by contemporary English playwrights tended to be unexceptional; the well-made play model created a great deal of formulaic work. Translations and adaptations of French plays were popular, as were melodramas and burlesques. Burlesques—the broadly played spoofs of operas, dramas, fairy tales, and myths—and the closely related genre of extravaganza, which featured lavish costumes and scenery, had broad appeal. As theatre became increasingly accessible due to the technological and social changes of the nineteenth century, that is, increased urban population, the advent of the railroads, shorter working days and better wages, it was seen in many quarters as pandering to the lowest common denominator. The rise of railroads contributed to the death of regional "circuit" theatres, like the one that had supported Robertson's family, by centralizing theatre in the cities at the expense of the countryside.

Upon Robertson's arrival in London in 1849, he tried to support himself as a writer, but he also depended on acting jobs to make ends meet.[19] In 1851, he received what should have been his big break as a writer—his play *A Night's Adventure* was produced at the Olympic, a major West End theatre. Barrett speculates that the Olympic's manager, William Farren, may have agreed to produce it as a favor to Robertson's father, or may simply have been short on available scripts at the time.[20] The play opened August 25, 1851, to bad reviews and closed after just four performances.[21] The always-temperamental Robertson exchanged heated words with Farren at the time, responding to the manager's charge that it was "a d—d bad play," with "Not so bad as the acting."[22]

And so, at age twenty-two, Robertson had already failed on a grand scale, "and with the terrible hall-mark of 'failure' stamped boldly upon him, its luckless author had to fall back to earn his living as best he might among those who do duty in the rank and file of stagehand."[23] Four months later, Robertson made his London acting debut in a burlesque titled *The Mandarin's Daughter or Willow Pattern Plate*, at Punch's Playhouse. It is difficult to trace Robertson's early stage career: He was working in 1851 and 1852 and was apparently unemployed in 1853, and this is likely when Byron entered his life. In 1854, Robertson worked as prompter at the Lyceum Theatre, and that summer he received positive reviews for playing Tom Gradgrind in a stage version of Charles Dickens *Hard Times* at the Strand.[24]

With the Lincoln circuit at an end, the rest of the Robertson acting family migrated to London. In the 1854–55 theatre season, Robertson, his parents, his brother Craven and sister Madge were all appearing at London's Marylebone Theatre. This engagement was followed by an ill-fated tour that involved bringing a company of actors to Paris to produce *Macbeth* at the Théâtre des Italiens. Robertson's parents were part of the acting company, and Robertson was hired as "general acting manager and interpreter" and was the only member of the company to speak French.[25] The producer reneged and left the company stranded in France with barely enough money to get home. Despite these tribulations, a bright spot in Robertson's life during this period occurred in 1855; he performed in a benefit performance held at the Queen's Theatre in Tottenham Street—this would later become the Prince of Wales's Theatre. In this engagement, he met his future wife, actress Elizabeth Burton.[26]

Robertson married in August 1856. The new Mrs. Robertson was a talented actress, and her employment often supported the couple. Shortly after their engagement, both were hired at the Theatre Royal Dublin, "she as leading lady, and he as assistant stage manager and eccentric comedian."[27] In the summer of 1857 they returned to England, where Robertson appeared at the Surrey Theatre in August and both were engaged at the Marylebone during the season.[28] On December 2, 1857, their son Thomas William Shafto Robertson was born. Elizabeth may have been unable to work at this time. Goldfarb states that Robertson was having difficulty getting hired as an actor in this period, and subsequently, he turned once again to prompting and stage management to earn a living. Around this time, Robertson worked for dramatic publisher William Hailes Lacy, translating French plays into English. In an era before strict copyright laws, publishers could make money by creating new translations of French plays, even if the plays had already been produced in England. These versions were then offered to East End and provincial theatres.[29] Robertson is believed to have translated at least sixteen plays for Lacy.[30] For Robertson, translating plays for Lacy was both a last resort and an apprenticeship in dramaturgy. His talents and ambitions had little outlet in the theatre of his time: Acting was not his forte and the modern role of director, which perhaps would have suited him well, did not exist. The closest analogues to the contemporary role of director—those of prompter and stage manager—were neither steady nor lucrative pursuits. Early on, Robertson had tried to write the popular fare of the day but had been unsuccessful; while translation was essentially hack work, it also seems that by closely reading and adapting the work of others, Robertson found his own voice as writer and critic.

In the 1858–59 season, Mr. and Mrs. Robertson were both hired at the Theatre Royal Plymouth. In 1859, Mrs. Robertson gave birth to a daughter, Betty. During the next few years, the Robertsons worked at the Theatres Royal in Woolwich, Rochester, and Windsor. During their engagement at Windsor, in January 1862, Betty died.[31] "It was after this that Robertson made up his mind to leave the stage and devote himself wholly to literature, his wife continuing to act whenever the opportunity offered."[32] Robertson's turn to literature is where Byron's friendship would come into play.

In contrast to Robertson, who took a great deal of time and travail to find his métier, Byron found his voice as a writer early. He encountered even less success as an actor than Robertson; his biographical essay in *Nineteenth Century British Dramatists* states, "His early attempts at acting, including the role of Isaac of York in his own burlesque of Sir Walter Scott's 1820 novel *Ivanhoe*, and a monologue titled *A Bottle of Champagne, Uncorked by Horace Plastic*, failed miserably."[33] Writing, and specifically comedic writing, seemed to be his strength: Byron tried his hand at writing burlesque in 1857 and quickly found an audience. His first attempt, *Richard of the Lion Heart*, was produced at the Strand Theatre. The Strand was known as the home of burlesque and an especially exuberant playing style that one contemporary writer characterized as "riotous mirth."[34] It was successful enough that the Strand produced his second, *The Lady of Lyons; or, Twopenny Pride and Pennytence*,[35] in February 1858. Byron's third burlesque, *Fra Diavolo Travestie, or the Prince, the Pirate and the Pearl*, "proved an enormous hit and contributed greatly to the early success of the Strand as a centre for burlesque."[36] Besides providing a ready outlet for Byron's work, the Strand brought Byron and Wilton together.

Burlesque as a genre had not yet acquired the salacious overtones we now associate with the term. The burlesques of Byron's era were essentially parodies of operas, melodramas, myths, and fairytales. They were built on a formula of nearly endless puns, broad comedy, and popular songs with rewritten lyrics. Cross-dressed roles were also a feature, especially women playing boys in "breeches roles." The shows often contained magical transformation scenes that allowed for spectacular scenery and costumes. Burlesques were short—most ran about an hour with no intermission—fast-paced, and lighthearted; they were popular, low-brow comedies. Byron had found his theatrical form and became extremely successful with it.[37] He married in 1856, and perhaps under pressure to earn a stable living, entered the Middle Temple to study law in January 1858.[38] With the success of *Fra Diavolo*, however, his legal studies went the way of his naval and medical careers before, and Byron gave himself over to being a burlesque writer.

Fra Diavolo was followed six months later by *The Maid and the Magpie*, which helped establish new Strand company member Marie Wilton as a star. Wilton was new to the company but not to the stage. Her background is in many ways similar to Robertson's; the eldest daughter of a traveling actor, she first went on the provincial stage at age five. As a child, she played Fleance to Charles Macready's Macbeth, and Prince Arthur in *King John*. She made her London debut at age seventeen, in 1856, playing the lead character's son in the melodrama *Belphegor the Mountebank*. During that engagement, Wilton was asked to fill in for another actress in an extravaganza on the same bill, a burlesque of *The Winter's Tale*, playing Perdita, the Royal Milkmaid. Wilton's heretofore unseen comedic talent, small stature, and lively energy were well suited to playing "burlesque boys," and this type of role became her specialty. Following her debut, she went on to act in eighteen such productions, playing a boy in thirteen of them.[39]

Wilton had just been asked to join the Strand company when Byron presented *The Maid and the Magpie* to the Strand management in 1858.

> When I first received the part of Pippo in the *Maid and the Magpie*, I was disappointed at its being another boy and wrote to ask if any change could be made in the cast. Miss Swanborough kindly agreed for me to meet her as well as Mr. Byron, whose acquaintance I thus made for the first time.[40]. . . He said he had written the part of Pippo expressly for me, and that he was distressed I did not like it. I explained that I did not wish to play burlesque boys, and that I objected to the part on that account. Miss Swanborough seemed to be perplexed and anxious, and Mr. Byron remarked that he was a young author, and my not acting Pippo would mean a serious loss to him, that there was no-one else in the theatre to whom he could entrust it, and that he could "see me in every line of it." He added, "I am

> only a beginner, you know, and this burlesque may make or mar me." This appeal decided me; I could hold out no longer, so promised to play Pippo.[41]

Wilton describes Pippo as "saucy and amusing,"[42] and this characterizes most of the burlesque roles she was called on to play—an energetic, sometimes sassy youth who could reel off puns in rapid-fire. At age eighteen, Wilton was already weary of it and longed to play a female character in a traditional comedy, rather than a boy in burlesque. Byron had created a role with Wilton in mind and pressured her to accept it; Wilton was already feeling limited by her "line" as a burlesque boy and wished to have an opportunity to play other types of roles. It is significant that Wilton and Byron's relationship began as a struggle over artistic judgment, though in this instance, Wilton deferred to Byron's judgment and he was correct. Wilton writes in her memoir that *The Maid and the Magpie* was as "an immense success, and I established myself as a leading favourite."[43]

Byron was in demand; Boxing Day, December 26, was a traditional opening day for burlesques; Byron had two shows open on Boxing Day in 1859, three in 1860, two in 1861, four in 1862 and 1863, and three in 1864. Burlesques were not limited to the holidays, however: between *Fra Diavolo* at the Strand in 1858 and the founding of the Prince of Wales's Theatre in 1865, he had thirty-eight shows produced in a span of seven years.[44] Byron also did not limit his talents exclusively to the theatre: In 1861, he helped to found *Fun* magazine, a rival to the humor magazine *Punch*. "The men who started and contributed to *Fun* considered themselves Bohemians and opposed the snobbishness engendered by the 'gentlemen' of *Punch*. These men always called themselves the *Fun* gang, for if the gentlemen of *Punch* could have a circle, the Bohemians, though always a loosely knit group, could have a gang."[45] He also edited *Comic News*, the *Wag*, and *Mirth* at various times in the 1860s, as well as writing for other publications.

Act II: Complications

As Byron's star was rising, he used his success to help his still-struggling friend Robertson. In February 1861, Robertson's one-act farce, *The Cantab*, was produced at the Strand Theatre.[46] It was Robertson's first original work since the ill-fated *A Night's Adventure* a decade earlier; his playwriting efforts to this point primarily consisted of adaptations and translations of French plays for Lacy. It is not known if Byron had any influence on getting Robertson's work produced; but by February 1861, the Strand had produced six of Byron's burlesques, and his recommendation—if offered—may have carried some weight.[47] Whatever income or recognition *The Cantab* may have offered Robertson, it was not sufficient. Alan Fischler notes that payment for playwriting had reached its nadir in the mid-nineteenth century; Robertson's contemporary Tom Taylor received only £150 for *Our American Cousin* and £200 for *The Ticket-of-Leave Man*, two of the most successful plays of the era. New playwrights fared even worse: Robertson's friend W. S. Gilbert earned only £30 for his second play in 1866. Writers usually sold their work outright to a theatre and collected no royalties. "The only way to make a living from such poorly paid work was to turn out a vast quantity of it."[48] Robertson was not a prolific writer, and in June 1862, he wrote to a friend: "I have abandoned my former unremunerative and nomadic calling and now hate theatricals and all things thereunto pertaining with a hearty intensity only to be appreciated by those who have been connected with the dreadful business and unsuccessful in it's [*sic*] pursuit."[49]

He may have been pushed to this sentiment by the circumstances of his family: His daughter Betty died in January 1862 and a second daughter, Maud, was born.[50] The family depended on Elizabeth's income as an actress; though she had been in ill health since the birth of Betty, she had continued to work.[51] Although "leaving the stage" was something Robertson had frequently threatened to do out of frustration throughout his life, he essentially did so during this period. Thanks to Byron's assistance, he turned to journalism and became a frequent contributor to Byron's *Fun*, as well as to other papers, such as the *Welcome Guest*, the *Liverpool Porcupine*, the *Glowworm*, *Beeton's Dictionary*, *Beeton's Englishwoman's Domestic Magazine*, the *Boy's Own Magazine*, *Colman's Magazine*, *Saturday Night*, the *Wag*, *London Society*, and the *Illustrated Times*.

Because of *Fun* magazine and his successful burlesques, Byron was part of London's bohemian society. In "Performing Bohemia," author Richard Schoch writes: "Bohemia was still understood as the cultural space for the experiences of unconventional artists, writers, and performers. In nineteenth century London the chief institutions of Bohemia were literary and artistic clubs (Savage, Arundel, and Reunion), newspaper and magazine offices (*Punch*, *Fun*, and the *Welcome Guest*), song-and-supper rooms (Evans's, The Coal Hole), and the minor West End theatres located on and around the Strand (Adelphi, Strand, Lyceum, Olympic, Gaiety, and Globe). Bohemian culture was characterized above all by fraternity, whether in clubs, press offices, art studios, or theatrical green rooms."[52] Byron provided an entrée into this society to his friend Robertson and kept him employed during a particularly trying time in his professional life. Additionally, both men enjoyed the bohemian world of literary club life—Byron was a founder of the Arundel Club. This world later served as the inspiration for a scene in Robertson's play *Society*.

As a journalist, Robertson wrote reviews and theatre-related pieces during this time. In 1864, the *Illustrated Times* ran a series of Robertson's humorous essays on "various acting lines and theatre personnel."[53] The articles are satires and are clearly written by someone with a lifelong association with the stereotypes in question. Robertson's first piece in the series appeared January 9, 1864, and poked fun at "London Managers."[54] His column the next week was a paean to "Burlesque Writers" and could very well be based on his friend Byron's experience: "During the last seven years burlesques and extravaganzas have taken so strong a hold on public favour that their authorship has become a distinct and separate form of dramatic writing. More than this; it has become a lucrative one, and is therefore much followed. That very large majority of persons who are not burlesque writers, burlesque actors, theatrical managers, and amateurs, would be astonished if they knew what serious importance is attached to the production of these rhymed travesties, what crowds they attract, and what large receipts they bring."[55] The article goes on to parody the conventions of the form as well as its production, imagining a harried writer creating a Christmas show out of Lord Byron's tragic poem *Lara*.

In Robertson's article, the burlesque writer deals with unimaginative management, prima donna actors, and choreographers and scenic artists working at cross-purposes. Barrett quotes the original, noting Robertson's statement that burlesque is "a mettlesome, audacious, *too* clever child, who, despising the wholesome restrictions of the nursery, is *de trop* in the drawing-room, a-straddle on the staircase, and a stumbling-block in the hall."[56] That Robertson had Byron in mind when he wrote the piece can be inferred by the fact that Byron was already an established burlesque writer at the time and was related to the poet Byron. While some historians point to the piece as a critique of burlesque (and, indirectly, Byron), the author's sympathies lie with his beleaguered burlesque writer-hero, who is doing his best to create under difficult circumstances. The piece can be read as a critique of the theatrical conditions that perpetuated the lowbrow commercialism of burlesque. At the same time, it is not unreasonable to expect that Byron may have personalized some of Robertson's critique of burlesque.

Despite his friend's evident disdain for burlesque, Byron was more than happy to provide the Strand with a steady stream of them. At the same time, Marie Wilton's dissatisfaction with playing boys in them continued to grow. Wilton writes of this period of her career, "Now and then I had a part in a comedietta given to me, and I was so successful in it that I pined more and more for that class of character."[57] Her use of the word "class" in this context is telling; Burlesque was considered "illegitimate drama." Prior to 1843, the "legitimate" forms of farce, tragedy, and comedy were performed only at theatres holding letters patent from the crown—Drury Lane and Covent Garden. The forms of burlesque, melodrama, and "light comedies with songs" developed as a challenge to the monopoly held by the major theatres. These forms were relegated to the smaller theatres in the West End and Surrey-side of the Thames, which "attracted audiences supposedly a cut below the audiences of Drury Lane, Covent Garden, and the summer operation of the Theatre Royal in the Haymarket."[58] Although the Theatre Regulations Act of 1843 had largely erased these legal distinctions, and in Wilton's era, any theatre could perform any type of play, the class distinctions remained. Burlesque was a lower-class form than comedy. Wilton wanted to expand her range as an actress by appearing in comedies (and as a woman), as well as raise her social status.

Deborah Pye writes about Wilton's particular issues with class by analyzing how she presents herself in her autobiographies: "She begins the story of her life by carefully establishing the respectability of her grandparents (one grandfather was a newspaper proprietor, the other a clergyman), then acknowledges that both her parents had lost caste, her father by going on stage rather than entering the clergy, and her mother by eloping with him. . . . From an early age Bancroft seems to have been both professionally ambitious and sensitive about the pariah social status bestowed on her by her family's occupation."[59] This class-consciousness drove her professional ambitions; Wilton wanted respectability, and she recognized that as long as she appeared onstage wearing pants, this was not going to happen.

Wilton states that during her time at the Strand, between 1858 and 1865, she frequently asked Byron to write comedies for her to appear in. Byron agreed to but never did. Wilton appeared in several more Byron burlesques at the Strand: *The Miller and His Men and Cinderella; or The Lover, the Lackey and the Little Glass Slipper* in 1860, and *Alladin; or The Wonderful Scamp*, *Esmerelda; or, The "Sensation" Goat!* and *Miss Eily O'Connor* in 1861, playing a boy in all of them.[60] As time went on, Wilton's patience wore thin. "Season after season, I found myself still a boy."[61] During the 1862–63 season, Wilton was asked to reprise the role of Karl in a revival of *The Miller and His Men*. She declined to do so, knowing it would result in her dismissal from the company: "According to the rules and regulations of the theatre, 'by refusing to act a part which was in accordance with my agreement' (and especially one which I had played originally), I forfeited my engagement. I determined to do this, at all risks, in the hope of obtaining somewhere the position I coveted. But alas! I soon found that I had made a mistake, for there was not that eagerness on the part of the managers to secure my services I thought there would be, and the difficulty to get out of the beaten track was greater than I anticipated. I applied everywhere and nowhere could I get an engagement for comedy."[62] Wilton was eventually forced to take more "burlesque boy" roles at other theatres in order to work at all. At the end of 1863, she was asked to rejoin the Strand company for a Byron burlesque of *Orpheus and Eurydice*. It is unknown if Byron played any role in getting her reinstated, but given his successful track record of writing roles specifically for Wilton, it is conceivable that he put in a word on her behalf. Wilton stresses that she was never on bad terms with Strand manager Miss Swanborough, "It was only my impatient desire to improve my position that parted us."[63] Her bid for freedom unsuccessful, Wilton returned and remained at the Strand for another season. While her gamble did not pay off at the time, it shows the risks Wilton was willing to take in order to improve her circumstances.

Act III: Climax

The mid-1860s mark a turning point for the careers of our three lead characters. Robertson resumed writing plays, and Byron and Wilton became business partners. In 1864, Robertson's play *David Garrick* attracted the attention of actor E. A. Sothern. It opened in Birmingham in April 1864 and later moved to London.[64] It was a long-running success for Sothern, so Robertson wrote a second play with Sothern in mind, titled *Society*: "Struck with the combined power and humour of Sothern's acting in 'David Garrick,' Robertson immediately conceived for him the character of a gentleman of the day, with a strong dash of bohemianism in his nature, well suited to the easiness of manner for which the actor was famous, and giving him a scene in which he, overwrought by nerves and a little champagne, becomes heroically and sentimentally intoxicated."[65] Sothern liked *Society*, but John Buckstone, the manager of the Haymarket Theatre where Sothern was under contract, famously called the play "rubbish" and refused it.[66] Robertson then offered the script to other London theatres, only to have it rejected by all.[67]

Buckstone and other London managers refused the play on the basis of content rather than quality: specifically, two scenes set inside a bohemian literary club. The "Owl's Roost" was modeled on the Arundel and Savage Clubs, to which both Byron and Robertson belonged, along with most of the London theatre critics. Barrett writes, "Buckstone believed . . . that the reviewers who frequented such clubs would be offended by these scenes, and the public might respond similarly. Since the Owl's Roost was too integral a part of the plot to cut or patch, Buckstone's only recourse was to reject the play." Barrett notes how often the word "danger" was associated with *Society* before its production.[68] The danger lay primarily in offending the critics with a comedic portrayal of the inside of their private club.

As Robertson met with small success followed by significant setback, Wilton attempted to once more establish a career for herself beyond burlesque. In 1865, she again wrote to the managers of theatres seeking roles in comedy, and again she found herself typecast. "Mr. Buckstone, I remember, replied that he could only associate me with 'the merry sauciness of the wicked little boy Cupid.'"[69] Wilton had had enough, and therein lies the genesis of the Prince of Wales's company. With the financial assistance of a brother-in-law, she established her own theatre company. In her memoirs, Wilton presents it as if the idea of founding her own company originated with her brother-in-law; but given Wilton's force of will, this seems somewhat disingenuous. Robin A. Werner, writing on the subject of Wilton's performance of femininity both onstage and off, notes that "most presentations of Victorian theatre gloss over the few and often brief female managements, but even the fact that some women attempted this authoritative position is significant in relation to the strictness of mid-Victorian hegemonic conceptions of gender roles."[70] Regardless of whether the idea was hers, Wilton's venture into management was less unique because of her gender than because of her age and relative independence; female managers had existed in London since Madame Vestris managed the Olympic Theatre in 1830, and Wilton had been working for the Swanborough family at the Strand for several seasons. Instead, Wilton was significant in that she was all of twenty-six at the time, and her management was unconnected to a father or husband.

Wilton's brother-in-law loaned her a thousand pounds with the understanding that it would be repaid only if the theatre was successful. Wilton writes that she proposed a partnership with Byron, "who I knew was about to sever his connection with the Strand Theatre. He thought it would be a very dangerous experiment, but I urged that if I failed, I should at least have the opportunity of showing the managers what I could do, and might afterwards have less difficulty in getting an engagement."[71] Why Byron wanted to sever ties with the Strand is not known, but Wilton was offering him a deal that would have been difficult to refuse. He was not required to invest any money, was indemnified against losses, and was to be paid ten pounds a week in exchange for his exclusive services as a playwright, with the understanding that he would write comedies for Wilton to appear in as well as burlesques.[72] Wilton was to be paid twenty pounds a week, ten of which went toward paying her brother-in-law. Wilton and Byron would share any profits after expenses.

The decision-making powers within the company seem to have lain primarily with Wilton, although this is not spelled out in her description of their partnership agreement and only becomes evident in light of subsequent events. She found an available theatre—the Queen's Theatre on Tottenham Road, which would be renamed the Prince of Wales's. The theatre was small by the standards of the day, both in terms of stage dimensions and audience capacity—seating about 560 and run down, it was nicknamed the "Dusthole."[73] It was also poorly located to attract the upscale audiences Wilton desired. She recounts being told by others that "the distance was too great from the fashionable world."[74] Nevertheless, Wilton and Byron committed to a two-year lease on the space, which was also the length of their partnership agreement.[75]

The Queen's theatre had catered to the working-class people of the neighborhood. Wilton had the theatre repainted and redecorated to appeal to a middle- and upper-class audience: "Curtains, carpets, in fact all the appointments, were of the cheapest kind, but in good taste. The stalls were also blue, with white lace antimacassars over them. This was the first time such things had ever been seen in a theatre."[76] Deborah Pye notes that in her autobiographies, Wilton portrays her role in the founding of the theatre more as that of a housewife or hostess—making an inviting domestic environment in which to entertain—than as manager, yet Wilton was the driving force behind the venture. "By means of antimacassars and other signifiers of respectability, Bancroft transformed The Prince of Wales's Theatre from a seedy commercial venue into an extension of the domestic sphere."[77]

Wilton was eager to open her theatre by playing in a comedy, but "Mr. Byron grew less sanguine, and—wisely, I think—entreated me to appear in burlesque."[78] Wilton somewhat reluctantly agreed to this, and the new theatre opened on April 15, 1865, with the comedy *A Winning Hazard* by J. P. Wooler and a Byron burlesque, *La Somnambula!; or The Supper, The Sleeper, and the Merry Swiss Boy*.[79] Wilton was the "merry Swiss boy" in the burlesque and did not appear in the comedy.[80] Byron was reluctant to run the risk of thwarting audience expectations: His writing and Wilton's performance in it were the draw for the young company. This speaks to Byron's caution and to Wilton's willingness to defer to his judgment at this point in their partnership.

For their second program, Byron wrote the kind of comedy Wilton wished to appear in, *War to the Knife*, which opened on June 10, 1865.[81] The play was only noteworthy for the fact that it was a three-act comedy that did not require

Wilton to be dressed as a boy; "Byron showed some restraint, too: he does not rely on farcical incidents and puns for cheap laughs, as in so many of his comedies. But the play is impressive only by contrast. On its own merits, it seems eminently conventional, full of the trappings of the well-made-play. . . . The play could have been (but was apparently not) another French adaptation."[82] The Prince of Wales's premiere season was short, since the theatre opened at Easter. Their second season—their first full season—began on September 25, 1865, with Wilton appearing again as a boy in another Byron burlesque: *Lucia di Lammermoor; or The Laird, the Lady and the Lover*.[83] In describing the founding days of the company in their joint autobiography, *Mr. and Mrs. Bancroft On and Off the Stage*, published in 1888, Wilton presents Byron as a hands-on partner, recounting their initial horrifying visit to the run-down, déclassé Queen's Theatre and placing him at early company rehearsals and backstage on opening night. In their second book, *The Bancrofts: Recollections of Sixty Years*, published in 1909, significantly less mention is made of Byron's early involvement, despite the fact that it is in many cases simply a reprinting of the earlier volume. The first autobiography was published within a few years of Byron's death and perhaps Wilton felt more compelled to include him in it than she did in the later edition.

At this point—the 1865–66 theatre season—the stories of our three leading characters begin to converge. Robertson was still hoping to have his play *Society* produced, and his friend Byron again came to his aid. Byron recommended the play to the manager of a theatre in Liverpool; it was produced in May 1865 and was a success.[84] Robertson's happiness was short-lived, however. His wife, Elizabeth, died in August. Her health had been in a decline since the death of their first daughter in 1861. A devoted father and husband, it is said that he was never again in good health after the loss of his wife.[85] Robertson's son states that it was shortly after his mother's death that Byron "induced" Marie Wilton to read *Society*.

Byron's motivation in bringing the play to Wilton's attention becomes somewhat problematic: As Wilton describes it, Byron was never enthusiastic about doing the play, leading one to suspect that he may have offered or promised to help Robertson and then have had second thoughts about it. Here we may be seeing the crux of Byron's problem: his personal feelings for his friend coming into direct conflict with his business interests. While Byron was instrumental in getting *Society* produced in Liverpool, where the London critics would *not* see it, he was by this time theatrically savvy and risk-averse enough to wish to avoid offending or antagonizing the London critics by representing them onstage. Wilton clearly did not share this view, as she writes of her first encounter with *Society*:

> I now approach a most important event in my career as a manager. Mr. Byron called upon me one day to tell me that an old friend, Mr. Robertson, wished him to read a comedy of his to me, which had been recently acted with success in Liverpool; he added that the play had been offered in turn to Sothern, Alfred Wigan, and to nearly all the London managers, but they would have nothing to do with it. Mr. Buckstone wrote his opinion that it "must fail wherever it was produced." They were chiefly afraid of it, Byron told me, on account of a scene which the journalistic world would take offence at, and the critics would, beyond all doubt, condemn, as it contained sketches of men well known to the author and in "Bohemia." Mr. Byron also feared its chance of success himself, but as he had known Tom Robertson, who was at the time in very low water, for many years, he was anxious to do his old friend a good turn; he dwelt on the danger he saw in the play, and thought that, as young managers, we could not afford to risk offending the critics. I said danger was better than dullness; the next day, Byron read the comedy to me; and, when he had finished it, he expressed himself more and more afraid of it. I at once offered to risk its production; the whole piece seemed to me so clever and original, that I felt sure of its success. Mr. Byron was astonished at my urging our acceptance of the play. At last he agreed that at all events it was worth the trial.[86]

Despite Byron's reluctance, Wilton overruled him, and *Society* went into rehearsals with Wilton playing the lead role. Rather than frightened, Wilton seemed drawn to the "risk" and "danger" involved in producing the piece. One can further speculate that had Byron convinced Wilton otherwise, he could then go back to Robertson and blame the rejection of the play entirely on her. Wilton's enthusiasm for the piece put Byron in an awkward position.

Those writing in the decades following the success of *Society*, such as Robertson's son T. W. S. Robertson, biographer T. Edgar Pemberton, and the Bancrofts in their two joint autobiographies, tended to dismiss Byron's concerns regarding the reception of the play and record only positive critical responses to the play. Barrett's research indicates otherwise: "Actually, the majority of critics responded negatively to Robertson's colorful, ideal club, where the members appeared to be genial eccentrics and social misfits who follow only two rules: moneymaking and fame are to be scorned, and drunkenness is an unmistakable sign of genius."[87] Barrett cites negative reviews that ran in the *Era* and the *Morning Post* and confirms that Byron's original fears were not misplaced.[88] While Byron was not mistaken, he was ultimately proven wrong: The negative critical reaction to the play helped to spark audience interest. In addition, the "realism" of the acting, costumes, and scenic design seemed striking and innovative to Victorian audiences accustomed to bombastic acting and furniture painted onto backdrops. "*Society* succeeded because it struck playgoers as a sophisticated, witty, charming, comedy thoroughly in tune with its time, a comedy that one simply had to see."[89] While it may have received mixed reviews, critics were not immune to its charms: drama critic Clement Scott, also an Arundel Club member, recounts attending the opening night of the play with fellow *Fun* writer Tom Hood and playing a guessing game as to which of their clubmates were being portrayed.[90]

In many respects, Robertson and Wilton were kindred spirits: Both were the eldest children in theatrical families, raised on the provincial acting circuits; both came to London while in their late teens to make their way in the London theatre, Wilton with great success, while Robertson starved and struggled. They were also both ambitious in what would prove to be symbiotic ways: Wilton wanted to change her image from that of burlesque boy to comedic leading lady, and Robertson had, through the years of hardship and rejection, developed definite ideas about theatre that he wished to put into practice. His association with the Prince of Wales's finally allowed him to put these into practice. Being allowed to direct his own work was key. Wilton says of *Society*: "The rehearsals advanced, and I liked the play more and more; my views of acting so entirely agreed with Mr. Robertson's that we encountered no difficulties whatever, and everything went smoothly and merrily, although Byron, to the last, dreaded the effect of the 'Owl's Roost' scene. My faith remained unshaken, and acquaintance with the author soon ripened into friendship."[91] It is important to remember that at this time, the position of director was unconceptualized in the English theatre. Booth writes that the person in charge of running a rehearsal—whether this duty fell to the lead actor, theatre manager, stage manager, or prompter—did not involve themselves with helping an actor develop or discover a character. Rather, they dealt with cues, blocking, and movement. "The Victorian theatre did not possess such a thing as a governing idea of a play in the mind of one person, who sought by collaboration or imposition to bring it out prominently in performance."[92] Robertson *did* have a governing idea and vision for his work, and Wilton gave him the opportunity to put it into practice.

Wilton was known as a conscientious and fair manager but not a particularly generous one, due to the financial circumstances of the new company. Robertson negotiated a smaller, per-performance payment for the performances of *Society*, in exchange for the chance to "stage-manage" it, which included running rehearsals and having dominion over costumes, setting, and props. This kind of deal may not have been appealing to anyone other than Robertson at the time, but it allowed him to see his work staged the way he envisioned it. He stressed realism and detail throughout his work with the Prince of Wales's, from having functional doorknobs and coat hooks on the walls to scenes built around the serving of tea or the making of a pudding. These minute details of properties, blocking, and scenery in turn demanded an understated style of acting and led to the description of his work as "cup and saucer plays."

Beyond this attention to scenic detail, as a lifelong theatre person he knew how to communicate with actors, who often struggled to portray his "realistic" characters. Prince of Wales's company member John Hare (also present at the Waterloo scene), remarked: "He had a gift peculiar to himself, and which I have never seen in any other author, of conveying by some rapid and almost electrical suggestion to the actor an insight into the character assigned him. As nature was the basis of his own work, so he sought to make actors understand it should be theirs. He thus founded a school of natural acting which completely revolutionized the then existing methods, and by so doing did incalculable good to the stage."[93] Due to the financial limitations of the Prince of Wales's company, Robertson was able to negotiate his ideal position, which ultimately combined authorship with what we would now recognize as the position of director.

Robertson's ideas on theatre, and specifically on what was wrong with it, were made clear in a series of essays he had written for the *Illustrated Times* in 1864. As mentioned earlier, the "Theatrical Types" were intended as a series of humorous essays, each focused on a line of business within the theatre: "Leading Ladies," "Tragedians," "Low Comedians," and so forth, presented with Robertson's characteristic acerbic wit. Barrett notes that most are "couched in a generally moderate and sympathetic tone,"[94] but Robertson does use some of the essays, particularly "London Managers" and "Burlesque Writers," as a soapbox to critique the current state of the London stage. Robertson largely refrains from proposing change, with the notable exception of the "Stage Managers" essay:

> The Stage-Manager is the man who should direct everything behind the scenes. He should be at one and the same time a poet, an antiquarian, and a costumier; and possess sufficient authority, from ability as well as office, to advise with a tragedian as to a disputed reading, to argue a wardrobe-keeper as to the cut of a mantle. He should understand military science like a drill-sergeant, and be as capable of handling crowds and moving masses as a major-general. He should possess universal sympathies: should feel with the sublime, and have a quick perception of the ludicrous. Though unable to act himself, he should be able to teach others, and be the finger-post, guide, philosopher, and friend of every soul in a theatre, male or female, from the manager and author to the call-boy and the gasman, from the manageress and principal soprano to the back row of the extra children's ballet and the cleaners.[95]

Robertson could well be describing his own experience and qualifications. The Prince of Wales's gave him the opportunity to test it out, and the results were pleasing to all parties. Except, perhaps, to Byron.

It was not uncommon for the author of a new play to take part in rehearsals; Wilton writes humorously of *A Winning Hazard's* playwright J. P. Wooler attending rehearsals.[96] In contrast to Robertson's eagerness, Byron notoriously did *not* like attending rehearsals. In the preface to *Plays of H. J. Byron*, Jim Davis writes: "Byron's attitude to rehearsals was as idiosyncratic as his attitude to writing. Even though he was unwilling to alter his plays once they were written, he seems to have been more adaptable with burlesque. He wrote anything into the piece that was wanted, reminisced John Hollingshead, on the spur of the moment, then left the task of putting everything together to the actors, the stage manager, the musical director and the manager. He used to arrive late at rehearsals, slope off into little corners and tell jokes and, at the first opportunity, creep out of the theatre unobserved. He detested rehearsals and would often spend the afternoon wandering around Covent Garden or drinking in a nearby bar."[97] Byron's laissez-faire attitude toward his own work could not but have irked the diligent Wilton, and made Robertson's passion and work ethic seem like a breath of fresh air.

Booth notes that in form, content, and message, Robertson adhered closely to existing conventions of comedy, melodrama, and the well-made play. He was innovative in his ability to write love scenes that juxtaposed the conversations of two contrasting couples and in presenting characters and conversations that seemed recognizable to his contemporary audiences.[98] Robertson, Wilton, and her company developed a collaborative method of working, in which the playwright partnered with performers to develop and deepen character. Sollars writes that Robertson "created characters to fit individual cast members and often accepted the actors" suggestions for alterations to his scripts.[99] He did this to the extent that Wilton and her company were essentially cocreators of the work. In terms of his dramaturgy, E. J. West states: "his innovations were not of plot or of character, but of occasional scenes (especially love scenes), of incidental details, of the use of the 'trappings and trifles of realistic every-day,' essentially a realism of milieu, a milieu which dictated the manners of the people who appeared in it."[100] Wilton for her part was happy to let Robertson stage-manage *Society* and all of his subsequent plays for the Prince of Wales's—*Ours* (1866), *Caste* (1867), *Play* (1868), *School* (1869), and *M.P.* (1870). "We were of mutual value to each other: he knew it, and certainly our good stars were in the ascendant when Tom and I were 'first acquaint.'"[101]

Society played for 147 performances in its initial run and would be revived by the company three times: in 1868, 1874, and 1881.[102] Its success led to Robertson writing his next play, *Ours*, specifically for the Prince of Wales's company. At the end of the 1865–66 London season, the company was engaged for several weeks during the summer in Liverpool. Robertson joined the company at the seaside to work on revisions. The scene recounted in the prologue of this article, on the beach at Waterloo, occurs in this period. It was during this summer that Byron became "entangled" with the management of a theatre in Liverpool—the Theatre Royal.[103] This quickly escalated to include two other venues, the Alexandra and the Amphitheatre. Elisabeth More notes that Byron's management of the Theatre Royal and Amphitheatre was reported in a London newspaper in late September 1866.[104]

What compelled Byron to go into management in Liverpool is unclear, but it may have its roots in burgeoning collaboration between Robertson and Wilton. Byron had been reluctant about doing Robertson's play, overruled on the matter, and then proven wrong—the show was a hit despite everything he had said. Taking on the management at Liverpool may have been an opportunity for Byron to prove himself as a theatrical manager, either to himself or to others.[105] As Robertson's star rose at the Prince of Wales's, there was less call for Byron's contributions. Wilton's goal in founding the company was to perform in comedy, and Robertson's refined domestic plays were exactly the type of work Wilton wished to be associated with, while Byron's burlesques were what she wanted to leave behind. This too perhaps drove Byron to Liverpool; his contributions were no longer wanted at home.

For *Ours*, Robertson took inspiration from his favorite book, Thackeray's *Vanity Fair*, and used one of his favorite subjects, military life and hardships faced by soldiers in wartime, to create a romantic comedy set during the Crimean War.[106] Parts were written with specific actors in mind; unfortunately, Wilton's intended role, Mary Netley, did not meet her expectations. Other company members were disappointed or upset as well. Robertson was in Waterloo during the summer of 1866, rewriting the play. Barrett reconstructs a near rebellion among the acting company, with many being unhappy with their assigned parts. Importantly, Robertson not only persuaded company members to accept the parts, but he also allowed them to improve upon them. This type of collaborative approach would characterize not just *Ours* but all of the Prince of Wales's subsequent productions. Wilton writes; "Robertson always gave me a carte blanche to do what I liked with the parts he wrote for me, and often said 'he knew full well that he could trust to my good taste and discretion.'"[107] This would characterize their entire working relationship: Robertson wrote roles with specific actors in mind, then allowed the actors to fit the roles to their personalities.[108] Wilton wrote of this: "Mary Netley is not a good part to read in the book, and had not Tom Robertson asked me to 'build it up,' she would have fallen comparatively flat upon the audience. When he had finished reading the piece to us, he begged me to do all I could in the scene which concerned me in the last act, for somehow he felt unable to make Mary as prominent as he wished, so at the rehearsals I set to work, and invented business and dialogue, which, happily, met with his approval; he declared I greatly helped the act, which was not only improbable, but in parts very weak."[109]

At the end of the summer of 1866, Byron remained in Liverpool managing the theatres, which, Wilton noted, "took him much from London and laid an unfair strain of work and responsibility upon me: although, I am glad to say, without destruction to our friendship." Wilton hired actress Lydia Thompson to replace her in the burlesques for the 1866–67 season, which would become another point of contention with Byron.[110] Robertson's *Ours* opened on September 19, 1866, and was an immediate success, running for 148 nights.[111] In October, Byron's burlesque, *Der Freischütz; or The Bill! The Belle!! And the Bullett!!!* featuring Thompson, played in conjunction with *Ours*. Wilton states that Thompson did well, but "it showed a distinct falling off in the writing, partly owing, perhaps, to his 'losing heart,' as he expressed it, through my refusal to act in it, but very much to divided interests caused by his Liverpool speculations."[112] She adds rather tersely, "Fortunately the great popularity of the comedy excused the weakness of the after-piece."[113]

Byron's final burlesque for the Prince of Wales's, *Pandora's Box; or, the Young Spark and the Old Flame*, ran at Christmas 1866. Again, Wilton did not appear in it. "Candor compels the admission that it never burnt brightly, and, indeed, hurt the receipts of the theatre instead of improving them."[114] The situation came to a head in February 1867, when Byron wrote to Wilton that he wanted out of their partnership: "I consider that by refusing to play in burlesque you have done me an irreparable wrong, and yourself considerable harm; however, I have met your views always, and it is no doubt too late for me to repeat what I have so often said, and what is the general opinion of the public."[115] That opinion being that Wilton should remain in burlesque, and the Prince of Wales's was primarily a burlesque house. Wilton, in her reply to Byron, answers his charge regarding her "refusal" to play burlesque by telling him, "All my acting in either *Der Freischütz* or *Pandora* would have done very little good for them, beyond saving my substitute's salary. I can't help it if my candour wounds you, my dear Byron, but neither of the pieces has been worthy of you."[116] She goes on to remind him that despite the fact that he has only written for one theatre during their partnership, he has been paid regularly for his efforts, and has been indemnified against any financial risk.

In their exchanges within the letters, reprinted by Wilton in her autobiography, it becomes clear that Byron always saw himself as a silent partner in the Prince of Wales's: In his defense, he states that he has deferred to her judgment in terms of casting and "dressing" of pieces and admits that the management of the theatre has "devolved" on her.[117] Byron indicates that the two had discussed matters during the summer of 1866, regarding both his management of the Liverpool theatres and renewing their partnership: "Your conduct in the matter of my taking these theatres was truly admirable, and was fully appreciated by me, so much so that you will remember I said at the time I should not consent—on a renewal of our management after two years—to take *half* the profits as my share, considering my frequent absence and divided duty. This I strongly impressed on you at Waterloo, and if we had remained in partnership, I should have insisted on your receiving the lion's share of the reward."[118] Wilton felt that Byron had abdicated his responsibilities to the Prince of Wales's, and Byron evidently felt betrayed or misled by Wilton's desire to leave burlesque behind. They agreed to dissolve their partnership effective April 15, 1867, one week after the premiere of what is considered Robertson's masterpiece, *Caste*.[119] In the final analysis, Wilton and Byron's partnership agreement appears to have been exactly what it was always intended to be—a two-year lease on the space of the theatre, during which time Wilton was to be the public face of the theatre and Byron its resident playwright.[120] The division of managerial duties seems to have been less clearly laid out.

At base, Byron and Wilton seem to have been at cross-purposes in their partnership from the start: She wanted Byron's services because he was a successful burlesque writer who could and would also write the types of comedies she wished to appear in. Byron held up his end of the bargain—writing *War to the Knife* and *A Hundred Thousand Pounds* for the Prince of Wales's. Byron expected Wilton to continue to appear in burlesques; he clearly felt that his last two burlesques for the company would have been better had Wilton appeared in them. Wilton's intentions for the company had always been to get out of doing burlesque, a fact that Byron may not have been fully aware of at the time. It is fair to say that in Byron, Wilton came to see all that she wished to leave behind, and in Robertson, both in his plays and in his views on theatre, all that she wished to become.

As Wilton's partnership with Byron unraveled, the collaboration with Robertson on *Caste* intensified: "Before *Caste*, Robertson's credentials as a dramatic author were still open to question. After *Caste*, he was almost universally acknowledged as the leading dramatist of the English stage, worthy (in the opinion of some) to take his place alongside Sheridan and Goldsmith in the pantheon of the immortals."[121] Today, it may be a stretch to place Robertson in the "pantheon of the immortals," but his work seemed nuanced and intelligent and appeared innovative to Victorian audiences. He learned his lesson with *Ours* and did a better job of tailoring *Caste*'s characters to the actors in the company; by this time, too, the company members knew that they would be given the freedom to develop their roles to suit their talents. William Kleb writes that Robertson took inspiration from life as well as from the rehearsal hall. He cites the mock trials presided over by Wilton during the Waterloo summer as the inspiration for the scene in *Caste* in which Wilton's character pantomimes a ballet. "This climactic scene, so dependent for its effect on Wilton's talent for mimicry, represents perhaps the most striking example of the collaborative nature of her work with Robertson; it 'grew' out of improvisations ('impromptu entertainments') the preceding summer, while Wilton's company and Robertson were preparing *Ours* for its previews in Liverpool."[122] *Caste* focuses on the issue of social class—specifically inter-class marriage. Robertson allows one of his upper-class characters to find a happy marriage with a working-class ballet dancer, "and Robertson does not deem it necessary to strengthen her credentials with a last-minute legacy or revelation of aristocratic lineage." However, only one set of "cross-class" lovers is allowed a happy ending; another male character's pursuit of a higher-caste woman is doomed. While the play only partially challenges the status quo, Barrett notes that for its time "a play that brought people from different classes into conversation allowed for a free exchange of ideas on the caste system, and ended with a commoner being accepted into the upper societal ranks was considered quite daring and, to some viewers, disturbing."[123] The subject of the play likely held appeal to the class-conscious Wilton, who originated the role of Esther, the ballet dancer.

It is not known how the end of the Wilton-Byron partnership impacted relations between Byron and Robertson. It had to have created some tension; at the Prince of Wales's, Robertson found his work appreciated and valued, while Byron's work, popular and successful almost everywhere else, was criticized and his professional judgment called into questioned. Byron had once again given his friend an opportunity, yet in this instance it had worked out well for everyone except Byron himself. The Prince of Wales's shift in programming, from a theatre that presented burlesque to one that presented witty and fashionable comedies, was emblematic of Victorian theatre's quest for respectability. Byron's burlesques were lowbrow entertainment and did not fit the image of middle-class respectability that Wilton sought to create. Wilton's judgment on this front proved to be correct. The Prince of Wales's became exactly what she hoped it would: a fashionable and respectable theatre.

Byron's involvement in the management of theatres in Liverpool can perhaps be viewed as an attempt to prove—either to Wilton or to himself—that he did, in fact, know what he was doing in terms of management. Unfortunately, his subsequent bankruptcy in March 1868 belies this. Elisabeth More, writing about Byron's career, states that it is difficult to determine why his Liverpool adventure failed. "I suspect that the most plausible explanation for Byron's failure is simply that he spread himself too thinly and lost the firm control necessary for the successful management of the three Liverpool theatres. Many critics believed this tendency to spread his focus too widely was also detrimental to his work as a playwright."[124] This is a charge, one might add, that Wilton evidently agreed with. Despite the bankruptcy, Byron recovered and remained popular and successful as a playwright. He made a return to acting in 1869 with a role in his play *Not Such a Fool as He Looks* and enjoyed a second career acting in his own shows. He died in 1884.

Play, the show that followed *Caste*, opened February 18, 1868, and was less successful, both dramatically and financially.[125] Robertson, who had lost his wife, Elizabeth, in 1865, married a German woman while writing the play. Barrett indicates that perhaps this was both a distraction (in that the play is not strong as his previous efforts) and an inspiration for the piece, as the play is set at a German spa (the title itself refers to gambling). It ran for forty-seven performances and was never revived. By contrast, *School*, his fourth play for the Prince of Wales's became "the most successful play he ever wrote."[126] The Bancrofts admit that it was not his best—that honor belonged to *Caste*—but was his most beloved, perhaps due to the growing reputation of the author and the company. That it was a sentimental comedy about an all-girls school, based on the Cinderella story, helps explain its appeal to Victorian audiences. The "pastoral, dreamy setting" of the play was a new quality in Robertson's work and also contributed to its popularity.[127]

In the final analysis, it is difficult to separate Robertson's plays from the Prince of Wales's productions of them; they were really a collaboration between the playwright/director and the ensemble. Robertson himself recognized the plays as a joint creation, and he expressed his appreciation and indebtedness to Wilton and company in a letter on the occasion of the 1870 revival of *Ours*:

> My dear Marie,
> 11/27/1870

"Ours" was acted so excellently last night that, as I may not see you for the next few days, I write to express the great gratification it gave me to see that the "light troupe" had distinguished themselves more than ever.

You know that I am not given to flattery, and that my standard of taste for comedy is somewhat high. I was really *charmed*; and I was very ill the whole night in discomfort and annoyance. The remark of everyone I heard was, "What wonderfully good acting!" And I was pleased to find Boucicault descanting on it to a chosen few. He said that not only was the general acting of the piece equally admirable, but that he had never—including Paris—seen such refinement and effect combined as in the performance of the second act. He said, too, that the actors who had played in the piece before, acted better than ever. I mention this, because the same thing struck me. Bancroft was most excellent; and I have never seen him succeed in sinking his own identity so much as in the last act. For the first time in my life I felt grateful to the folk on the stage side of the foot-lights, and I am not given to that sort of gratitude.

I was terribly late last night. If the revival should draw, and it should be worth while, could not the first and third acts be relieved of some ten minutes' talk? Cut wherever you like. I shan't wince; for I don't care about either the first or last acts. If they had been less perfectly acted they would have missed fire, and deservedly.

Yours very sincerely,
T. W. Robertson.[128]

That Robertson acknowledged Wilton as a cocreator of the work is best illustrated in the dedication of *Caste*, "To Miss Marie Wilton (Mrs. Bancroft) this comedy is dedicated by her grateful friend and fellow-labourer, the author."[129]

Act IV: Denouement

Robertson was known to have had a heart condition, and his health had been in decline since the death of his first wife. He was bedridden as he worked on his final play for the Prince of Wales's, *M.P.* Unable to attend rehearsals, he dictated the final scenes of the show to others. Wilton and her husband came to his house to "show him, act by act, what they hoped to do with his work, he being a little better in the fine weather, and able to reach his drawing room."[130] Wilton, Bancroft, and company were aware at the time that the play was not as strong as his previous work: however, out of devotion to Robertson they gave it an unheard of six-week rehearsal period to ensure the best production possible.[131] Robertson was so ill at the time that even the task of naming the play fell to Wilton; the title *M.P.* refers to "Minister of Parliament," and the action of the play centers on a parliamentary election. *M.P.*, despite its weaknesses, was well-received at the time. This was due in part to the fact that Robertson's ill-health was well-known, and no one seemed willing to say a bad word in the press regarding what proved to be his final play.

Robertson died on February 3, 1871. He was thirty-six when *Society* opened at the Prince of Wales's theatre, and he died just six years later. In a short span of time, he wrote and directed five plays that offered audiences a new experience: a less bombastic and overwrought style of acting, accurate and detailed scenery and costumes, and, by Victorian theatre standards, realistic dialogue. This move toward realism predates Ibsen on the London stage by twenty-five years, but Robertson's innovations were not picked up by any other playwrights at the time. This was a problem acutely felt by Wilton and Bancroft, who had a difficult time finding suitable material for their company after Robertson's death. They resorted to frequent revivals of his *Society*, *Ours*, *Caste*, and *School* (*Play* and *M.P.* were never revived). Booth remarks, "Never was a Victorian management more dependent upon the work of one writer."[132] Despite these limitations, the Bancrofts managed the Prince of Wales's theatre for fourteen years, before moving to the much-larger Haymarket in 1880, and retiring from the stage in 1885. During the course of their careers, they had performed Robertson's work nearly 2,900 times.[133]

After many unsuccessful years in the theatre, Robertson finally found an artistic home with Wilton's company. Wilton operated her company as an ensemble, despite the fact that she was initially the star attraction. Although both Robertson and Wilton were rather headstrong individuals, they developed a mutual respect and admiration for one another. "He and I never once during our acquaintance knew what it was to have an angry word: a delightful reflection!"[134] Robertson taking an active role in the production of his plays, and on top of this being an effective director, he impressed everyone who encountered his work. As a manager, Wilton allowed Robertson free rein as "stage manager," and Robertson in turn gave his actors carte blanche with regard to developing their roles. This mutual respect, which seems to have largely come about by accident rather than by design, created both a collaborative working approach and a new type of stage language, one that presented an idea of "realism" for its audiences, an idea that first coalesced on the beach at Waterloo in the summer of 1866. While we would likely not recognize it as such today, it no doubt contributed toward what followed with the advent of Ibsen on the London stage in the 1880s.

Epilogue

Returning once again to the image of Wilton, Byron, Robertson, and the Prince of Wales's company playing by the seaside, this moment at Waterloo emerges as the watershed moment for the Victorian theatre; it was a moment when something new began. Beneath the placid surface, changes were taking place that would alter the course of three lives and careers and determine the direction of the popular theatre for decades. As the scene unfolds, tension already exists between Byron and Wilton over managerial duties. Byron, perhaps upset over Wilton's decision to produce Robertson's play, and perhaps even more chagrined to have been in the wrong, was in the midst of becoming involved in managing theatres in Liverpool, maybe in the hopes of proving his own competence. Wilton was struggling to come into her own as an actress and manager—she was in the process of shedding her burlesque past, marrying Squire Bancroft, who will become her partner in the theatre, and becoming one of the most successful women of her time, in large part because of her collaboration with Robertson. Robertson was present and working on polishing *Ours* for the company. It was a melancholy time for him: After years of rejection and failure, he had finally had a success with *Society* and found a theatre willing to let him direct his own work, but he was still mourning the recent loss of his wife.

Theatre is a collaborative and social art; it is made by people working together, either harmoniously or at cross-purposes. It is also a product of its time. This particular moment—the Waterloo summer of the Prince of Wales's company—is a moment of both fracture and coalescence, in which a business partnership and possibly a friendship unraveled, and an artistic collaboration spontaneously developed. Out of this, a new way of working and a new type of work emerged. This may be a lot to read into a brief passage about a group of Victorian theatre people playing on the beach, but this moment seems to have been significant to the participants as well, as it echoes through their subsequent work and correspondence for several years.

Byron and Robertson found in each other's companionship a friendship that sustained both of them through the lean times of their early careers. Robertson and Wilton most likely found themselves in accord over their common experience as lifelong theatre people and their desire to bring an aura of respectability to the theatre and the drama. Without Byron's assistance over the years, it can easily be argued that Robertson may never have written the work he is best remembered for, let alone to have had it produced. Robertson died young, at the height of his career; and both Byron and Wilton outlived him by many years. Wilton and Robertson were working together at the time of his death, but there is no mention of Byron in connection with Robertson's death. One could infer that they were no longer close at that time. I would hope that this is not the case; in doing this research I have come to like my three subjects—the determined Wilton, the loyal and cautious Byron, and the cynical visionary Robertson—and would like to believe that they were all good enough friends to put their differences aside. Wilton makes it clear that no hard feelings existed between her and Byron.[135] Byron even wrote another play for the Prince of Wales's, *Wrinkles*, in 1876.[136]

With regards to Robertson and Byron, the end is less clear. Robertson's sister, Dame Madge Kendal, recounts an incident between the two that is indicative of their depth of feeling toward one another, an exchange that I hope was repeated between the two men later in life:

> On one occasion he and Tom quarreled bitterly, and did not speak for some time. One day, however, quite unexpectedly they did meet and Harry, as I, like all his friends, called Byron, went up to my brother and holding out his hands said, "It's a long time since we met, Tom."
> My brother grasped the proffered hand and the hatchet was buried for all time.[137]

Plays are written and theatre is made by people, in relationship to one another; and it is ultimately these relationships—more than work or success—that matter in the course of daily life. Through the interactions of Byron, Robertson, and Wilton—in friendship, in business, in collaboration, and at times in opposition and discord—a new kind of writing emerged: A collaborative authorship combined with a modern idea of the director as the guiding vision of a production. Concurrently, this process evolved a new type of play, which captivated its contemporary audience through its depiction of the ordinary, through scenic verisimilitude and through its dramatic understatement. The "Robertsonian" plays of the Prince of Wales's Theatre are the legacy of this interaction between three artists of the Victorian theatre.

Notes

Editor's note: The historical theatre where Wilton, Robertson, and Byron worked spelled its name Prince of Wales's. London's current Prince of Wales Theatre is unrelated to the theatre established by Byron and Wilton and does not use the possessive.

1. Squire Bancroft and Marie Bancroft, *Mr. & Mrs. Bancroft On and Off the Stage* (London: R. Bentley, 1888), 207.
2. The actor John Hare, a member of the Prince of Wales's company.
3. W. S. Gilbert, of Gilbert and Sullivan fame. At this point in time, he was a practicing lawyer.
4. Bancroft and Bancroft, *Mr. & Mrs. Bancroft On and Off the Stage*, 209.
5. T. W. S. Robertson, *The Principal Dramatic Works of Thomas William Robertson with Memoir by his Son* (London: Sampson Low, Marston, Searle and Rivington, 1889), xxv.
6. Robertson, *The Principal Dramatic Works*, xx.

7. Ibid., xxii.
8. The actual number of Robertson children is unclear: some sources indicate eleven children, others twenty-two. In either case, it is safe to say that the Robertsons were a large family.
9. Clement Scott, *The Drama of Yesterday and Today, vol. 1 and 2* (London: Macmillan, 1899), 504.
10. Maynard Savin, *Thomas William Robertson* (Providence: Brown University Press, 1950), 25.
11. Ibid., 25.
12. Angela Courtney, *Nineteenth-Century British Dramatists* (Detroit, MI: Thomson Gale, 2008), *MLA International Bibliography*, EBSCO*host*, accessed December 15, 2012.
13. Jim Davis, *Plays by H. J. Byron*, (Cambridge: Cambridge University Press, 1984), 33.
14. Robertson, *The Principal Dramatic Works*, xxv.
15. T. Edgar Pemberton, *The Life and Writings of T. W. Robertson*, (London: R. Bentley, 1893), 50.
16. Robertson, *The Principal Dramatic Works*, xxvi.
17. Pemberton, *The Life and Writings*, 58.
18. Oscar Brockett, *History of the Theatre* (Boston: Allyn and bacon, 2003), 354.
19. Daniel Barrett, *T. W. Robertson and the Prince of Wales's Theatre* (New York: Peter Lang, 1995), 34.
20. Ibid., 36.
21. Robertson, *The Principal Dramatic Works*, xxiv.
22. Barrett, *T. W. Robertson and the Prince of Wales's Theatre*, 36.
23. Pemberton, *The Life and Writings*, 46.
24. Alvin Goldfarb, "Thomas William Robertson, Actor." *Theatre Survey* 20, no. 2 (1979): 64.
25. Robertson, *The Principal Dramatic Works*, xxx.
26. Ibid., xxxi.
27. Ibid., xxxii.
28. Goldfarb, "Thomas William Robertson, Actor," 65; Savin, *Thomas William Robertson*, 31.
29. Barrett, *T. W. Robertson and the Prince of Wales's Theatre*, 38.
30. Ibid., 229.
31. Robertson, *The Principal Dramatic Works*, xxxiii.
32. Ibid., xxxiii.
33. Courtney, *Nineteenth-Century British Dramatists*.
34. Davis, *Plays by H. J. Byron*, 3.
35. Courtney, *Nineteenth-Century British Dramatists*.
36. Davis, *Plays by H. J. Byron*, 2.
37. Ibid., 3.
38. Courtney, *Nineteenth-Century British Dramatists*.
39. Willaim Kleb, "Marie Wilton (Lady Bancroft) As An Actress," *Theatre Survey* 20, no. 1 (1979): 46.
40. The Strand Theatre was initially managed by Henry Valentine Swanborough. His daughter Louisa managed it in the late 1850s, and this is likely the "Miss Swanborough" that Wilton refers to. After Henry's suicide in 1863, his wife, Mary Ann, managed the Strand until 1883. This "Mrs. Swanborough" was well-known for her malapropisms and was the butt of jokes between Byron and Robertson.
41. Bancroft, *Mr. & Mrs. Bancroft On and Off the Stage*, 37.
42. Ibid., 79.

43. Squire Bancroft and Marie Bancroft, *The Bancrofts: Recollections of Sixty Years* (London: John Murray, 1909), 16.
44. Courtney, *Nineteenth-Century British Dramatists.*
45. Edward Stewart Lauterbach, *"Fun" and Its Contributors: The Literary History of a Victorian Humor Magazine* (PhD diss., University of Illinois 1961), 3.
46. Scott, *The Drama of Yesterday and Today*, 194.
47. Courtney, *Nineteenth-Century British Dramatists.*
48. Alan Fischler, "Guano And Poetry: Payment For Playwriting In Victorian England." *Modern Language Quarterly* 62, no. 1 (2001): 43, *Academic Search Complete*, web, July 11, 2016.
49. Barrett, *T. W. Robertson and the Prince of Wales's Theatre*, 45.
50. In *The Principal Dramatic Works of T. W. Robertson*, written by Robertson's son, a second daughter, Maud, is named, although no birth date is given. From the context, she appears to have been born between 1862 and 1865. According to this source, Robertson had two children, Tom and Maud, when his wife died in 1865.
51. Robertson, *The Principal Dramatic Works*, xliv.
52. Richard Schoch, "Performing Bohemia," *Nineteenth Century Theatre and Film* 30, no. 2 (2003): 1.
53. Daniel Barrett, "T. W. Robertson [1829–1871]: The Dramatist as Critic," *Victorian Periodicals Review* 14, no. 4 (1981): 145.
54. Ibid., 148.
55. Pemberton, *The Life and Writing*, 108.
56. Barrett, *T. W. Robertson and the Prince of Wales's Theatre*, 28.
57. Bancroft and Bancroft, *Mr. & Mrs. Bancroft On and Off the Stage*, 83.
58. Michael R. Booth, *Theatre in the Victorian Age* (Cambridge: Cambridge University Press, 1991), 6.
59. Deborah Pye, "'Irreproachable Women and Patient Workers': The Memoirs of Victorian Leading Ladies," *Texas Studies in Literature & Language* 45, no. 1 (2003): 79.
60. Bancroft and Bancroft, *Mr. & Mrs. Bancroft On and Off the Stage*, 90—98.
61. Ibid., 82.
62. Ibid., 101.
63. Ibid., 108.
64. Robertson, *The Principal Dramatic Works*, xxxix.
65. Pemberton, *The Life and Writings*, 65.
66. Robertson, *The Principal Dramatic Works*, xl.
67. Robertson, *The Principal Dramatic Works*, xl; Pemberton, *The Life and Writings*, 166.
68. Barrett, *T. W. Robertson and the Prince of Wales's Theatre*, 56.
69. Bancroft and Bancroft, *The Bancrofts: Recollections of Sixty Years*, 56.
70. Robin A. Werner, "The Angel in the Theatre: Marie Wilton, the Performance of Femininity and Intertheatrical Playwrighting," *Theatre History Studies* 21 (2001): 43–59, *Historical Abstracts*, web, July 11, 2016.
71. Bancroft and Bancroft, *Mr. & Mrs. Bancroft On and Off the Stage*, 175.
72. Bancroft and Bancroft, *The Bancrofts: Recollections of Sixty Years*, 55.
73. Richard L. Lorenzen, *The History of the Prince of Wales's Theatre* (Hertfordshire: University of Hertfordshire Press, 2014), 139.
74. Bancroft and Bancroft, *The Bancrofts: Recollections of Sixty Years*, 56.

75. Ibid., 57.
76. Bancroft and Bancroft, *Mr. & Mrs. Bancroft On and Off the Stage*, 186.
77. Pye, "Irreproachable Women and Patient Workers," 79.
78. Bancroft and Bancroft, *The Bancrofts: Recollections of Sixty Years*, 57.
79. Bancroft and Bancroft, *Mr. & Mrs. Bancroft On and Off the Stage*, 186.
80. Lorenzen, *The History of the Prince of Wales's Theatre*, 130.
81. Bancroft and Bancroft, *Mr. & Mrs. Bancroft On and Off the Stage*, 190.
82. Barrett, *T. W. Robertson and the Prince of Wales's Theatre*, 65–6.
83. Bancroft and Bancroft, *Mr. & Mrs. Bancroft On and Off the Stage*, 195.
84. Robertson, *The Principal Dramatic Works*, xli.
85. Ibid., xliv.
86. Bancroft and Bancroft, *Mr. & Mrs. Bancroft On and Off the Stage*, 200–201.
87. Barrett, *T. W. Robertson and the Prince of Wales's Theatre*, 76.
88. Ibid., 78.
89. Ibid., 80.
90. Scott, *The Drama of Yesterday and Today*, 505.
91. Bancroft and Bancroft, *Mr. & Mrs. Bancroft On and Off the Stage*, 204.
92. Booth, *Theatre in the Victorian Age*, 108.
93. Pemberton, *The Life and Writings*, 200.
94. Barrett, *T. W. Robertson and the Prince of Wales's Theatre*, 13.
95. Pemberton, *The Life and Writings*, 122.
96. Bancroft and Bancroft, *Mr. & Mrs. Bancroft On and Off the Stage*, 184.
97. Davis, *Plays by H. J. Byron*, 29–30.
98. Booth, *Theatre in the Victorian Age*, 182.
99. Michael D. Sollars, "T. W. Robertson (9 January 1829–3 February 1871)," in *Nineteenth-Century British Dramatists*, vol. 344, ed. Angela Courtney (Detroit: Gale, 2009), 315–26, *Dictionary of Literary Biography Vol. 344. Dictionary of Literary Biography Main Series*, web, July 11, 2016.
100. E. J. West, "From a Player's to a Playwright's Theatre: The London Stage, 1870–1890." *Quarterly Journal of Speech* 28, no. 4 (1942): 430.
101. Bancroft and Bancroft, *The Bancrofts: Recollections of Sixty Years*, 82.
102. Barrett, *T. W. Robertson and the Prince of Wales's Theatre*, 83.
103. Bancroft and Bancroft, *The Bancrofts: Recollections of Sixty Years*, 67.
104. Elisabeth A. More, "Henry James Byron: His Career and Theatrical Background," *Theatre Studies* 26–27 (1979): 56.
105. More also notes that Byron booked Wilton and the Prince of Wales's company to perform at the Royal Alexandra in 1867. Wilton notes that *Ours* was produced by Robertson in Liverpool, but it is unclear if it occurred this summer or at a later date.
106. Barrett, *T. W. Robertson and the Prince of Wales's Theatre*, 85.
107. Bancroft and Bancroft, *Mr. & Mrs. Bancroft On and Off the Stage*, 415.
108. Barrett, *T. W. Robertson and the Prince of Wales's Theatre*, 87.
109. Bancroft and Bancroft, *Mr. & Mrs. Bancroft On and Off the Stage*, 414–15.
110. Ibid., 211–12.
111. Barret, *T. W. Robertson and the Prince of Wales's Theatre*, 99. *Ours* was revived and ran for nine months and would become the most frequently revived of the Robertson plays, with productions in the 1875–76, 1879–80, 1881–82, and 1884–85 seasons. Wilton and

her husband would eventually perform the play more than seven hundred times, and it served as their final stage appearance, at a charity event in 1896. Wilton said of this, "My husband and I have always looked upon the second act of *Ours* as the best the author ever wrote, an opinion which we are sure Robertson shared. It was fit and proper that it should so fall out that our last appearance should be in this fine scene." (*The Bancrofts: Recollections of Sixty Years*, 319).

112. Bancroft and Bancroft, *Mr. & Mrs. Bancroft On and Off the Stage*, 213.
113. Ibid., 213.
114. Ibid., 216.
115. Ibid., 217.
116. Ibid., 218.
117. Ibid., 220.
118. Ibid., 220.
119. Ibid., 218; Barrett, *T. W. Robertson and the Prince of Wales's Theatre*, 111.
120. Bancroft and Bancroft, *Mr. & Mrs. Bancroft On and Off the Stage*, 178.
121. Barrett, *T. W. Robertson and the Prince of Wales's Theatre*, 111.
122. Kleb, "Marie Wilton (Lady Bancroft) as an Actress," 57.
123. Daniel Barrett, "Freedom of Memory v. Copyright Law: The American Premiere of Caste," *Theatre Research International* 8, no. 1 (1983): 45.
124. More, "Henry James Byron: His Career and Theatrical Background," 60.
125. Barrett, *T. W. Robertson and the Prince of Wales's Theatre*, 137.
126. Bancroft and Bancroft, *The Bancrofts: Recollections of Sixty Years*, 104.
127. Barrett, *T. W. Robertson and the Prince of Wales's Theatre*, 154.
128. Pemberton, *The Life and Writings*, 278–79.
129. Ibid., 206.
130. Ibid., 262.
131. Bancroft and Bancroft, *The Bancrofts: Recollections of Sixty Years*, 115.
132. Booth, *Theatre in the Victorian Age*, 53.
133. Ibid., 53.
134. Bancroft and Bancroft, *The Bancrofts: Recollections of Sixty Years*, 82.
135. Ibid., 67.
136. Bancroft and Bancroft, *Mr. & Mrs. Bancroft On and Off the Stage*, 199.
137. Madge Kendal, *Dame Madge Kendal by Herself* (London: John Murray, 1933), 44.

Chekhov's *Three Sisters*

A Proto-Poststructuralist Experiment

—SARAH WYMAN

In Anton Chekhov's *Three Sisters* (1900), the domestic scene may appear estranged, both static and understated, but it becomes increasingly familiar the longer one looks. Characters, like well-tuned instruments, echo, harmonize, and clash as they seek meaning in each other's words and gestures. In an impressionistic polyphony of voices, one hears soundings of desire, outrage, and self-revelation above a basso continuo of longing, loss, and regret.[1] Borrowing terms from painting and music, critics have called this play both impressionistic and symphonic, descriptors that point to how Chekhov's writing works in a new way or changes the structures of dramatic storytelling. Indeed, more than realism or formalism, Chekhov's mosaic approach, an experiment in representation, ushers in stylistic techniques that enable the technical innovation of artists to follow and project well beyond his own moment. Considered radical in its day for its true-to-life effects, Chekhovian drama continues to engage contemporary theatre publics due to the freshness of its approach to writing the human condition and to staging the problem of representation itself.

Raymond Williams indicates that with Chekhov one witnesses "a writer of genius beginning to create a new dramatic form, but in ways so original and so tentative that it is in constant danger of breaking down."[2] Like a painting whose array of brushstrokes merge into meaning when beheld from a distance, Chekhov creates a play whose intricate system of verbal and visual signifiers requires a particular perspective. The work captures ordinary life as it is lived, the ostensibly *real*, in a manner revolutionary for its time. As a theatrical work, *Three Sisters* marks a new kind of verisimilitude that is, paradoxically, realistic in its estrangement.[3] Chekhov's four major plays remain relevant to discussions of new works for theatre because they self-reflexively engage hermeneutical questions of meaning-making even as they conjure convincing illusions of the real. Furthermore, their dialectical approach to complex questions sets similarity and difference against each other in ways that destabilize easy, normative thinking. Chekhov's plays testify to art's relevance as an arbiter of culture, as demonstrated by their astonishing popularity and many contemporary adaptations.[4]

As visual/verbal/aural performance, *Three Sisters* engages an array of touchstones that will come to describe the trope of early-twentieth-century modernism. Although various scholars have noted Chekhov's attention to formal structures and his convincing characterization, they have not recognized the way the playwright's approach to rhetorical choices prefigures poststructuralist concerns. I will examine Chekhov's self-reflexive attention to aspects of dramatic writing, to human being, and to discursive effects as perceived by those who people his plays. He plays with dialectics of real and virtual time as he foregrounds and defamiliarizes the dramatic genre and affective experience. Both thematically and structurally, Chekhov's new writing, metadiscursively concerned with its own meaning-making, goes beyond the cohesive systems described by formalism and structuralism to approach questions now considered the purview of poststructuralism and even postmodernism.

Chekhov's approach to playwriting epitomizes Fredric Jameson's celebrated notion of *multiple* narratives of modernism that have dominated critical theory from the mid-nineteenth century until today. The critic identifies *modernism* itself as a representation, a signifier whose referent is so multivalent as to be nearly untenable. For Jameson, modernism escapes representation, and only *situations* of modernity, those that Chekhov captures eloquently onstage, can be narrated. Chekhov's work weaves many of the strands Jameson includes in his definition of modernity as trope: the fetish of the new; a self-reflexive reification of language such that it operates beyond its communicative function; a dissociation from the present (due to an emphasis on past and future); a celebration of chance; a critique of *progress* and causality; the (illusory) autonomy of the aesthetic system, still lodged firmly in culture; the self grasped as a construction knowable only through inadequate representations; and the emergence of formal abstraction.[5] Through its participation in this conceptual aesthetic arena, one whose grip on critical theory remains strong today, Chekhov's new writing ensures its cultural foothold as historical phenomenon and radical experiment. For example, dialectical investigations into the place and relevance of particular truths, and the concept of socially constructed, yet dynamic identities in flux retain contemporary relevance as the high and low arts merge into popular culture. Chekhov figured a reality onstage that asserts its autonomy as construct, yet maintains a contingent link to the cultural moment in which it is experienced.[6]

Various aspects of dramatic writing are made new as well in Chekhov's art. Rather than Aristotelian plot structures in which action rises to a climax and falls to a satisfying denouement, Chekhov employs minimal plot and uses alternative elements to create form and integrity. Instead of progress toward goals or resolution, the play displays process without result, activity without outlet, percolating onstage as one complex and intricate sign. Thematic and rhetorical structures repeat and reflect, calling attention to the play's own artifice, much the way later jazz structures produce the illusion of spontaneous invention and growth. As in a free-verse poem, each act creates its own rules of repetition and emphasis. The effect is spatial and visual as much as it is philosophical and psychological. Chekhov's new writing shifts the focus from *what* happens to *how* elements of the human condition and experience can be captured and signified by verbal and visual means. His main interest lies with the way humans perceive reality and thereby form their understanding of it. The emotional valences that guide these perceptions influence their responses. By foregrounding discourse itself, Chekhov dramatizes the human urge to make sense of a confusing world, a world reflected and doubly estranged through its representation onstage. At the endpoint of this journey lies each character's self-critique or notion of self. As humanistic as Chekhov's portraits of individual struggle appear, his approach anticipates poststructuralist notions of identity as unstable and unknowable. His characters depend upon depictions in the faulty language of self-description and in the reflections and reactions of others. So keen is Chekhov's attention to these aspects of human experience that the activity of the play moves forward, act-to-act, yet achieves an effect of stasis.

Indeed, for much of the play, nothing happens. Thematically, each of the play's four acts offers an extended moment in time in which alienated characters attempt to make sense of their lives, desires, and impulses. These figures inhabit a limbo land, a stilled interval in which the loss of parents, their Moscow home, dreams, treasured objects, friends, and lovers overshadows all. Their explicit and inferred renunciation of the present tends to compromise both action and dialogue as one expects them. Instead of moving the plot along, these fundamental aspects of dramatic form eddy in two dimensions, forming images of inaction and miscommunication. Characters often achieve little more than stasis onstage, while many dialogues collapse into monologues or non sequiturs. A subterranean logic yokes the characters together; their flailing attempts at happiness weave an ultimately convincing fabric of verisimilitude, a surprisingly dynamic tableau. Chekhov may be the most Zen of the moderns, as he asks his audience to spend two concentrated hours attending to characters who pay little-to-no attention to the present moment.

Yet, how rich that moment may be, when its articulations in sight and sound coalesce in the audience's imagination. Many of the pivotal greats of modern drama in the West, including Chekhov's favorite author, Henrik Ibsen, as well as George Bernard Shaw and Samuel Beckett, insist that to represent life, to show us ourselves, our experiences, and our lives reflected onstage, one must present the banal and the mundane in stripped-down, everyday language.[7] As Paul Schmidt remarks, Chekhov's "entire art is the creation of extraordinary human depths out of the surface banalities of everyday life."[8] Liesl Olson has elaborated on the paradox of early-nineteenth-century modernism in that the writer/artist aims to present that which is overlooked (ordinary life) by means of close examination and accurate portrayal. So, once negligible elements achieve significant value, even as they act as counterpoint to the more memorable epiphanic moments of awareness.[9] As Martin Esslin has observed, "Paradoxically, the resolve to reproduce the casualness and triviality of ordinary life led to a higher rather than a lesser degree of 'artificiality.'"[10] Despite the seemingly transparent surface, semantic implications build into new webs of meaning. For example, in *Three Sisters*, what it means to *see* becomes a corollary for what it means to live authentically, or to love. What it means to *hear* another person becomes the key to connection (for the lucky few who manage) and the signal of absurdity for those who fail. In response to a legacy of Romantic melodrama, Chekhov calls for a verisimilitude that reflects his perspective and emphasis, "On stage everything should be just as complicated and just as simple as in life. People eat their meals, and in the meantime their fortune is made or their life ruined."[11] Indeed, Chekhov revolutionizes the remaking of the real in terms of linguistic structures such that his work intersects with the many realisms and tropes of modernism that developed in the twentieth century.

Chekhovian drama transforms the theatrical genre itself, as it presents a proto-poststructuralist iteration of the human condition. As a radical playwright, Chekhov's main mode of distinguishing himself from the forms and figures he inherits, those of the well-made play, is through the process of estrangement. Consequently, the audience becomes aware of their own eyes, ears, touch, and frustrated expectations as they struggle to piece together the fragments of action and affect displayed onstage. *Three Sisters* appears as the third of Chekhov's four major plays, including *The Seagull* (1896), *Uncle Vanya* (1899), and *The Cherry Orchard* (1904). *Three Sisters*, the only one he did not call a tragedy, premiered at the Moscow Art Theatre on January 31, 1901. In this play, a language of semantic ambiguity, disillusion, and dialectical differentiation conjures a more remarkably abstracted remaking of the real than audiences had seen onstage before. Remarkably progressive for its time, the play acknowledges the power of discourse to shape reality, as characters seek clarity and understanding. The action of Chekhov's play inhabits the interstitial spaces that both connect and delimit human bodies, their affective states, and their physical/temporal locations.

Like the formalists and structuralists of his time, Viktor Shklovsky, Roman Jakobson, and Jan Mukarovsky, Chekhov attends to the exposed or *bared* device; he points to the artificiality or constructed nature of his play when he foregrounds the media of drama: dialogue, gesture, sound, image, and embodied affect onstage. Rather than a straight delivery of content as promised by the seeming realism, the audience stumbles over the tools of the trade, scattered upon the sisters' bench. Because the playwright works to estrange and abstract each of these aspects, the audience must engage more rigorously than ever in the interpretation of action. Verbal and visual effects along with staged self-presentation work together to figure an illusion of the *real* as arena and as experience, energized by tensions between repeating similitudes and differential variations. Chekhov's publics, at home and abroad, enjoy a particular and lasting relationship of personal investment in the significations he has daringly elected to leave open. As Robert Shimko has argued, these self-selecting groups function alongside the more mysterious workings of culture to regulate norms and standards of public taste.[12] Chekhov carefully structures the arc of his tale, yet he undermines the sense of progress or solid foundation in a way that destabilizes familiar messages drawn up in neat, binary schemas typical of early-twentieth-century thinkers in the West.

From a twenty-first-century perspective, this playwright seems to have his finger on the philosophical pulse of a century before the critics rushed in to describe it. Chekhov engages classical philosophical questions about the meaning of life and our place in it with the characters' repeated pronouncement, "What difference does it make?" Nevertheless, the play's overarching concerns fall more squarely with the critique of discourse and meaning-making that begins with Bertrand Russell and Ludwig Wittgenstein and dominates critical theory to this day. Although today's critics have ventured beyond Chekhov's traditional labels as *realist* and *symbolist*, the playwright's affinities with late-twentieth-century theoretical approaches deepen the significance of those terms. By examining *Three Sisters* through a structuralist/poststructuralist lens, one can dissolve misleading limits between masterful form building on the playwright's part and the deconstructive tendencies inherent in his analytical view.[13] It is nothing new to use art to critique cultural norms and values. Yet, Chekhov's emphasis on the power of verbal/visual discourse to mediate human experience and his attention to related delicacies of human perception and interaction are noteworthy. His sense of the fluidity and flexibility of the self, situated in society, seems to surpass even Michel Foucault's notion of socially constructed identity.

The playwright's own approach to the craft of drama combines formulaic recipes for success and survival, for control, and for minimalist revelation that depend upon minute attention to emotional valences and a rejection of the humanistic notion of integrated selfhood. As a practicing physician self-trained as well in the burgeoning fields of psychology and sociology, he sees the human condition as utterly mediated through contextualized, perceptual experience and thus contingent on both embodied activity and intellectual interpretation.[14] People know the world as they know each other's bodily spaces, as Sara Ahmed has elaborated, through the senses: sight, sound, smell, taste, and touch. They struggle, above all, to know themselves as beings in time. Yet, they necessarily experience a disconnect between sense impressions and the meanings attributed to them due to their respective subject positions, the fallibility of the language systems they inhabit, their lack of engagement with the present moment, and their inability to fully understand their own being. According to the poststructuralist theories Jameson describes and Chekhov anachronistically echoes, the self must be grasped as a construction.[15] Many of the characters enact this struggle for self understanding, especially Andrei and Chebutykin, as they squirm within restrictive categories such as husband, father, doctor that impose conceptual constructs on their identities. They confront others or the mirror itself, in search of a totalizing narrative of integrated selfhood, the red herring humanism Jameson rejects wholesale, in the name of poststructuralist/deconstructive theory. In a related way, one could argue that Chekhov acts as a poststructuralist when he dismantles the humanist illusion of intersubjectivity between Másha and Vershinin.[16] Despite the logical conclusions they arrive at together, that "no one will remember us," their union fades out with little resistance due to practical impediments.

Within the emotional landscapes Chekhov constructs and the mood he famously conjures, characters react as though reflecting the audience's own lived perceptions vis-à-vis the aesthetic space.[17] Chekhov holds up a mirror not to life but to the audience. As he wrote in his notebook, "Man will only become better when you make him see what he is like."[18] So, the playwright presents a slice of life in which only a rare viewer would miss seeing a reflection of his or her own dissolving self. The absurd and the understated coalesce, as one witnesses the Chebutykin's mild denial of the difference between peace and war, love and loneliness, life and death. In *Three Sisters*, Chekhov thus meditates on the inner machinations of the human psyche by foregrounding his characters' searching, circling thought processes as they struggle, despite limits of discourse, to understand the reality they inhabit. As Jameson has pointed out, in the early twentieth century, emotions and feelings come to exist as concrete experiences rather than as primary abstract knowledge, lending both an existential freshness and horror to aesthetic depictions.[19] Rather than align each character with a particular emotion, Chekhov exhibits distinctive personalities as they experience the range of sensations available to them, each in his or her own way. Másha's heights of romantic elation[20] hardly resemble Anfísa's joyous relief over securing shelter in her old age,[21] yet the commonality between these affective responses creates a patterning that solidifies the text and evades linguistic description. Consequently, objectified affective content, reified to a degree via aesthetic transformation, builds atmosphere and ultimately structures the play. Readers and viewers use this material not only in the semantic decoding of the work but also as expressive phenomena that resist easy interpretation. Functioning as surface grammar, the articulations of emotion that can be named and described, such as joy, fear, and anger, give way to a deeper affective level of experience that shares a physiological aspect but resists verbal/visual representation.[22]

Chekhov serves up a new beast on a deceptively familiar platter of domestic drama. He creates a carefully structured aesthetic sign out of ostensible themes as well as articulations of emotion ("I'm so happy today," "I'm feeling a little depressed"); phenomenal motifs (trees, birds, timepieces); behaviors (contradictory activities, conversational curiosities, and mood swings); affective content (sensations of anticipation, of regret); and repeating conversation topics (progress, work, marriage). In his 1889 "Advice to Playwrights," he instructs, "The more of a *mosaic* the work is the better."[23] The patterns of repetition and contrast that develop from these juxtaposed elements become as important as the webs of story line on which they hang. As Schmidt explains, in this play, as in *The Cherry Orchard*, "the actor's role is subordinate to the extraordinary dramaturgy that Chekhov invents."[24] Nevertheless, each character becomes a fascinating and roundly developed being due to the accuracy with which Chekhov interprets the life of the mind.

A transitional figure, Chekhov rejects the overt stylization of the melodrama of the well-made play, known for its exaggerated emotional content, and employs a more covert and intricate element of artifice. Yet his celebrated repudiation of established theatre calls for a return to it in a sense, to justify his own difference.[25] On the surface, one watches a standard middle-class family drama. The playwright eschews typical dramatic elements such as plot, dialogue, and character development, however, in favor of an organic, minimalist focus on the phenomena of everyday life, emotional valences, and existential preoccupations with problems of being in a rapidly changing world. Stock characters such as the fetching soldier and the buffoon experience subtle feelings reified as structural elements that repeat and modulate. Chekhov upsets the notion of theatre in order to deconstruct commonly held beliefs about family happiness, class structures, notions of progress and social cohesion, and other naturalized ideological phenomena. Binary divisions between good and bad dissolve as characters grapple with complex emotions and practical decisions.

Three Sisters capitalizes on the notion of defamliarization (*ostranenie*) that Viktor Shklovsky would describe in *Art as Technique* years later (1916/17). The playwright seems to subscribe anachronistically to Shklovsky's dictum that art forces people to notice and thereby rescues them from a robotic life of mindless repetition: "Habitualization devours works, clothes, furniture, one's wife, and the fear of war. . . . And art exists that one may recover the sensation of life; it exists to make one feel things, to make the stone *stony*."[26] Ludwig Wittgenstein reiterated this ontological fact in his *Philosophical Investigations* when he wrote, "The aspects of things that are most important for us are hidden because of their simplicity and familiarity. (One is unable to notice something—because it is always before one's eyes)."[27] Time and again in Chekhov's fiction and drama, life is rendered palpable by the process of estrangement, by presenting both the subject matter and the medium in unexpected ways.[28] As though to dramatize Shklovsky's scenario of habituated blindness, Chekhov's characters fail to fully experience the present moment as they live it. Instead, they long for an illusory *Moscow!* and lose themselves in chatter about fashion details and the salvation of work.

Chekhov succeeds in making the stone stony by defamiliarizing the material of language, sound, visible image, and gesture. Rather than attempting mirror-like mimesis, the playwright insists on the artificiality of the theatre; he foregrounds the dramatic device when he uses the stuff of comedy and tragedy, such as a marriage proposal, villainous threat, or suicide, but refuses to let events transpire in expected ways. He employs dialogue to befuddle and delay as much as to convey information or to move the plot along. As though to emphasize the artificiality or constructedness of three actors upon a stage, *Three Sisters* begins and ends with freeze-frame tableaux of the female siblings, at first dispersed across the living room but ultimately united on an outdoor bench. Thus, Chekhov's bracketing scenes emphasize the visual and signify a move toward greater solidarity and mutual understanding as any hope for progress wanes.

How risky to attempt steps away from realism's illusions within the deceptively familiar theatre of the everyday! Chekhov achieves the effects of the real not through Stanislavsky's tricks of convincing sound effects, animal noises, and train whistles but by foregrounding the materiality of the medium: language and people onstage, as emotive, self-searching beings. Instead of mimicking typical life events, he uses characters, events, and conversation to conjure the chaos and emotional conflict of actual life, in familiar modalities. He creates intricate structures and systems, yet metadiscursively questions the functionality of language, its capacity to represent the world, its pragmatic use-value in context, the arbitrariness of the signifier, and its role in necessarily imperfect representation and communication. Chekhov thus creates a highly literary, ART-ificial verbal/visual presentation by using language in unexpected, estranged ways. He acts as a proto-poststructuralist artist who manages to build structures even as he dismantles false binary distinctions between life and art, between literary and vernacular language, between highbrow and lowbrow art. He makes ordinary life itself literary with complex turns of phrase and with a recognition of the repeating patterns and predictable structures of our thoughts and behaviors. To transform ordinary subject matter into art, Chekhov insists upon the artificiality or literariness of the play itself and blurs the limit between aesthetic figure and the reality and culture in which it exists. Conversations swerve comically between misunderstandings and non sequiturs, yet forcefully negate Chebutykin's nihilistic quip, "What difference does it make?" with the exquisite delicacy of the quiet present moment. As a result of Chekhov's estranging devices, the dramatic genre seems distorted, but not in the direction one might expect, for it moves via abstraction closer to, not further from, life as experienced. Thus the realist core to Chekhov's so-called modernism affirms multivalent human experience through its dialectical strategy of evoking similarity and difference at once.[29]

The so-called absurd in Chekhov's work can be read as a breakdown of representation based on similitude and equivalence between real-world referents and their signifiers. The pervasive reiteration of comments, motifs, and mirrored gestures in *Three Sisters* asserts both similarity and difference at once. Abstraction emerges via this "conceptual coordination of incommensurabilities," in Jameson's words, be it sisters, sashes, or death wishes.[30] The play as sign becomes energized by formal tensions between items that can be simultaneously designated same or different or, in Susanne Langer's words, complements to space-tensions and space-resolutions.[31] The characters themselves experience fluctuating degrees of conflict and calm as they probe questions and challenges of human existence. Rather than functioning mimetically, the play thus engages formal and intellectual dimensions that allow it to be representational of life's energies without being necessarily pictorial.[32] Furthermore, the language of the play establishes its own logic, and accordingly, words, gestures, and affective elements find their meaning in context embedded within a cultural moment that shifts with the reader/viewer. Rather than building empirically from facts to logical conclusions, the repetition of phrases, actions, and affective expressions creates confusion. These rhythms constitute a patterning toward abstraction that fosters dialectical tension between parts and wholes, between verbal/visual/aural elements and the dramatic text as culturally embedded object. As cocreator of potential meanings, Chekhov depends upon the audience, the reader/viewer as scripter, to transmit the aesthetic event from its virtual space to the historical moment in which they experience it.[33] In these ways, Chekhov's estranged orientation toward the aesthetic project further resonates with poststructuralist and present-day aesthetic theories.

Chekhov paints a world peopled with bodies attempting to come to terms with its ambiguities in a new language wrought in unfamiliar visual and verbal forms that destabilize representation itself. To take the title, for example, the three sisters share a familial designation, swim in sibling similitude as sisters, but could not be more different from one another. Even their designated dress in blue, black, and white emphasizes this. In Chekhov's antiempiricist realm, such neat categories do not lead to comforting distinctions or greater clarity. Jameson develops an explanation, linked closely to Foucault's, of the way similarity and difference can be seen to coexist to the degree that representations conceived on the order of resemblance between object (e.g., word; category) and referent must fail. As Foucault writes and Jameson quotes, "Similitude is no longer the form of knowledge but rather the occasion of error."[34] Chekhov's clever word play in which one word can designate multiple referents, and his echoing structural repetitions, signal that he thinks along similar lines. Since communication falters and characters are unable to read the signs of their world consistently, they, like the audience, become stymied by the play-world as verbal/visual sign. Chekhov toys with the negation of meaning even as he insists on the value of the present moment.

Also in the manner of a poststructuralist, Chekhov challenges scientific reasoning and asserts the unreliability of observational data. Instead of constructing empirical arguments, he undertakes a dialectical approach that plays the possibilities of reference. Referring to the flight of birds, Másha insists, "But there has to be some meaning in it," to which Tuzenbach retorts, "Meaning? Look out the window: it's snowing. Is there any meaning in that?"[35] Here, structures and themes that seem authentic to both phenomenological and metaphysical experience manifest onstage, often in terms of difference and with a twentieth-century eye to discursive inquiry and symbolic analysis. Any *truths* the characters and audience may locate in this culturally mediated space remain ultimately allusive. Instead, the characters' quest for comprehension mimics that of the audience for whom the initial experience of the play includes numerous interpretive errors and aporias that may persist when the full contexture unfolds. Therefore, the complete meaning of the play as representation comes to them by way of mistaken first encounters and semantic ambiguities as they gather information progressively to build contexture that will mediate meanings.[36]

Conventional structures of motif, foreshadowing, intertextual reference, and mirrored events weave a tight fabric upon which Chekhov makes his more experimental strokes. Certain phenomenal objects punctuate the stage with such frequency that they create a sense of regularity. Trees, birds, and timepieces, for example, evoke similarity and difference each time they appear or sound. While the characters hesitate to deal with future practicalities, the text itself nearly obsesses over events to come, via foreshadowing. Solyony seems most prescient of all, as he tells Tuzenbach outright that he will shoot his head off, or Irina that he will tolerate "no happy rivals."[37] Both events do, indeed, come to pass—Solyony kills Irina's fiancé the day before their wedding—yet this melodrama transforms stylistically in a way that says more about human sexuality and relationship than it furthers the plot. Tuzenbach's avowed desire to "sacrifice [his] life" for Irina, foreshadows his own arguably suicidal demise.[38] When Másha recalls Vershínin as "the love-sick major," she predicts their own romance to come.[39] Likewise, the early rumors that Natasha is to marry Protopópov turn out to be true with a twist: They carry on a glaringly obvious adulterous affair that few notice later on. Each of these logical structures, meanings, and events, which reflect across lines of verbal prediction and depicted action, helps constitute the virtual reality of the play and contributes to the systematized import of the art-sign as a whole.

Despite the structural logic of the text, Chekhov orchestrates a remarkable sense of spontaneous semichaos that corresponds to his deconstruction of causality, progress, and logic. Describing the nature of Absurdist theatre, Esslin comments on this typical effect of a heterogeneous genre, "Real randomness would be totally meaningless, it was merely the *appearance* of randomness and triviality that had to be evoked by creating a structure of which every element contributed to the production of meaning."[40] The apparent discontinuities and intentional confusion that Chekhov creates serve to involve the audience in the process of analysis and interpretation, including the production of meaning-making, alongside characters engaged in the same activity. A lapse in attention or a look away, and all could collapse. According to Murray Krieger, the integrity of a literary work depends on an understanding of the work's potential destruction: "Built into the mystical dialect of organicism, with its magical imposition of unity, is a negative thrust that would explode it."[41] Howard Moss's discussion of *Three Sisters* delineates networks of "interlocking triangles" to form a solid framework against which he sets up similar dialectics.[42] For example, Moss describes the climactic third act according to familiar schemas of difference: "The sense of danger, a hairsbreadth away from the cozy, becomes actual in the fire of Act 3."[43] In addition, the sisterly triumvirate, Ólga, Másha, and Irina, paralyzed due to gender-based social restrictions and psychological circumstances, holds the play together.

In similar fashion, vestiges of plot dissolve and recombine as well. Instead of a storyline that propels the action forward with suspense and mystery, one regards a patchwork of episodes in the everyday life of a family and their associates. Rather than a hero to win hearts or capture imaginations, a multiplicity of flawed protagonists intersect visually and verbally in a cohesive structure of meaning that none of them seems able to understand. For this constellation of characters tends to renounce the present, focusing rather on the past and the future as though roped in by imagined narratives or myths that prove illusory. Even the repeated cry, "To Moscow!" becomes a conceptualization, an illusory totality cut off as a tiny story-seed within the play. With this repeated wish, Jameson would argue, the past is created as an idealized and nostalgic vision by way of its "energetic separation from the present" in an act of dissociation.[44] Isolated as a totality, the sisters' urge to return to a moment lost in time and space cuts them off from the "living moment in the continuum" reflected onstage.[45] As this motif punctuates the surface of the play, it pulls the parties involved and the following audience both backward in time and forward to a utopian future.[46] The "To Moscow!" refrain becomes a figure of resistance to consolation as well, as Howard might argue. The three daughters use this epithet as a means of escape, not to do the work of mourning for the lost parents who lived there or their own lost youths. Their evident melancholy arises from this cyclical return to an ephemeral moment reified in language.

Chekhov thus studied the forms of artistic expression as well as the structures of the human heart contextualized within a cultural moment. The playwright connected with his theatre public on the levels of private anguish and collective unrest as a burgeoning middle class migrated from rural areas to city centers. Written the same year Sigmund Freud published *The Interpretation of Dreams* (1900), this play features unconscious impulse and psychic conflict as painterly strokes that repeat and vary dialectically. Each character reacts to some stock event, such as Másha's kiss or Anfísa's geriatric panic, in a way that ties in with the play's concerns with social and political themes, including marriage, progress, and class structures in upheaval.[47] By extension, these isolated expressions comment on the lack of freedom in a small, provincial town. Másha's forbidden extramarital love and the complete disenfranchisement of the aged, unmarried servant Anfísa demonstrate the plight of women Chekhov knew well as a traveling doctor in similar regions. Rather than taking collective or public action, Chekhov's deeply internalized characters remain at the level of the isolated individual, as each reveals him/herself less by actions or conversation than by ongoing self-analysis.[48]

Even the lone outsider-instigators of action in the play, Solyony and Natasha, exhibit their easily diagnosable neurotic symptoms with differing levels of insight linked to specific ideological concerns and structural patterns of verbal and affective gestures.[49] Solyony's disordered personality borders on a psychotic break, so closely does he identify with the Romantic poet Lérmontov. His confession to Tuzenbach of social unease and his unexpected profession of love to Irina foil the violent explosions over trivial topics or simple misunderstandings that make him memorable.[50] His sarcastic disparagement of philosophy and maternal sentimentality display his contradictions, as he seems to proffer rationality and truth in the face of cultural instability and his own impassioned heart.[51] He and Chebutykin enact a ridiculous dispute over the descriptions of *chekhartmá* and *cheremshá* when they do not seem to notice that they are discussing two different dishes designated by different names.[52] Thus, his obsession with distinctions based on facts about an onion dish (misunderstood as a plate of meat) or the number of Moscow universities contrasts with the "what difference does it make?" refrain that crescendos as the play unfolds.[53] The tyrannical, narcissistic Natasha, on the other hand, forsakes her modest roots to align herself through marriage to the unstable yet comfortable upper middle class. These two characters stand out from the others not only because of their consistent engagement with the present moment but also for the corollary to this orientation: a lack of ennui.

Chekhov's arguably existentialist approach to his assembly of atomized characters allows for their sense of isolation as they search for meaning and possibility in their lives. Again, the work appears precocious, activating ideas that gained popularity in the mid-nineteenth century but became fundamental to mid-twentieth and twenty-first-century theatre and its publics. Svetlana Evdokimova has identified Chekhov's thematic emphasis on fully conscious being, a state that requires more than logic to attain and thus evokes the intuition Langer emphasizes in perceptual experience. Evdokimova critiques *Three*

Sisters in terms of twentieth-century existential philosophy as it "engage[s] philosophical ideas and inquiries that placed human existence or the *conditio humana* at the center of attention." She also notes the self-reflexivity of the characters' search for meaning in their own lives and links Chekhov's approach to Heidegger's ideas of the "unfolding of being in its temporality."[54] As the time of the play slowly unfolds, so does the characters' metatemporal discussion of their place in the grand scheme.

Aside from clocks and seasonal migrations, time functions thematically in additional, abstracted ways. Upon their first meeting, in act 1, Vershínin and Másha agree:

> VERSHÍNIN: True. No one will remember us. That's fate, there's nothing you can do about it. Things that seem important to us, serious and significant things—the time will come when they'll all be forgotten—or they won't seem so important anymore. (*Pause*) And the interesting thing is, there's no way we can guess what will be considered important and serious, and what will be considered petty and silly.[55]

While the audience sees little in the way of progress, events that lead to change or impact on character development, the personas remain fascinated and perplexed by their own lives that transpire according to a Bergsonian sense of experiential time.[56] Boris Zingerman has gone so far as to claim that "drama in Chekhov is to be found not so much in the event but rather in time, in that which takes place between the events."[57] Time functions as the negation of action in Zingerman's view but becomes a positive and arguably spatial value in the play-sign's field of action, an element both formally and technically concrete that articulates the web of affective and physical events.

The radical isolation of these characters reflects in their lack of engagement with the present moment until love yanks them to attention. In a fit of pique, Másha quotes Gogol, "Life is a bore."[58] By evoking Gogol even obliquely, she welcomes into Chekhov's work the main concerns of Gogol's oeuvre, including the challenge to overcome ennui and to find value and knowledge in minor events. Once Vershínin's attraction to her is made known, Másha changes her tune. As a social construct, love, like their philosophizing, becomes a stay against the banality of everyday life rather than a transcendental ideal. In short stories such as "About Love," Chekhov also revels in the ironies of attraction, the ebb and flow of desire, and, most notably, love's divorce from logic: "I realized that when you love someone, your reasoning about that love should be based on what is supreme, on what is more important than happiness or unhappiness, sin or virtue, in the way that they are usually understood, otherwise it is not worth reasoning at all."[59] Chekhov's defamiliarization of the play genre itself parallels in the sublime illogic that estranges love and its object in many of his stories. He treats the mysterious phenomena of love in a way that feels authentic in its staged representations but simultaneously deconstructs ideologies or grand narratives, with his wry look at illusions of individuality and his shift of focus to social praxis.

For example, Chekhov satirizes the institution of marriage as antithetical to love's vicissitudes when he presents the wedded state as a tease and a tyranny rather than a smooth passage to happiness. Disappointed husbands Vershínin and Andrei denounce their bonds.[60] Kulygin claims contentment but entertains other possibilities, imagining unions with both Ólga and Irina.[61] Marriage never aligns with love in the play, at least not for long. In a lucid moment, Chebutykin counsels Andrei to drop everything and run from family life while he still can.[62] Yet, the sometimes-cynical doctor nests comfortably in the arms of the Prózorov children. Having worshipped their mother, he may have fathered one or two, as Másha comes to suspect toward the play's end. Indeed, this drama is full of love, from the familial, to the platonic, to the sexual. Varied statements that defamiliarize and denounce the marital institution only foil the more convincing, fluctuating instances of love in its many forms: Chebutykin's paternal solicitude; the sisters' devotion to each other; Fedotik's playful adoration of Irina; Másha's passion for Vershínin, and his for her.

The characters fail to achieve fully conscious being, only to end up isolated and perplexed due to a lack of perspective on their chaotic environment. Chekhov seems to predict as well the Derridean/Jamesean emphasis on an outside space from which to achieve the requisite perspective to create a *totalizing narrative* and project a sense of order on the environment (or cultural moment).[63] Various characters attempt to define some sense of logic or order on the world and events. But just as often, one finds metadiscursive commentary on this very human impulse. For instance, the highly self-reflexive text betrays a certain fascination with the theme of coherence. Working dialectically from wholes to parts, the playwright dismantles supposedly logical thinking. Kulygin, the wise-fool, delivers Chekhov's metadiscursive aesthetic message:

> When things lose their form, they lose their identity—and in our daily lives it is precisely the same. (*Puts his arm around Másha's waist and laughs*) Másha loves me. My wife loves me. And the window drapes should be stored with the rugs.[64]

Irony lies in Chekhov's subtlety, his simultaneous celebration and rejection of the very notion Kulygin proffers via his laughable pedantry. Másha doesn't love Kulygin, and his statements equate his wife with the banalities of arbitrary domestic protocol. By merging form and identity, Kulygin parrots the idea that the manner by which people intuitively understand the world depends on form, on metaphors we live by, to conjure Lakoff and Johnson.[65] This intellectual act of conceptualizing concrete and abstract phenomena determines their being for us but also reveals something about our own identity. Through juxtaposition, Kulygin conceptualizes his wife as a household object.

In contrast, Konstantin Treplev's call for new forms in *The Seagull*, the first of Chekhov's major plays, refers more specifically and metadiscursively to Chekhov's challenge to the well-made play. His self-reflexive play within a play signals the work's hermeneutical attention to its own workings and sets up a dialectic between not only old and new forms (embodied by mother and son) but also simultaneously layered realities: "The contemporary theater is nothing but the same old thing, the same old conventions. The curtain goes up, those bright lights come on, and you have a room with three walls!. . . The high priests of that sacred art will demonstrate for you how people eat, drink, love, walk, wear their coats! From those sad little pictures and words, they try to squeeze a moral. . . . We need new forms!"[66] Within the illusion of *The Seagull* lies the illusory reality of the unnamed play Treplev composes and directs in *The Seagull*'s virtual time. The minimalist stage, "real theater," in his words, comprises "a curtain, two wings, and an open playing space. No scenery."[67] He calls emphatically for "new forms or nothing," such that form itself aligns with reality, and both stand opposite the void. Illusion and world-as-illusion become indistinguishable.[68]

When the action of *The Seagull* develops and Treplev loses hope for both love and his revolutionary art, his vision displays the void of the future, as though reality can be nihilistically equated with nothingness in a Beckettean sense, and (far more radically) *shown* onstage: "Then show us that nothing."[69] For Nina, the dead seagull Treplev presents to her constitutes a dead signifier without referent, just as he becomes a dead body whose referent (life-project or identity) remains unfinished and unknowable. The reification of language, coarsely depicted in the bird corpse/play/life merger, and the formal abstraction that emerges from this collocation both figure as features of early-twentieth-century modernist tropes.[70] This play may end with the obliteration of Treplev's suicide, but Chekhov goes on to achieve the new forms he sought. As though in answer to Treplev's bold call, *Three Sisters* delivers radical content in more subtle ways through a multiplicity of protagonists.

In *Three Sisters*, where many theatregoers have joked that nothing happens, Chekhov appears to have achieved the goals Treplev set for himself as a young and eager playwright. As a new writer for the stage, Treplev envisions a total theatre complete with a sulfur smell, years before Federico Garcia Lorca's rural tragedies.[71] In *Three Sisters*, when the titular sisters project themselves into a "To Moscow!" mirage, they actually lurch into a void in the play/text, much the way Treplev's stage, perched on the lakeside, comes to ruin by *The Seagull*'s end. The trick is, of course, that much does indeed transpire, visually, linguistically, and affectively on both stages, real and illusory. Chekhov, through his protagonist Treplev, demands new modes of representation for contemporary life, and uses Treplev to highlight aspects of human life that may not be apparent to the eye.

In Chekhov's *The Seagull* and *Three Sisters*, those who cannot achieve adequate perspective on the present moment, who prefer illusions of a utopian past or future instead, end up either failing to recognize themselves or longing for self-annihilation. The drunken Doctor mistakes his reflection in the mirror and Irina questions the irritable woman she has become at her unfulfilling job.[72] Both characters move from such moments of disorientation to more extreme states of potential nonexistence. Chebutykin exclaims, "Oh, I wish I didn't exist!" and the bright, young Irina states, "I don't know why I still exist, I should have killed myself long ago."[73] Yana Hashamova has argued that the playwright "turned from the word to silence as a means of expressing the problems of existence, paying particular attention to the problem of alienation and self-alienation."[74] Andrei bares his soul before Ferapont, who fails to hear him, so that his most poignant moment of self-awareness tumbles into the abyss of noncommunication.[75] Thus, thematic elements, including the passage of time, ontological questions, and a sense of alienation that will fuel the characters' emotional responses, structure the text as formal repetitions and aporia.

From a twenty-first-century perspective, the play's plentiful intertextual borrowings signal a remarkably familiar conversation on origins and semantics in context. Literary historiographers have fully annotated quotes that solidify the text as a collage of appropriations set in a precise Slavic European cultural moment.[76] Másha quotes the opening of Pushkin's poem *Ruslan and Liudmilla*, and Solyony references an Ivan Krylov fable, "He didn't catch his breath before the bear jumped on him," translated by Schmidt as, "Said the dog to the flea, don't jump on me."[77] Prescient Solyony then goes on to quote his beloved model Lérmontov, "But every rebel seeks a storm, as if a storm will bring him peace."[78] Vershínin's lines from Tchaikovsky's opera *Eugene Onegin*, "Love is appropriate at any age, its delights are beneficent,"[79] allow Chekhov to layer in yet another ironic love theme according to a strategy of overt if disjointed intertextual reference that will become a staple of so-called high modernism and a (shifting) foundation for the theoretical deconstruction of origin as idea.

Along with the conventions of repeating motifs, foreshadowing, and literary appropriation, Chekhov mirrors events, again working with a structure of similarity and difference, original and permutation, that has become a fundamental of poststructuralist analysis. For example, in the final scene, Natasha recapitulates early moments of the play when she evokes the tree motif, comments on Irina's fashion faux pas of an unbecoming belt, displaces occupants from their bedrooms, expresses her surprising depths of mother-love to the motherless/childless sisters, and throws another violent tantrum, this time over a fork left in the garden. Thus, Chekhov employs conventional cyclic structure to draw his play's conclusion back to the beginning so that origin, even of the play itself, may become confused with (non)resolution. Instead of perfectly mirrored repetitions, contingent situations (with striking similarity between events) conjure an insistence on difference. Jameson describes the way the fetish of the *new* in the many narratives of modernism gives way, with poststructuralism, to a fetish of difference upon which deconstruction builds its palace.[80] Difference emerges necessarily alongside the new with Chekhov's proto-poststructuralist approach, and he reflects these ruptures and discontinuities within the fabric of his plays.

Chekhov's new mode of writing employs basic elements of drama, including dialogue, in ways that necessarily signal novelty through their unexpected effects. Through enacted conversations, he leads his audience into absurdist realms that rub multiple meanings against each other. For example, he refashions dramatic dialogue to enact difference between purpose and playfulness, between intended and received meanings. Paradoxically, the estranged effects he employs convincingly mimic lived experience. Conversation often serves to isolate rather than connect characters, emphasizing the sense of modernist alienation and a fragmented psyche.[81] As Irving Deer has observed, often the dialogue in Chekhov's plays rambles on, full of seemingly disconnected, irrelevant commentary: "Conventionally, speech in drama is a device for simultaneous two-way communication: the characters talk directly with each other and at the same time they talk indirectly to the audience. But in Chekhov, these two functions of dialogue seem often separated. The characters seem to be talking to themselves in a daze primarily for the purpose of giving the audience direct exposition."[82] For example, speech creates separation rather than solidarity when Andrei bares his soul, rehearsing his own existential crisis in act 2 (discussed previously), and again in act 4.[83] In both cases, Andrei's near-deaf interlocutor Ferapónt misses the entire message. In a related way, Chebutykin's act 3 soliloquy of self-revelation delivered drunkenly to his own reflection in the mirror demonstrates language in the service of articulating thought rather than facilitating communication.[84] Nevertheless, these seemingly solipsistic utterances communicate important information to the audience, as they paint in aspects of character and deliver affective content impossible to render otherwise.

Another common Chekhovian dialogic technique involves juxtaposing discontinuous conversations for absurd or comic effects. In these instances, the playwright's mosaic of fragmentary statements produces the cohesive sense of a shadowy, quasinarrative presence that conveys irony.

ÓLGA: This morning I woke up and realized it was springtime, everything was so bright, I felt such a wave of happiness inside me, and I wanted so much to go back home.
CHEBUTYKIN [to Tuzenbach]: The hell you say!
TUZENBACH: You're right, it's all a lot of nonsense.[85]

Moments later, a telling juxtaposition contributes cynically to one of the play's main themes:

ÓLGA: I think if I'd gotten married and could stay home all day long, that would be better somehow. (*Pause*) I would have loved my husband.
TUZENBACH [to Solyony]: Nothing you say makes any sense.[86]

In this second example, the use of a pause indicates Chekhov's minute attention to rhythm. This empty space functions as well as a positive signifier, if only via the absence of sound. Emotional import rests in the prescribed void, as Chekhov represents thought by the very absence of language, depending on Ólga's simple presence onstage. While any artist working in the dramatic form necessarily considers effects of the multivalent visual/verbal activity (except in the case of miming), this artist capitalizes on the effects of such openings in a way that predicts techniques developed by twentieth- and twenty-first-century dramatists from Samuel Beckett to Suzan-Lori Parks.

Talk serves as a fundamental human activity in the play, and rarely in the service of effective communication; instead, it often functions as a gateway to the imagination, in the productive forms of hypothesis and reflection. In addition, monologue and dialogue become the platforms for many of Chekhov's metadiscursive observations within the play. Vershínin manages to inhabit the present moment via the very activity of speech: "Let's make up things. For instance, let's talk about what life will be like after we're gone, say in two hundred or three hundred years."[87] The hyper-self-conscious characters tend to comment reflexively on topics of expression and communication, even as they fumble to get the words out. "Arguing is a bore," whines the dejected Tuzenbach.[88] Vershínin makes a Nietzschean assault on truth: "Remember the discoveries of

Copernicus, or let's say, Columbus, how they seemed silly and unnecessary at first, while a lot of nonsense was propounded as eternal truth? So in time perhaps this life of ours, the one we're so proud of, will seem strange, stupid, messy, perhaps even sinful."[89] Vershínin's act 3 reprieve of the theme, "they'll laugh, and the things we do today will seem strange and complicated and impractical," now contextualized in a moment of despair over his daughters' future, seems no longer even mildly amusing but holds hints of tragedy.[90] When Solyony observes metadiscursively, "This is the first time I've ever talked about my love for you," he suggests that simply articulating his emotions in words will not change Irina's position.[91]

The self-reflexive quality of dialogue invites further investigation into the way the real and the literary intersect in terms of representation and expression. However familiar Chekhov's staged events appear, they never constitute a perfect reproduction of the real. Instead, the playwright constructs an illusion of contemporary life with such attention to patterning gestures, phrases, and affective content that these aspects appear more visible or *foregrounded* once the contexture of the play unfolds in its entirety.[92] In reference to Ibsen, Toril Moi makes a convincing case for the meta-discursive qualities of late-nineteenth-century realist drama when she argues against any "fundamental opposition between realism and metatheatrical reflection, between theatre as illusion and representation, and theater as investigation of theater." Following Jameson, she explains, "realism is perfectly compatible with aesthetic self-consciousness."[93] Chekhov's experiments with dialogue, with the display of misunderstanding and use of nonsense words, for example, allow him to participate in the variety of modernism Jameson identifies in terms of "the reification of language and the emergence of formal abstractions."[94] Again like a poststructuralist, Chekhov plays with meanings and playfully challenges social constructs when he says he's not a dramatist and calls his beloved Ibsen no dramatist either.[95]

In Chekhov's four major plays, the absurd and nonsensical elements depend upon a rational-intuitive background. Chekhov may have had much to say to Wittgenstein on his theory of the *way* particular sentences convey meaning beyond the implications of surface grammar. The bid for a cup of tea, for example, may signify anything from desire for comfort to a declaration of love, depending on context.[96] Form and ground both shatter as in an analytic Cubist painting, and shadowy emphasis appears with a sense of randomness in the intersecting realms. Similarly, Chekhov achieves an all-over effect of randomness or consistent texturing within his four discrete acts. In act 3, especially, anxiety courses through like a character and manifests against a backdrop of petty troubles and an offstage disaster. This way, the affective spaces around the iconic forms—sister, tree, dinner table—start to function on an equal plane with the objects.

In this climactic third act, Chekhov dispenses with plastic representations of the physical crisis and signifies the fire abstractly with reddened windows and the clang of fire alarms and passing engines. Color and sound evoke destruction in arguably naturalistic, even iconic, ways but with such a minimalist touch that the signified fire (but also panic, loss, defeat, etc.) becomes highly abstracted. Fire is red in some states, and pumper trucks do sound that way, yet this dramatic artist capitalizes, as expected, on the effect of saying less. As with Gotthold Lessing's theory of the pregnant moment, the evocation of catastrophe at the expense of naturalistic portrayal creates the most powerful effect and invites the reader/viewer/scripter's imagination.[97] Consequently, the audience does not see the ragged victims amid the flames nor Vershínin's panicked daughters but rather witnesses Ólga's empathy for them and Versínin's anguish over his offspring's imagined future. Thus, Chekhov's objectification of affective content, achieved by building intense atmosphere, constitutes an important dimension of abstraction in the play. Whereas *emotion* suggests a connection to descriptive narrative (historically contextualized as it must be within culture), *affect* does not necessarily subscribe to narrative and thus stands apart from culture or ideology. According to Brian Massumi, affect defies representation "prior to an indexed articulated referent. Affect describes an energetics that does not necessarily emerge at the level of signification."[98] While Chekhov can engineer the illusion of fiery catastrophe onstage, the added dimension of affective atmosphere emerges from the verbal/visual structures of the sign.

The thematic rejection of rationality and logic, along with the dissonant structure of negations, creates an alternative culture within the play. The absurdity of Chebutykin's philosophical obliterations provides a backdrop against which the characters and themes contend. While Andrei, Másha, Tuzenbach, Solyony,[99] and others echo the line that so clearly belongs to the Doctor—what difference does it make?—the text itself resists him by affirming the solidarity of the three sisters, true if fleeting love, and the value of emotional life.[100] With supreme irony, Chebutykin questions existence itself at the same moment that he demands his companions' attention to the truth: "Natasha's having a little affair with Protopópov, but you can't see that."[101] Natasha's blatant violation of a weak social code (fidelity) hardly harms her upward trajectory. For others, a failure to *see* serves as a key corollary to the inability to *act* and thus thrive within the culture of the play.

The absurd plays out as well in the characters' blindness to the present moment, leading to acts of nonsensical behavior in Freudian terms of repression, displacement, and traumatic returns. When Vershínin returns to his suicidal wife, for example, Másha redirects her fury toward the innocent servant Anfísa and Chebutykin, the two surrogate parental figures in the play.[102] A more existential absurdity allows for Vershínin's earlier Zen moment in which he sorrows over our inability to appreciate the flight of birds unless we are in prison, deprived of them to the extent that we crave their presence.[103] Recapitulating this emphasis on contextualized meaning or constructed experience in other terms, he tells Másha, "Once you're actually living in Moscow you won't notice it anymore either."[104] Chekhov here explicitly predicts Shklovsky's revolutionary call of the renewal of human perceptual experience via the social function for art that radically deconstructs the art/life divide.

Due to Chekhov's strategies of newness, it may take a while to understand the whole of *Three Sisters*, to see the way textures of feeling and the rhythms of repeating sounds and gestures form a unified work. Rather than reflect our own reality back to us, he creates so complete an illusion of such kinship, that one can hardly look away. Chekhov manages to conjure an affective complex via his extraordinary combination of not only thematic content and depicted (in) activity, but by way of his rhetorical strategies of composition and linguistic performance. As he works with units of human perceptual experience and maintains focus on flawed human attempts to communicate, he presents deeply alienated characters cut off from each other and from their own connection to the present moment. The boundaries of the play weaken as one hears lines layered in from Pushkin poems and pop songs, newspaper snatches, and recipes, in a mash-up of what mattered then, in 1900, when the playwright, wracked with the tuberculosis that would kill him, threw a world upon the stage and found his beauty there.

Chekhov's *Three Sisters* demonstrates the "flawed narrative" of a break between realism and modernism, or two theoretical categories that each crumble under closer inspection.[105] The play also destabilizes distinctions between structuralist and poststructuralist modes of analysis that focus on the vagaries of linguistic expression and semantic interpretation without or with cultural implications. Like a structuralist, Chekhov foregrounds his media, attends to the effects of unfolding contexture, and conceives an intricate form such that his play functions as an interlocking sign system. Characters, comments, affects, and events combine into an elaborate structure. Like a poststructuralist, however, his delight seems to come from the destabilization of meaning, from the play of signifiers, birds, clocks, kisses, cut free from their accustomed referents. He goes beyond the descriptive tendencies of the structuralist approach, to actively critique the deployment of linguistic material at a precise historical and cultural moment that varies with the audience/scripter. The playwright founds no new knowledge on phenomenological experience or systemic structures of thought. Even the savvy Vershinin finds no resolution; even Tuzenbach's work-dream falls like a brick. Yet, Chekhov's profound discoveries in new horizons for realist illusion, or the artifice of a convincing depiction of human perceptual experience, continue to inform new writing today. One sees Chekhov playing the dynamics of similitude and difference like a deconstructionist. Through his characters, he demonstrates dialectical differentiation between utterances and their interpretation, between flashes of self-knowledge and the dissolving sense of self, known only through imperfect representations. He even delves into in-between spaces between situated bodies and their affective experiences in ways still being theorized by today's critics, such as Sara Ahmed.

Chekhov's legacy continues to inspire artists and inform new writing. The realist formulations he engendered within the multivalent modernisms of his artistic world still open possibilities for novel modes of verbally and visually signifying the human experience. Chekhov's plays enjoy many adaptations on the contemporary stage, from Mustapha Matura's *Trinidad Sisters* (1988) to Timberlake Wertenbaker's *The Break of Day* (1995).[106] These productions give renewed life to his works and update his innovative style. As Linda Hutcheon insists, adaptation is "a derivation that is not derivative—a work that is second without being secondary."[107] Historical distance lends a new perspective as theatre publics continue to piece together his ever-intriguing forms, his depicted situations of *modernity*, paradoxically *realist* in their very estrangement of human existence, and the world itself. Chekhov presents a coherent image of life, one that convinces by way of its very confusions, that sets three searching sisters back on their bench and engenders new writings to come.

Notes

1. See Laurence Senelick, *The Complete Plays: Anton Chekhov* (New York: Norton, 2006), xviii; Philip Callow, *Chekhov: The Hidden Ground* (Chicago: Ivan R. Dee, 1998), 341; George Steiner, *The Death of Tragedy* (Oxford: Oxford University Press, 1961), 300.
2. Raymond Williams, "Anton Chekhov," in *Anton Chekhov*, ed. Harold Bloom (Philadelphia, PA: Chelsea House, 1999), 45–55, 55.
3. Jacqueline George, conversation May 24, 2012.
4. In English-speaking countries, Chekhov productions are outnumbered only by Shakespeare plays. See Clayton, J. Douglas, and Yana Meerzon, eds., *Adapting Chekhov: The Text and its Mutations* (New York: Routledge, 2013), 23.
5. Fredric Jameson, *A Singular Modernity* (London: Verso, 2012), 55, 48.

6. For this conceptualization, I am indebted to W. Scott Howard's notion of *figural historicity*, described in relation to the elegies of Robert Hayden. See W. Scott Howard, "Resistance, Sacrifice, and Historicity in the Elegies of Robert Hayden," in *Reading the Middle Generation Anew: Culture, Community, and Form in Twentieth Century American Poetry*, ed. Eric Haralson (Iowa City: University of Iowa Press, 2006), 133–52.
7. Williams, "Anton Chekhov," 46.
8. Paul Schmidt, trans., *Anton Chekhov: Three Sisters* (New York: Theatre Communications Group, 1992), ix. All textual citations and the accents in characters' names refer to this translation, abbreviated *TS*.
9. Liesl Olson, *Modernism and the Ordinary* (London: Oxford University Press, 2009), 7, 3.
10. Martin Esslin, "Chekhov and the Modern Drama," in *Anton Chekhov*, ed. Harold Bloom (Philadelphia: Chelsea House, 1999), 139–50, 143.
11. Anton Chekhov, quoted in Esslin, "Chekhov and the Modern Drama," 141.
12. Robert B. Shimko and Sara Freeman, *Public Theatres and Theatre Publics* (Newcastle upon Tyne: Cambridge Scholars, 2012), 3.
13. Most clearly, one can find links to the poststructuralist projects of Michel Foucault, Roland Barthes, Julia Kristeva, and Jacques Lacan. I will limit my discussion to that of discourse-dependent social constructs (Foucault) and semiotics of the text (Barthes). Derridean deconstruction also comes into play with the courtship semantic indeterminacy and characters' limited perspective on their own situation. Looking forward, new materialist and critical affect theories (especially Brian Massumi, Lauren Berlant, Patricia Clough, Lawrence Grossberg) inform my approach to embodied perception and affect situated in a precise cultural moment. Although this is not the primary focus of this essay, I am particularly interested in how Chekhov's *Three Sisters* can be informed by a consideration of affect as autonomous from language, conscious perception, and emotion, as defined by Massumi and developed by Clough in her discussion of "The Affective Turn: Political Economy, Biomedia, and Bodies," in *The Affect Theory Reader* (Durham, NC: Duke University Press, 2010), 209.
14. According to Callow, in preparation for his visit to Sakhalin prison, Chekhov spent three months of study in sociology, geography, geology, and meteorology; see Callow, *Chekhov: The Hidden Ground*, 139.
15. Jameson, *A Singular Modernity*, 48; 54.
16. Ibid., 55.
17. As Fredric Jameson insists, this aesthetic space is not autonomous, as in the narratives of modernism, but firmly ensconced in the world as cultural object; Jameson, *A Singular Modernity*, 173.
18. Anton Chekhov, *Notebook of Anton Chekhov*, trans. S. S. Koteliansky and Leonard Woolf (New York: B. W. Huebsch, 1921), 94.
19. Fredric Jameson, *The Prison-House of Language: A Critical Account of Structuralism and Russian Formalism* (Princeton: Princeton University Press, 1972), 50.
20. *TS*, 69.
21. Ibid., 87.
22. While I will not focus on affective theory here, it is well to point out Brian Massumi's groundbreaking investigations and to claim that his emphasis on in-betweenness and constant fluctuation would have fascinated Chekhov. As Massumi explains, *affect*, equated with *intensity*, resists narrative or any other linguistic representation. Chekhov's

strokes of affective intensity that mark and modulate his discrete acts likewise resist any schema of empirical analysis. See Massumi, "The Autonomy of Affect," *Cultural Critique* 31, *The Politics of Systems and Environments, Part II*, (1995): 83–109, 88. Because affect "emerges out of muddy, unmediated relatedness and not some dialectical reconciliation of oppositional elements or primary units," according to Gregory Seigworth and Melissa Gregg, it has helped displace structuralism and poststructualism from the theoretical limelight ("An Inventory of Shimmers," *The Affect Theory Reader* [Durham, NC: Duke University Press, 2010], 1–25, 4–5). Perhaps my proto-poststructuralist claim is too modest indeed, and Chekhov pushes beyond even deconstructive treatises to the "not yet of never-quite-knowing" that affect theory embraces (ibid., 9).

23. Anton Chekhov, "Advice to Playwrights" [1889], in *Playwrights on Playwriting: The Meaning and Making of Modern Drama from Ibsen to Ionesco*, ed. Toby Cole, 23–29 (New York: Hill and Wang, 1960), 24. Italics mine.
24. *TS*, ix.
25. See Jameson, *A Singular Modernity*, 6.
26. Viktor Shklovsky, "Art as Technique," *Russian Formalist Criticism: Four Essays*, trans. Lee T. Lemon and Marion J. Reis, 5–22 (Lincoln: University of Nebraska Press, [1917] 1965), 4.
27. Ludwig Wittgenstein, *Philosophical Investigations*, 3rd ed., trans. G. E. M. Anscombe #129 (Englewood Cliffs: Prentice Hall, 1973), 50e; quoted in Liesl Olson, *Modernism and the Ordinary* (London: Oxford University Press, 2009), epigraph.
28. Using Shklovsky's and Wittgenstein's ideas, Liesl Olson makes the important observation that the ordinariness of modernism resists the very defamiliarization that seems to make it work. As she explains, "The representation of the ordinary *as* ordinary counterbalances the understanding of it as something that demands aesthetic defamiliarization" (5). Shklovsky's focus on perceptual experience and on the way humans make sense of the world alerts us to the paradoxical way art of this period can both engage and resist ordinary experience and circumstances.
29. Jameson identifies the realist core within modernism's supposed break or rupture with nineteenth-century realism, a "flawed narrative" (*A Singular Modernity*, 120–122). The "obscurity" and "incomprehensibility" (i.e., the absurd) moments in *Three Sisters* depend on expectations of verisimilitude according to established modes of illusion.
30. Jameson, *A Singular Modernity*, 64.
31. Susanne Langer, *Feeling and Form* (New York: Scribner's, 1953), 371. Barbara Hernstein-Smith would rather locate these tensions in the reader-viewer; see Barbara Hernstein-Smith, *Poetic Closure: A Study of How Poems End* (Chicago: University of Chicago Press, 1968), 3.
32. Arthur Danto has described the project of post-Wittgenstein semantics in just this way in *The Transfiguration of the Commonplace: A Philosophy of Art* (Cambridge, MA: Harvard University Press, 1981), 82.
33. Susanne Langer describes the virtual space of the aesthetic work, as a relatively autonomous field of investigation (divided yet connected to the space in which we live and act); see Langer, *Feeling and Form*, 72. Fredric Jameson, on the other hand, will vehemently warn against the "utopian" and misguided tendencies of theories of (the multiple) modernisms to cut the work free from the cultural moment in which it exists, as did such misguided critics as Clement Greenberg. Jameson, *A Singular Modernity*, 161.
34. Michel Foucault, *Les Mots et les Choses* (Paris: Éditions Gallimard, 1966), 62; Michel

Foucault, *The Order of Things* (New York: Vintage, 1973), 51; Jameson, *A Singular Modernity*, 67.

35. Anton Chekhov, *Three Sisters*, trans. Paul Schmidt (New York: Theatre Communications Group, 1992).
36. See Jameson, *A Singular Modernity*, 111.
37. *TS*, 8, 51.
38. Ibid., 65.
39. Ibid., 13.
40. Esslin, "Chekhov and the Modern Drama," 143.
41. Murray Krieger, *A Reopening of Closure: Organicism Against Itself* (New York: Columbia University Press, 1989), 3.
42. Howard Moss, "Three Sisters," in *Anton Chekhov*, ed. Harold Bloom (Philadelphia, PA: Chelsea House, 1999), 121–37, 133.
43. Moss, "Three Sisters," 135.
44. Ibid., 25.
45. Ibid., 24.
46. Affect theorists Seigworth and Gregg would call the "To Moscow!" refrain an "affective bloom-space of an ever processual materiality," one that holds both promise and threat, embodied in those who experience it (9). For Lauren Berlant, this recurring memory/dream constitutes a "cluster of promises," one that resists structuralist binaries of good/bad or here/there, but also goes beyond poststructuralist thinking as its referent—the impulse that articulates it exists in a shifting, in-between state, yet appears to endure in the object, here, a phrase each repeats in his or her way. Lauren Berlant, "Cruel Optimism," in *The Affect Theory Reade*, ed. Gregory Seigworth and Melissa Gregg (Durham: Duke, 2010), 93–117, 93.
47. *TS*, 35, 56.
48. Irving Deer, "Speech as Action in Chekhov's *The Cherry Orchard*," *Educational Theatre Journal* 10, no. 1 (March 1958): 30–34.
49. Moss, "Three Sisters," 221.
50. *TS*, 45, 50, 46–7.
51. Ibid., 15, 43.
52. Ibid., 46.
53. Ibid., 47.
54. Svetlana Evdokimova, "Being as Event, or the Drama of Dasein: Chekhov's *The Three Sisters*," in *Chekhov for the Twenty-First Century*, ed. Carol Appollonio and Angela Brintlinger, 57–78 (Bloomington, IN: Slavica, 2012), 65, 57, 58.
55. *TS*, 14–15.
56. See Anatoly Sobennikov, "Classical Ideas of Fate in Chekhov's Dramaturgy," in *Chekhov for the 21st Century*, ed. Carol Apollonio and Angela Brintlinger (Bloomington, IN: Slavica, 2012), 79–87, 79.
57. Boris Zingerman, *Teatr Chekhova i ego mirovoe znachenie* (Moscow: RIK Rusanova, 2001), 16–17; qtd, Evdokimova, 59.
58. *TS*, 40.
59. Anton Chekhov, "About Love," in *About Love and Other Stories*, trans. Rosamund Bartlett, 158–66 (London: Oxford University Press, 2004), 166.
60. *TS*, 20, 81.

61. Ibid., 58–59, 76.
62. Ibid., 82.
63. Jameson, *A Singular Modernity*, 40.
64. *TS*, 21.
65. George Lakoff and Mark Johnson, *Metaphors We Live By* (Chicago: University of Chicago Press, 1980).
66. Anton Chekhov, *The Seagull*, in *Chekhov: The Four Major Plays*, trans. Curt Columbus, 15–81 (Chicago: Ivan R. Dee, 2005), 24–25.
67. Ibid., 23.
68. Ibid., 25.
69. Ibid., 30.
70. Jameson, *Modernity*, 32.
71. Chekhov, *Seagull*, 27.
72. *TS*, 59, 36.
73. Ibid., 59, 67.
74. Hashamova, Yana. "Alienation as Structure: The Cases of *Hedda Gabler* and *Three Sisters*," *Elementa* 3 (1997): 341–48, 341.
75. *TS*, 85–86.
76. See, for example, Cynthia Marsh, "The Implications of Quotation in Performance: Másha's Lines from Pushkin in Chekhov's *Three Sisters*," *Slavonic and East European Review* 84, no. 3 (2006): 446–59.
77. *TS*, 82.
78. Ibid., 82.
79. Ibid., 98–100.
80. Jameson, *A Singular Modernity*, 5.
81. Leslie Kane, *The Language of Silence* (Plainsboro, NJ: Associated University Press, 1984), 5.
82. Deer, "Speech as Action in Chekhov's *The Cherry Orchard*," 31.
83. *TS*, 31–33, 85–86.
84. Ibid., 59–60.
85. Ibid., 4.
86. Ibid., 5–6.
87. Ibid., 38.
88. Ibid., 40.
89. Ibid., 14–15.
90. Ibid., 63.
91. Ibid., 50.
92. Jan Mukarovsky, *Structure, Sign, and Function: Selected Essays by Jan Mukarovsky*, trans. John Burbank and Peter Steiner (New Haven: Yale University Press, 1978), 74.
93. Toril Moi, *Henrik Ibsen and the Birth of Moderism* (London: Oxford University Press, 2006), 25–26.
94. Jameson, *A Singular Modernity*, 32.
95. Philip Callow, *Chekhov: The Hidden Ground* (Chicago: Ivan R. Dee, 1998), 341, 335.
96. *TS*, 53, 33.
97. Gotthold Lessing, *Laokoön: An Essay on the Limits of Painting and Poetry*, trans. Edward McCormick (Indianapolis: Bobbs-Merrill, [1766] 1962), 20–21.

98. Quoted in Jenny Edbauer Rice, "The New 'New': Making a Case for Critical Affect Studies," *Quarterly Journal of Speech* 94, no. 2 (2008): 200–212, 201.

99. *TS*, 48, 35, 40, 90, 41, 51.

100. Ibid., 49.

101. Ibid., 62.

102. Ibid., 44.

103. Ibid., 43.

104. Ibid., 43.

105. Jameson, *A Singular Modernity*, 122.

106. Kristin Johnsen-Neshati, "Chekhovian Transformation: *Three Sisters* and Timberlake Wertenbaker's *The Break of Day*," in *International Dramaturgy: Translation and Transformations in the Theatre of Timberlake Wertenbaker*, ed. Maya E. Roth and Sara Freeman (Brussels: P.I.E. Peter Lang, 2008), 123–33.

107. Linda Hutcheon, *Theory of Adaptation* (London: Routledge, 2006), 9. Quoted in Victoria Petterson Lantz, "What Comes 'After Chekhov'? Mustapha Matura and West Indian Reiterations of *Three Sisters*," in *Adapting Chekhov*, 161–79, 164.

Historicizing Shakesfear and Translating Shakespeare Anew

—LEZLIE C. CROSS

"Bless thee, Bottom! bless thee! thou art translated."
A MIDSUMMER NIGHT'S DREAM (ACT 3, SCENE 1)

In 2011, the Oregon Shakespeare Festival (OSF), helmed by artistic director Bill Rauch, started an experimental project to "translate" Shakespeare's plays into contemporary English. The project was funded by tech entrepreneur Dave Hitz and led by Dr. Lue Morgan Douthit, then director of literary development and dramaturgy at OSF. The experiment started with a single text: *Timon of Athens*. Poet and translator Kenneth Cavander, known for his work translating Greek plays into English, was chosen to undertake a trial "translation" of this lesser-known play into twenty-first-century English.[1] In approaching this translation, Cavander did not paraphrase and worked to maintain the poetic integrity of the original, without writing in iambic pentameter.[2] It was important for Douthit and Cavander that the new version not fall into the realm of either revision or truncation. They wanted "no editing, no cutting, no fixing, no personal politics, no regionalisms," any of which might transform the translation into an adaptation.[3]

The experiment became reality when Cavander's version of *Timon* was produced at the Alabama Shakespeare Festival in April 2014, where it was, in Douthit's words, "incredibly well-received by critics and audiences."[4] Indeed, Rick Harmon, the reviewer for the *Montgomery Advertiser*, called it "brilliant," "sleek, understandable and affecting" due to Cavander's "updating some of its language."[5] Bolstered by the apparent success of this venture, Douthit, with the financial support of Hitz, commissioned thirty-six playwrights (each partnered with a dramaturg) to create translations of all thirty-nine of Shakespeare's plays into modern English.[6] To promote the idea that this project is simply a new way to play with, and thereby get to know, Shakespeare's works, the project was called *Play on!* Artistic Director Bill Rauch reassured skeptics that "The *Play on!* translations are not being commissioned because we despair that people will never understand the original language" but rather to create a new arena of engagement with Shakespeare's texts.[7] This newness is twofold: (1) the nature of the project, which calls for translation rather than adaptation and (2) the demographics of the translation teams. More than half of the thirty-six playwrights are people of color and more than half are women.[8] The aims of the *Play on!* project are to allow these important and emerging theatre practitioners a chance to intimately know Shakespeare's language and to have Shakespeare interpreted by a diverse body of artists.

When the *Play on!* project was formally announced in September 2015, there was an instantaneous outpouring of both censure and support. On one side of the debate, the initiative was lambasted as a disturbing, misguided travesty. These detractors feared that translated Shakespeare would once again take the great playwright from the stage, as in the eighteenth-century adaptations of Shakespeare. On the other side of the debate, the project was praised as a solution to the dread that Shakespeare, a treasure of Anglophone culture, was quickly disappearing from American life due to the density of his language. As the articles appeared one after another, the fear on both sides of the debate was palpable. Ultimately, both proponents and opponents of the translations were afraid of losing Shakespeare. In this article, I examine three of the major Shakesfears stimulating the *Play on!* controversy and place those anxieties in historical context to demonstrate how these concerns have fueled the Shakespeare industry since the Restoration.[9]

Fear One: Audiences

As students are taught in introductory drama classes, an audience is essential to theatrical performance; per Eric Bentley's famous formula, "A impersonates B while C looks on."[10] For theatremakers, the audience is not only the consumer of the theatrical product but also the fuel that keeps the theatre running. According to *American Theatre*'s 2014 "Theatre Facts," ticket sales account for 53 percent of the earned income of theatres in the United States.[11] This significant figure means that artistic directors and producers need to estimate accurately the appeal of each title and playwright offered in their season to insure fiscal solvency. One of the major fears motivating the *Play on!* project is that if audiences no longer understand Shakespeare, if his word choice and syntax are too archaic for modern playgoers, they will choose to attend other, lighter, offerings, rather than expend their mental energy on trying to understand Shakespeare. This fear is not new.

As early as 1668, John Dryden admitted that "*Shakespeares* language is likewise a little obsolete," preferring the more regular and linguistically clear plays of Beaumont and Fletcher.[12] In the early 1700s, both literary editors and theatre artists labored to alter Shakespeare's plays to make them palatable to a general audience. In his 1709 edition of Shakespeare, Nicholas Rowe promised readers that he had "rendered many places intelligible that were not so before."[13] These alterations to Shakespeare's texts began the popularization of Shakespeare that developed through the eighteenth century. Yet, about twelve years later, in 1721, Bishop Francis Atterbury wrote to editor Alexander Pope, "I protest to you, in a hundred places I cannot construe him, I don't understand him."[14] Pope, for his part, agreed. The preface to his 1725 edition of Shakespeare's works included the pronouncement: "It must be own'd that with all these great excellencies he has almost as great defects; and that as he has certainly written better so he has perhaps written worse than any other."[15] Accordingly, Pope's edition of Shakespeare features emendations, amendments, and even additions to the text, as well as moving into the footnotes any passages Pope felt were "excessively bad."[16] In this way, the early editors of Shakespeare mimicked the stage versions of the same period.

Eighteenth-century theatre artists also saw the obscurity of Shakespeare's language and his old-fashioned characters as the reasons his plays did not succeed. Nicholas Rowe, in the prologue to *The Ambitious Stepmother* (1781), worried that native playwrights "Shakespear, Fletcher, and laborious Ben" Jonson would "be left for Scaramouch and Harlequin," accessible foreign clowns.[17] A similar fear existed in the prologue to Charles Gildon's adaptation of *Measure for Measure*:

> To please this Winter, we all Means have us'd;
> Old Plays have been Reviv'd, and New Produc'd.
> But you, it seems, by Us, wou'd not be Serv'd;
> And others Thrive, while we were almost Starv'd.
> Our House you daily Shun'd, yet Theirs you Cram'd,
> And Flock'd to see the very Plays you Damn'd.[18]

Gildon's preface demonstrates the centuries-old perfidy of audiences, who say they want Shakespeare and the classics but actually attend farces and light entertainments.

Eighteenth-century theatre practitioners therefore felt the need to alter the language, plots, and characterizations in Shakespeare's plays and to embellish them with songs and dances, to provide the "diversion" the audience craved.[19] Alteration became the way Shakespeare survived on the stage, the way "Old Plays" competed with contemporary comedies. As David Wheeler has pointed out, between 1660 and 1820, all of Shakespeare's plays were revised (and rewritten) for production in more than 123 adaptations.[20] For eighteenth-century theatre makers, the only way to keep audiences coming to Shakespeare was to adapt them into a contemporary context. It was this reshaping of Shakespeare, tailoring the works to the social and moral expectations of audiences, that caused Shakespeare to become the most popular playwright in England and America.

By the late nineteenth century, adaptations had been driven from the stage in favor of relatively faithful cuttings and rearrangements of Shakespeare's plays, presented with meticulous historical accuracy. Yet, most audiences were still looking for entertainment, not education, in the theatre. They missed the old adaptations. When actor Edwin Booth attempted to "restore" *Richard III* from Colley Cibber's adaptation, actress Rachel Noah, of the Boston Theatre, complained, "T. B. Aldrich and some other highbrows have talked Mr. Booth into doing Shakespeare's *Richard III*. Oh, it reads well enough, but Cibber's Richard *acts*."[21] Noah was not alone in this estimation; many actors believed that the Cibber version of *Richard III* was simply more performable than Shakespeare's original. Even Booth admitted that Shakespeare's version was "a far more difficult part to handle effectively than the old Cibber," speaking to the theatricality of Cibber's text.[22] Audiences therefore, as they had in the early eighteenth century, started turning from Shakespeare toward light entertainment, comedies, farces, and the newest theatrical form: musicals.

This shift in audience loyalty away from Shakespeare's plays caused F. B. Chatterton, manager of the Drury Lane Theatre, to famously lament that "Shakespeare spells ruin" for theatrical producers, as his plays were no longer profitable in the theatre. By the end of the nineteenth century, theatre managers only attempted Shakespearean production at their financial peril. This pronouncement became a common cry. Edwin Booth wondered in 1887 "Is Shakspere dead? Is the drama utterly depraved, or overwhelmed by the high jinks of variety-shows and the maudle of society plays?"[23] In 1898, manager Daniel Frohman asserted that Shakespeare was no longer popular, as "the great mass of the American people . . . are impatient of stage performances that tax too severely the intellect or the attention."[24] The fear that audiences would not attend Shakespeare caused fewer producers to risk mounting the plays, and production of Shakespeare dropped radically. Simultaneously, the literary Shakespeare became a mainstay of the educational system. As actor-manager Augustus Pitou observed at the turn of the twentieth century, "Shakespeare was never so widely read and taught as now; in all our schools and colleges he is foremost in classes of English literature, and if he is less popular on the stage it is the fault of his interpreters. His students evidently find him more impressive in the classroom and in the library."[25] The majority of audiences now encountered Shakespeare as a poet, a creator of literature, not as a playwright.

As the twentieth century progressed, theatre makers attempted to draw audiences back to productions of Shakespeare by heeding Ezra Pound's modernist dictum to "make it new."[26] The plays were made "more accessible" by employing contemporary dress and presenting them as allegories for current social and cultural issues. As director Peter Brook expressed it, "The problem is adapting this material to the present moment . . . the moment when people are sitting here in the audience."[27] Accordingly, Brook's landmark productions at the Royal Shakespeare Festival in the 1950s and 1960s, which were visually stunning and played with theatrical form, often used only about half of Shakespeare's words. Orson Welles's popular adaptations of Shakespeare for the Mercury Theatre in the 1930s and 1940s, especially his 1937 fascist-themed *Caesar*, responded to contemporary tensions with radically streamlined texts. Joseph Papp, founder of the New York Shakespeare Festival, notably staged a one-act, twelve-actor *Hamlet* in 1968 to free the play from the centuries of interpretations that "encrusted" it.[28] Edith Oliver, in her review of Papp's *Hamlet*, observed of the text: "Most of the words are Shakespeare's and many of them are from *Hamlet*, but the speeches are broken up and scattered all over the play."[29] Actor Martin Sheen, who played Hamlet, recalled that this fresh approach to the language meant that audiences "were listening, some of them for the first time . . . to things that had been in the literature for four hundred years."[30] The freshness created by radical cutting and reinterpretation began to bring audiences back to the plays, yet the language remained a barrier for many playgoers.

For the last few decades, translation of Shakespeare's plays into "modern English" has been touted as an answer to the fear that audiences don't understand the plays. In his 1998 book *Word on the Street, Debunking the Myth of a "Pure" Standard English*, African American linguist and author John McWhorter called for Shakespeare to be translated into modern English. McWhorter's solution was motivated by the fear that "the foremost writer in the English language, the most precious legacy of the English-speaking world, is little more than a symbol in our actual thinking lives" because of the density of Shakespeare's literary, poetic language.[31] He points to the many popular productions of Shakespeare across the globe as evidence of what translation can offer; readers and audiences in Germany, Russia, and Japan experience Shakespeare in their modern vernacular. Importantly, it is theatregoers, those that *listen* to Shakespeare, who concern McWhorter: "Overall, Shakespearean language is alarmingly opaque to modern listeners except in careful excerpt."[32] McWhorter's call for translation was an inspiration for Dave Hitz, the financial backer of the *Play on!* project. The initiative amplified McWhorter's vision to include the entirety of the canon and create a new arena of "improved" Shakespeare, one that addresses playgoers' fear of feeling stupid in the theatre.

The selective translating of Shakespeare has been a practice since the Restoration. For instance, in his 1878 acting edition of *Hamlet*, Edwin Booth insisted on changing the antiquated term "mobled queen," in act 2, scene 2, to the clearer "ignobled queen," as that word choice "expresses both the condition of *Hecuba* in her fallen stage, and the Queen of Denmark's degradation."[33] Today, most theatre companies continue to silently update or cut archaic words, phrases, and passages in Shakespeare's plays. The *Play on!* project's complete translation of the Shakespearean canon is shocking due to the scale, but not the type, of the endeavor.

Perhaps the reason theatremakers are so certain they need to alter Shakespeare for their audiences is that even they, alleged experts, have moments of incomprehension in listening to Shakespeare's plays. Nicholas Hytner, the artistic director of the National Theatre in England, admitted in the *Guardian* that he "hardly ever [goes] to a performance of one of Shakespeare's plays without experiencing blind panic during the first five minutes," sitting in the audience fearing that he has "no idea what these people are talking about."[34] Emma Rice, the recent artistic director of the Globe Theatre in London confessed that Shakespeare on the page makes her sleepy.[35] In an article on *Howlround* announcing the aims of the project, Lue Douthit, the director of *Play on!*, opened with a confession: "My name is Lue. And when it comes to Shakespeare, I'm afraid I might be just a little bit tone-deaf."[36] If top employees at the largest Shakespeare-producing theatres in the world feel this apprehension, it is natural for them to assume they share this trait with audiences and that something must be done with Shakespeare if audiences are going to keep coming back. For, as Matt Trueman argued in the *Telegraph*, Emma Rice's admission that she doesn't "'get' Shakespeare wasn't philistinism or stupidity. It was an invitation. It said, loudly, 'I'm not fluent and I'm running the place. Come on in.'"[37]

Fear Two: Dethroning the God of My Idolatry

In September 1769, David Garrick, with his Shakespeare Jubilee in Stratford-upon-Avon, inaugurated what George Bernard Shaw would later call "Bardolatry," the worship of Shakespeare as a secular deity.[38] Garrick's celebration of Shakespeare as the "god" of the theatrical firmament was a deliberate ploy to reclaim the playwright from literary editors. For, as editor George Steevens noted, "A perfect edition of the plays of Shakespeare requires at once the assistance of the Antiquary, the Historian, the Grammarian, and the Poet," but not the actor.[39] Garrick's promotion of Shakespeare, however, had the unintended consequence of imbuing the language of the plays with a kind of biblical reverence. From that time, understanding Shakespeare has become a religion to which many people devote their lives, as evidenced by the members of the Shakspere Society of Philadelphia in 1861 referring to themselves as the "Shakspere Apostles." One fear occasioned by the *Play on!* project is that translation will topple Shakespeare from his consecrated pedestal.

In the fifty years following the Shakespeare Jubilee, as Bardolatry spread, theatre artists came to realize that Shakespeare devotees saw their alterations of the plays as blasphemous. However, as the "Advertisement" to the 1813 adaptation of *Anthony and Cleopatra* articulated, the changes were "a profanation, which may, possibly, be the only mode of continuing some of [Shakespeare's] Plays before a modern Audience."[40] Or, as the preface to Charles Johnson's *Love in a Forest*, a version of *As You Like It*, phrased it, adaptation allowed "The Scene from Time and Error to restore, / And give the Stage, from Shakespear one Play more."[41] These artists feared that without restoration through adaptation, Shakespeare's works would retreat into obscurity. Bardolators, on the other hand, maintained that the language of "the divine William" should not be tampered with by mere players. As Charles Lamb put it, no one with "a proper reverence for Shakespeare" would have "admitted into his matchless scenes such ribald trash as Tate and Cibber . . . have foisted into the acting plays of Shakespeare."[42]

As Daniel Pollack-Pelzner has argued, Bardolatry rose in the nineteenth century as a secular answer to "the challenge to biblical literalism that came from Darwin's theory of evolution," put forward in his 1859 *The Origin of the Species*.[43] What arose in its place was Shakespearean literalism, a devotion to his words and syntax (or "beauties") as well as the historical and cultural context of the plays. This devotion was manifested in two forms: (1) what might be called the cult of the First Folio and (2) in theatrical productions featuring Shakespeare's own text in the midst of historically accurate splendor.

The First Folio as the true source of Shakespeare stems from editor Edmund Malone's insistence in his 1790 variorum that it was "the only authentick edition."[44] The veneration of the First Folio continued to grow during the following centuries. James Boaden, the biographer of John Phillip Kemble, records that the actor's copy of the First Folio was reverently "purified from all stains . . . inlaid into a royal paper and superbly bound. . . . Thus sumptuously equipped, it was deposited in the neat case with a lock and key," where it remained "the most precious copy of that folio."[45] In the 1870s, following the printing of Howard Staunton's *Exact Fac-Simile of the Famous First Folio* (1866), Clement Mansfield Ingleby declared that "Shakespeare's immorality can be guaranteed by only one event—the continued practice of reprinting verbatim the First Folio edition."[46] At the turn of the twenty-first century, actor-training manuals such as Don Weingust's *Acting from Shakespeare's First Folio* (2006) and Graham Watt's *The Case for Staging from the First Folio* (2008) established the First Folio as the only true text for actors and theatrical production. This was reinforced when editors Jonathan Bate and Eric Rasmussen chose the First Folio as the base text for *The RSC Shakespeare: The Complete Works* (2007), arguing that it is "the most important single book in the history of world drama."[47] The most recent manifestation of the cult of the First Folio is the Folger Shakespeare Library's 2016 touring exhibition "First Folio! the book that gave us Shakespeare," in which ten of the Folger's eighty-two First Folios made one-month stops in each state across the United States. At each location, Shakespearean pilgrims can view a copy of the First Folio, reverently displayed in a large glass case, open to Hamlet's "To be or not to be" speech. As Adam G. Hooks phrased it, the First Folio has come to be considered "the true text of a secular scripture."[48]

When the First Folio became religious doctrine in the nineteenth century, those theatre artists who presented something other than Shakespeare's language were rebuked by critics and chided by educated audiences. When actor Frank Mayo, known for his portrayal of Davy Crockett, played Hamlet at San Francisco's California Theatre in 1878, the reporter from the *San Francisco Call* scathingly reported that the actor "misread the text in many important passages, and in others omitted lines altogether."[49] To escape similar censure, theatre artists heeded the cry of literary critics and Bardolators and worked to "restore" the text of Shakespeare to stages. In William Macready's preface to his adaptation of Cibber's *Richard III*, he stated, "To restore the Character of Richard and the

Language of Shakespeare to the Stage has been the sole object of this re-arrangement."[50] Similarly, the advertisement to George Lamb's *Timon of Athens* declared that his goal was "to restore Shakespeare to the stage, with no other omissions than such as the refinement of manners has rendered necessary."[51] John Phillip Kemble, according to biographer James Boaden, never simply adopted the text of "some old mutilated prompt copy" but considered "attentively the author's genuine book," likely his sanctified copy of the First Folio.[52]

In January 1887, American theatrical producer Augustin Daly "restored" Shakespeare's *The Taming of the Shrew*, producing the "original" rather than David Garrick's popular adaptation *Katherine and Petruchio*, which condensed the action down to a short fifty-minute afterpiece featuring the quarreling lovers. On opening night, Daly's brother Joseph wrote him a letter praising his courage and calling *Shrew* "a forgotten and condemned play" that "many generations of theatrical magnates had consigned to oblivion" but that, in reality, had received a healthy stage life in Garrick's truncation.[53] In the print edition celebrating the one-hundredth performance of his *Shrew*, Daly triumphantly declared: "I could not help thinking that when Shakespeare wrote it, he knew what was best, and so, to vindicate Shakespeare, I set my judgment against that of Garrick and you have the result. Shakspere [*sic*] was right."[54] For Daly, the absolution of Shakespeare, through a successful production of *Shrew*, reinforced the inviolability of the great dramatist's works.

Yet, all of these "restorations" were still edited for theatrical presentation. Theatre artists continued to fear their audiences. As dramatic critic and theatrical editor William Winter wrote to Daly: "It seems almost a sacrilege to touch with editorial hand the works of Shakespeare: but we very well know that there is scarcely one of them which can be put upon the stage in its original form."[55] In May 1868, Edwin Booth confessed to publisher Henry L. Hinton in reference to his cutting of *Romeo and Juliet*: "I have *desecrated* Shakespeare a little—here + there—by changing or transforming a word or two."[56] While Booth was committed to restoring Shakespeare's texts, he still knew the limits of his audience's attention. He explained to Hinton, "I deem it safer to risk the critic's 'd—n' than bore my auditors" with an overly lengthy and poetic play.[57] Accordingly, nineteenth-century producers truncated and rearranged the plays "as suiting the time of the representation to the habits of [their] audience."[58] As additional material was rarely added, however, the producers could claim the plays were "restorations" and that they were, thereby, honoring Shakespeare.

The nineteenth-century shift in stage Shakespeare from eclectic design to unified, historically accurate productions was another manifestation of Bardolatry on the stage. English actor-manager Charles Kean staged lavish productions of Shakespeare's history plays, particularly *King John* (1852) and *Henry VIII* (1854–5), that were hugely popular with audiences and earned him the moniker "prince of theatrical antiquities."[59] Soon, other theatre artists in England and the United States began mimicking Kean's production values and his commitment to the full realization of Shakespeare's rich imagination on the stage. In these theatrical exhibitions of Bardolatry, the settings of Shakespeare's plays became sacred. Today, when audiences clamor for "traditional" productions of Shakespeare, they long for the historically motivated pageantry of the nineteenth century.

In the early twentieth century, the nineteenth-century passion for historical correctness was taken a step further as scholars and producers attempted to stage Shakespeare's unadulterated plays in "authentic" spaces, with "traditional" clothing, and even "original" pronunciation. For William Poel, the founder of the Elizabethan Stage Society, "One of the debts we owe to Shakespeare is to present his plays in their authentic form" without any cuts, reorganization, or even act breaks to interrupt the flow of action.[60] For linguist David Crystal, Original Pronunciation "brings us as close as possible to how old texts," particularly Shakespeare's plays, "might have sounded" without the "modern social connotations" of speaking the language with contemporary accents.[61] Many theatre companies in England and the United States, including OSF, adopted this ethos through the 1950s.[62] As OSF founder Angus Bowmer argued, "There was a tremendous practical advantage in doing the plays on an Elizabethan stage."[63] In the latter half of the century, companies such as Shakespeare's Globe, in London, and the American Shakespeare Center in Staunton, Virginia, devoted themselves to producing "authentic" Shakespeare. In October 2016, when the board of the Globe announced the departure of artistic director Emma Rice, they argued that Rice's aggressively modern vision did not fit with the aims of the theatre, which was constructed as a "radical experiment to explore the conditions within which Shakespeare and his contemporaries worked," and which they believed "should continue to be the central tenet of our work."[64]

As Victorians wrestled with the idea that the Bible was not the word of God, modern Bardolators have wrestled with the idea that the words of Shakespeare are not sacrosanct. Developments in textual studies throughout the twentieth century demonstrated the instability of Shakespeare's texts and revealed the collaborative nature of early modern playwriting. Because of these revelations, we can no longer consider Shakespeare to be a divinely inspired, individual genius. Even Harold Bloom, who claimed that Shakespeare was a "mortal god," acknowledged that "there cannot be a definitive Shakespeare."[65] The *Play on!* project capitalizes on this new conception of Shakespeare as a collaborator, as a playwright with whom modern theatre practitioners can join artistic forces. Yet, it is also founded on a kind of Bardolotry, a certainty that Shakespeare should be a central part of modern culture. In this way, the *Play on!* project echoes John McWhorter's fear that Shakespeare, "the most precious legacy of the English-speaking world," was retreating into obscurity.[66] The fear of losing the Bard of Avon, our "precious legacy," became a reason to promote translation of his works.

Yet, for opponents to translation like James Shapiro, "the only thing Shakespearean about his plays *is* the language," as he commonly borrowed his plots and characters from other sources.[67] By stripping the original language from the plays, opponents argue, translators are robbing them of their essential "Shakespeareanity." They fear that the erosion of Shakespeare's language through translation might be the beginning of the end of Shakespeare as a secular deity. Familiar with this fear, McWhorter wondered if those resistant to translation assumed he was "questioning the worth of Shakespeare as an artist," and thereby attempting to knock the Bard of Avon off his cultural pedestal.[68] This act, a feared result of translation, would be tantamount to sacrilege.

Fear Three: The Literary Elite

John Heminges and Henry Condell, the compilers of the First Folio were, above all, attempting to sell an expensive and risky book. Therefore, in the prefatory material to the volume, they emphasized the importance of reading Shakespeare: "Reade him therefore; and againe, and againe: And if then you do not like him, surely you are in some manifest danger, not to understand him."[69] What Shakespeare's contemporaries unwittingly established with this scolding dictum is a hierarchy between Shakespeare the poet, who is read and reread in the study, and Shakespeare the player, who is experienced fleetingly on the stage. One modern manifestation of this hierarchy is the preservation of Shakespeare within English, rather than theatre, departments on university campuses. As with all cultural hierarchies, there is fear attached to trespassing from the lower echelons (here, the theatrical) to higher levels (here, the literary). Those at the bottom fear rejection and scorn for their temerity and those at the top fear that their elevated position will be disrupted. The theatrically based *Play on!* project flagrantly trespasses these boundaries in daring to rewrite Shakespeare, the supreme poet of English literature.

In the introduction to Henry Irving's 1888 edition of Shakespeare, titled "Shakespeare as a Playwright," the actor opened with the observation that "it will appear to some readers a profanation of the name of Shakespeare to couple it with the title of playwright," instead of that of poet.[70] The nineteenth-century backlash against stage Shakespeare, despite the restoration of texts for stage production, had become so virulent that Irving felt impelled to argue that "surely the end of all plays is to be acted, and not to be simply read in the study" and to defend the profession of acting as a whole.[71] His defense of the stage did not extend to a vindication of Shakespearean adaptations. To set himself apart from other producers of Shakespeare, Irving joined literary critics in disparaging earlier stage adaptations, figuring them as "commonplace . . . mutilated versions of the works of our greatest dramatist."[72] Irving, as fearful of his audiences as the eighteenth-century theatrical managers, knew "the popular taste nowadays would not permit an actor to take such liberties with the text as were once thought not only pardonable but commendable."[73] Literary Shakespeare, the bible of Bardolotry, had trumped theatrical, adapted, and truncated Shakespeare.

As I mentioned previously, when literary editing began in the eighteenth century, both editors and actor-managers altered and reshaped Shakespeare. Both were popular forms of disseminating Shakespeare to a mass audience. By the end of the eighteenth century, the expensive variorum editions by George Steevens and Edmund Malone, founded on historical methodologies and meticulous scholarship, established literary Shakespeare as "legitimate." Theatrical Shakespeare, by default, became the bastard offshoot. Working against a legitimated, literary Shakespeare, theatre artists had to be clear about the extent of their trespass into Shakespeare's poetry.

In the early 1770s, publisher John Bell devised an ambitious plan to bring together the many popular acting editions of Shakespeare in a single, unified series of plays "as now performed at the Theatres Royal in London." In doing so, Bell was offering the reading public the chance to experience theatrical Shakespeare as well as giving amateur actors access to theatrical texts. The series openly admitted that it presented Shakespeare "improved," as evidenced by the "Advertisement" in volume one: "Shakespeare's admirers, even the enthusiastic ones, who worship him as *the god of their idolatry*, have never scrupled to admit that his most regular pieces produce some scenes and passages, highly derogatory to his incomparable general merit; he frequently trifles, is now and then obscure, and, sometimes, to gratify a vitiated age, indelicate."[74] The theatrical editors featured in Bell's edition therefore endeavored to amend these faults, to "render" what they called "the essence of Shakespeare, more instructive and intelligible; especially to the ladies and to youth; glaring indecencies being removed, and intricate passages explained."[75] By offering explanations for difficult passages, the Bell series was mimicking the use-value of the literary editions of Shakespeare.

Almost 250 years before OSF Artistic Director Bill Rauch reassured audiences that the *Play on!* translations are "companion pieces (*not* replacements) to the original texts,"[76] Bell's edition assured readers that "to expect any thing more of this work, than as *a companion to the theatre*, is to mistake the purpose of the editors."[77] They were therefore careful to have "carefully preserved in the notes" those "passages, of great merit for the closet," which "are never spoken" in stage representation.[78] When approached about the publication of his scripts as part of the Bell's edition of Shakespeare, David Garrick expressed a "delicate fear" that the "prunings, transpositions, or other alterations" he was obliged to make "for the convenience of representation, or accommodation to the powers and capacities of his performers, might be misconstrued into a critical presumption of offering to the literati a reformed and more correct edition of our author's works."[79] In other words, Garrick was afraid that uneducated readers might read Bell's edition and mistake it for an authentic edition of Shakespeare.

Other eighteenth-century theatrical editors were similarly trepidatious. Richard Cumberland, in his alteration of *Timon of Athens*, marked his additions by placing commas around them. In George Granville Lansdowne's *The Jew of Venice*, a 1701 adaptation of *Merchant of Venice*, the additional lines were marked with an apostrophe, so "that nothing may be imputed to Shakespear [*sic*] which may seem unworthy of him."[80] Colley Cibber, in his long-running alteration of *Richard III*, was equally careful to set off Shakespeare's language from his own. In his 1700 edition, he "caus'd those [lines] that are intirely [*sic*] *Shakespear's* to be Printed in thick *Italick Character*; and those lines with this mark (') before 'em, are generally his thought, in the best dress I could afford 'em. What is not so mark'd, or in a different Character is intirely [*sic*] my own."[81] The authors' desire to mark, in print, the distinction between their own additions and Shakespeare's "original language" indicates their subservience to the literary Shakespeare.

When the First Folio was printed in 1623, it sold for about fifteen shillings and was mainly purchased by "noblemen and 'commoners of standing,' so it was not strictly an elite item."[82] By the end of the nineteenth century, the First Folio was an edition of Shakespeare "accessible only to princes and merchant princes."[83] The First Folio became a symbol of the wealthy's ability to "own" Shakespeare. The financial inflation of the First Folio was matched by the rise of Bardolatry and the restoration of Shakespeare's language to the stage in historically correct settings. Cultural historian Lawrence Levine describes this nineteenth-century elevation of Shakespeare as a transition from lowbrow, popular Shakespeare to highbrow, elite Shakespeare.[84] Levine argues that in the early decades of the nineteenth century, Shakespeare (in eighteenth-century adaptations) was popular entertainment, enjoyed by audiences of all classes, but by the end of the century, his works were consumed solely by the upper classes.

The authorship debate, which blossomed in the nineteenth century, was a leading indicator of the changing economic status of Shakespeare in the popular imagination. From Delia Bacon, who wondered if "this crowning literary product of that great epoch" could be a "stupid, illiterate, third-rate play-actor," to J. Thomas Looney, who was convinced that the author of the plays must have been a member of the higher aristocracy, the authorship debate was based on classist notions.[85] As Andrew Murphey argued in *Shakespeare for the People*, when "working-class activists" in the early nineteenth century "comprehensively claimed Shakespeare as their own," the authorship debate provided "a reactionary denial of the possibility that the working class could ever produce a figure of Shakespeare's magnitude."[86] While the authorship debate flourished, Shakespeare was ensconced in the upper echelons of society. As Virginia Mason Vaughn phrased it, "At the height of America's 'gilded age' a gentleman (or a lady) could acquire cultural cachet . . . not simply by brushing up but by knowing and understanding his Shakespeare."[87] These class divisions held through the twentieth and into the twenty-first century. According to OSF's 2013 audience survey, almost half of their playgoers make more than $100,000 a year.[88] Class distinctions have even invaded Joseph Papp's grand vision of free Shakespeare in Central Park, as a $200 donation provides the donor with one "free" ticket, which cannot be guaranteed through the Public Theatre's lottery system.[89]

Access to education is another barrier to Shakespeare for many audience members. One goal of the *Play on!* project is to democratize Shakespeare, to make his works accessible to playgoers and readers of all backgrounds—especially those without educational opportunities and those for whom English is a second language. In this way, *Play on!* is a threat to the Shakespeare of the Ivory Tower. It prompts an anxiety: if Shakespeare's works are translated and accessible to all, the many years of laborious study put into understanding his language will be lost. Those of us who are adept in Shakespeare's language, and make our livings transmitting that knowledge in print, in the classroom, and in the rehearsal room, fear translation might put us out of a job.

One of the claims of the literary elite is Shakespeare's universalism, or his ability to provide truths about all humanity.[90] This caused high school English teacher Dana Dusbiber to worry "that as long as we continue to cling to ONE (white) MAN'S view of life as he lived it so long ago, we (perhaps unwittingly) promote the notion that other cultural perspectives are less important."[91] The *Play on!* project wrests Shakespeare from the hands of the white, male establishment with its inclusive array of playwrights and dramaturgs. As Bill Rauch explained, the project "will bring a range of diverse voices and perspectives to the works of Shakespeare."[92] These new interpretations of Shakespeare may also create opportunities to bring new audiences to the theatre. According to the Broadway League, "almost eighty percent of all tickets were purchased by Caucasian theatregoers" and, in 2013, 84 percent of OSF audiences identified as "Anglo/White."[93] By inviting playwrights of color to have such an immersive engagement with Shakespeare's language, *Play on!* empowers them to take ownership of his works and, as Andrew Hartley has argued, "ownership of Shakespeare, it seems, necessitates a degree of refashioning."[94]

Conclusion: Facing Our Fears

The controversy surrounding the *Play on!* project is motivated by a cocktail of Shakesfears. The fear that audiences will reject Shakespeare's complex works; the fear of destroying Shakespeare, the god of Bardolatry; and the fear of trespass upon the literary elite all fuel the controversy surrounding the *Play on!* project. As I have demonstrated, none of these fears are new but have been constant points of contention for hundreds of years.

These anxieties about the place of Shakespeare in our culture have fueled the Shakespeare industry since the Restoration. Generations of people have responded to their Shakesfears by creating stage productions, both authentic and radical; film adaptations; literary offshoots such as novels and comic books; dictionaries and printed scholarly editions; Shakespeare kitsch and relics of Bardolatry; and the plethora of popular, critical, and scholarly articles and volumes published each year. As each anxiety about Shakespeare reached a flash point, a new body of Shakespearean work arose in answer. The *Play on!* project, the newest manifestation of this phenomenon, answers the fear that Shakespeare's language is too impenetrable for audiences and even readers. It seeks to establish what Helen Krich Chinoy calls an "evolving, new, inclusive canon."[95]

My identification of the historical tensions surrounding *Play on!* in this article leads me to wonder: Can Shakesfear be overcome? As a Shakespearean scholar and dramaturg, I have experienced each of these fears firsthand. Jaimal Yogis, the author of *The Fear Project*, argues that "exposure therapy is generally accepted as the most successful in alleviating phobias, anxiety disorders, and everyday fears of any sort" through positive experiences of the object of fear.[96] When the *Play on!* project was first proposed, I was not in favor of it. Like many skeptics of the project, I feel that Shakespeare's genius (note my Bardolic terminology) is in his inventive use of language. I worried that if the language was stripped away, the plays would be deflated, like a flat tire. I am now facing these concerns head-on as the dramaturg on two of the translations: *As You Like It* with David Ivers, artistic director of the Arizona Theatre Company, and *Twelfth Night* with Alison Carey, director of OSF's successful American Revolutions initiative. Perhaps supporters and detractors of the translation of Shakespeare will join me in exposing themselves to their Shakesfears to expand understanding of the ever-changing position of Shakespeare's works in our society.

Notes

1. Douthit chose Cavander due to OSF's successful production of his translation of *The Trojan Women* in 2000, and the two decided on *Timon* as it is one of Shakespeare's lesser-known works. ("Spelunking with Shakespeare," *Howl Round*, September 30, 2015).
2. Scott Kaiser describes Cavander's translation as being in "poetic verse." See "Translating *Timon*: The Oregon Shakespeare Festival's Shakespeare Translation/Adaptation Project," http://scottkaisershakespeare.com/pdf/essays/kaiser-translating-timon.pdf.
3. Douthit, "Spelunking with Shakespeare."
4. Ibid.
5. Rick Harmon, "Review: ASF 'Timon' Premiere Superb," *Montgomery Advertiser*, May 7, 2014. Cavander and director Jim Helsinger also rearranged several scenes of the play for this production.
6. This number includes *Two Noble Kinsman* and *Edward III*.
7. Bill Rauch, "Why We're Translating Shakespeare," *American Theatre*, October 14, 2015.
8. While the playwrights chose most of the dramaturgs, they are a similarly diverse group: 61 percent women, 39 percent men, 79 percent white, and 21 percent people of color (Taylor Bailey, e-mail message to the author, October 15, 2016).
9. I am building on Ralph Alan Cohen's coined term "Shakesfear," which he defines as modern readers' and playgoers' fear of the density and apparent impenetrable nature of Shakespeare's language. See Ralph Alan Cohen, *Shakesfear and How to Cure It* (Clatton, DE: Prestwick House, 2007).
10. Quoted in Christopher Balme, *The Cambridge Introduction to Theatre Studies* (Cambridge: Cambridge University Press, 2012), 2.
11. Zannie Giraud Voss and Glenn B. Voss, with Ilana B. Rose and Laurie Baskin, "Theatre Facts 2014," 8, http://www.tcg.org/pdfs/tools/TCG_TheatreFacts_2014.pdf.
12. John Dryden, *An Essay of Dramatick Poesie* (London: Harry Herringman, 1668), 89.
13. Quoted in Harry M. Geduld, *Prince of Publishers: A Study of the Work and Career of Jacob Tonson* (Bloomington: Indiana University Press, 1969), 136.
14. Quoted in Brian Vickers, *William Shakespeare: The Critical Heritage*, vol. 2 (New York: Routledge, 1995), 7.
15. Alexander Pope, ed., *The Works of Shakespear*, vol. 1 (London: Jacob Tonson, 1725), 8.

Accordingly, Pope's edition included more emendations than any other literary edition before or since. Many subsequent editors have adopted Pope's emendations.

16. Pope, *The Works of Shakespear*, 34. Pope blamed actors and the theatre for the errors, whereas theatrical editors blamed Shakespeare's times. See Pope, *The Works of Shakespear*, 19.
17. Nicholas Rowe, "Prologue," *The Ambitious Stepmother: A Tragedy; As It Is Acted at the Theatres-Royal in Drury-Lane and Covent-Garden. By Nicholas Rowe, Esq*. (London: Harrison & Co., 1781), 2.
18. Charles Gildon, "Prologue," *Measure for Measure Or, Beauty the Best Advocate As It Is Acted at the Theatre in Lincolns-Inn-Fields* (London: D. Brown, 1700).
19. See, for instance, the preface to *The Comick Masque of Pyramus and Thisbe*: "As Diversion is the Business of the Stage, 'tis Variety best contributes to that Diversion. The Reader therefore, or Auditor rather, thos' the Severest Critick, 'tis hoped will accept of the following Entertainment."
20. David Wheeler, "Eighteenth-Century Adaptations of Shakespeare and the Example of John Dennis," *Shakespeare Quarterly* 36, no. 4 (Winter 1985): 438.
21. Quoted in Katherine M. Goodale, *Behind the Scenes with Edwin Booth* (Boston: Houghton Mifflin, 1931), 57.
22. Edwin Booth to William Winter, November 11, 1877, Folger Shakespeare Library Y.c.215_251.
23. Quoted in Edwina Booth Grossmann, *Edwin Booth: Recollections by His Daughter Edwina Booth Grossmann, and Letters to Her and to His Friends* (London: Osgood, McIlvaine and Co., 1894), 271.
24. Quoted in "Will the People Have Shakspere?" *Munsey's Magazine* 18 (New York: Frank A. Munsey, 1898), 925.
25. Augustus Pitou, *Masters of the Show* (New York: Neale, 1914), 67.
26. See Ezra Pound, *Make it New: Essays* (New Haven: Yale University Press, 1934). As Jay L. Halio has argued, "Modern dress settings are ultimately a superficial means of coming to grips with a play in an attempt to 'make it new.'" See Jay L. Halio, "*Romeo and Juliet* in Performance," *Shakespeare in Performance: A Collection of Essays*, ed. Frank Occhiogrosso (Newark: University of Delaware Press, 2002), 66.
27. Peter Brook, *Evoking Shakespeare* (New York: Theatre Communications Group, 1998), 32.
28. Kenneth Turan and Joseph Papp, *Free for All: Joe Papp, the Public, and the Greatest Theater Story Ever Told* (New York: Anchor Books, 2009), 200.
29. Quoted in Turan and Papp, *Free for All*, 199.
30. Ibid., 204.
31. John McWhorter, *Word on the Street: Debunking the Myth of "Pure" Standard English* (New York: Basic Books, 1998), 107–8.
32. John McWhorter, "Translating Shakespeare into English: A Debate," *A World of Voice, Voice and Speech Review* 7, no. 1 (2011: 38–51, 46).
33. Edwin Booth to William Winter, July 27, 1879, Folger Shakespeare Library Y.c.215_342.
34. Nicholas Hytner, "With Shakespeare, the Play Is just a Starting Point," *The Guardian*, April 12, 2013, https://www.theguardian.com/culture/2013/apr/12/nicholas-hytner-shakespeare-play.
35. Mark Brown, "The Globe's Emma Rice: 'If Anybody Bended Gender It Was Shakespeare,'"

Guardian (London), January 5, 2016. Rice is a proponent of adapting and translating Shakespeare, with the mission of stripping "away generations of bafflement" to "bring Shakespeare really, truly, to the masses." See Hannah Furness, "Emma Rice: 'A Lot of Shakespeare Feels Like Medicine," *Telegraph* (London), January 25, 2016.

36. Douthit, "Spelunking with Shakespeare."
37. Matt Trueman, "The Globe's Freezing out of Emma Rice Is Snobbery That Defies Commercial Sense," *Telegraph* (London), October 26, 2016.
38. George Bernard Shaw, *Three Plays for Puritans* (London: Grant Richards, 1901), xxxi.
39. Quoted in Andrew Murphy, *Shakespeare in Print: A History and Chronology of Shakespeare Publishing* (Cambridge: Cambridge University Press, 2003), 89–90.
40. *Shakespeare's Tragedy of Anthony and Cleopatra with Alterations, and with Additions from Dryden; As Now Perform'd at the Theatre-Royal, Covent-Garden* (London: J. Barker, 1813). The word "Advertisement" here signifies a foreword—a section of the book—not an advertisement in the modern sense of an announcement meant to sell something.
41. Charles R. Johnson, "Prologue," *Love in a Forest: A Comedy As It Is Acted at the Theatre-Royal in Drury-Lane, By His Majestys Servants* (London: W. Chetwood, 1723).
42. Charles Lamb, "On the Tragedies of Shakespeare, Considered with Reference to their Fitness for Stage Representation," *Essays of Charles Lamb*, ed. George Armstrong Wauchope (Boston: Ginn and Company, 1904), 249.
43. Daniel Pollack-Pelzner, "*Play On!* Convening," lecture, *Play on!* Public Seminar, Ashland, OR, September 11, 2016.
44. Edmund Malone, "Mr. Malone's Preface," (London: J. Rivington and Sons, 1790), 208.
45. James Boaden, *An Inquiry into the Authenticity of Various Pictures and Prints* (London: Robert Triphook, 1824), 5.
46. Clement Mansfield Ingleby, *Shakespeare: The Man and the Book* (London: Trübner and Co., 1877), 112.
47. Jonathan Bate, "General Introduction," *The RSC Shakespeare: The Complete Works* (Houndmills: Macmillan Publishers, 2007), 53.
48. Adam G. Hooks, "Afterword: The Folio as Fetish," *The Cambridge Companion to Shakespeare's First Folio*, ed. Emma Smith (Cambridge: Cambridge University Press, 2016), 186.
49. "Mr. Frank Mayo as Hamlet," *New York Times*, November 3, 1878.
50. W. C. Macready, "Preface," *King Richard III* (London: R. and M. Stodart, 1821), iii.
51. George Lamb, "Preface," *Shakespeares Timon of Athens, As Revived at the Theatre Royal, Drury-Lane, on Monday, Oct. 28, 1816; Altered and Adapted for Representation, by the Hon. George Lamb* (London: C. Chapple, 1816).
52. James Boaden, *Memoirs of the Life of John Philip Kemble, Esq. Including a History of the Stage from the Time of Garrick to the Present Period* (Philadelphia: Robert H. Small, 1825), 259.
53. Joseph Daly to Augustin Daly, April 20, 1887, Folger Shakespeare Library Art Vol a14_017–19.
54. William Shakespeare, *Taming of the Shrew: A Comedy by Shakspere* (New York: Privately Printed for Mr. Daly, 1887).
55. William Winter to Augustin Daly, June 21, 1883, Folger Shakespeare Library Y.c.5244_11.
56. Edwin Booth to Henry L. Hinton, N/D, Folger Shakespeare Library Y.c.215_129.
57. Ibid.

58. William Winter to Augustin Daly, June 21, 1883, Folger Shakespeare Library Y.c.5244_11.
59. *Leader*, September 6, 1856, quoted in Richard W. Schoch, *Shakespeare's Victorian Stage: Performing History in the Theatre of Charles Kean* (Cambridge: Cambridge University Press, 2006), 30.
60. William Poel, *Shakespeare in the Theatre* (London: Sidgwick and Jackson, 1913), 44.
61. Originalpronunciation.com, accessed September 19, 2016.
62. OSF built the first replica Shakespearean theatre in America, based on the "dimensions mentioned in the contract for the construction of the 1599 Fortune Theatre." See Kathleen F. Leary and Amy E. Richard, *Images of America: The Oregon Shakespeare Festival* (Charleston, SC: Arcadia Publishing, 2009), 31.
63. Angus L. Bowmer, *As I Remember Adam: The Autobiography of a Festival* (Ashland: Oregon Shakespeare Festival Association, 1975), 71.
64. Quoted in Matthew Hemley, "Emma Rice to Step Down as Artistic Director of Shakespeare's Globe," *The Stage* (London), October 25, 2016.
65. Harold Bloom, *Shakespeare: The Invention of the Human* (New York: Riverhead, 1998), 3, xiii.
66. McWhorter, *Word on the Street*, 107–8.
67. James Shapiro, "Shakespeare in Modern English?" *New York Times*, October 7, 2015.
68. McWhorter, *World of Voice*, 46.
69. John Heminge and Henrie Condell, "To the Great Variety of Readers," *The Norton Facsimile: The First Folio of Shakespeare, ed. Charlton Hinman* (New York: W. W. Norton, 1996), 7.
70. Henry Irving, "Shakespeare as a Playwright," *The Henry Irving Shakespeare* (London: Blackie and Son, 1888), xvii.
71. Ibid., xviii, xxiii.
72. Ibid., xx.
73. Ibid., xxi.
74. Francis Gentleman, "Advertisement," *Bell's Edition of Shakespeare's Plays as They Are now Performed at the Theatres Royal in London Regulated from the Prompt Books of Each House by Permission; with Notes Critical and Illustrative; by the Authors of the Dramatic Censor*, vol. 1 (London: John Bell, 1774), 5.
75. Ibid., 9.
76. Bill Rauch, "Why We're Translating Shakespeare," *American Theatre Magazine*, October 14, 2015.
77. Gentleman, "Advertisement," 8.
78. Ibid., 8.
79. Ibid., 8.
80. Richard Cumberland, *Timon of Athens Altered from Shakespear: A Tragedy As It Is Acted at the Theatre-Royal in Drury Lane* (London: T. Becket, 1771); "Advertisement to the Reader," *The Jew of Venice: A Comedy As It Is Acted at the Theatre in Little-Lincolns-Inn-Fields by His Majesty's Servants* (London: Ber. Lintott, 1701).
81. Colley Cibber, "Preface," *The Tragical History of King Richard III* (London: B. Lintott, 1700).
82. Hooks, "Afterword," 192.
83. Ingleby, *Shakespeare*, 112.
84. See Lawrence W. Levine, *Highbrow/Lowbrow: The Emergence of Cultural Hierarchy in America* (Cambridge, MA: Harvard University Press, 1988), 11–81.

85. Delia Bacon, "William Shakespeare and His Plays," *Putnam's Magazine* 7 (January 1856): 2, 19.
86. Andrew Murphy, *Shakespeare for the People: Working-class Readers, 1800–1900* (Cambridge: Cambridge University Press, 2008), 175.
87. Virginia Mason Vaughan, "Shakespeare in America's Gilded Age," *Shakespeare in the Nineteenth Century*, ed. Gail Marshall (Cambridge: Cambridge University Press, 2012), 345.
88. See https://www.osfashland.org/~/media/Files/PDF/About-OSF/Audience_Survey_13.ashx?la=en.
89. Artistic director Oskar Eustis is working to reverse this trend with several initiatives to provide free theatre to audiences as a form of audience development.
90. See, for instance, Bloom, *Shakespeare*, 1–17.
91. Valerie Strauss, "Teacher: Why I Don't Want to Assign Shakespeare Anymore (Even Though He's in the Common Core)," *Washington Post*, June 13, 2015.
92. Rauch, "Why We're Translating Shakespeare."
93. See https://www.broadwayleague.com/research/research-reports/.
94. Andrew James Hartley, *Shakespeare and Political Theatre in Practice* (New York: Palgrave Macmillan, 2013), 54.
95. Helen Krich Chinoy, *Women in American Theatre* (New York: Theatre Communications Group, 2006), 396.
96. Jaimal Rogis, *The Fear Project* (New York: Rodale, 2013), 37.

A New Noble Kinsmen

The *Play On!* Project and Making New Plays Out of Old

—MARTINE KEI GREEN-ROGERS
AND ALEX N. VERMILLION

When evaluating any play, dramaturgs ask of it: "Why this play? Why this play now?" The answers to these questions are complicated when evaluating the purpose and power of a play that is a retelling of a currently existing dramatic story. What does it mean to make a "new" play out of an "old" play? Why do we need to make a new play out of an old one? This line of questioning belies subtextual questions such as, What is the issue with the older version of the play that hinders an audience's understanding of or appreciation for the story being told? Has something changed about our society and the way we view the older version of this story that needs to be addressed for the story to resonate with contemporary audiences? How do our answers to these questions shift if we are talking about one of the most revered playwrights of the early modern era? To engage these questions, this article discusses Tim Slover's "translation" of *The Two Noble Kinsmen*, commissioned as part of the Oregon Shakespeare Festival's *Play on!* project and supported by a workshop and production process at the University of Utah during the 2015–16 and 2016–17 school years. It seeks to document the successes and challenges facing Slover, the dramaturgs, the students at the University of Utah, and the leaders of the *Play on!* project at the Oregon Shakespeare Festival (OSF) involved in this experiment to modernize the language of the canon of Shakespeare. What adds to the difficulty of this *Play on!* project is that Shakespeare and Fletcher's version of *The Two Noble Kinsmen* is a modernization and dramatization of another "old" text: Chaucer's "The Knight's Tale." Slover's translation of Shakespeare and Fletcher's *The Two Noble Kinsmen* continues their precedent by making "new" writing out of "old" writing, and that positions his resulting new play as a dramatic metanarrative that continues the bold statement foregrounded by Shakespeare and Fletcher's original version. We explore these iterations of old and new texts to argue that for the continued relevance and survival of some stories, those stories must be changed and updated as language shifts and evolves. We also challenge a contemporary academic assumption that early modern English is close enough to contemporary English that it is easily understandable to a lay audience. The OSF project sets up a paradoxical task—to preserve Shakespearean text by rewriting it—and therefore opens debate about the general comprehensibility of early modern plays left unchanged, the continued role of Shakespeare in contemporary culture, and the type of newness desired in contemporary American theatre created by focusing on contemporary language.

Slover's task is a heavy one: The goal of the OSF project is translating Shakespeare's plays in a way that requires examining the language "with the same kind of rigor and pressure that [Shakespeare] did" and keeping in mind the poetical, metaphorical, and thematic elements of the original text while rediscovering the play in contemporary language.[1] Dramaturg Martine Kei Green-Rogers is assisting Slover in an experiment that involves students in the Theatre Department at the University of Utah in pursuing that goal, and already the artists and students are discovering the difficulty of accomplishing this paradoxical task. For example, if the point of the project is to leave as much of the play intact as possible, do precedents such as trimming Shakespeare for time still apply when a production is attached to the commission (and if so, at what point does it venture out of the realm of translation and into the world of adaptation)? In addition, what techniques do actors use to help them determine the meaning and intention behind a line when the verse and punctuation is, for one reason or another, not reinstated in a section of text in the translation? These kinds of dilemmas demonstrate the nuts-and-bolts decisions facing artists at work on *Play on!* commissions, and they carry particular weight because of the controversy that surrounds OSF's project.

Controversy over *Play on!*

From its inception, the OSF's enormous three-year project has provoked vigorous and thoughtful expressions of support and skepticism from the media, academia, and theatre audiences and practitioners alike. Many critics of OSF's project express fear that it will replace the original texts and/or that the artists involved are complicit in "dumbing down" the language. James Shapiro, a professor of English and comparative literature at Columbia University and author of critically acclaimed books on Shakespeare such as *Contested Will: Who Wrote Shakespeare?*, claims the project is "a waste of money and talent," arguing that commentary that Shakespeare's language is "unintelligible goes back to his own day" and that that did not stop audiences from attending the performances.[2] As detailed below, the most contested issue in these debates is whether or not Shakespeare's language presents a legitimate barrier to most contemporary audiences. Green-Rogers takes it as a foundational precept, however, that Shakespeare was *not*, in fact, writing to confuse, trick, or dazzle audiences with confounding wordplay as evidence of his own cleverness. Shakespeare wrote of subjects familiar to the audiences of his time using both colloquial and very elevated language. The subject and language of his plays were *accessible* to all who attended the plays or could afford to purchase a copy of a quarto of his work—a quality the Oregon Shakespeare Festival is determined to emulate in their new scripts. In addition, the Oregon Shakespeare Festival's partnering with the University of Utah emphasizes how these new texts can be used as a learning tool alongside the original texts to break barriers in the comprehension, especially of verse, and illustrate the historical and performative significance of the older texts.

Despite a rocky start and initial negative publicity, the project has blossomed into a process that Bill Rauch, artistic director of the Oregon Shakespeare Festival, states is "about creating a new body of work, one that represents what we hope will be a fruitful encounter between contemporary writers and the English-language dramatist who is frequently considered the greatest that has ever lived."[3] Rauch hopes that, as a result, the project will "specify up" the language of Shakespeare to "excavate some of the specificity and detail that may be lost to contemporary audiences. The clarity we aspire to get from the translations will make us better appreciate the vibrancy of the original."[4] The idea of "specify up" has resonated at the University of Utah, as the students in working on the project with Slover and Green-Rogers debated the nature of the "insanity" of the Jailer's Daughter (act 3, scene 2). Providing more specific framing for her contexts may allow an actor to make a stronger choice in terms of that character's development.[5] Small revelations like this in the classroom allowed for a better understanding and appreciation of the story that the original text revealed and followed the parameters outlined for the *Play on!* projects.

Parameters for a New *The Two Noble Kinsmen*

To each artistic pair invited to participate in the project, OSF Director of Literary Management and Dramaturgy Lue Douthit presented the same challenge, which reflects parameters she developed after pilot "translations" by Ranjit Bolt and Tim Cavendar: "First, do no harm. There is language that will not need translating and some that does. Each team is being asked to examine the play line-by-line and translate to contemporary modern English those lines that need translating. There is to be no cutting or editing of scenes and playwrights may not add their personal politics. Second, put the same kind of pressure on the language as Shakespeare put on his. This means the playwright must consider the meter, rhyme, rhythm, metaphor, rhetoric, character action and theme of the original. These translations are not adaptations. Setting, time period and references will remain unchanged."[6] In this same press release, Douthit stated, "'Translate' is an inadequate word because it implies a word-for-word substitution, which isn't what we're doing. I'm going for something much more subtle. But I like the rigor that 'translate' implies. What excites me the most about this is who will dig into these texts."[7] *Play on!* at its core therefore embraces the idea of creating new writings out of old writings. The artists commissioned by OSF for this project understand that the goal of the project is to create companion texts to Shakespeare's plays that are meant to help illuminate the original text while also standing on their own as pieces of new writing that may be performed.

In a way that benefits the context for *The Two Noble Kinsmen*, Slover is known for writing "history plays."[8] As David Ivers, former coartistic director of the Utah Shakespeare Festival, notes about another one of Slover's plays, *March Tale*, which is set during the English Renaissance and is about Shakespeare's troupe, "it's a very difficult thing to write a period play, and Tim's natural dexterity with language and understanding of structure make 'March Tale' a must-see."[9] Slover's skill set includes an ingrained sense of Shakespeare's history and an understanding and respect for the language, style, and rhythm of Shakespeare. Slover states: "Recent scholarship has focused on Shakespeare as a collaborator with other writers—a subject which also interests me—and *The Two Noble Kinsmen* certainly fits that category. . . . Many think of *The Tempest* as Shakespeare's farewell to the stage, but it was *The Two Noble Kinsmen* that he actually wrote last. What drew him to this final collaboration? What about Chaucer's 'Knight's Tale' attracted his attention? Perhaps the answer to these questions can be found in the script, itself."[10]

The other half of this artistic pairing is Green-Rogers, one of Slover's former colleagues at the University of Utah and a freelance dramaturg who works on reimaginings of Shakespeare in performance. Green-Rogers brings to the process of creating a new text a clear reverence and need for understanding the old text, all bathed in a healthy dose of playfulness. She is working on two of the scripts in the *Play on!* project (*The Two Noble Kinsmen* and *The Comedy of Errors*).[11]

In spring 2016, students in the New Play Workshop course at the University of Utah aided Slover in developing the first draft of the script. His companion piece was workshopped within this class in the way new plays are often workshopped in theatrical settings. This course, taken by students in the BA in theatre studies and the BFA in actor training program at the University of Utah, creates a space in which new plays by playwrights of professional and student backgrounds may have access to student directors, actors, and dramaturgs to facilitate a playwright's lab experience. Slover and the University of Utah Department of Theatre's administration felt strongly that it would be ideal to use this pool of actors during the script-creation phase of the project. In fact, many of the people in this class may end up acting in the scheduled spring 2017 production of the play at the University of Utah and could help collaborate on the new language they will eventually present onstage.

Alex Vermillion, a senior in the English Department and a theatre studies minor, is the student dramaturg assigned to aid Green-Rogers on this project. Green-Rogers and Vermillion created a dramaturgical website and workbook that was used to study (and scrutinize) Slover's language choices. This workbook presents a side-by-side view of the quarto version of the original text, the Arden version of the text, and Slover's version of the text. This comparison of the three texts allowed Green-Rogers and Vermillion to assess how closely Slover adhered to the rules set by the project during the first draft and may be useful as a pedagogical tool for those studying Shakespeare and Fletcher's work in comparison to Slover's modernization. As of this writing, the script for *The Two Noble Kinsmen* is still in development. An adaptation created specifically for the production (supported by the New Play Workshop class) occurred ahead of the translation of the entire script because of the need to prepare for the spring 2017 production at the University of Utah.

Shakespeare and Language

We ground our process at Utah in the observation that when a playwright creates a new play, as Shakespeare and Fletcher did when they penned *The Two*

Noble Kinsmen, he or she crafts the story, characters, and language with a target audience in mind. These tasks are no different when a playwright translates a classic text; language and adaptation choices must consider the audience. There is an implied contract between the audience and the performance (regardless of whether the performance is a new, contemporary play, or classic text) that the language onstage will not impede the audience's understanding of the performance, unless the audience is watching in a country in which they do not speak the language. However, as time passes, and the Western canon ages, this implied contract has been broken; words fall into disuse or a word's denotation or connotation shifts. Examples of these words and phrases in act 3, scene 1 of *The Two Noble Kinsmen* include: "laund" (clearing), "house-clogs" (shackles), and "gyves" (fetters). Slover replaced the antiquated words with the contemporary words found in the parentheticals and then, if needed, adjusted the sentence to account for its new rhythm. This small action made those lines easier for the students to comprehend during the workshop.

One critique of the objectives of *Play on!* is that audiences are already able to understand Shakespeare's words, through either sufficient education and preparation or simply by dint of clear and vivid performances. Yet, the fact that we *do* have, and need, specialized training and additional books when it comes to understanding, theorizing, and performing Shakespearean texts serves as the proof that the Bard's language is not as natural and comprehensible as some argue. And in fact, this challenge with regard to language has, perhaps, shaped *The Two Noble Kinsmen* from its inception: Chaucer's *The Canterbury Tales* was written in the 1380s, during a period of transition between Old English and Middle English, and Chaucer used words from these two types of English interchangeably in this work. For this reason, by the late fifteenth and early sixteenth centuries, Chaucer's use of language may have been as confusing to those studying and reading his work during the English Renaissance as Shakespeare's early modern English is to some now.

In addition, Shakespeare was using language that was "new" to his audience as well. He transformed nouns into verbs and verbs into adjectives, was liberal and creative in his use of prefixes and suffixes, and, on occasion, created new words entirely.[12] However, while noting Shakespeare's creation of "new" language that we continue to use, we must also recognize that there are words Shakespeare created (or used liberally) that have crept out of common usage. Those words leave us with a gap in terms of meaning and understanding in the language of Shakespeare's plays, just as a gap existed between Chaucer's tale and Shakespeare and Fletcher's reimagining of that text. What, in theory, *Play on!* hopes to achieve is the same feeling of "newness" of *The Two Noble Kinsmen* from Shakespeare's time period for a contemporary audience by embracing modern slang (when appropriate), updating archaic terminology, and searching for equivalent and effective idioms, just as Shakespeare and Fletcher did with the text of Chaucer, thereby bringing subtle or hidden jokes in Shakespearean texts to life with language modern audiences will understand and embrace.

Take, for example, 2.3, when the Jailer arrives to inform Palamon that he must move jail cells because the windows "are too open," making him a flight risk.[13] Palamon resists this move because it would mean he would not be able to see the garden, and therefore, the woman he has fallen for, Emilia, when she is out for a walk. The Jailer threatens him with additional shackling and Palamon's response in the original text is "Do, good keeper!/ I'll shake 'em so, ye shall not sleep; I'll make ye a new morris" (274–76). Slover's translation turns that line into "Then I'd shake them so loud you'll never sleep—I'd Morris dance in them!" This small shift in language allows for a clearer understanding of the joke (that Palamon is referring to a dance with the word "morris"). Even if a reader is not familiar with a "Morris dance," the clue that it *is* a dance will allow a reader (or performer) to infer that the joke is born out of the noise the chains would make during that type of dance (not just the shaking of the chains that the first part of that line sequence implies). This embedded help in understanding Palamon's statement allows a production to avoid removing the line "I'll make ye a new morris" or delivering a "bad joke" (which may happen in a production of the original text) and allows a reader to understand what is occurring without having to look for a footnote, an endnote, or a dictionary.[14]

Despite the clarity that has come from these changes, there have also been challenges with the language in translation. During the New Play Workshop class, there were numerous instances in which the dialogue between the two lead characters, Palamon and Arcite, felt stilted. Changes were made to no avail. However, some dramaturgical digging held the key to the problem. Later in the process, it was discovered that Slover's translation had removed the verse and shared lines in those passages. Dialogue that was meant to be rapid fire was being delivered at a much slower and unmeasured pace, which detracted from the emotion of the scene. Although the changes to the verse and shared lines will remain in the adaptation performed at the University of Utah in 2017, discussion about the translation text and how these lines will read in the final version submitted to the *Play on*! project is ongoing.

From Language to History

Translating the language of a historical text can be interpreted as an act of violence against the history and context of the play. Changing a term from its original language loses the cultural and historical vocabulary of that period. However, Shakespeare, by manipulating some of the historical events represented in his plays, also played with the "old" way of telling history and made way for a "new" manner of viewing these events. Felix C. H. Sprang says that Shakespeare's histories "invited early modern Londoners to position themselves as 'modern' vis-a-vis ancient Rome and medieval England. . . . His late plays seemed less concerned with 'medieval' themes or ideas than with an exploration of narrative structures and generic boundaries."[15] Through his writing, Shakespeare sought to do what many modern directors and playwrights aim to do when producing historical plays: Tell a story with a setting and characters so fully realized that any new or unfamiliar information becomes an easily digested part of a compelling, propulsive narrative. After all, for the audience one of the most seductive pleasures of a play is being transported to locations and situations far outside themselves, and Shakespeare accomplished this by taking on the role of educator as well as entertainer. For instance, Shakespeare often has a minor character enter his plays *first* (e.g., Rumor, in *Henry IV, Part II*) to capture the rather rowdy and loud audience. During these speeches, the minor characters provide the audience with background information for the play they are about to watch. If a contemporary audience of a Shakespeare play is prevented from understanding the historical background provided by this opening speech, due to a language barrier, then the meaning and the reception of the production is threatened (since a contemporary audience does not have the information needed to understand the play as members of Shakespeare's audience would have).

In the case of *The Two Noble Kinsmen*, a contemporary audience's ability to understand the language of the play is troubled from the start because of the stylistic differences between Shakespeare and his Chaucerian source text. Chaucer used didactic repetition and little to no imagery and saved old stories by rewriting them as literature, while Shakespeare used repetition for style or to set the mood, combined history with modern stories to dramatize them for his audience, and provided many details about the setting of his scenes. Although they both used historical sources from classical Greek and Roman literature, Chaucer was more likely than Shakespeare to reference his sources in his works. While Chaucer and Shakespeare both spoke and wrote in English, there were significant differences in language and language structure between the late 1300s and early 1600s—much like Shakespeare's language differs greatly from our modern language, owing to the four-hundred-year gap between Shakespeare and the writing of this article. Slover embraces these precedents to bring the world that Chaucer began and Shakespeare and Fletcher dramatized to contemporary audiences.

Shakespeare took a risk, just as Slover and the other playwrights participating in the *Play on!* project are doing, by incorporating twists on words and meanings that move between historical and linguistic contexts. Peggy A. Knapp, in *Time-Bound Words: Semantic and Social Economies from Chaucer's England to Shakespeare's*, states: "Semantic and social changes must be seen in a dynamic and fluid relationship, in which new social formations modify the range or inflection of verbal signs and those signs in turn impel or retard social change,. . . . for example, the shift from a primary meaning for *thrift* as feudal proprietary to one which stressed economic frugality under Calvinist influence. But other kinds of semantic participation in social transformation are more gradual and diffuse. *Kynde*, for example, slowly loses its medieval connection with *kin*, and its early modern spelling *kind* begins to appear as the neutral 'category' or 'sort,' in an intellectual climate inclining toward systematicity and away from birthright."[16] The words in Knapp's study are "bound to and bounded by the social formation in which they occur, the horizon of what is imaginable in a particular time and place," and because they are bound by time and place, they are "headed somewhere—not necessarily for glory. . . . but headed for new territory."[17] Words continually change because they are signifiers. Language is not natural or inherent; Shakespeare knew this, and the artists involved in *Play on!* are tasked with taking great care to preserve the deep meaning and significance conveyed by every aspect of Shakespeare's language and legacy.

Moreover, because *The Two Noble Kinsmen* is an adaptation itself of Chaucer's "The Knight's Tale," Shakespeare and Fletcher begin the text by establishing that adaptation is a boon, rather than a liability, in the creative process. In the prologue of the play, they state:

> New plays and maidenheads are near akin:
> Much followed both, for both much money gi'en,
> If they stand sound and well. And a good play,
> Whose modest scenes blush on his marriage day
> And shake to lose his honour, is like her
> That after holy tie and first night's stir
> Yet still is Modesty and still retains

More of the maid, to sight, than husband's pains.
We pray our play may be so, for I am sure
It has a noble breeder and a pure,
A learned, and a poet never went
More famous yet 'twixt Po and silver Trent.
Chaucer, of all admired, the story gives;
There, constant to eternity, it lives.
If we let fall the nobleness of this
And the first sound this child hear be a hiss,
How will it shake the bones of that good man
And make him cry from under ground, 'Oh, fan
From me the witless chaff of such a writer
That blasts my bays and my famed works makes
lighter
Than Robin Hood!. . .[18]

Alex Davis's article "Living in the Past: Thebes, Periodization, and *The Two Noble Kinsmen*" establishes that "the point of the prologue of *The Two Noble Kinsmen* is to stage a form of historical awareness that is predicated on a sense of the difference of the past. And yet, perhaps the most immediately striking thing about these lines is just how lightly they historicize the figure of Geoffrey Chaucer. . . . Chaucer is presented as above all grave and noble: a laureate poet. . . . He is presented, in fact, as something like an English Petrarch."[19] That kind of reverence for Chaucer is lampooned and yet still supported by Shakespeare and Fletcher. This attitude remains in Slover's translation, since Slover is evoking the same sense of the difference from the past to which Davis refers. Slover's translation of *The Two Noble Kinsmen* participates in this lineage of positive "adaptation" across history, as illustrated by Slover's reworking of that same section of text:

New plays and new brides are much the same:
Both much desired and both expensive to maintain.
And a play, if good, when first it meets your sight
Is like the blushing bride after her blissful opening night:
Happy, modest, content, and smiling a lot
A good new play, like her, is again as eagerly sought.

This one's father was a poet of fame:
Geoffrey Chaucer, lively and profound
This story was his and bears his name.
Ours is its child, and if the sound
That first it hears is hiss of blame,
His voice will cry from underground,

> "Who has dared to blaspheme me for gain?
> Who threats to blast my poet's crown?"[20]

Although Slover is prohibited from lampooning Shakespeare and Fletcher's lampooning of Chaucer in his translation, due to the rules of the *Play on!* project, the humor in this moment was not lost on the students working with Slover and Green-Rogers on the translation. Students chuckled during their first read of Slover's script, getting the joke that might have been lost on them had they been reading the original text.

Which Story Is Being Told?

A final problem for new plays made out of old ones concerns the potential for changes to the through lines of the plot and characters. *The Two Noble Kinsmen* combines factual history with mythological figures from ancient Greece; it begins with three queens whose husbands have been killed in battle by Creon of Thebes. Creon is an evil tyrant who refuses to properly bury the kings. The queens plead with Theseus and Hippolyta, the rulers of Athens, to avenge their husbands' deaths, and he accepts their request. As history imparts, Ancient Thebes fought for its freedom for many years, going back and forth as enemies and allies of Sparta. During this time, Thebes invited Philip II of Macedon to aid in their fight, but once given power Philip II decides to conquer Thebes for himself and rule Thebes with his son, Alexander the Great. However, in 335 BCE, the citizens revolt against Alexander the Great and Philip II, which results in Alexander the Great and Philip II destroying the city and subjecting the Thebans to slavery. The citizens revolt again in 292 BCE, ushering in the Siege of Thebes.[21] It is this battle that the three queens allude to in *The Two Noble Kinsmen*.

This source material raises a question: which version of the story is being adapted by Shakespeare and how does that affect what Slover is translating? Chaucer's "The Knight's Tale" is not the first literary account of the Siege of Thebes in the manner described in *The Two Noble Kinsmen*. Boccaccio first retold the story of Palamon, Arcite, and Emilia (characters found in Shakespeare and Fletcher's version) in his epic poem *Teseida delle Nozze d'Emilia* (1340). Chaucer began writing *The Canterbury Tales* at some point in the 1380s and "read a number of works by Giovanni Boccaccio (1313–75) in this period, and as his poetry grew increasingly ambitious he turned to Boccaccio again and again for source material and inspiration."[22] Richard Allan Underwood notes that Shakespeare's adaptation is more similar to Chaucer's than to Boccaccio's. Underwood states that "the Theseus character in Boccaccio is relatively kind," "Chaucer's Theseus is a sterner figure," and "Shakespeare's Theseus is more complex."[23] He goes on to state, "Shakespeare's depiction of Theseus begins in public spectacle. . . . In Fletcher's scenes especially . . . Theseus is forever marveling at the combatants who will help decide which man marries Emilia. . . . On the other hand, as in Chaucer, he is an angry Theseus who must be knelt to. . . . Shakespeare's Theseus of *The Two Noble Kinsmen* is often arrogant and angry, impatient to dispose of Emilia."[24]

Shakespeare and Fletcher's characters resemble those of Chaucer's "The Knight's Tale" more so than those of Boccaccio's *Teseida*. The character of Emilia, for example, gains more autonomy with each revision/adaptation of her story. Although Boccaccio's Emilia may possess more "three-dimensionality"[25] in a literal sense, it is Chaucer who deemphasizes Emilia's physical description and chooses instead to shape her character through voice and dialogue. Chaucer's Emilia delivers a full-length speech to the goddess Diana, in which she prays to keep her virginity. Dissatisfied with a mere three descriptive dimensions or, indeed, a single impassioned speech, Shakespeare picks up where Chaucer left off. The Emilia of *The Two Noble Kinsmen* is active, complex, likable, and opinionated. She delivers multiple speeches and openly speaks of the love she feels with one of her ladies. Her "decision to be a participant is crucial to her role in the play. . . . Shakespeare goes beyond Boccaccio and Chaucer in having her think feelingly of other women who will condemn her [for the bloodshed of these two cousins]."[26] The nuances of how these characters have evolved into Shakespeare and Fletcher's version must remain in Slover's script, because the rules of the *Play on!* project discourage Slover from shifting the characters in his own ways. Although this prevents Slover from following in Shakespeare and Fletcher's footsteps in terms of bringing something new to his version of the story, it also underlines the importance of Slover's work as a companion text. Slover's text allows a reader to more easily understand the adjustments Shakespeare and Fletcher made to the characters in this story from an English Renaissance perspective when compared to Chaucer's text.

Shakespeare and Fletcher combined the previous versions of this story to add dimension to the characters, to provide more historical context, and to bring a story to life by adapting these poems into a play. Created for Jacobean audiences, *The Two Noble Kinsmen* provided a story that incorporates themes of love, honor, lust, kinship, and virginity—all of which lent urgency, currency, and entertainment value to a familiar tale. However, for Shakespeare to adapt Chaucer's works (or indeed, for Chaucer to adapt Boccaccio's), the process had to begin with an in-depth understanding of the language of the original text and from there start the process of making new texts out of the old writing. Created for twenty-first-century audiences, Slover's new *The Two Noble Kinsmen* begins with a similar in-depth understanding of the source text to create, again, a new text from the old.

Performance History and the Future of *Kinsmen*

The performance history, or lack thereof, of *The Two Noble Kinsmen* illustrates how a text and the perceptions of that text can impede the performance of a play and exacerbate confusions in audience comprehension. Called "a deeply flawed play" by people such as Michael Kahn, the artistic director of Shakespeare Theatre Company, *The Two Noble Kinsmen* has within the past fifty years begun to fascinate Shakespeare scholars and performers more. Despite high-profile productions such as the one at the Royal Shakespeare Company in 2016, the play still suffers from the stigma of being one of the last plays of debatable Shakespearean authorship.[27] The editors of the Folger Shakespeare Library's most recent publication of the play, Barbara A. Mowat and Paul Werstine, acknowledge the difficulties this play presents, stating that people who do not have a background in Latin or poetry would "need to develop the skills of untangling unusual sentence structure and of recognizing and understanding poetic compressions, omissions, and wordplay. And even those skilled in reading unusual sentence structures may have occasional trouble with the words in the play."[28] For this reason, producers of Shakespeare tend to shy away from this play, despite the growing enthrallment. Even the Oregon Shakespeare Festival has produced this play only once, in 1994, as an additional piece, because they do not view it as part of the canon.[29]

Despite this play's complicated authorship and production history, OSF decided to include it in Shakespeare's canon when selecting works for the *Play on!* project. In an interview, Douthit explained the reasoning behind the play's inclusion: "There have been other plays that some scholars have been advocating for [inclusion in Shakespeare's canon] but *Edward III* and *The Two Noble Kinsmen* seemed the most legitimate not only in terms of language but in production history with Shakespeare's company. . . . There is something about the feel of the play that I think is in Shakespeare's wheelhouse. . . . Formally, it ranges all over the place, and has a bit of a throwback to the morality plays that influenced Shakespeare at the beginning of his career. I liked the fact that he returns to his early morality roots infused with the Jacobean masques."[30] Slover's journey toward creating a companion text for this play begins from this place of revering the text, its history, its range, and the lack of attention shone upon it.

Adhering to the rules of the project has so far presented the playwright and dramaturgs with many challenges, but these are challenges they all embrace. As Slover states, "The most challenging aspect has been working with archaic metaphors in the dialogue. They are not likely to communicate sense and meaning to a contemporary audience—and moreover, the concepts that the metaphors are being employed to make vivid are also likely to be obscure. In those cases the policy I have adopted is to create both metaphors and the ideas which are being illuminated that are as close as possible to the originals but more likely to communicate to a modern audience in performance." Resultantly, Emilia's line in 1.3 of Shakespeare and Fletcher's original text—"Thanks, sir. Remember me / To our all-royal brother, for whose speed/ The great Bellona I'll solicit; and, / Since in our terrene state petitions are not/ Without gifts understood, I'll offer to her / What I shall be advised she likes. Our hearts / Are in his army, in his tent"[31]—becomes in Slover's text "I thank you, sir. Remember me to my royal almost brother-in-law. For his sake I go to lay on the altar of the great Goddess of War whatever gifts she likes best. Our hearts are in his army, in his tent."[32] The students in the New Play Workshop class noticed how much easier it was to comprehend that passage in Slover's version, and this made the students even more interested in comparing the original with Slover's text.

Despite these challenges, the process of excavating Shakespeare and Fletcher's use of language is proving to be a rewarding exercise. Slover continues, "In accordance with guidance from Lue Douthit—and my own inclination—I have adopted as a guiding principle being very respectful to the script as written. What that means is that my goals are always simply clarification and 'dramatization,' that is, making the new script both accessible and playable without changing the content, characters, or tone. J. R. R. Tolkien writes usefully about the need for employing heightened language when writing modern fairy stories. *The Two Noble Kinsmen* is akin to a fairytale, and so, I believe, calls for that kind of language."[33] Slover's employment of fairy tale–like language in his script becomes apparent in the Jailer's Daughter's speech in 2.1.: "They seem to think no more about their captivity than I think about ruling Athens. They have good appetites, they're cheerful, they talk together of many subjects—but never of their shackles or misfortunes. Every now and then, one or the other begins to sigh, but stifles it quickly. And then the other rebukes it so gently and sweetly that I could wish I was that sigh—or, better yet, someone to be so rebuked."[34]

Play on! has its own deadline for delivery of the final *The Two Noble Kinsmen* script, December 31, 2018, but Slover accelerated his process to meet the public reading of his version of *The Two Noble Kinsmen*, in April 2016, and the production in April 2017. Slover and Green-Rogers found that working with student actors to facilitate the crafting of language during the process was invaluable. Some students remarked that they entered the process assuming the language would be easier to deliver because it was modernized, only to realize that because Slover followed Shakespeare and Fletcher in employing heightened language, they needed the same skills they were learning in their Shakespeare class to perform Slover's text. This information was useful not only to Slover but also to the *Play on!* project, in terms of the efficacy of the rules in place for the project. We learned that the rules of the *Play on!* project also function to maintain the rigor of the language.

The controversial premise and launch of *Play on!* does not seem to affect the energy and excitement of the students working on the project at the University of Utah—and for that reason, the project may be well on its way to achieving its goal of inspiring a new love of Shakespeare (and a new text), as desired by the David Hitz, Lue Douthit, and the Oregon Shakespeare Festival. Most importantly, in the New Play Workshop class at the University of Utah, the irony is not lost on any of the participants that a process normally used to support the development of "new" texts has now become an avenue by which a deep engagement with an "old" text may occur.

Notes

1. "*Play on!* Further Reading," Oregon Shakespeare Festival, accessed March 5, 2016, https://www.osfashland.org/experience-osf/upcoming/play-on/play-on-faq.aspx.
2. James Shapiro, "Shakespeare in Modern English?" *New York Times*, October 7, 2015, https://www.nytimes.com/2015/10/07/opinion/shakespeare-in-modern-english.html.
3. Bill Rauch, "Why We're Translating Shakespeare," *American Theatre*, October 14, 2015, http://www.americantheatre.org/2015/10/14/bill-rauch-why-were-translating-shakespeare/.
4. Ibid.
5. During the class, the students spent time debating whether the Jailer's Daughter was going insane because of her love for Palamon or whether she began to play "insane" because of the situation she had put herself and her father in by releasing Palamon without Theseus's consent. Many students felt that the clarity that came with Slover's translation of 3.2. placed the Jailer's Daughter character on a clearer path as to why she acts the way she does later in the play.
6. "OSF Launches Three-Year Shakespeare Translation Commissioning Project," Oregon Shakespeare Festival, accessed October 14, 2015, https://www.osfashland.org/press-room/press-releases/play-on.aspx. In April 2014, the Alabama Shakespeare Festival

presented Cavander's *Timon of Athens*. This was the watershed moment for the project. Rick Harmon of the *Montgomery Advertiser* wrote in his review of the production, "Cavander has streamlined this plot, which strengthens its characters. At the same time, he has made the lines more understandable to modern audiences while retaining the feel and eloquence of Shakespeare's language." Rick Harmon, "Review: ASF's 'Timon' premiere superb." *Montgomery Advertiser*, May 7, 2014, http://www.montgomeryadvertiser.com/story/life/2014/05/01/review-asfs-timon-premiere-superb/8589499/.

7. Douthit, qtd. in "OSF Launches Three-Year Shakespeare Translation Commissioning Project."
8. Ellen Fagg Weist, "Utah Playwright Makes Shakespeare's Love Story Come Alive," *Salt Lake Tribune*, January 14, 2016, http://www.sltrib.com/home/3391564-155/utah-playwright-makes-shakespeares-love-story.
9. Ibid.
10. Timothy Slover, e-mail communication with Green-Rogers, February 26, 2016.
11. Christina Anderson is the playwright on the *Play on!* translation *of The Comedy of Errors*.
12. Rachael Scarborough King, "Coined by Shakespeare? Think again," *Boston Globe*, August 18, 2013, https://www.bostonglobe.com/ideas/2013/08/17/coined-shakespeare-think-again/tWFE6b8qTD5gnybL5fOn8H/story.html.
13. Line 265.
14. The authors acknowledge that some of this confusion could be cleared up in a performance by way of the actor performing a piece of a morris dance. However, this does not clear up this confusion for someone reading the original text rather than viewing its performance. This small shift in the language clears up the ambiguity no matter how you encounter Slover's text (on the page or on the stage).
15. Felix C. H. Sprang. "Never Fortune Did Play A Subtler Game." *European Journal Of English Studies* 15, no. 2 (2011): 115, accessed January 5, 2016, doi:10.1080/13825577.2011.566692.
16. Peggy A. Knapp, *Time-Bound Words: Semantic and Social Economies from Chaucer's England to Shakespeare's* (London: MacMillan, 2000), 6.
17. Ibid., 8.
18. John Fletcher, William Shakespeare, and Lois Potter, *The Arden Shakespeare: The Two Noble Kinsmen* (London: Bloomsbury, 2015), 117–78.
19. Alex Davis. "Living in the Past: Thebes, Periodization, and the Two Noble Kinsmen." *Journal of Medieval and Early Modern Studies* 40, no. 1 (2010): 173–95, accessed January 5, 2016, doi: 10.1215/10829636-2009-018.
20. Timothy Slover, *The Two Noble Kinsmen*, draft, June 27, 2016.
21. See *A History of Macedonia: 336–167 B.C.*, by Hammond and Walbank, for more information about the Siege of Thebes.
22. Geoffrey Chaucer and David Wright, *The Canterbury Tales*, Oxford World's Classics (London: Oxford University Press, 1986), xiii.
23. Richard Allen Underwood, *The Two Noble Kinsmen and Its Beginnings*, (Salzburg, Austria: Salzburg University, 1993), 11–12.
24. Ibid., 13.
25. Ibid., 14.
26. Ibid., 19.
27. John Pancake, "Shakespeare's 'Two Noble Kinsmen' a Pleasant Surprise to Find—and Watch," *Washington Post*, August 19, 2011, https://www.washingtonpost.com/

lifestyle/style/shakespeares-two-noble-kinsmen-a-pleasant-surprise-to-find—and-watch/2011/08/15/gIQAR6I1PJ_story.html.

28. William Shakespeare and John Fletcher, "The Two Noble Kinsmen," ed. Barbara A. Mowat and Paul Werstine, *The Folger Shakespeare Library* (New York: Simon & Schuster, 2010), xix.
29. Lue Douthit, e-mail communication with Green-Rogers, August 24, 2016.
30. Ibid., February 15, 2016.
31. Lois Potter, "The Two Noble Kinsmen/John Fletcher and William Shakespeare," *MLA International Bibliography*, EBSCO*host*, accessed August 27, 2016.
32. Timothy Slover, *The Two Noble Kinsmen*, first draft, March 27, 2016.
33. Timothy Slover, e-mail communication with Green-Rogers, March 2016.
34. Timothy Slover, *The Two Noble Kinsmen*, first draft, March 27, 2016.

Making New Theatre Together

The First Writers' Group at the Royal Court Theatre and Its Legacy within the Young Writers' Programme

—NICHOLAS HOLDEN

The reconstruction of the Royal Court between 1996 and 2000 saw the theatre relocated to the heart of London's West End. The Court's delayed return to Sloane Square, along with the arrival of Ian Rickson as the theatre's new artistic director (1998–2006), allowed for a period of reflection and adjustment as the theatre approached the new millennium. Under Stephen Daldry's leadership (1992–1998), the Royal Court enjoyed one of the most successful periods in its history, with new plays by exciting young playwrights such as Sarah Kane, Joe Penhall, Mark Ravenhill, and Rebecca Prichard all contributing to what was hailed as the "renaissance of new writing."[1]

Through Rickson's appointment, the Royal Court returned to Sloane Square with new intentions that rejected the "stack 'em high, sell 'em cheap" 1990s paradigm, which saw around fifty new plays produced for short runs in the Court's Theatre Upstairs between 1994 and 1997. Rickson's administration replaced it with a more considered culture of growth and development for new playwrights at the theatre.[2] The rebranding of the Court's long-standing Young Peoples' Theatre as the Young Writers' Programme (YWP) and the subsequent relocation of that initiative to a building adjacent to the Royal Court known as the Site proved to be an early sign of Rickson's aspirations for a more unified theatre. Launched in 1998, the Young Writers' Programme sought to focus the Court's work with young people on playwriting, and this implemented what Catherine Love calls a "culture of development" that, importantly, aligned with the Court's identity as a writers' theatre.[3] In the first decade of the twenty-first century, the Young Writers'

Programme provided the foundation to the careers of playwrights such as Lucy Prebble, Duncan Macmillan, Polly Stenham, and Mike Bartlett, and those writers, in turn, featured regularly on the stages of the Royal Court and in British theatre more widely. The inception of the Young Writers' Programme, therefore, went on to provide an unsurpassed model of success for the Court that has since proved invaluable to the theatre's production of new plays by new writers.

The achievements of the writers who have emerged out of the Royal Court's Young Writers' Programme can be measured through the production of their plays in the United Kingdom, the United States, and across Europe. In addition, the work of the Court's International department, headed by Elyse Dodgson, has ensured that the theatre's work with writers has become a truly international endeavor. But in spite of the YWP's significant accomplishments in its fourteen-year history, academic engagement within this area of the Court remains limited. Indeed, it is only Love's 2015 article that has looked to bring some much-needed focus and scholarly analysis to what she describes as the "overwhelmingly successful" structure of the Royal Court's Young Writers' Programme.[4] But the YWP is not the Royal Court's first attempt to provide an infrastructure that would offer support for a new generation of playwrights at the theatre. Such ambitions can be traced back to 1958, two years after the English Stage Company first began its residency of the Royal Court, where a writers' group was first established by George Devine in an attempt to further relationships between the Royal Court and a number of aspiring young playwrights of the time. In contrast to the Young Writers' Programme, whose history, as I have noted above, is in the early stages of academic analysis, the purpose, practice, and impact of the first Writers' Group at the Royal Court can be largely comprehended from the recollections of that time in the autobiographies of the group's members and through many of the publications on the history of the Royal Court.[5]

It is the purpose of this article, therefore, to revisit what should be regarded as the first attempt to bring a new generation of young playwrights to the Royal Court, through the Writers' Group in 1958, and to place the group's inception, methodology, and legacy within the contemporary context of the Young Writers' Programme. The article draws on existing information on the first Writers' Group and combines it with original insights from theatre practitioners who have worked closely with the Royal Court, such as William Gaskill (artistic director, 1965–1969), Ola Animashawun (director of the Young Writers' Programme, 1998–2008), and Simon Stephens (Young Writers' Programme writers' tutor; 2001–2005) to create a new analysis of the Royal Court's long association with young writers.

As I have already suggested, the objective of the Young Writers' Programme—to provide support for the next generation of playwrights for the Royal Court—shares some fundamental commonalities with the earlier initiative implemented by the theatre in 1958. This article developed out of an interview that I conducted with the late theatre director William Gaskill, which took place in January 2015, just over a year before Gaskill's death, in February 2016. It is through this interview that I started to reconsider both the purpose of a writers' group within a theatre such as the Royal Court and the impact of such initiatives on their participants. I had arranged to meet with Gaskill initially to discuss his involvement with the origins of the Young Peoples' Theatre, which Gaskill had pioneered along with Jane Howell, in 1966. However, as our conversation evolved, it became evident that much of our hour-long dialogue would be focused on the beginnings, methodology, and legacy of the Court's first Writers' Group. Indeed, it is upon these three aspects of the Writers' Group—its beginnings, methodology, and legacy—that this essay builds, as it reflects and engages with the origins of a notion that remains fundamental to the approach used by the Royal Court in its work with new playwrights, today. It argues that the Writers' Group was set up by George Devine to proactively source new writers for the Royal Court in an attempt to replicate the early success garnered by John Osborne's *Look Back in Anger*. However, what emerged instead was a group of writers who were far removed from the autonomous process of writing a play, as demonstrated by John Osborne, and instead driven by mutual support, collaboration, and community that carved an unexpected legacy for the group's participants and the Royal Court in the decade that followed. In positioning this argument within the context of the Young Writers' Programme, this article is able to confirm and expand previously established parallels that have been made between the Royal Court of the 1950s and the theatre in the 1990s. Further, it begins to articulate and elucidate the competing models of success that functioned across two generations at the Royal Court, as the theatre looked to build and sustain its reputation as a leading producer of new writing in the United Kingdom.

As Aleks Sierz and Jacqueline Bolton have previously alluded to, it is possible to draw similarities between these two significant periods in the theatre's history, particularly through the models of commissioning and production deployed in the 1950s that were echoed through Stephen Daldry's artistic directorship in the mid 1990s, "a period commensurate in the public imagination with 'the right to fail': the right to take risks, the right to show daring, the right to take a punt on a play despite the playwright's anonymity."[6] But by 1998, Ian Rickson had started to prepare the Royal Court for life beyond Kane, Ravenhill, Penhall, and so on, and out of this emerged the Young Writers' Programme, a tangible space in which a new generation of playwrights could be supported and developed. From the perspective of George Devine's Royal Court, the 1958 Writers' Group was created for much the same purpose: as a bridge that aimed to connect and familiarize new writers with the Royal Court in an attempt to maintain the theatre's ability to generate a constant output of new plays by a range of young writers.

Beginnings: A Paint Shop on Flood Street

The eventual success of Osborne's debut brought public interest and financial stability in the early years of the English Stage Company's tenure at the Royal Court. But the Court's aspiration to produce a season of work made up entirely of new British plays was yet to materialize.[7] As a result, the theatre's artistic director, George Devine, unwilling to rely on Osborne as the sole contributor to the Court's new writing ambitions, began to seek new plays and new writers through alternative means. Out of this developed the Sunday Night Productions without Décor, a financially austere initiative, beginning in 1957, that saw the chosen productions afforded no budget, the actors paid a small amount, and the writers asked to relinquish all rights to their work for just five pounds.[8] Sunday Nights provided aspiring writers with the opportunity to present their work on the Royal Court Stage in a "simple way without scenery."[9] It was through their involvement with the Sunday Night Productions that some of the first members of the Writers' Group were found.

The desire to formulate a Royal Court Writers' Group was first put forward by George Devine in a letter to the English Stage Company chairman, Neville Blond, on January 2, 1958. Here, Devine suggests that "a small group of young writers" be invited to meet regularly with each other and with members of the Court staff.[10] Within the month, the first meeting had been arranged. The limited space at the theatre meant that an alternative location at a paint shop on Flood Street was secured as the group's base, and here the participants "sat on boxes, creaking chairs, anything to hand, in a strict circle surrounded by debris and draughts" as Devine got the first meeting underway.[11] It is a less than glamorous picture and, unsurprisingly, given the working environment, the initial meetings of the first Writers' Group are remembered by those involved as being "tentative and a little stiff."[12] These early impressions were only exacerbated by those present in the room, as emerging young playwrights such as Anne Jellicoe, Keith Johnstone, and John Arden mixed with the Court's core of Devine and Lindsay Anderson, along with John Dexter and Devine's close friend Michel Saint-Denis.[13] As Gaskill recalls, Devine "didn't really know how to run [the group] or what to say and, although he was a wonderful man, he was often almost shy in his relationships with people."[14]

The early life of the Young Writers' Programme in the late 1990s also suffered some teething problems. The role of the writers' tutor evolved in the 2000s to become integral to the achievements of the program, but prior to that point, the tutor's post had been governed on an ad hoc basis by playwright Nicola Baldwin.[15] With the appointment of Simon Stephens to the role full-time in 2001, a turning point occurred in the Young Writers' Programme that afforded much-needed structure and vision to the initiative. It is because of this that Stephens and his successor, Leo Butler, are often credited for their positive influence "on a generation of young writers."[16]

The writers' tutor figure in 1958 is visible within George Devine's role in the group, but with the artistic director proving unable to provide the vital attributes of structure and leadership to the group, the meetings on Flood Street often lapsed into aimless discussion on the state of the theatre. It became evident that the combination of the paint shop backdrop coupled with the absence of any real vision for the group was not entirely conducive to a successful working environment that would be of benefit to those writers in attendance.[17]

Devine aimed to use the Writers' Group as "a means of creating a more formal structure to which young and promising writers could be invited and where they would come to know other writers and members of the Court staff."[18] For Devine this structure should be regarded as less about honing writing skills and more about networking and community building between young writers and Royal Court staff. The facilitating of these relationships through the Writers' Group meetings can be seen as an attempt by Devine to both safeguard the theatre's future in terms of its output of new plays and further the Court's intentions to function as a writers' theatre. But without any real purpose to the weekly gatherings, within the year Devine's presence was seen as a hindrance to the group's progression, and, as a result, the director, along with John Dexter, withdrew from the group. With no one immediately available to replace Devine, a temporary disbandment of the Writers' Group followed.

By creating the Writers' Group, Devine had hoped to systematically source a new cohort of Royal Court writers who would seemingly go on to support other writers, such as John Osborne, in producing work for the Royal Court stage. But his status within the Royal Court together with the sessions' lack of purpose exposed some early flaws in the initial meetings that led to its premature demise. In addition, what Devine had failed to take into account was that the Osborne model of success—the single authored play with an original, previously unheard voice that would ultimately bring both critical and box-office acclaim to the Court along with the potential to transfer to the West End—could not be easily replicated. Further, the solitude that accompanies the life of a playwright is isolating to some but welcomed by others, and the invitation to take part in a group with other playwrights is not always the most appealing opportunity for a writer. Gaskill explains that "some people thought of their work as individual, which I think is true of Beckett or Pinter, and N. F. Simpson, and that they had nothing to learn from being part of a group."[19] The Writers' Group, therefore, split opinion and was the source of some of the earliest divides at the Royal Court.

Methodology: Reconceiving the Writers' Group

The breakdown of the group was short-lived because the aspirational Gaskill, "in one of his unemployed periods," took charge of the group following Devine's exit.[20] At that point, the venue also changed from the draughty paint shop on Flood Street to the "cozy and relaxing Georgian mansion" of fellow group member Anne Piper in London's Hammersmith.[21]

It was here that, as Gaskill recalls, the relaunched Writers' Group "very quickly formed itself into a specific group of people who met every week."[22] With a new leader at the helm, the group expanded to include Edward Bond, who was "very keen and would come every week without fail," along with Arnold Wesker and Wole Soyinka joining Jellicoe, Arden, and Johnstone as its most devoted members.[23] The group met regularly on a Wednesday evening and quickly developed an ethos that was far removed from Devine's discussion-based sessions and instead founded upon Johnstone's belief that "things should be shown happening in the theatre, not analyzed and talked about."[24] Johnstone's practice-based work ethic became central to the operation of the group, leading to a format that was largely improvisational in content and focused almost entirely on the physical exploration of the theatre.[25] Gaskill remembers this shift in focus from discussions to practice: "The basis of the group was that we basically did acting exercises, it wasn't like people read their plays, we had different themes for example one week George Devine taught them the use of the character mask and then I would hold sessions on Brecht . . . and the writers themselves would supply ideas and we would work on them through improvisation."[26] This move from discussion to practice-based sessions became central to the group as it moved forward over the next two years. It allowed writers to receive "direct experience [of] what it was like to get up on their feet rather than sit down and write":[27] "The moment anyone began discussing anything, Gaskill, Keith, or another writer would say, 'Go and show us.' And that is how improvisation became [the Writers' Group's] primary tool of exploration. Over the next two years [the group] would become very close and collaboratively develop moments for performance through improvisational means."[28] Both Gaskill and Johnstone scholar Theresa Robbins Dudeck note above how Johnstone's "no-discussion policy" was strictly enforced by the group.[29] But the improvisatory nature of the sessions served as an important catalyst for writers such as Jellicoe and Arden, who were experiencing some difficulties translating their ideas to the page.[30] As is indicated from his above account, Gaskill also introduced themes for the members to explore alongside the improvisational work of the group, as a way of broadening their understanding of theatre. As part of this, Gaskill led workshops on Brecht, and Devine returned with a series on mask work that is now regarded as one of the defining moments of the Writers' Group.[31] The writers, too, were often given responsibility for the sessions and later, as Gaskill's burgeoning directorial career began to affect his attendance, Jellicoe and Johnstone were charged with continuing the group's work in his absence. This insight into the practice of the Writers' Group is significant as it appears far removed from what might be expected from the self-titled "Writers' Theatre" and its work with new playwrights. That the meetings were concerned with the exploration of improvisation and the practical nature of the theatre as opposed to the creation of an environment that allowed writers to hone their playwriting skills is an unusual approach to adopt. In addition, the shared leadership and fluctuating numbers of the group imparted an unusual dynamic to the sessions that offered a sense of communal ownership of the group's work.

The introduction of weekly themes to the Writers' Group became central to the structure and methodology of the Young Writers' Programme as it evolved in the 2000s, as Simon Stephens attests: "Each week I would take a theme, and the theme would be what I considered to be a key element of the playwright's craft, which might be: dramatic action, writing dialogue, writing stage imagery, character, narrative, structure, re-writing, something like that and I would plan the session based on those things . . . and I'd plan a series of exercises based on those themes."[32] Stephens's approach for the Young Writers' Programme, more than forty years after the first Writers' Group at the Royal Court, is driven by what he calls "element[s] of the playwright's craft." As he describes above, the structure of the program is framed by a series of key components that he deems necessary to the fundamental composition of a play, and these are then delivered through writing exercises that the participants are expected to complete.

Although, as I have pointed out above, the concept of theming each workshop existed within the first Writers' Group, much of the work contained within the 1958 group's meetings was centered on the practical exploration of the theatre. The writing exercises delivered by Stephens in the Young Writers' Programme juxtaposed with the acting and improvisatory exercises present within the first Writers' Group are indicative of the differing approaches to and indeed knowledge of playwriting that existed at the time.

The methodologies of the Writers' Group and the Young Writers' Programme conflict on this account, but they are ultimately driven by a shared goal: to produce a script that could be considered for production by the Royal Court. In the same way that the participants of the Young Writers' Programme were expected to produce a script in the weeks that followed their completion of the course, the members of the Writers' Group, even if their work had been inspired by the improvisations carried out during the workshops, would also go on to develop those improvisations into the form of a script. It was not until the late 1980s and early 1990s that specific structures and guidelines with regards to what Stephens terms the "playwright's craft" began to articulate a more tangible pedagogy of playwriting. This paradigmatic shift in approaches to writing for the stage is reflected in the creation of specific playwriting courses within higher education, such as the renowned MA in Playwriting Studies at the University of Birmingham, United Kingdom, pioneered by playwright David Edgar in 1989, and these courses have contributed to a new understanding of the components necessary to write a play. Through the Young Writers' Programme, the Court, too, had recognized the potential to capitalize on the area of playwriting pedagogy and, with Simon Stephens's tutelage, carved a new model of success at the theatre whereby young writers could emerge through the Young Writers' Programme and the Young Writers' Festival and subsequently onto the main stages of the Royal Court Theatre.

However, this model of success, aligned to Devine's original objectives for the group, differs significantly from what was actually achieved by Gaskill's writers in the 1950s and beyond. With the Writers' Group headed by a director and focused on acting and improvisation rather than writing, a communal attitude and dedication by the group's members to work together generated a sense of unity that was grounded in mutual interests and shared experience: "The group had strength and cohesion because we were all much of an age, of the same calibre of personality and at the same time not too egotistical. We recognized each other's talent and supported it. This is said to be rare among writers. We were extremely careful whom we invited into the group—not from exclusiveness, but because we were aware that anyone too argumentative or destructive would upset the balance. Unsympathetic people would sometimes come in for a few meetings, but they tended to fall away: the central core was probably too strong for them."[33] Under Gaskill's guidance, and away from Devine's "overawing" presence, the group had gained more focus and it was at this point that membership in the Writers' Group shifted from its ad hoc origins, apparent under Devine, to a strict "by invitation only" policy.[34] This change in policy severely restricted the group's intake for the remainder of its existence, as the selective core members looked inward to protect the group from unwanted colleagues and threats to its potential future.

The exclusion of those who could be seen by the rest of the group to have the potential to "rock the boat" led to accusations of exclusivity from outsiders.[35] Indeed, analyzing Jellicoe's choice of words when describing the policy of the group under Gaskill, it is difficult to understand how such a group could be affiliated with the Royal Court. Adjectives such as "argumentative" and "destructive," alongside phrases such as "upset the balance" and "rock the boat," had already and would continue to be readily applied to the Court's work in the future, including to the plays of some of the group's members. In excluding those playwrights who, in the group's opinion, demonstrated the aforementioned features, a contradiction of the fundamental purpose of the Writers' Group had emerged that effectively prevented a new generation of Royal Court playwrights from having the Writers' Group experience, which had proved invaluable to its original members. Further, as playwright Donald Howarth suggests, there was a growing belief that involvement in the Writers' Group was the only way for a playwright to be programmed by the Court: "I think one of the reasons I went to the meetings was that I thought, 'If I don't go I'm not going to get my plays on. If I do go, I might.' So, I thought, 'I'll go and join in.' I tried hard, but it wasn't worth it."[36] For Howarth, the group "felt like school" and the improvisations made him feel "very self-conscious" and "a fool," which caused him to leave.[37]

Accusations such as this only served to fuel an emerging "them and us" division by the end of the 1950s between those at the Court who were involved in the group and those who were not. Gaskill himself recalls that "nobody liked us," and John Osborne affirms this belief when he describes his view of the group's function as "committee wanking."[38] This, coupled with the confusion as to the exact purpose of the Writers' Group, as a supportive writers' network or as a gateway to the Royal Court stage, only served to strengthen the discord. And while it is without doubt that those members of the Writers' Group had ambitions for their work to be produced by the Royal Court, many of which were realized over the next ten years, it was the sense of community and "the ritual of going to see one's friends" that had evolved into the central function of the first

Writers' Group.[39] Indeed, it is often the social benefits that are remembered by those who have participated in future iterations of writers' groups at the Royal Court. The notion that a playwright could attend a group "every Monday night, after whatever shitty job you were doing for a living" and be with like-minded people remains a vital support to many aspiring playwrights.[40]

The Writers' Group offered a unique opportunity for many playwrights at the start of their careers to feel part of something, and what had begun as a writers' group had ultimately transformed into the regular meeting of a close-knit group of friends. Where the group had failed was in their inability to recognize the value of a regular meeting place for young writers "to make new theatre together" in a supportive environment, and as a consequence this had prevented any future opportunity for other writers who could have also benefitted from the writers' group structure.[41]

There is without doubt value in the notion that playwriting groups can provide a much-needed sense of camaraderie in the often solitary life of a writer. But the concept of a group, also, by etymological necessity breeds a sense of exclusivity and elitism and this has been a point of contention and criticism throughout much of the Court's history and specifically in its work with young playwrights. An analysis of the Young Writers' Programme's practices and its influence on the Royal Court more widely, particularly in the mid-2000s, should be reserved for a separate article, but it is important to note here that the exclusion of others, especially those who are perhaps not suited to a group environment, and the consequences of this is an ever-present factor in the history of writers' groups at the Royal Court.

Legacy: A Diaspora of the Writers

Whether new members coming into the group "tended to fall away," as Jellicoe describes, or were pushed out by what Gaskill terms "a certain sort of elitism" within the group is a matter of opinion.[42] However, the primary aim of introducing a select number of young writers to the Court had been a successful exercise. Subsequently, when Gaskill returned to the theatre as artistic director in 1965, he would look to make these writers "absolutely central" to his aspirations.[43] And with a battle against the Lord Chamberlain on the horizon, Edward Bond became a significant Writers' Group alumnus in Gaskill's Royal Court. Gaskill admits, somewhat self-critically, that the censorship struggle overshadowed his commitment to the writers of the group. Nevertheless, the appearance of these writers' work in the programming of the Royal Court, often to the theatre's financial and reputational detriment, in the decade that follows reveals a legacy that outlives the group itself. Gaskill remembers feeling "very attacked" for his firm commitment to those writers during his tenure of the Royal Court, but the Court's contribution to the abolition of censorship remains the most significant aspect of his directorship at a time when very few new playwrights emerged out of the Royal Court.[44]

The Writers' Group continued to run until 1960, at which point the group separated for the final time. Gaskill remembers how: "Things [had] started to happen elsewhere and John Dexter and I went to the National in 1963 but [the group] had died before then. I had also started what we called the 'actors' studio,' which was specifically for actors, it wasn't a writers' group, which was almost completely improvisation based."[45] Jellicoe reveals the reason for the dissolution as simply "the need had past."[46] Indeed, for writers such as Jellicoe, Wesker, and Arden, the need *had* past, as the objective for the group to facilitate a much-needed link between young writers and the Royal Court had been fulfilled. But as Gaskill explains, it had become clear that "the writers were not going to go on to be successful in the way that John Osborne had been a success," and despite Gakill's efforts to reinvigorate their careers as Royal Court writers during his tenure as artistic director, it was evident that these writers would make little impact on the Royal Court stage.[47] Speaking more than fifty years after the beginning of his artistic directorship at the Court, Gaskill reflects on the notion of success and the early model through which the Court had survived its early life as a result of the production of John Osborne's *Look Back in Anger*. Indeed, that type of success would never be replicated through the work of those members of the first Writers' Group. It is worth noting here, that, somewhat ironically, the model of success first achieved by Osborne can be realized in the achievements of a number of participants from the Young Writers' Programme, as plays such as Polly Stenham's *That Face* (2007) and Laura Wade's *Posh* (2010) brought box-office and critical acclaim to the Court before transferring to the West End.[48] The achievements of these so-called graduates of the Young Writers' Programme demonstrate the potential of a model of success that had first been identified by George Devine as a fundamental function of the first Writers' Group back in 1958. Although that initial vision was never fully realized in Devine's Royal Court, the contribution that the members of the first Writers' Group have made to theatre both in and out of the United Kingdom should not be measured by their limited success within the confines of the Court itself.

In his autobiography *A Sense of Direction: Life at the Royal Court*, Gaskill describes how the Writers' Group "had played an important part in all our lives": "I had started to learn about teaching, which was to become very central to my work, and the writers had explored new approaches to theatre and, more important, had shared creative experiences with friends. To others outside the group it sounded pretentious and cliquey, but to us it was a warm and fertile time."[49] Gaskill's account recalls how writer after writer from within the group had "been savaged by the critics" and how he would often have to fight for the writers against the opposition of George Devine and Tony Richardson.[50] But as the director highlights above, the group's "shared creative experiences with friends" had become an influential feature of the group's limited life. For reasons grounded in those experiences within the Writers' Group and in what Gaskill terms as a "diaspora of the writers," many of the Writers' Group's core membership left London in the 1960s and early 1970s to fulfil newfound aspirations: "They all went off to do things that were community based: Ann Jellicoe went to Dorset and did work *in* communities, made plays in communities, very successfully, John Arden went to Ireland, Keith Johnstone went to Canada and started *Theatre Sports* and so the work sort of went towards a community based life."[51] The sense of what Gaskill terms "embattled community" that was first realized at the Royal Court more generally and then developed through the work of the Writers' Group had caused a number of the group's original members to consider the potential of theatre beyond the stages of the Royal Court. By 1966 a Schools Scheme at the Royal Court had been developed, and out of this came the Young Peoples' Theatre, which served as an important stepping-stone particularly for the likes of Bond, Jellicoe, and Johnstone between the Royal Court and their later community endeavors. Bond and Johnstone worked closely with the young people involved in this initiative and led a number of workshops both for the Schools Scheme and Young Peoples' Theatre. With Johnstone continuing to focus his workshops on improvisation, Bond offered sessions on the representation of violence in the theatre, alongside the Court's production of *Saved*.[52] Bond's work here signifies the beginning of a decade-long relationship with the Court's outreach program that culminated in the premiere of his play *The Worlds* by the Scheme's youth theatre company the Activists in 1979.[53] Jellicoe also wrote for the Schools Scheme, and her play *The Rising Generation* (1967) was produced by the Scheme and included a cast of more than 150 young people aged twelve to seventeen.

By 1975 Jellicoe had moved to Dorset in South West England, where she established the Colway Theatre Trust, a company designed to explore and develop plays in the community.[54] In the previous year, Johnstone too had relocated from London to take up a visiting professorship in Canada. Following his move to Canada, Johnstone developed his teaching of improvisation and, significantly, the theatresports form. Theatresports—an improvisational game inspired by British prowrestling in which teams of improvisers battle against each other for points and audience approval—has taken form across the world. In the same way as many other more conventional sports, Theatresports encourages team building, participation, and spectatorship, which in turn encourages social interaction with a community. John Arden, whose plays were "box office disasters" at the Royal Court, had also begun working outside of London by the 1970s. Settling in Galway, Ireland, Arden contributed "frequently to community drama" and along with his wife, actress Margaretta D'Arcy, founded the city's arts center.[55]

The benefits of "sharing creative experiences" during their time in the Writers' Group at the Royal Court had exposed the group's members to the benefits and possibilities of theatre. It is by no means a coincidence that many of the group's original members, galvanized by the feeling of camaraderie attained during that period as young writers, went on to pioneer projects in the community. Their success should not, therefore, be measured against that of other Royal Court writers, as their achievements and contributions to the field more widely exceed the boundaries of the Royal Court and the West End.

Conclusion

The mass production of new plays by new writers at the Court in the 1990s has seen critics and academics alike quick to draw close links between the Royal Court of the 1990s and that of the 1950s. As this article has uncovered, the commonalities between the two periods can also be extended to the Court's attempts to attract young writers to write for the Royal Court stages. Being in the fortunate position to now engage with the work of the first Writers' Group at the Royal Court retrospectively can lead to some disgruntlement that the group disbanded without any discernable attempt to preserve this unique feature of the Court's work for future playwrights. Indeed, the landscape of British theatre in the years that followed could have been significantly different had this feature been properly managed and developed in the way that the Young Writers' Programme was forty years later. Instead, due to Gaskill's fierce loyalty to those members of the first group, the Royal Court of the 1960s was largely concerned with the production of those writers and, as a result, garnered little commercial success for the theatre during those years. It was not until the creation of the Young Writers' Programme that the full potential of an environment that could be used to support and stimulate new writers was fully seen to benefit the Royal Court. Through the Young Writers' Programme, the outline of the model of success first represented by John Osborne in 1956 can be applied to writers who have emerged through the program, such as Laura Wade, Jack Thorne, Lucy Prebble, and Duncan MacMillan, who began their careers as participants on the program and have gone on to see their work produced at the Royal Court, the West End, and beyond. Ultimately, Devine's desire to find additional playwrights to follow the successes of John Osborne failed to materialize, but the achievements of those writers occurred beyond the Writers' Group and beyond the Royal Court. Instead, a new model of success was made as a result of what had occurred in the Writers' Group that was far from the theatre's intentions. The group had facilitated, and consequently the participants had benefitted from, the togetherness that a community-based environment had provided, and ultimately, for those involved, this would come to be an inspiring experience that would influence their career choices as artists in the future.

Upon Gaskill's death in February 2016, one obituary described Gaskill as "a fighter who always stayed loyal to the writers in which he passionately believed." Whether that was with Bond and his battle with the censor or Jellicoe and her experimental style, the director was steadfast in his support.[56] The first Writers' Group at the Royal Court is often analyzed by its members' contribution in terms of plays to the theatre. But to examine this period in Court history in such a way overlooks what was really achieved and does not accurately represent a key feature of the Court's early work with young writers. Through their participation in the Writers' Group, these writers were made aware of the value of community and the place of theatre within that, and how this can often lead to opportunities and possibilities that spanned far beyond the walls of the Royal Court.

The Young Writers' Programme ceased in this iteration following the last Young Writers' Festival in 2012. It has been replaced with writers' groups, which function in a similar way but look beyond the youthful connotations presented by initiatives such as the Young Writers' Programme and new writing more widely following the influx of young writers in the mid-1990s. In his 2011 survey of British theatre, *Rewriting the Nation: British Theatre Today*, Aleks Sierz points out how "new writing is almost always associated with youth," and the Court's decision to conclude the Young Writers' Programme could be grounded in Sierz's assertion. Indeed, it could be argued that new writing's long association with youth has been prompted largely by the Royal Court's own ambitious programming of young writers in the 1990s and the subsequent establishment of the Young Writers' Programme in 1998, which put young writers at the core of the theatre's ambitions. The Royal Court under Vicky Featherstone's artistic directorship (2013–) has created a theatre actively concerned with notions of identity, representation, and inclusivity, which can be traced through the Court's current infrastructure, its staffing, and its initiatives. The Young Writers' Programme, which focused its attention primarily on writers aged eighteen to twenty-five, could be seen to be restrictive in its reach, acting in contrast to the remit through which the Court functions today. Just as the Young Peoples' Theatre made way for the Young Writers' Programme in 1998, writers' groups, which have hosted participants from eight to eighty years of age since their reintroduction in 2012, continue to provide for the ongoing development of the playwright at the Royal Court today. As Stephen Berwind remarked on the Court's return to Sloane Square in 2000: "Periodically, the Royal Court, like a snake, must shed one skin and emerge in another." Therefore, the Court and its artistic team, to retain its fundamental identity as a writers' theatre, must also continue to challenge and question the ways in which it works with its writers so as to remain central to the future of new writing.

Notes

1. Aleks Sierz, *Modern British Playwriting: The 1990s* (London: Methuen, 2012), 56. Sierz documents that "following cuts in state subsidy during the 1980s, the 'genre' of new writing was widely perceived to be in trouble at the start of the decade" (54; quotation marks are my own). However, with theatres such as the Bush, Hampstead, Royal Court, and Soho in London along with Edinburgh's Traverse, Newcastle-upon-Tyne's Live Theatre, and touring theatre companies such as Paines Plough and Out of Joint all demonstrating a clear commitment to new writers, important contributions were made to the revival of new writing in the years that followed.
2. Jack Bradley, interview with Jacqueline Bolton, August 29, 2008. See also Ruth Little and Emily McLaughlin, *The Royal Court Theatre Inside Out* (London: Oberon, 2007), 294.
3. Catherine Love, "A Culture of Development: The Royal Court and the Young Writers' Programme," *Theatre Notebook*, 69, no. 2 (2015), 113–24.
4. Ibid., 123.
5. Most notably: Richard Findlater, ed., *At the Royal Court: 25 Years of the English Stage Company* (Derbyshire: Amber Lane Press, 1981), 52–57; Gresdna A. Doty and Billy J. Harbin, *Inside the Royal Court Theatre, 1956–1981* (Louisiana: Louisiana State University Press, 1990), 84–90; Philip Roberts, *The Royal Court Theatre and the Modern Stage* (Cambridge: Cambridge University Press, 1999); Ruth Little and Emily McLaughlin, *The Royal Court Theatre Inside Out* (London: Oberon, 2007), 43–44; William Gaskill, *A Sense of Direction: Life at the Royal Court* (London: Faber and Faber, 1988), 31–41; Arnold Wesker, *As Much as I Dare* (London: Century, 1994), 515. It is important to note here, however, that much of what is known about the Writers' Group is through retrospective engagement with the group's work as opposed to documentation obtained from records made during the meetings of the Writers' Group itself.

6. Jacqueline Bolton, "Capitalizing (on) New Writing: New Play Development in the 1990s," *Studies in Theatre and Performance*, 32, no. 2 (2012), 209–25 (214), and Aleks Sierz, *In-Yer-Face Theatre: British Drama Today* (London: Faber and Faber, 2001), xi and 15.
7. In Terry Browne's book *Playwrights' Theatre*, the first publication on the English Stage Company's work at the Royal Court, the author writes, "One persistent problem continued to plague the Company: the lack of worthwhile new British plays." Browne goes on to note how several members of the Court's management had "expressed 'serious alarm' that the Company was as yet unable to announce a new season of plays" and "although over 1,000 new plays had been received, very few had in fact merited production" (Terry Browne, Playwrights Theatre, [London: Pitman, 1975], 31).
8. William Gaskill, interview with the author, January 15, 2015.
9. Philip Roberts, *The Royal Court Theatre and the Modern Stage* (Cambridge: Cambridge University Press, 1999), 58.
10. Ibid., 63.
11. Findlater, *At the Royal Court*, 52.
12. Ibid.
13. It is also important to acknowledge that when discussing the first Writers' Group at the Royal Court, much of the primary source material is available from what has been written and said by Ann Jellicoe. Jellicoe was a central figure in the first Writers' Group and has been the most publicly vocal about her experience during that time of all the group's original members. These accounts can be found in Jellicoe's contribution to Findlater, ed., *At the Royal Court*, 52–57, as well as *Inside the Royal Court Theatre, 1956–1981* (Baton Rouge: Louisiana State University Press, 1990).
14. William Gaskill, interview with the author, January 15, 2015.
15. Ola Animashawun, interview with the author, June 16, 2016.
16. Dan Rebellato, *Modern British Playwriting, 2000–2009* (London: Methuen, 2013), 68.
17. Irving Wardle, *The Theatres of George Devine* (London: Jonathan Cape, 1978), 199.
18. Findlater, *At the Royal Court*, 52.
19. William Gaskill, interview with the author, January 15, 2015.
20. William Gaskill, *A Sense of Direction: Life at the Royal Court* (London: Faber and Faber, 1988), 36.
21. Coincidentally the home of Anne Piper was situated two doors down from Devine's home on Lower Mall Street, Hammersmith. Arnold Wesker, *As Much as I Dare* (London: Century, 1994), 515.
22. William Gaskill, interview with the author, January 15, 2015.
23. Ibid.
24. Findlater, *At the Royal Court*, 54.
25. These ideas are expanded upon in more detail in Johnstone's *Impro: Improvisation and the Theatre* (London: Routledge, 1987).
26. William Gaskill, interview with the author, January 15, 2015.
27. Doty and Harbin, *Inside the Royal Court Theatre, 1956–1981*, 86.
28. Theresa Robbins Dudeck, *Keith Johnstone: A Critical Biography* (London: Methuen, 2013), 42.
29. Ibid.
30. Doty and Harbin, *Inside the Royal Court Theatre, 1956–1981*, 88. Anne Jellicoe's *The Knack* (1962) and John Arden's *The Happy Haven* (1960) both feature extracts that were

formulated as a direct result of what had occurred through improvisations and sessions within the Writers' Group. In her 2013 book *Keith Johnstone: A Critical Biography*, Theresa Robbins Dudeck also notes that a project staged as a Sunday Night production by Gaskill and Johnstone titled *Eleven Men Dead at Hola Camp* also "evolved in part because of the improvisational processes [that had been] explored in the Writers' Group" (46).

31. Ibid., 86.
32. Simon Stephens, interview with the author, July 1, 2016.
33. Findlater, *At the Royal Court*, 55.
34. Irving Wardle, *The Theatres of George Devine* (London: Jonathan Cape, 1978), 199; and Doty and Harbin, *Inside the Royal Court Theatre, 1956–1981*, 87.
35. Doty and Harbin, *Inside the Royal Court Theatre, 1956–1981*, 88.
36. Ibid.
37. Ibid.
38. William Gaskill, interview with the author, January 15, 2015, and Findlater, *At the Royal Court*, 22.
39. Findlater, *At the Royal Court*, 56.
40. Joe Penhall, in Harriet Devine, *Looking Back: Playwrights at the Royal Court, 1956–2006* (London: Faber and Faber, 2006), 326.
41. William Gaskill, interview with the author, January 15, 2015.
42. Doty and Harbin, *Inside the Royal Court Theatre, 1956–1981*, 87, and William Gaskill, interview with the author, January 15, 2015.
43. William Gaskill, interview with the author, January 15, 2015.
44. Ibid.
45. Ibid. The Royal Court Actors' Studio opened in the Jeanetta Cochrane Theatre in London's Kingsway in February 1963. The Studio specialized in improvisation and operated under Gaskill and Keith Johnstone's direction. With improvisation at its core, the Studio, which operated from 1963 until the end of 1965, would build on many of the ideas that had originated in the Writers' Group in the years before (Little and McLaughlin, *The Royal Court Theatre Inside Out*, 73). For a detailed account of Keith Johnstone's work with the Studio, see Robbins Dudeck, *Keith Johnstone*, 58–65.
46. Findlater, *At the Royal Court*, 56.
47. William Gaskill, interview with the author, January 15, 2015.
48. *That Face* premiered at the Royal Court on the April 27, 2007, before transferring to the West End opening at the Duke of York's theatre on May 1, 2008. *Posh* opened at the Royal Court on April 15, 2010, with an updated version of the play premiering at the Duke of York's theatre on May 11, 2012.
49. William Gaskill, *A Sense of Direction: Life at the Royal Court* (London: Faber and Faber, 1988), 39.
50. Ibid., 40.
51. Ibid., 39.
52. Graham Saunders explores the ethical implications of this event in his chapter "Kicking Tots and Revolutionary Trots: The English Stage Company Young People's Theatre Scheme, 1969–70," in *Ethical Speculations in Contemporary British Theatre* (Basingstoke: Palgrave Macmillan, 2014).

53. *The Worlds* premiered on the November 21, 1979, and was performed in the YPT's own space known as the Garage by members of the Activists. It was directed by Edward Bond.
54. In 2000, and under the direction of Joe Oram, Colway Theatre Trust was renamed Claque Theatre and its base relocated from Dorset to the South East. It continues to develop community plays across the United Kingdom and the Western world.
55. In his autobiography, John Osborne writes, "John Arden became an in-house joke for box-office disaster" (*Looking Back: Never Explain, Never Apologise* [London: Faber and Faber, 1999], 378) and author unknown, John Arden obituary, *The Telegraph*, accessed September 30, 2016, http://www.telegraph.co.uk/news/obituaries/culture-obituaries/theatre-obituaries/9177000/John-Arden.html.
56. Michael Billington, "William Gaskill: A Fighter Who Stayed Loyal to His Writers," *Guardian*, accessed February 5, 2016, http://www.theguardian.com/stage/2016/feb/04/william-gaskill-appreciation-obituary-royal-court-artistic-director-theatre.

New Writing in a Populist Context

A Play, a Pie and a Pint

—DEANA NICHOLS

While in Glasgow during a May 2012 research trip, I took many cabs. Glasgow cab drivers are known, in my experience, for asking two questions: "Where are you from?" and "What brings you to Glasgow?" In the case of every cab driver but one, the driver's immediate response upon learning that I was studying Scottish theatre was to ask whether I'd been to Òran Mór. More often than not, my affirmative reply would be followed by the driver rattling off a list of plays he had seen there, frequently including a personal critique of the best and worst plays. And in the one case in which my cab driver had not yet been to Òran Mór, he told me he was going the next day. The plays that these cab drivers, and throngs of Glaswegians of every other trade, had seen were part of David MacLennan's A Play, a Pie and a Pint (PPP) series, which has been described as having "broken the mould in terms of theatre-making in this country."[1] And for this series of productions, breaking the mold has entailed embracing the practice of theatrical populism to propel the production of new plays. This essay will investigate the populist impetus behind and the practice of A Play, a Pie and a Pint, before drawing conclusions concerning the series's ramifications in the arena of new writing.

The notion of populist theatre is ubiquitous in attempts to define contemporary Scottish theatre. Aleks Sierz defines Scottish theatre as "hard-headed realism with a populist vaudevillian flair,"[2] while Trish Reid defines it as "politicised populism."[3] Playwright David Greig has written, "I believe there is such a thing as 'Scottish theatre.' At its best, it is a unique distillate of meaty poetry, playful intellect and the democratic populism of the variety theatre."[4] In Aleks

Figure 1. David MacLennan in the Òran Mór performance space, 2005. The audience space now consists of rows of long rectangular tables rather than the smaller circular tables seen here. Image courtesy of PPP photographer Leslie Black.

Sierz's article "'Can Old Forms Be Reinvigorated?': Radical Populism and New Writing in British Theatre Today," the practitioners interviewed concerning radical populist theatre repeatedly reference Scottish companies and Scottish works. Defining populism in general, and theatrical populism specifically, is crucial, then, to appreciating the political and theatrical context for A Play, a Pie and a Pint. While the term "populism" is used today, often pejoratively, to describe a variety of discourses—often those of the Right—the definition perhaps most applicable to the current project is that of Kenneth Roberts, who writes that "populism is a specific type of response to crises of political representation, which can themselves take a number of different forms. It is a natural—though hardly an inevitable or exclusive—political strategy for appealing to mass constituencies where representative institutions are weak or discredited, and where various forms of social exclusion or political marginalization leave citizens alienated from such institutions."[5] In theatrical populism, then, one can equate the "representative institutions" against which political populism rallies with the traditional institutions of literary theatre: theatrical populism seeks to dispel the myth, persistent today, that theatre is a medium for the supposedly cultured elite, providing theatrical entertainment for the "mass constituencies" who are perceived to be excluded from that elite.

In the case of Scottish theatre practitioners, populism might be said to be entrenched in their theatrical DNA, a DNA infused with the traditions of variety theatre, music hall, and pantomime. Femi Folorunso argues that "the music hall occupied the middle space in a direct line from seventeenth-century popular entertainment to contemporary drama in Scotland."[6]

Indeed, the two most oft-cited works in the Scottish canon reference the two ends of that direct line and are telling in their populist characteristics: Sir David Lyndsay's sixteenth-century morality play *Ane Satyre of the Thrie Estaites*, and 7:84 (Scotland)'s 1973 play *The Cheviot, the Stag and the Black, Black Oil*. The former has been described by Trish Reid as being "the earliest example (and . . . one of the most vivid) of a distinctive combining of popular forms with political invective that was to become a signature of the Scottish performance tradition."[7] The play contains song, music, direct address, and a mixture of high and low language. Also seen as foundational is the play's ideology: Eschewing the religious themes of the medieval morality play, Lyndsay's play instead addresses the then-current abuses of power by Scotland's spiritual leaders, as well as closes by upending the hierarchies of Scottish society.

Even more formative in the populist theatrical tradition is *The Cheviot, the Stag and the Black, Black Oil*, which toured to more than thirty thousand people throughout Scotland—focusing its efforts on the otherwise theatrically underserved Highlands—and connected the sweeping history of the Highlanders' oppression at the hands of the English to current issues of land ownership. *The Cheviot*, devised by playwright John McGrath with the 7:84 company, was based largely on the Scottish tradition of the *ceilidh*, an evening of entertainment consisting of song, dance, and storytelling that was instantly recognizable to potential audience members.[8] The ceilidh was "a genuinely ethnic and vital form of entertainment . . . which crossed class barriers and which still played an important part in the lives of often geographically isolated Scottish communities."[9] McGrath, then, utilized the form's story-telling potential to create a "ceilidh-play." Part of this potential stemmed from the ceilidh's use of stirring music and song; *The Cheviot*'s use of traditional, well-known songs, as well as new, satirical songs following familiar melodies, took advantage of this affecting quality of traditional Scottish music. Additionally effective in terms of emotive reference points was the frequent use of the Gaelic language throughout the play; according to Randall Stevenson, the Gaelic provided "a still greater lever on the sympathies of Highland audiences, who might never have encountered it in live theatre performance—than the use of Scots at that time for Lowland audiences."[10] *The Cheviot*, then, successfully addressed Roberts's "mass constituencies" of populism: In terms of access, even the smallest of Highland villages was able to experience the production; in terms of history, the production staged the otherwise marginalized history of Highlands oppression; and in terms of cultural forms, the production was inclusive in both its formal and linguistic means.

The populism inherent in Scottish theatre, from Lyndsay's sixteenth-century *Satyre* through the 1970s work of 7:84 (Scotland), is also inherent in the career of A Play, a Pie and a Pint's creator, David MacLennan; his work before A Play, a Pie and a Pint might be best described as a thirty-year extravaganza of political, populist theatre. He was a cofounder of 7:84 (Scotland) and codevised and performed in *The Cheviot*. Five years after the production, MacLennan and fellow 7:84 member David Anderson split off from the company to form Wildcat Stage Company, which shared 7:84's socialist goals but highlighted more contemporary popular music in its productions. Wildcat would, in 1996, coproduce John McGrath's contemporary adaptation of Lyndsay's *Satyre, A Satire of the Four Estates*. Following the 1996 cut to Wildcat's funding, MacLennan went on to work with Mayfest, Glasgow's festival of political theatre, before working as a freelance director.

The impetus for A Play, a Pie and a Pint stems from a trip MacLennan made to Cuba. As he was driving through the country around lunchtime, he "passed a sugar field where the cutters were lying around with their sandwiches and their flasks, and there was a jazz band on a loader at the side of the field playing music. And it had a *huge* impact on me. And I thought how wonderful it is to see some artistic cultural experience happening in just a normal part of life, while you're having a bite to eat."[11] Later, in 2003, MacLennan worked on a production with David Anderson at Bewley's Café Theatre in Dublin, seeing firsthand the enormous possibilities inherent in lunchtime theatre, in a way that hadn't been explored as consistently since the 1960s and 1970s alternative theatre movement.[12] Just weeks later, MacLennan had a chance meeting with Colin Beattie, with whom MacLennan had previously worked on Glasgow's Mayfest. MacLennan learned that Beattie had recently purchased a converted church in Glasgow's West End that he was renovating as a pub and that happened to have a sizeable basement space. MacLennan asked Beattie if he "would like to have a lunchtime theatre. And that was it."[13] In 2004, MacLennan produced his first season of plays, and in June 2016 the series celebrated its four-hundredth play.[14] This staggering output has made the series "the largest de facto commissioning body for playwrights in Scotland"[15] and "perhaps the biggest commissioner of new drama in Europe."[16] But perhaps most startling, particularly in the context of the subsidized Scottish theatre, is that the series began with no public funding whatsoever.[17]

The premise of A Play, a Pie and a Pint is simple: In the basement of the church-turned-pub Òran Mór, spectators pay a flat fee—the current price is between £10.00 and £12.50, depending on the day of the week[18]—and they receive a lunch consisting of a pastry and a pint of beer (or other beverage), as well as viewing a new, one-act play with a run time of around fifty minutes. A new play is on offer each week during the fall and spring seasons, totaling up to thirty-eight new plays per year. The plays vary widely in subject, tone, and, as would be expected given a rehearsal period of two weeks per play, quality. However, the sheer number and variety of theatrical experiences has made the series a triumph of theatrical populism. Additionally, for Scottish writers (whose work comprises approximately 70 percent of the series's plays),[19] the series serves three vital functions: It provides new writers with an avenue for their work to be seen, it offers opportunities for established writers to experiment with form, and it allows both nonplaywright theatre artists and writers of other genres to gain the experience of writing for the stage.[20]

Given the series's output, it is obviously impossible to accurately and thoroughly document the range of plays that have been produced in a short article; this is made more difficult, indeed, by the fact that only a small percentage of the plays produced have been published. Thus, I will spend the next few pages describing one production that exemplifies the populist potential inherent in the A Play, a Pie and a Pint format: 2012's *The Jean-Jacques Rousseau Show*. This production incorporated both the 7:84/Wildcat generation of writers and a new generation of political theatremakers: Credited writers included David Anderson, Davey Anderson, Alan Bissett, Catrin Evans, Mike Gonzalez, Sean Hardie, Kieran Hurley, David MacLennan, Gary McNair, Amanda Monfrooe, and Julia Taudevin. This generational blend was seen earlier in and inspired by the MacLennan-curated "Thorn in Their Side: Nurturing the Thistle of Scottish Political Theatre," an evening of political theatre provocations produced by the National Theatre of Scotland as part of its 2011 *Staging the Nation: A Conversation about Theatre in Scotland* program, a yearlong series of productions and discussions.[21] MacLennan invited "Thorn in Their Side" contributors to collaborate on *The Jean-Jacques Rousseau Show*, a production that for MacLennan demonstrated a return from the days in which "the use of agit-prop was considered the lowest form of life, and past its sell-by date."[22] *The Jean-Jacques Rousseau Show* also demonstrated, moreover, that the difficult, complicated questions of contemporary social equality, independence and freedom, now colored by the postmodern failure of partisan ideology, could still be effectively addressed via the variety, agitprop form.

MacLennan produced *JJR* as the 250th PPP production. As mentioned in the play's opening song, "We googled 2- / Hundred and 50 / But we came up / With nothing nifty / We typed 'Two-fifty years ago' / And there it was: / Jean-Jacques Rousseau!"[23] Rousseau's *The Social Contract* had indeed been published in 1762, 250 years before the MacLennan production. (Although, as playwright

Figure 2. *The Jean-Jacques Rousseau Show*: Brian James, David Anderson, George Drennan, Julia Taudevin, Kirstin Maclean. Image courtesy of PPP photographer Leslie Black.

Figure 3. *The Jean-Jacques Rousseau Show*: Brian James, Julia Taudevin. Image courtesy of PPP photographer Leslie Black.

Gary McNair notes, "had he googled 250 years ago, and it said the inventing of the sausage press, he'd have run with it."[24]) The writing process involved the writers reading Rousseau's works and incorporating them into their writings: "We would all meet up, we would talk about the landscape of Scottish theatre but simultaneously looking at the readings and writings of Jean-Jacques Rousseau."[25] Particularly focused were discussions of how *The Social Contract* compared to contemporary Scotland, both in terms of Rousseau's call for equality as related to present-day struggles toward social democracy in Scotland and in terms of the work's role in precipitating the French Revolution versus Scotland's impending independence referendum in September 2014. As McNair describes, the writers utilized the "American sitcom writers model" of contributing ideas and pieces of writing: "you get to kind of flex your muscles, as a writer: you're writing short scenes and throw[ing] them in a roomful of artists who, in a really supportive and generative way . . . just kind of took ownership over everyone's work."[26]

The finished product was a performance that began as soon as spectators entered the space: a character called General Will greeted patrons as they lined up at the bar for their pies and pints, explaining that "I've been trying to please everyone, and so because some people don't drink alcohol, we thought it would be most fair if there were only soft drinks, that way everyone is happy, that's great. Also, because not everyone can eat meat, we've just got veggie pies today, that way everyone will be happy, so that's great too." Meanwhile, a "wheeler-dealer type" of character offered patrons black-market beer and meat pies. When spectators reached their tables, the placemats in front of them were printed with a modern-day Social Contract, sufficiently entertaining to be quoted here in full: "I (insert name . . .) being of sound mind, average intelligence and only mildly intoxicated at this hour of the day, do hereby undertake to enter into a SOCIAL CONTRACT whereby I, (insert name . . .), hereinafter referred to as The Punter, agree to be set free from my chains, whether I like it or not, in return for which I do solemnly undertake at all times and in all places to put the interests of society as a whole before my own greed, ego, personal needs, indulgences, whims, binges, grudges, jealousies, appetites (gastronomic and sexual), sullen resentments, sure-fire racing tips, zany self-enrichment schemes etc, so help me God."[27] Also printed on the placemat was an invitation to "draw a picture of the kind of Scotland you would like to see" and a direct reference to *The Cheviot*: While the McGrath/7:84 play begins with the statement that the play is "a story that has a beginning, a middle, but, as yet, no end,"[28] the *JJR* placemat stated that "this is a story with umpteen beginnings, a short middle 8 but, as of yet, no final chorus. We need you to help us write the lyrics." As the spectators ate their pies, drank their pints, and created crayon drawings of a future Scotland, two sansculottes milled about, one singing such songs as "Ca Ira" ("It'll be Fine"), "Bandiera Rossa" ("The Red Flag"), and "The Internationale" and the other reading extracts from *The Social Contract* and bantering with the audience: "'It will be said that the despot assures his subjects civil tranquility. . . . Tranquility is found also in dungeons; but is that enough to make them desirable places to live in?' Bit of a dungeon this, eh? Used tae be a church [but] we strung up all the priests we could lay oor hauns oan."[29] Finally, as has been the case with most PPP productions, MacLennan welcomed the audience to the performance, which he explained was written "by a bunch of politically biased, socialist minded ne'er-do-weels and their fellow travellers." The performers confirmed his description by responding to MacLennan's mention of the production's sponsors, Heineken and the *Evening Times*, with a shout of "Sell out!"[30]

The play proper is a mixture of song, sketch, and direct address, with the performers periodically taking it in turns to don the personage of Jean-Jacques Rousseau. Following the opening song quoted above, Rousseau chides the audience: "Well you voted away your parliament, didn't you? You became North Britain. You became one with your English neighbours. Perhaps that is an exaggeration. You became one tenth of your English neighbour." Rousseau then quotes himself concerning the relationship of land to the *men* who own it, and Julia (Taudevin, who along with David Anderson was a performer as well as cowriter) objects to the absence of women in Rousseau's writings, resulting in a song in which she asks, "So we want a world free from inequality? / Then we'd better get working on the patriarchy. . . . The fruits of the earth belong to us all / And the earth to no one, aye I'm on board Rousseau / Man must not live in chains to another / So how is it different for your sister and your mother?"[31] This is followed directly by a monologue telling the story of Brian, who was accosted by a begging family after returning from a bookie and whose generosity was rewarded by the family following him down the street, badgering him for additional money. After shouting them down, he wonders, "How I can now be feelin so bad aboot something that was meantay make me feel gid. See this world man. Wha got us intay this fuckin mess?"[32]

At two different points in the performance, the contrasting characters of General Will and Freer Admiral BawFree interact with the audience.[33] General Will arrives with supposed solutions to the problems of inequality. First, to counter the "unfair distribution of wealth in this room," he proposes the idea of passing around a bucket so that all spectators can empty their wallets, and he will then "divide it up by the amount of people in the room and then redistribute it evenly amongst you, then we'll all have the same, then it will all be fair. Come on, what could be fairer than that?! No?" Later he returns with a new idea: "It goes deeper than money—It's the barriers we put up between us that cause the world to be unfair, all the locked doors keeping society separated."[34] His solution again involves a bucket: Each spectator will put his/her keys into the bucket, and Will in turn will copy the keys for everyone else in the room. This solution too is met with a negative response by the audience, much to the exasperation of Will. Meanwhile, Admiral BawFree welcomes soldiers home from war with Loyalty Cards allowing them to access free television, "because I know what it's like to want the freedom to stand up and be counted and say 'No! I will not accept substandard viewing quality. As a free citizen of the free world I claim my right to enjoy *Spooks* on blu ray in plasma screen without additional charge.'"[35] And later the Admiral instructs the audience to "vote with your heart": "Vote for being told you're the only country in the world that could not possibly survive and that without us you'd fall to pieces like children abandoned in the wild, caked in faeces. Vote Empire. Vote Tradition. Vote for Glasgow having the highest knife crime and lowest life-expectancy in Europe due to our generosity. You may thank us at your leisure. Vote for the absence of your history in our schools. All Brits together. Vote for The Iron Lady. Such a strong leader, gave this country backbone (you didn't really want the unions, industries or council homes, just made the place look tatty)."[36]

Interspersed with these sketches and monologues are several songs and poems addressing the social inequality of contemporary Scotland. A courtroom scene in which a character is accused of theft features a rap in which the accused connects his crime with inequality and white-collar crime: "Not guilty / I did it / But I plead no contest. . . . But what I done / It was an act of pure / Political protest. . . . Every day / Stuff is shoved in my face / I cannae afford / While cunts like you just seem tae earn / More and more / Aye / I know the score / You want something / You take it / See it every night on the news. . . . Seems to me / There's a wan or two bankers / Should be standing in the docks / They got a few billion / Out the public purse / Don't imagine that's something they'll reimburse." Later the issue of economic equality is addressed even more overtly in a poem: "Britain is broken / Trouble on the streets / Cost of living / Getting higher every week / How do we solve these / Economic scares / Simple / We must have / Tax breaks for millionaires." Following the sequence, in which the performer has successfully enjoined the audience to join in on the refrain of "tax breaks for millionaires," he implicates the spectators in the economic crisis when he invites the audience to "give yourself a round of applause. You've been a wonderfully compliant audience."[37]

Also addressed in the poems and songs, however, is the question of what independence might mean for Scotland, particularly in terms of equality. One song references the success of the devolution referendum of 1997, highlighting the fact that "You thought that things were changing / But really they just stayed the same / Red turned to blue / Now what's left to do, but / Rip it up and start again. . . . But if we separated / What would really be changed?" Later, in a mock television interview with First Minister Alex Salmond, Salmond asks the interviewer, "If Scotland is such a total basket case why are you little England nationalists so keen to preserve the Union and hang on to us?" This in turn is followed by a poem addressed to Salmond, which directs the First Minister to "tell these good people of North Britain / What they're voting for. / A radical change? / Or just more of the same / Under a new name? / What's the ultimate aim / Of this referendum game?"[38]

The play's ending contains elements that serve to drive home the questions of equality and independence. In "The Possible Endings Show," the performers relate several possible futures for Scotland's independence, ranging from the serious to the silly:

KIRSTIN. Scotland votes itself out of the Union and becomes a beacon of social democracy transforming Europe, and thus the World, through the power of its radical and persuasive example.

. . . .

JULIA. Scotland votes itself out of the Union and uses its autonomy to lower corporate taxes in a vain attempt to attract multinational corporations, actually increasing the gap between rich and poor.

. . . .

GEORGE. Donald Trump is chased—literally chased—out of the country after government forces evict him from his holiday mansion and send him running to his private jet in just his pants: an historic moment which is immortalised forevermore in the annual . . .

ALL. Great Trump Run![39]

Before the performers exit in triumph, however, Rousseau dampens their spirits with a reminder that fulfilling his words in practice will prove more difficult than they realize. The finale song, then, asks the production's key questions: "Has winning independence / Set any country free? / Did US independence / End US slavery? / Will putting up a border / Bring true democracy / Will winning independence / Set all the people free?"[40] The song's refrain of "Which side are you on?" makes for an interesting means of "closure" (or lack thereof) for the piece, in that it appears to pit social democracy against independence. Thus, while the play as a whole seems to endorse independence, the correlation between that independence and improved social conditions for Scotland is troubled.[41] What is clear, though, is that the overall format of the lunchtime theatre experience served as a potent vehicle for debating Scotland's future, combining as it did new writing and traditional forms.

Douglas Maxwell's 2013 play *A Respectable Widow Takes to Vulgarity* is in some ways on the opposite end of the theatrical spectrum from *The Jean-Jacques Rousseau Show*, as it was written by a single playwright and has a cast of only two, characteristics that make it somewhat more typical of a PPP play (if, indeed, one can use the word "typical" in reference to the series's productions).[42] It shares, however, a predilection for populism, this time of the linguistic variety, for it carries the distinction of being the only play I know of whose inciting incident is the word "cunt." Thus, in addition to examining such questions as the intersection of class and language, one's need to speak and be heard, and contemporary linguistic taboos, it provides a useful primer to contemporary Scots' swearing habits.

Maxwell's play begins, in true comedic fashion, at a funeral. Annabelle, widow of the deceased, chances to meet Jim, an employee of her dead husband, and Jim, in the anxiety that comes with being at a funeral in general and speaking to the boss's wife in particular, unleashes the dreaded c-word when he tells Annabelle that her husband "was a really, really lovely old cunt."[43] Annabelle is

Figure 4. *A Respectable Widow Takes to Vulgarity*: Scott Fletcher, Joanna Tope. Image courtesy of PPP photographer Leslie Black.

fascinated rather than horrified and follows him across the street to a Burger King, where her lessons in swearing begin. Jim explains that "cunt" is not necessarily a negative term: "It's not always a hingbee. A bad word. I mean, it is. Obviously. I shouldnae've said it. But. With Scottish guys it can mean like, a geezer, a lad, a good . . . kinda . . . guy."[44] Annabelle is thus ushered into a new linguistic world that, in her life as a middle-class wife, has eluded her to this point.

She also appreciates Jim's referral to her husband as a cunt, because "it felt true. You were the only one who managed that today. The only one who even came close."[45] Annabelle later reveals that her life has been one of verbal meaninglessness, in which her acquaintances ignore the content of her speech and she does the same for them ("My friends are clearly not listening to a word I bumming say."[46]). She attempts to incorporate her newly acquired word, but is unsure of the appropriate context:

ANNABELLE. I've been wondering too, about cunt. (*That stops him.*) Your little revelation that there is a Scottish usage which is positive rather than negative got my old brain going I'm afraid. I was wondering, would it be correct, for example, if someone was, I don't know, very good at playing the organ, to say: "Lillian is a cunt on the organ"?. . . I find this fascinating. I really do. I fight for the language.

JIM. Well. I think, it's kinda, no right if it's a woman. . . . And it doesnae mean "good at something." You'd have to say. . . "see that cunt John, he's fucking amazing on the organ."[47]

Not only does Annabelle then incorporate her new language into her daily conversation, an incorporation that offers up a wealth of profanity-centered malapropisms, but she comes to notice that language is intimately tied to power relations: "We use language—bad language—as a mode of control. Not just to insult, but as a way to pen those who use certain words: 'they are coarse and vulgar, do not regard them!' etc. But if people are defeated by a word—squashed and repulsed and shocked by a word—then they lose. Don't they?"[48] This new insight is coupled with her desire to speak like her dead husband, who was working-class and therefore used such terms freely. Swearing, for her, is then about both interrogating linguistic assumptions and connecting with her husband in the only way that she feels is open to her. As Maxwell states, the play is "about what happens if you don't have the vocabulary to express how you feel. So you're left with two choices: one is you don't express how you feel, and two is you go and find ways to speak, which is what she does."[49] In fact, the most moving moment of the play occurs when, in the final scene, Annabelle equates losing language with losing a loved one. Jim asks whether she misses her husband, and she replies in absolute sincerity: "I don't just miss him. I fucking miss him."[50] The simple truth of the statement, and the friendship that has developed between the two otherwise disparate characters, marks the greatest subversive force of which language, even profane language, is capable.

Maxwell points to other linguistic issues in his play, including the taboos that exist even in a world comfortable with swearing and the negative stereotypes that accompany languages marked as Other. Jim experiences a communicative crisis when he needs to tell his doctor about the pain he is experiencing in a particular portion of his penis for which, unfortunately, he only knows a euphemistic and racist term. Annabelle offers the sensible solution of "urethra" but also invents a new list of possible terms, including "Spouter," "Slit-tube," and "Piss-Gub."[51] Annabelle's desire to create a new, original swear word, even if such creation yields such results as "slit-tube," demonstrates her creativity in stretching the vocabulary with which Jim has provided her, pointing to the imaginative possibilities inherent in swearing. However, Annabelle learns that there are limits to her freedom in vulgarity when she attends a football match with Jim in an effort to free her remaining verbal inhibitions. At first she is successful, shouting awkward gems such as "Fuck off you fucking devils! You're an ugly arse! Go to hell! I hate you!" She then, however, includes the word "Catholic" in her verbal rampage, to Jim's and the rest of the imagined football spectators' horror.[52] Earlier in the play, moreover, Jim questions linguistic stereotypes as he explains to a coworker that a new worker whose first language is not English should not be disparaged on the assumption that he is underqualified to perform his job: "Fucking, hing is, you cannae just lift some cunt out ay his natural hingmee and fucking drop him here and expect him to be as fucking ace as he wis back home, fucking straight away." He then connects this worker's plight to his own experience with "aw they cocks in Portsmouth giving it 'aw we can't understand you Scots. You need to speak slower.' I'm like that: naw man, you need tae listen quicker. How come I can understand every fucking thing you say? Geordie, Yorkshire, Cockney, but they cannae even fucking *hear* me. But still, when I put the phone down, I'm the one that feels stupit. Naw. Give him time man. Let the words come."[53] Thus, even in a play whose inciting incident is the use of the word "cunt," Maxwell acknowledges that contemporary society is not without its linguistic limitations and preconceptions.

As evidenced by the above plays, the PPP series has produced a wide range of plays, from the comparatively large cast, direct-address format of *The Jean-Jacques Rousseau Show* to the more conventional two-hander of *A Respectable Widow Takes to Vulgarity*. The series has also demonstrated innovative practices in terms of series format and coproduction: Spring 2007 saw the PPP series offer a new evening version of its lunchtime theatre. The series, titled A Dinner, a Drama and a Dram, offered spectators who could not attend the lunchtime plays the opportunity to view each week's plays on Thursday evenings. The Dinner, a Drama and a Dram format has continued periodically since its 2007 inception. Further, Spring 2009 marked a key moment in the evolution of PPP: The series partnered with the Traverse Theatre in Edinburgh for a series of five plays that, after being staged at Òran Mór, transferred to the Traverse. The Traverse has followed the PPP format, though spectators must eat their pies either before or after the performance in the theatre café. While the initial season of transfers featured such established writers as David Greig, David Harrower, and Jo Clifford, the transfers have since included works by newer playwrights. They have also included coproductions with the National Theatre of Scotland (see below) and England's Paines Plough, and 2015 saw PPP's first Welsh coproduction, with Cardiff's Sherman Cymru Theatre. Further, the Fall 2013 season marked a new first: Catronia Lexy Campbell's *Doras Dùinte* became the first Gaelic (or Gàidhlig) play to be staged in the series. The inclusion of the Gaelic language for an urban audience whose predominant languages are English and Scots was a key step in acknowledging the importance of this native language in PPP's populist setting.

While the majority of PPP plays have been written by Scottish playwrights, the series has demonstrated in multiple miniseasons within its regular seasons that it is international in dimension as well. Fall 2011 saw a short series of six new plays from Latin America, each adapted by a prominent Scottish playwright. The series was coproduced with the National Theatre of Scotland and was so successful that the PPP-NTS coproduction was repeated the following year, this time with a season of plays from the Arab world. Curated by David Greig, who has spent much time in the area while mentoring young writers, the mini-season was titled *One Day in Spring*, referencing the Arab Spring revolts of the previous year. As Greig describes, "I found that many of the playwrights with whom I'd worked were on the streets: some in Cairo, some in Damascus and some in Tunis. And they were writing about it, and they were talking about it on Facebook. And it seemed an extraordinary opportunity. . . . Suddenly this was a generation who were at the heart of something important politically in their part of the world, but also it felt to me at that time and still does, emblematic of a generation around the world who are bridling against various political, social, economic restrictions."[54] Because of Greig's desire to involve as many playwrights as possible, the season offered two multiauthor works in addition to plays by single authors. The first, *Dear Glasgow*, consisted of letters written by the established generation of writers in the various Arab countries; in performance, the letters were read aloud by established Scottish writers such as Liz Lochhead and Alan Bissett. Closing the season was a montage of very short plays titled *One Day in Spring*, assembled and directed by Greig. Subtitled "24 Hours in the Middle East or How to Stage a Revolution in 18 Easy Lessons," the resulting piece resembled agitprop sketches and was very powerful, the audience learning that in some countries the act of throwing a tennis ball over a dictator's fence, with the words

"We do not love you" written on the ball, is an act of revolutionary aggression.[55] The international season repeated in 2013, this time featuring plays from China and in partnership with both the National Theatre of Scotland and the National Theatre of China. The 2014 international season featured Commonwealth writers from Zimbabwe, Nigeria, and Jamaica, while the 2015 season staged three plays from Russia and Ukraine.

While the international seasons have provided continuity within larger seasons of diversity, additional continuity has been displayed through PPP's season-ending pantos, also known as A Panto, a Pie and a Pint. Panto is a tremendously popular theatrical form; contemporary Scottish panto generally starts from a well-known fairy tale and turns the material on its head, with the addition of contemporary (generally lowbrow) cultural references, parodies of popular songs, outrageous costumes, and a drag-wearing Dame character. While traditional panto is kid-friendly, PPP's pantos are decidedly for adults—in fairness, it is perhaps difficult to imagine small children lining up for their pints. These productions both celebrate and send up the form, and because they are the creation of MacLennan, the productions are rife with political references. In *Snow White and the Seventh Dwarf* (2011), for example, the Occupy and other protest movements are evoked when the Queen faces her own protest. As critic Joyce McMillan quotes, "'Their demands are so vague!' she shrieks; while the protesters chant some crystal-clear demand, like 'Make the Bankers Pay Their Taxes.'"[56] And *Alice in Poundland* (2012) sees the heroine shopping in the eponymous store (equivalent to American dollar stores) when she finds herself transported to Plunderland, "a parallel universe where everything costs £1m but you don't have to pay if you are rich."[57]

PPP returned its political focus to the question of Scottish independence in June 2014, when it served as the hub for the National Theatre of Scotland's *The Great Yes, No, Don't Know Five-Minute Theatre Show*, an event that asked people to write five-minute plays in response to the question of independence, plays that were performed and broadcast live online over a 24-hour period to over twenty-six thousand people worldwide.[58] The *Five-Minute Theatre Show* was cocurated by MacLennan and David Greig, who were anti- and proindependence, respectively. Greig described the importance of the event in terms of its democratic format: "The show takes the Scottish Variety tradition and propels it into the internet age. The live hubs around the country and beyond will provide an exciting environment for lively debate, one-off performances and thoughtful reflection. At this key moment in the nation's history it's a way for Scotland to speak to itself—not in formal political tones—but in a relaxed, rambunctious, celebratory and personal way; and crucially, it's a chance for everyone to contribute, not just a political or artistic elite."[59] Sadly, MacLennan was not able to see the *Five-Minute Theatre Show* in performance: he announced in February 2014 that he had been diagnosed with a motor-neuron disease, and on June 13, a mere ten days before Òran Mór was to host the culmination of his and Greig's project, he passed away.[60] Perhaps, though, this most egalitarian of theatrical productions, in which literally anyone with Internet could participate as writer, performer, and/or audience member, served as a fitting final project for a director and producer who so strongly championed populism in the theatre.

For MacLennan, his years as producer of PPP demonstrated the power of populist theatre: "I think one of the things that A Play, a Pie and a Pint has dispelled is the myth that there is not an appetite in theatre audiences for new work. . . . We do forty-two weeks a year, six days a week, average perhaps 130 people a day. So it is a myth."[61] Although he has acknowledged that the work produced is not always of the same high quality—he allowed in 2005 that "there's probably been one real turkey per season along with a couple of fairly plucked birds; the rest I think have been fairly creditable"[62]—his ethos of providing new theatrical experiences each week, within a Pie and a Pint environment that is informal, welcoming, and frankly fun, has stood the series in good stead. Further, his relationship with his daily audience is to my view a key element in the series's success—the majority of performances have featured MacLennan's own personal welcome. Because of the camaraderie he has established with his audiences, those audiences are willing to take the small weekly risk, in terms of time and money, to see new theatre. Additionally, as MacLennan remarked during the lead-up to the *One Day in Spring* season, "There are things I do now that I would never have dreamed of doing back in that first season. Because what I've learned is that once you build up this strong connection with an audience, everything becomes possible. Their appetite for new experiences is astonishing, and it means we can do so much more than I ever imagined, seven years ago."[63] Nor have the fruits of his labor been limited geographically to Glasgow or even to Scotland: In addition to the numerous coproductions mentioned above, the series has inspired similar programs around the world: the West Yorkshire Playhouse in Leeds has its own series of A Play, a Pie and a Pint productions, and Philadelphia's Tiny Dynamite theatre company has been producing its offshoot seasons of PPP shows since 2011—in the latter case, the pies served are of the pizza rather than the pastry variety.[64] And franchises in Venezuela and Brazil are in process. Further, many plays that started their production lives at PPP have gone on to be produced internationally, as listed on the series's website: "Plays from A Play, a Pie and a Pint have been seen at: Edinburgh Festival Fringe; Belfast Festival; Brighton Festival; Adelaide Festival; Island Festival,

Tasmania; Golden Mask Festival, Moscow; and Last Frontier Theatre Festival, Alaska. We've also had plays from Òran Mór performed in Newcastle, Manchester, Coventry, Bristol, London, Seoul, Beirut, Milan, Amsterdam, Dublin, Bermuda and New York."[65]

There exist in the realm of new writing multiple models for play development.[66] The PPP is simply one of these models, but a model that can provide exciting and fruitful inspiration for both writers and programmers. The casual, comparatively low-risk context of production means that writers can play with ideas and forms that they might not otherwise attempt.[67] It also means that works can be more easily placed in front of audiences, who are, after all, the point of live theatre. Additionally, in a contemporary context in which the notion of dinner theatre is frequently met with derision, the PPP model offers opportunities for reviving and reconfiguring the concept: dinner theatre frequently carries with it an assumption of companies "trotting out" tired plays that are guaranteed to please, and the insertion of new writing into the mix has the potential make the notion of dinner (or lunch) theatre exciting again. Perhaps, though, the greatest potential lies in the same inspiration that MacLennan experienced in the sugar fields of Cuba: The experience of theatre "in just a normal part of life, while you're having a bite to eat."

Notes

1. Neil Cooper, "Drama to Get Your Teeth Into," *Herald* (Glasgow), December 6, 2005, Lexis-Nexis Academic.
2. Alex Sierz, *Rewriting the Nation: British Theatre Today* (London: Methuen, 2011), 44.
3. Trish Reid, *Theatre & Scotland* (Basingstoke, UK: Palgrave, 2013), 32.
4. David Greig, "Our New National Theatre . . . Like an Elephant Let Loose Upon the Machair," *Sunday Herald* (*Glasgow*), March 14, 2004, 1–2.
5. Kenneth M. Roberts, "Populism, Political Mobilizations, and Crises of Political Representation," *The Promise and Perils of Populism: Global Perspectives*, ed. Carlos de la Torre (Lexington: University Press of Kentucky, 2015), 140–58. ProQuest ebrary, web, February 6, 2016, 141.
6. Femi Folorunso, "Scottish Drama and the Popular Tradition," in *Scottish Theatre since the Seventies*, ed. Randall Stevenson and Gavin Wallace, 176–185 (Edinburgh: Edinburgh University Press, 1996), 177.
7. Reid, *Theatre & Scotland*, 38.
8. The ceilidh form has been utilized more recently in David Greig's 2011 *The Strange Undoing of Prudencia Hart* and 2014's *Rantin'*, cowritten by Kieran Hurley, AJ Taudevin, Drew Wright, and Gav Prentice.

9. D. Keith Peacock, *Radical Stages: Alternative History in Modern British Drama* (New York: Greenwood, 1991), 91.
10. Randall Stevenson, "Border Warranty: John McGrath and Scotland," in *Freedom's Pioneer: John McGrath's Work in Theatre, Film and Television*, ed. David Bradby and Susanna Capon, 73–85 (Exeter, UK: University of Exeter Press, 2005), 75.
11. The Cuban practice of incorporating "some artistic cultural experience happening in just a normal part of life" is also dramatized in Nilo Cruz's *Anna in the Tropics*, in which workers in a Cuban-American cigar factory are read literary classics while they work.
12. MacLennan acknowledged the influence of Edinburgh's Pool Theatre, a lunchtime program that ran from 1971 to 1974. Nor was the Pool alone in the practice of lunchtime theatre during that period; as Rosalind Asquith describes, documenting lunchtime theatre in London during the 1960s and 70s: "The original intentions were numerous—from the blatantly commercial impulse to showcase the work of new writers and performers in circumstances that were relatively painless economically, to the much more radical motive that, by presenting plays at an unusual time of day, one was breaking through one of the paradigm conventions of Western theatre." See Rosalind Asquith, "Subversion at Lunchtime," in *Dreams and Deconstructions: Alternative Theatre in Britain*, ed. Sandy Craig, 145–52 (Ambergate, UK: Amber Lane Press, 1980), 145.
13. David MacLennan, interview with the author, May 31, 2012.
14. A Play, a Pie and a Pint. "Mini Musicals Season: The Day I Found the Blues," accessed June 25, 2016, http://playpiepint.com/plays/mini-musicals-season-day-i-found-blues/. For a complete list of the series's plays, see A Play, a Pie and a Pint, "Archived Shows," accessed June 25, 2016, http://playpiepint.com/archived-shows/. In comparison, the Royal Court's 1994–2006 period staged 266 productions, including several revivals. See "Plays: 1956–2007," in *The Royal Court Theatre Inside Out*, by Ruth Little and Emily McLaughlin, 461–469 (London: Oberon, 2007), 467–69.
15. Philip Howard, ed., *Scottish Shorts* (London: Nick Hern, 2010), viii.
16. R. W. Maslen, "Political Theatre from Greece to Glasgow," in *Fleeto*, by Paddy Cuneen, 5–9 (Edinburgh: Fairplay, 2009), 9.
17. The series has since its inception received periodic, indirect public funding through coproductions with such companies as the National Theatre of Scotland, Dundee Rep, and England's Paines Plough. And in 2014, Creative Scotland provided direct funding to the series for the first time. See Joyce MacMillan, "Budget Cuts Mean a Rethink Is Required at the Traverse," *The Scotsman*, November 8, 2014, LexisNexis Academic.
18. These figures are accurate as of April 2016.
19. MacLennan, interview with the author.
20. Howard, ed., *Scottish Shorts*, viii.
21. See National Theatre of Scotland, "Live Archives," Staging the Nation, accessed January 30, 2014, http://stagingthenation.com/live/live-archives/.
22. MacLennan, interview with the author.
23. David MacLennan, David Anderson, Davey Anderson, Alan Bissett, Catrin Evans, Mike Gonzalez, Sean Hardie et al., *The Jean-Jacques Rousseau Show* (unpublished manuscript, 2012), Adobe Acrobat file, 9.
24. Gary McNair, interview with the author, June 11, 2012.

25. Ibid.

26. Ibid.

27. MacLennan et al., *JJR*, 1–2.

28. John McGrath, *The Cheviot, the Stag and the Black, Black Oil* (London: Methuen, 1993), 2.

29. MacLennan et al., *JJR*, 2, 7.

30. Ibid., 8.

31. Ibid., 10–11.

32. Ibid., 14.

33. "Baw" is a Scots pronunciation for "ball," or testicle.

34. MacLennan et al., *JJR*, 15, 31–32.

35. Ibid., 31. *Spooks* is the original title for the British TV series known in some countries as *MI:5*.

36. Ibid., 33–34. This is a shortened version of Alan Bissett's poem "Vote Britain," which Bissett performed at several proindependence rallies. The text of the poem, along with a video of Bissett performing it, can be found on the writer's website, and several videos of his performances can be found on YouTube. See Alan Bissett, "My Contribution to the Debate on Scottish Independence," AlanBissett.com, accessed March 10, 2014, http://alanbissett.com/2012/01/13/my-contribution-to-the-debate-on-scottish-independence/.

37. MacLennan et al., *JJR*, 24–30.

38. MacLennan et al., *JJR*, 32, 35, 36.

39. This was, of course, before there was any inkling that Trump would become a presidential nominee in the United States or that he would win the election. Scots' derision for Trump is thorough and widespread, stemming from his building of a golf resort on the coast of Scotland near Aberdeen (documented in the 2011 film *You've Been Trumped* and again in 2014's *A Dangerous Game*); his protracted attempts to block a windfarm from being built in the resort's vicinity; and, most recently, his celebration of the Brexit vote while standing in that resort, apparently ignorant of the fact that Scots voted overwhelmingly to remain in the European Union.

40. MacLennan et al., *JJR*, 36–37, 40.

41. I would assume that this troubling is the work of MacLennan, who stated that he is in the No camp because he believes that the working classes and unions in England and Scotland stand a better chance of creating change by working together than by working separately.

42. *A Respectable Widow Takes to Vulgarity* was first staged in 2012 as part of the Traverse Theatre's first series of Breakfast Plays, a series that has been repeated each year since then and includes with the price of admission a coffee and a breakfast roll.

43. Douglas Maxwell, *A Respectable Widow Takes to Vulgarity*, unpublished manuscript, 2013, Adobe Acrobat file.

44. Maxwell, *A Respectable Widow*, 6. Having read numerous contemporary Scottish plays, I would add here that in fact the word is used in a wide variety of contexts: sometimes as Jim defines it here, sometimes with a rather more menacing connotation. It is rarely, however, used to reference its literal definition.

45. Maxwell, *A Respectable Widow*, 7.

46. Ibid., 14.

47. Ibid., 10–11.
48. Ibid., 14.
49. Douglas Maxwell, interview with Susie Armitage, YouTube video, 7:41, A Play, a Pie and a Pint, accessed November 10, 2013, http://playpiepint.com/?p=5224.
50. Maxwell, *A Respectable Widow*, 31.
51. Ibid., 25.
52. Ibid., 26.
53. Ibid., 7–8.
54. David Greig, interview with David MacLennan, YouTube video, 11:40, A Play, a Pie and a Pint, accessed February 17, 2014, http://playpiepint.com/?p=4333.
55. I viewed the piece on May 25, 2012.
56. Joyce McMillan, review of *Snow White and the Seventh Dwarf*, by David MacLennan and David Anderson, *Scotsman*, December 9, 2011, LexisNexis Academic.
57. Tom Shields, "Pounding the Boards," *Herald (Glasgow)*, June 7, 2012, LexisNexis Academic.
58. This event was the fourth incarnation of NTS's *Five Minute Theatre* series.
59. National Theatre of Scotland, "Latest News," Five Minute Theatre, accessed February 1, 2014, http://fiveminutetheatre.com/news/.
60. Michael Coveney, "Obituary: David MacLennan" *Guardian (London)*, June 18, 2014, LexisNexis Academic.
61. MacLennan, interview with the author.
62. Neil Cooper, "Drama to Get Your Teeth Into," *Herald (Glasgow)*, December 6, 2005, LexisNexis Academic.
63. Joyce McMillan, "On a Roll into Spring," *Scotsman*, January 19, 2012, LexisNexis Academic.
64. Tiny Dynamite, "What Is 'A Play, a Pie and a Pint'?" accessed February 17, 2014, http://www.tinydynamite.org/whatisppp.htm.
65. A Play, a Pie and a Pint, "About Us," accessed March 14, 2016, http://playpiepint.com/about/. New York's 59E59 Theatre alone has produced Kieran Hurley and AJ Taudevin's *Chalk Farm* (2014), Gerda Stevenson's *Federer Versus Murray* (staged at PPP in 2010 and in New York in 2012), and *A Respectable Widow Takes to Vulgarity* (2014). See E59E59, "Season 2011 Archive to the Present," accessed March 28, 2015, http://www.59e59.org/archivelist.php.
66. For an overview of new writing processes in Britain, including workshops, writers' groups, and rehearsed readings, see Jacqueline Bolton, "Capitalizing (on) new writing: New play development in the 1990s," *Studies in Theatre & Performance* 32, no. 2 (2012): 209–225, doi: 10.1386/stap.32.2.209_1.
67. Douglas Maxwell sees potential danger in the low-risk nature of the program: "Where's the risk? Can a play fail? Can the audience reject it? And if not, is it really professional theatre? That might be taking it too far, but risk is a big factor in professional theatre. . . . That risk is what we sharpen our skills on. Without it . . . if it doesn't need to [be] good . . . how the hell do we get better? Why should we care? How do we even *know* if it is good?" He does, however, acknowledge his own success with *Respectable Widow*, success that includes multiple productions in Scotland, one in New York, and an upcoming production in Quebec, in a Québécois translation. Douglas Maxwell, e-mail to the author, April 5, 2016.

American Playwriting and the Now New

—TODD LONDON

I write from the University of Washington's School of Drama, which celebrated its seventy-fifth anniversary during the 2015–16 academic year. It's a school that, like so many theatre programs, groped its way out of an English department long before colleges in the United States trained actors, directors, and designers for a living theatre, and a full two decades before American cities commonly housed permanent professional theatres. The "drama" in its name carries its origins as a literary art. As a result, it sounds rusty, a bit old-fashioned. The idea of writing about "new drama" feels oxymoronic. The study of dramatic literature long ago gave way the study of performance, and our notions of text expanded far beyond the mere playscript.

The days when theatre studies were a subsidiary teaching of English were the days, too, when professional playwriting had a single source: Broadway. Mainstream scholarship, like the mainstream theatre, described a unified field of then-contemporary dramatic writing, dominated by a triumvirate of major writers: Arthur Miller, Tennessee Williams, and the father of so much American playwriting, Eugene O'Neill. It would take until Lorraine Hansberry's *Raisin in the Sun* in 1959 and off-off-Broadway's boom in the 1960s for the complexion of the profession to begin to change and for the image of the playwright as a pipe-smoking white man in a narrow tie, banging away at his Underwood manual, to reach its endgame.

Jump to now. If drama is old-school, what exactly is new about it now? The answer, even when considering playwriting as a literary art, is "a lot." A lot is new, and if *Los Angeles Times* critic Charles McNulty is correct—and he is—we are living through a budding golden age for playwrights, a boom unlike any in the recent past. It's a boom of stories and who gets to tell them. It's a boom of formal experimentation, including those who would wrest playwriting away from the domination of story itself. It's a boom of talent, a *professional* boom. What follows is a quick tour: where new writing is in the United States, what it looks like, and some of the people who are doing it.

National geography has impact on contemporary drama. According to *Outrageous Fortune: The Life and Times of the New American Play*, the book that resulted from a study I led for New York's Theatre Development Fund from 2005 to 2009, 50 percent of our nation's playwrights live in New York City and another 25 percent in Los Angeles. The last quarter is spread across the other forty-eight states. In other words, 75 percent of our collective dramatic concerns are filtered through visions from these two urban poles—one constellated around Broadway, the other in the shadow of Hollywood.

This statistic might not matter in finance or mass media, but theatre is a local activity, and our cultural concerns change with the landscape. America looks very different from a Brooklyn subway, a freeway in Baja, California, or a bus in Seattle's International District. Audiences look different, too. Having relocated to Seattle in the summer of 2014 after twenty-nine years in New York, I crossed the threshold of Saul Steinberg's famous *New Yorker* cover and entered the flat, indistinct no-man's-land separating Midtown Manhattan from the Pacific Ocean. It has become apparent that everything I thought I knew about contemporary playwriting was partial. Changing location, I found, can change your eyes. The demographics of casts look different in New York or Minneapolis or Custer, South Dakota. Decades-old formal experimentation can seem shocking when you trade "downtown" theatre for regional centers, a geographic shift that sometimes feels like backward time travel, depending on what is actually new to the place you land.

What's new in the American drama is also shaped by the angle of vision of the theatrical industry that selects, produces, and reviews contemporary work in mostly nonprofit, institutional venues—the curatorial politics of the new. What feels natural and contemporary on the East coast may jar in Seattle. It's hard to know, because it often takes years for all but the most New York–visible plays to get seen elsewhere. In fact, the plays I'm about to discuss have yet to be seen in my new home of Seattle, so *angle of vision* is more of a *blind spot*.

While the new in American playwriting has sometimes referred to the form of drama, rather than its subjects, it makes sense today to begin with story. Despite long-running academic and scholarly arguments about what Aristotle meant, what he was upholding dramaturgically, and what he was promoting politically with his *Poetics*, contemporary theatres and theatregoers, like Aristotle himself, subscribe to his belief that the structuring of events—the plotting of story—is preeminent among the six constituent elements of tragedy: plot, character, verbal expression, thought, visual adornment, and song composition.

The mainstream tastes of our nation's theatre have consistently reinforced his view of theatre as a mimetic form, as mirror and representation. In the theatre more than any other performing or visual art, we privilege story above all. Do we "read" contemporary dance or sculpture for plot? Do we assess contemporary jazz on the basis of story arc or character trajectory? Of course not. But despite the passage of 2,400 years, despite a century of intense theatrical experimentation, when it comes to writing for the stage, story refuses to release its grip, regardless of writers' efforts to buck it. This is true for audiences, and it's true for the curators of our major stages.

Just as the idea of "the narrative" has come to dominate our artistic, political, and social discourse, in universities theatre training currently accepts the new-old designation as one of the "story arts." We are storytellers, we tell our students. We hold story circles with communities other than our own, as a way of creating work that speaks across cultures. We assess production choices by how well they "tell the story."

Moreover—and this is really important—as educators we agree that the viability of theatre as a storytelling art depends on the inclusion of stories previously denied access to the stage. In the era of the American playwright triumvirate of O'Neill, Miller, and Williams, or the second string of Odets, Inge, and Wilder, a pantheon that might have grudgingly been expanded to include Susan Glaspell or Lillian Hellman, the regularly produced and lastingly canonized storytellers were mostly men and, until Lorraine Hansberry, all white. Our playwriting community is now, by contrast, distinguished by its heterogeneity, by the leading examples of African American and Latinx playwrights, by Asian American writers of various origin, by a new critical mass of Arab American dramatists, and by what drag artist and playwright Taylor Mac teasingly calls LGBTQLMNOP, a joke that both embraces and pokes fun at gender fluidity and category proliferation.

New stories enlarge our concerns, enhance our capacity for empathy, and, thereby, increase our humanity. This is what we teach when we teach theatre. New stories also revitalize our language. Mac's own play, *Hir*, makes the point with verbal virtuosity.

The form of *Hir* is familiar: a traumatized soldier comes home from the war, this time Iraq, to a changed world. What's new is the substance of that world and the words it's made from. Taylor Mac dramatizes a family's transformation from a brutal patriarchy under the now-stroke-addled Arnold to a maybe equally abusive tyranny under a new regime led by Arnold's long-victimized wife, Paige. Where there was order under Arnold, there is now a hoarder's chaos. Where Arnold ruled with iron fist, Paige rules by dressing her disabled husband as a clown and spraying water in his face when he speaks. And as Paige's daughter transitions from one gender to a nonbinary other, nothing is guarded more ferociously than pronouns.[1]

PAIGE In these new genders, exists new pronouns. Max is no longer a she or a he. So you call Max, ze. You must use ze instead of the pronouns he or she and you must use the pronoun hir, H.I.R., in place of the pronouns her or him. Max gets very upset if you refer to hir as a she, he, her, or him. Ze wants you to refer to hir as a hir or ze. Ze also gets upset when you emphasize the ze as if commenting on the pronoun when speaking to hir. For example if you were to say, "What is *ZE* doing today?", ze will not like that. Ze, understandably, is not to be treated as a side-show oddity. Ze wants you to say ze or hir as if this had been part of your regular speaking vocabulary your entire life. Any breach in decorum will cause hir to write in hir blog about how awful hir troglodyte fascist hetero-normative mother is. It's fantastic.

Suffice to say, not all new stories are new at all. Some have been knocking at the door to be heard, and some have been previously told from a single, dominant point of view. The reclamation of stories is a major strain in contemporary playwriting. What's new now often stems from a deep engagement and revision of history. In Suzan-Lori Parks's *Father Comes Home from the Wars, Parts 1, 2, & 3*, the writer draws on structural elements from *The Odyssey* for a story of slave involvement in the Civil War. It's a heartbreaking work, in which the uncertain promise of freedom becomes the Hero's incentive for serving his master in the fight to save slavery.

In Part 2, the hero, named Hero, is left alone with Smith, a captured Northern soldier, a free black passing as white:

SMITH This world is such a mess. How's a Colored gonna make his way? Seems like we either get sold off by somebody or sell out our ownselves. You could be bought and sold and so could I.

HERO That'll end with Freedom.

SMITH But what if it don't somehow? Sometimes I get the feeling that the heart of the thing won't change easy or quick. Cause of the way we were bought and brought over here in the first place. Maybe even with Freedom, that mark, huh, that mark of the marketplace, it will always be on us. And so

> maybe we will always be twisting and turning ourselves into something that is going to bring the best price. That's the way we were born into this, so is it always gonna be like that for us, slavery or not? Freedom or not? Are we ever going to get us a better place in the marketplace?

Freedom when it does come comes with trauma and the damage of both slavery and war—a freedom that is anything but free.

We hear this story with twenty-first-century ears, in a world of marketplace and the mass incarceration of black American men. We hear the story of the Civil War not as a tale of triumph and emancipation, as it's usually told, but as one stage of African America's tortuous and stumbling odyssey toward an elusive and always incomplete freedom.

For all its urgency, dramatic power, and structural pull, story is, even in Aristotelian terms, only one element among many. Contemporary playwriting has long fought against story's dominance, struggling to raise up language, spectacle, song, debate—to train audiences to see the making of the work, its formal structures, its politics and art, separate from its narrative accessibility, human interest, or "relatability," a word that has seeped in from TV. The fight goes on to wrest story from the center of the spectacle.

Sybil Kempson's *From the Pig Pile* defies storytelling. *From the Pig Pile* unfolds in pageant-like processionals, beginning in the street outside the theatre. Audience members are corralled and assigned to groups by strange and hostile designations. The audience travels in separate small groups through a series of living dioramas. In the early phases of the spectacle, the audience is told stories, both by diorama figures and by tour guide/docents. But these stories are obscured by linguistic twists, by the cacophony of simultaneous scenes, by obstructed views.

Here's one such story, a prehistoric rant and feminist critique all matted together. The speaker's name is Whale Bone Hut Lady #1:

> One of our elder who some say was brought here at one time by a certain tribe of hagwitches who shall remain nameless was able to read the twigs and leaves by the way they fell in her cup. New group people to show up at our stead, each winter, elder said. They climb and travel over many landforms, she foretold in the way the twigs and leaves fell of briny twig tea. They arrive we knew from what she said, by boat, they were coming. . . . Each year, each winter, a boat. People come.
>
> Now it is winter here again—so here again. Bringing many tales and ways, heh.
>
> Don't bring? Wealth, money, riches. Right? Show up with no ATM cards, no credit cards. No wedding rings, no memories, no wallets even. Two or three winters later? We're drained. One skinbag memory yoghurt, that's it. Dark winter days ahead.

> Watch but don't listen and don't learn. So loud—put selves and own opinions into all observations made. Take a gift then criticize it. Rape a couple few of our women, say not staying long, don't marry the women. Same old story. And then come back the next winter and drain us again, always in winter when there is no work possibly to help with, only ways of keeping warm.
>
> Burn precious firewood just for partytime. Rub bodies against our bodies. 'Oh, I must sleep between you and yr. husband, else I freeze!' Hoh I heard that one before!

In addition to thwarting our desire to make story, the play, as you can hear, messes with our ability to make meaning from language. This is just one of the faux-archaic dialects in the play and among the more parsable. It is representative, though, of the way Kempson slip-slides with syntax, frolics with the highfalutin, and tickles with idiom. We always almost know what is being said to us, but just almost.

From the Pig Pile was developed in and for Austin, Texas, in cahoots with a group of six theatres there, through successive showings for the locals. These showings at Salvage Vanguard Theatre and Rude Mechanicals, among other venues, alternated with workshops at New York's New Dramatists. The play reveals, in its final form, the process of that making, the way an action painting does or the sculpture of a body only partially released from its originating marble. The artists who worked on the play get named in the text like the begetters in the Bible. Even the title refers not to the play's subject but to the collaborative team that early on dubbed itself the Pig Pile.

It's easy to find in contemporary playwriting this kind of fascination with the mechanism of storytelling, its blur of truth and fiction. Carlos Murillo's trilogy, *The Javier Plays*, revels in the meta. *The Javier Plays* center on a playwright genius named Javier C., a Columbian born in the late 1950s, recently dead. Murillo's plays, which include *The Thick Description of Harry Smith* and *Your Name Will Follow You Home*, are about Javier's missing plays, including a "lost" magnum opus that gives the third part of the trilogy its title: *Diagram of a Paper Airplane*. Javier is the charismatic enigma who his surviving friends and family must puzzle together; he is also as-if real, the object of his own creator, Murillo's, obsession. Is Murillo Javier? Are his plays Javier's plays? Is any of it true?

For the playful, the new can offer a funhouse of infinite mirrors—the self reflected on every surface. In *Yellow Face*, David Henry Hwang is both the playwright and the main character, and actual public events surrounding his earlier play *Face Value* are among the whirl of self-referential events at the heart of its action. In *The Inexplicable Redemption of Agent G* (2011), the self-proclaimed "geek theatre" playwright Qui Nguyen ups the meta on Hwang: not only does Qui appear as the playwright of his own play, but David Henry Hwang appears too, to put Qui in his place as a wannabe. The two playwrights have a rap battle in which "DHH easily beats [Qui's] ass to the ground." "I'M THE D DOUBLE H/PLAYWRIGHT MASTER HWANG/GONNA KILL YA WITH MY LYRICS/ GONNA SMASH WITH THIS SONG."

Branden Jacobs-Jenkins pulls out all these stops in *An Octoroon*: he deconstructs his own play as it goes; he reclaims an old story; and he sets in motion a metastasis of the meta. As a figure in his own play, Jacobs-Jenkins writes himself three times—triple doppelgängers—first as the playwright, BJJ (as in Branden Jacobs-Jenkins), and then, in whiteface, as both the hero (George) and the villain (M'Closky) of a play by another historical playwright, Dion Boucicault, who also appears as a character, The Playwright.

Jacobs-Jenkins employs and destroys *The Octoroon*, Boucicault's 1859 melodrama of life in Louisiana. The actual playwright prepares us for satire and a kind of head-spinning, self-referential undoing in BJJ's prologue monologue:

> "Black playwright."
> I can't even wipe my ass
> without someone trying to accuse me
> of deconstructing the race problem in America.
> I even tried writing a play about
> talking farm animals once—
> just to avoid talking about people—
> and this literary manager was like, "Oh my God!
> You're totally deconstructing African folktales aren't you?"
> I'm like,
> "No. I'm just writing about farm animals."

The plot is sheer melodrama: A white man wants to possess a beautiful octoroon slave, who is a slave only because she has one-eighth black ancestry. To have her he must take over the plantation she lives on. He does this by killing another slave and stealing the letter that could save the plantation from his clutches. He kills the slave using a tomahawk that belongs to a local "Indian of ambiguous background, and then pins the murder on Wahnotee, the Indian." By forcing the sale of the property, the killer forces the octoroon's sale as well. He buys her to possess her. What the white killer M'Closky doesn't know, though, is that the murder has been captured by the newest technology: a photographic plate in a nineteenth-century stationary camera.

This is the moment of revelation: the photographic plate carrying the image of the criminal in action. It's the moment of revelation, and The Playwright interrupts. "You know, it's really hard to describe how this scene works—," he says. "Because it actually would have been very exciting 150 years ago—having someone caught by a photograph," BJJ adds.

PLAYWRIGHT. They were a very novel thing.

BJJ. Which is why this whole plot is more or less centered around a camera. But photographs to us? Boring. It's a cliché, but we've gotten so used to photos and photographic images that we've basically learned how to fake them, so the kind of justice around which this whole thing hangs is actually a little dated—

PLAYWRIGHT. But part of the thrill, part of the "sensation" of the scene, was giving people back then a sense of having really witnessed something new and novel.

BJJ. And that's basically impossible for us to do now. If anything, the theatre is no longer a place of novelty. The fact is we can more or less experience anything nowadays. So I think the final frontier, awkwardly enough, is probably just an actual experience of finality, I think.

PLAYWRIGHT. Like—death, basically?

And so the playwright duo discusses ways to thrill the audience by bringing it closer to death. They could set the theatre on fire, but that would mean the play could be performed only once. Meanwhile, an assistant wheels out an overhead projector. BJJ tells us, "Anyway, I figured I'd try something. I hope it isn't too disappointing."

Finally, as Boucicault's plot's unravels, the assistant turns on the overhead projector so it displays a photo of a lynched black man. The silly melodramatic denouement is played out by the light of this horrific image, until BJJ complains, "I can't see anything. I'm sorry—Can we turn this off." From creaky melodrama to the rabbit hole of the referential self, suddenly we are, for a moment, in the blinding light of too real, too true, too still-with-us racism and death.

In another assault by the vitally theatrical on the merely literary, playwrights often wield time itself as a weapon. Theatrical events, of course, happen in real time, because in the shared, live, present of a physical theatre, the clock ticks for us all. Much has been made, for instance, of the duration of Annie Baker's silences and pauses in her Pulitzer Prize–winning *The Flick*, a play that, depending on how much time gets allotted to the quiet between characters and such tasks as sweeping up popcorn in an empty movie theatre, can take a couple of hours or, when I saw the premiere in New York, well over three hours. In contemporary playmaking, time—or what has come to us from performance art as "the durational"—has become a prevalent obsession, from earlier epic cycles by major writers Tony Kushner, August Wilson, Robert Schenkkan, and Suzan-Lori Parks, in which length, scope, and sweep signaled size of ambition, and the new epics by the likes of Murillo and Anne Washburn to the two-minute plays of the Chicago and New York Neo-Futurists, on the other side of the clock.

Anne Washburn's remarkable epic of ancient Rome, *The Octavia*, is intended to come in at no less than twelve hours long. Drag artist Taylor Mac, whose transgender family play *Hir* represents his more traditional playwriting side, premiered an epic twenty-four-hour performance in October 2016 that highlighted his work as a singer and performance artist. Mac performed a twenty-four-hour concert of American popular songs demonstrating twenty-four decades of our independence as a nation, a project many years and many months of physical and vocal endurance training in the making.

Following the burst of new playwriting at the birth of off-off-Broadway in the 1960s and early 1970s, new work in America went through a sweeping professionalization. New institutional theatres added new play development to their portfolios and introduced audiences to contemporary writing. The geography of our nation's theatre changed, and the center for new work became centers, with plays moving into New York instead of centrifugally out.

At the height of this institutional settling, though, the United States began to experience the economic, political, and cultural shifts described so well by historian Daniel T. Rodgers as "the age of fracture." As American life experienced what Rodgers calls "the disaggregation of the block categories of mid-century," so too did the work of the theatre break up. As cultural stability and organizational—or maybe narrative—singularity gave way to "choice, provisionality, and impermanence," so too did our artists explore numerous, disparate paths, what for some (I am not among them) still represents a sad fragmentation of the American theatre.

Creative energies turned to company-devised performance, to community-based social justice theatre, often blending professional and nonprofessional artists. Some playwrights looked for old, overlooked stories, some created the future, some—like playwright/performer Anna Deavere Smith—"wrote" plays from dozens of other people's voices, other people's stories. By the turn of the millennium, playwrights gathered in larger groups under smaller designations—by race, ethnicity, gender, region. Was it, in fact, an era of mortal fragmentation or of profusion? Disaggregation and disaffection or regrouping? And, if profusion, how do we tell that story? As old Aristotle knew, the singular journey is so much riper for narrative than the thousand stories difference leads us to.

When we ask, What's new? we are, in effect, asking, Who's new? Who is writing now? What are they writing? As someone who has worked with generations of writers working from an array of aesthetics, I know that there are so many names. These are boom days for playwriting, despite the nearly impossible economics of the profession. Sustained by new play theatres, labs, fellowships, and retreats, and nurtured by our finest generation of playwright-teachers—Maria Irene Fornes, Mac Wellman, Paula Vogel, Marsha Norman, and others—this profession of playwrights is as vibrant and varied as anytime in our history.

As it happens, though, it can take institutional culture a long time to catch up with the swifter movement of individuals. Our big awards are shameful: A third or more of Broadway's forty-five Tony-nominated plays between 2006 and 2016 were written by British playwrights or first produced in the subsidized British Theatre despite the boom here. Of these forty-five nominated plays, only five were written by women. Only one of these women, the French playwright Yasmina Reza, won; and only three of them, Nora Ephron, Sarah Ruhl, and the black Iowan-Zimbabwean playwright Danai Gurira, were from the United States. Only four or five of these same forty-five nominees were men of color. Two of them were August Wilson, and none of them won.

The Pulitzers are similar: between 2006 and 2016, three of the eleven winners were women, and four of the eleven winners were people of color (Lynn Nottage and Quiara Alegría Hudes get counted in both categories). Statistically, though, a full 50 percent of American playwrights are women, so I don't take much hope from "three out of eleven." The American Theatre Critics Association's Steinberg Awards are almost precisely as bad, despite having their eyes trained outside of New York. As an antidote, a group of playwrights, literary managers, and other artistic leaders formed the Kilroys, an annual list of un- or underproduced plays by female and trans authors of color.[2]

For years—inarguably—the wellspring of the new theatre's creative explosion has come from communities of color, many of whose writers have been heard only on small, local stages. The work isn't getting around. Some of our leading Chicano playwrights, for example—I'm thinking of such prolific writers as Luis Alfaro, Elaine Romero, Octavio Solis, and Tanya Saracho—influential and even celebrated on the West coast, remain largely unknown and unheralded in New York City and much of the country. Similarly, New York and the national theatre that looks to it to define the new has heard little from Chinese, Korean, or Japanese American playwrights, with notable exceptions like David Henry Hwang and Julia Cho, outside of pioneering Asian American theatres.

One of the most exciting groups of writers in America is housed in the playwrights lab of Ma-Yi Theater Company, a New York company dedicated to innovative Asian American writing. Few of these playwrights have had much mainstream opportunity, but, on a hopeful note, stay tuned. For instance, Seattle, where I am writing from, is starting to hear from several of them, including Lauren Yee, Kimber Lee, Susan Soon He Stanton, Dipika Guha, and Clarence Coo. Vietnamese American playwright Qui Nguyen, another member of the Ma-Yi Lab, who has pioneered a "geek theatre" aesthetic—comic-book-hero violent, rude-funny, genre-mixing, and video game–inspired—won the 2016 Steinberg-ATCA Award from the American Theatre Critics Association with *Vietgone*, which is making its way around the country, including in visible productions at Oregon Shakespeare Festival, Seattle Repertory Theatre, South Coast Repertory Theatre, and the Manhattan Theatre Club.

Our theatres don't always know where to look for the new or, even, how to assess it. Even as he proclaims "a budding golden age," *Los Angeles Times* theatre critic Charles McNulty marvels that so few of the new plays he finds so brilliant have been produced appropriately (in terms of scale) or at all in Los Angeles. I marvel, too, that our nation's institutional theatres are so slow on the uptake, passing around the same one or two of last year's New York stand-out plays and missing so much of the rest of it, unable to see the forest for a few *New York Times*–favored trees.

Indeed, contemporary playwriting could well be defined by what mainstream producing theatres have *missed*, as well as by what they've produced. The winner of 2014's prestigious James Tait Black prize for the best play coming out of Britain or America went to Gordon Dahlquist's *Tomorrow Come Today*. The play is a brilliant futuristic look at power and wealth in a world where the wealthy survive a ruined earth by building hypersecure and climate-proof fortresses for themselves and then downloading their very selves into new bodies to ensure lives hundreds of years long. Dalhquist's recurring themes of American imperialism and its sadistic domination, cast in violently theatrical terms, have proven prescient. The playwright, who has, since the 1980s, consistently spun out a singular body of genre-bending work, despite a paucity of production, turned his hand to fiction about ten years ago, becoming, in short order, an international bestselling author. Despite Dahlquist's novelistic success and the James Tait Black prize's 10,000 pounds at Edinburgh, *Tomorrow Come Today* has only had one small production—last season at Undermain Theatre in Dallas.

There are many other examples of playwrights writing ahead of our mainstream theatres and, so, being passed over by them. I wrote earlier about Carlos Murillo's "Javier" plays, but I didn't mention that in the town where Murillo lives and writes, the flagship Goodman Theatre spent enormous resources on theatricalizing the late Roberto Bolaño's epic novel *2666*, while ignoring the fact that, a couple miles away, the closest thing the American theatre has to a Bolaño was wondering how to get his great (my word) American trilogy produced. Indeed, when it comes to overlooking, the theatre's loss has been television's gain. Cable, network, and streaming TV thrive—often led by the very playwrights who've been unable to sustain careers in theatre or, even, to establish these careers in the first place.

I want to know what writing writers value. So I watch the new play reading lists that playwrights post—and gather suggestions for—on Facebook. I will finish with this list from Kristoffer Diaz, whose play *The Elaborate Entrance of Chad Diety* a few years ago made him easily list-worthy. These are the writers he teaches: Annie Baker, Rajiv Joseph, Stephen Adly Guirgis, Quiara Alegría Hudes, Dominique Morisseau, Tarell Alvin McCraney, A. Rey Pamatmat, Charise Castro Smith, Branden Jacobs-Jenkins, and Anne Washburn.

These names and the others I've mentioned, as well as many others I haven't gotten to here, tell the story of the new in American playwriting. I purposely overwhelm you with them, so you can know what it feels like to live in their abundance, so that you can sample their stylistic heterogeneity and the range of their concerns. There are plays of the mind and plays of the heart, playful plays and panoramically peopled plays, just as in recent fiction we have Bolaño and Alice Munro, Elena Ferrante and David Foster Wallace, Junot Díaz, Jhumpa Lahiri, Toni Morrison and Italo Calvino, Marilynne Robinson, Kazuo Ishiguro, Zadie Smith, Karl Ove Knausgård, and Philip Roth, each not only differently voiced but differently positioned in relation to self and story, sentence structure and novelistic experimentation. In fact, this aesthetic heterogeneity or range of voice may be the defining feature of contemporary playwriting.

This artistic biodiversity has been decades in the making; this profusion *is* what's new. These contemporary playwrights tell stories that have never been told and that have been aching to be told; they retell stories in new tongues. Sometimes they pick stories up, turn them inside out and blow them apart. What's new is that which is made new, including, unexpectedly, an old-fashioned thing called drama.

Notes

1. This paragraph appears in a slightly different form in my essay about Mac, in my howlround.com column "A Lover's Guide to American Playwright," October 5, 2016.
2. "The Kilroys are a gang of playwrights and producers in LA who are done talking about

gender parity and are taking action. We mobilize others in our field and leverage our own power to support one another." https://thekilroys.org/about/; 2017 Kilroys List at: https://thekilroys.org/list-2017/.

Part III

ESSAY FROM THE CONFERENCE

The Robert A. Schanke Award-Winning Essay

Black Folks's Theatre to Black Lives Matter

The Black Revolution on Campus

—LA DONNA L. FORSGREN

At a time when the value of a college education, particularly a humanities education, is under attack, the Black Lives Matter campus protesters of 2015 have shown, through their own display of historically informed and intersectional politics, that universities matter.

DR. JENNIFER WILSON

Introduction

Throughout the past three years social media has exploded with accounts of black student protests over racist administrative practices and ineffective responses to hate crimes at institutions of higher education. These protests emerge from a rich tradition of black student activism that spans nearly fifty years. "While the white student movement of the late 1960s has garnered much more attention, black student protest produced greater campus change," writes historian Martha Biondi.[1] Inspired by the leadership of Stokely Carmichael and the assassination of Malcolm X, black students across the United States mobilized and participated in roughly two hundred campus demonstrations between 1968 and 1969.[2] Driven by black power rhetoric of the era, black student activists demanded that universities revoke racist institutional policies and create an inclusive environment for underrepresented communities. At times, black student activists used theatrical and confrontational tactics to force universities to increase financial aid opportunities for minority students and establish or broaden affirmative action policies. While student activists often faced criminal prosecutions and retaliation from police and white students, their extralegal efforts resulted in a dramatic increase in black student enrollment on college campuses across the United States. Nearly fifty years later, the struggle to achieve an inclusive academic community continues.

This study privileges two seemingly disparate events in social movement history: the 1968 black student protest at Northwestern University and the 2015 black student protest at the University of Missouri (Mizzou). Collectively, these events demonstrate not only a rich tradition of black student activists staking their claim to education but also an important connection between performance and black student activism. In both cases, black students used performative demonstrations as part of their campaigns to affirm their right to attend college and influence faculty selection and university governance policies. In so doing, student activists created an important ideological space that helped transform their communities. This study begins by exploring the 1968 black student protest at Northwestern University and the subsequent formation of the black student union For Members Only and their artistic branch, Black Folks's Theatre.[3] The paper then analyzes the goals, organizational framework, and community outreach efforts of Black Folks's Theatre and how this relates to the Black Arts Movement (1965–1976) ethos of the time. The study concludes by drawing connections between this history and current challenges faced by black student activists at Mizzou. While the Black Lives Matter movement and the Legion of Black Collegians helped bring awareness and some institutional change to Mizzou, the struggle is far from over.

For Member's Only and Black Folks's Theatre

On May 4, 1968, exactly one month after the assassination of Dr. Martin Luther King Jr., 105 black students locked themselves inside the bursar's office at Northwestern University to protest the university's racist practices. Ironically, the black student protest primarily resulted from Northwestern's valiant efforts to recruit black students a few years prior.[4] Unfortunately, the university was unable or unwilling to cope with the concerns of their rising black student population. Many found Northwestern "hostile and callous," experiencing "many instances of fights, of whites refusing to room with Blacks, and of whites thinking the. . . Black [students] were maids."[5] These hostile conditions caused black students to mobilize.[6] Led by graduate student James Turner, all but fifteen of Northwestern's black student population chained themselves together in the bursar's office for thirty-six hours and presented a list of demands to university officials. This dramatic demonstration transformed a historic symbol of black oppression (i.e., chains of enslavement) into a symbol of black power (i.e., racial solidarity). After only eight hours of deliberation, Northwestern officials agreed to form several committees that would assist black students with their concerns over inadequate financial aid support, housing, and admission processes. Perhaps most important, student activists were able to transform Northwestern's curriculum to include more African American studies courses, as well as establish For Members Only, a black student alliance that fostered community and protested racism on campus.

For Members Only positioned its activism within the black nationalist tradition and used revolutionary theatre as a unifying force. Northwestern's *Black Student Handbook* describes the ideologies of For Members Only as follows: "We organize to meet the needs of Black students on our own. We have our orientation program, social outlets, choir, theater, newspaper, and committees such as admissions and financial aid to negotiate for Blacks in those areas. FMO maintains that it is not our purpose to integrate this University. We feel that our role is to commit Black Students to develop Black Institutions, rather than strengthening white ones. . . . F.M.O. then, seeks immediately to provide a social, cultural and intellectual outlet for the Black students of this community, and ultimately, to instill in Black students a sense of Black consciousness or awareness."[7] For Members Only established Black Folks's Theatre in 1971 to provide an intellectual and cultural outlet, as well as foster community.

Black Folks's Theatre's philosophy and production aims reflect the ethos of the Black Arts Movement and, in particular, the theories of Barbara Ann Teer and Amiri Baraka. A Black Folk's Theatre program states: "Our philosophy: 'Art is for people's sake'; it should serve a definite function in our struggle for liberation. The purpose behind establishing Black Folk's Theatre was to create another vehicle for the liberation of Black minds. We are students of Blackness, in all its aspects, politically, as well as spiritually. Our art emanates from a deep and abiding love and concern for ourselves. We do not wish to be known as actors, actresses and creative technicians in the conventional sense. We do not 'perform' or 'put on a show.' We view ourselves as 'liberators' and 'spirit/movers' and strive to live and see the world, in terms of the principles we teach."[8] In keeping with Barbara Ann Teer's theories of performance, members of Black Folks's Theatre viewed themselves as "liberators" and did not distinguish between their art and activism. As such, their art served as a vital force within the black community, raising awareness and inciting political action. Black Folks's Theatre produced the works of leading Black Arts Movement playwrights, including Ed Bullins, Sonia Sanchez, and Martie Evans-Charles. Sanchez attributes much of her success as a playwright to students producing her works. "I would go to universities and the plays were being done by students. That's what kept a lot of our plays alive. The student population," she remembers.[9] Black Folks's Theatre holds the distinction of producing the premiere of Sanchez's drama *Uh, Uh; But How Do It Free Us?* Told from the perspective of three young black women, *Uh, Uh* exposes destructive behaviors within the black community that were cloaked under the guise of so-called revolution.

Black Folks's Theatre's efforts to produce such dramas realize the sentiments expressed in Amiri Baraka's manifesto, "The Revolutionary Theatre" (1965). "The Revolutionary Theatre must EXPOSE!. . . It must stagger through our universe correcting, insulting, preaching, spitting craziness . . . but a craziness taught to us in our most rational moments. . . . We will scream and cry, murder, run through the streets in agony, if it means some soul will be moved, moved to actual life understanding of what the world is, and what it ought to be," writes Baraka.[10] Black Folks's Theatre likewise asserted that theatre was as a powerful tool that could expose, educate, and inspire the community on campus and in the greater Chicagoland area. To this end, Black Folks's Theatre often invited prominent Chicago artists such as Haki Madhubuti and Gwendolyn Brooks to speak at their events, as well as toured their revolutionary productions to Chicago correctional facilities. While ignored in contemporary Black Arts Movement and black nationalist scholarship, student theatre organizations did, in fact, play a vital role in fostering new works and disseminating black power politics to black communities.

The Legion of Black Collegians and Black Lives Matter at Mizzou

Unfortunately, history repeats itself. The 1968 black student protest at Northwestern mirrors student unrest at Mizzou in 2015, 2016, and 2017. Both protests follow years of battling racist incidents on campus and both were sparked by the racially motivated murders of black men. Indeed, the assassination of King and the more recent murder of unarmed civilian Michael Brown galvanized black students across the nation. As a predominately white public university with a total enrollment of thirty-five thousand students, Mizzou includes an 8 percent black student population. Despite their minority status, black students have labored for years to incite student protest against racial incidents on campus. In 2008, for example, black activists attempted to rouse student athletes to protest a ballot initiative that would eradicate affirmative action in the state of Missouri. While ultimately unsuccessful, their attempt demonstrates a keen awareness of the power of identity politics. Black students continued to lead protests after discovering cotton balls were placed on the lawn of the Gaines-Oldham Black Culture Center in 2010 and again when white students spray-painted racist epithets on campus statues. Their protests failed to capture massive student body mobilization. Black student organizations did not gain mass support until the murder of Michael Brown and the ensuing riots in Ferguson, Missouri, located just 120 miles from Mizzou's campus in Columbia. The organized protests of the Black Lives Matter movement following the one-year anniversary of Brown's murder not only exposed the long tradition of racism on campus but also galvanized students to action. Graduate student Jonathan Butler, who famously went on a hunger strike in protest of Mizzou President Tim Wolfe's leadership, credits "MU for Mike Brown," a student group affiliated with the Black Lives Matter movement, for initiating the demonstration that would bring about Wolfe's resignation.[11]

During the fall of 2015, tensions continued to mount as Wolfe consistently failed to effectively respond to racial incidents on campus. In September of that year, just weeks before the November 9 black student strike, Mizzou's student body president reported that white students in a pickup truck hurled racial epithets at him. His demand for justice was ignored. The following month, just days before Mizzou's homecoming game, members of the black student organization Concerned Student 1950 reported a similar incident to university officials. Again, nothing happened.[12] Finally, on October 10, members of Concerned Student 1950 confronted Wolfe after the homecoming game, surrounded his car, and demanded he take decisive action. He refused to leave his car and ordered Columbia Police to escort the protestors off university grounds. Unfortunately, several students were allegedly injured by Wolfe's car, bystanders, and the Columbia Police during the demonstration. As word spread throughout campus, student athletes joined the student protest. In a show of support, more than thirty black football players announced that they would not participate in team events until Wolfe resigned. With three remaining games in the season, this display of racial solidarity had the potential to cost Mizzou more than one million dollars for just one canceled game. The Legion of Black Collegians, a conglomeration of black student alliances, organized an official strike and presented a list of demands to public media outlets. Their first article calls for President Wolfe's resignation and handwritten apology to Concerned Student 1950. "Tim Wolfe must acknowledge his white male privilege, recognize that systems of oppression exist, and provide a verbal commitment to fulfilling Concerned Student 1950 demands."[13] Their campaign gathered support from hundreds of black students, faculty, Black Lives Matter affiliates, and national and social media outlets. Wolfe resigned his post, with the chancellor of Mizzou quickly following suit.

The Legion of Black Collegians' list of demands remains important because it demonstrates the ways in which black students continue to create ideological space to assert their rights in determining the dissemination of knowledge. Article IV states: "We demand that the University of Missouri creates and enforces comprehensive racial awareness and inclusion curriculum throughout all campus departments and units, mandatory for all students, faculty, staff, and administration. This curriculum must be vetted, maintained, and overseen by a board comprised of students, staff, and faculty of color."[14] Contrary to some conservative media coverage, these demands and subsequent demonstrations were not fueled by misplaced emotion. Rather, black student activists wanted to transform Mizzou into a more inclusive academic community. "It was not an overdramatic reaction by a couple of angry Black students, but a moment built up over time. . . . Many of us behind the scenes have been suffering and struggling with administration and students while trying to deal with class and work. The movement is not over. This is the beginning," states Mizzou senior Alanna Diggs.[15] These prophetic words suggest that although positive changes have been made, black students must prepare to engage in a much longer battle.

Two years after Wolfe's departure, tensions continue to simmer at Mizzou, as administrators willfully ignore racial divides on campus and fail to implement strategies for a more inclusive community. Working against institutional amnesia, Dr. Claire Syler, an assistant professor of theatre at Mizzou, created a course titled Adaptation of Literature for the Stage: Performance Praxis, "Race" and Education to challenge students to engage with the 2015 events that erupted across their campus. Throughout this fifteen-week course, students explored concepts such as community, personal narrative, and performance praxis and attended symposiums and lectures about social justice. Students were also required to read an early draft of this article and discuss student activism with me via Skype. During our hour-long discussion, students asked the following questions:

1. In your article, you mentioned that after the protests at Northwestern University it took only eight hours of deliberation for officials to form

committees and assist black students. Why, do you think, did it take so much longer for the administration at Mizzou?

2. Why do you think they [the Mizzou administration] no longer talk about the Fall 2015 events [on campus]? Why do they act like they never happened?
3. When talking about Mizzou, they [the administration] always say "we're getting better at preventing racial activity." How long do you think it will take to actually change and educate the racist individuals?

These questions, coupled with the students' tone and body language, lead me to surmise that feelings of frustration, anger, and distrust with Mizzou's administration continue to run high. While there are no simple answers to these questions, I urged these students not to wait for administrators to make positive change happen. I encouraged students to take the lead: form grassroots organizations, use social media to voice their concerns, build alliances, and create meaningful art. Finally, I let them know that despite the unique challenges that persist for this generation of black activists, Mizzou students continue to serve as a source of inspiration for student activists across the United States.

Conclusion

The road ahead will remain fraught with unique challenges for this generation of millennial activists. First, how does one foster intersectional politics and develop a historically informed constituency in a so-called postracial society? Second, how can black student activists maintain political and social relevance within the constantly shifting age of social media? Finally, what role will theatre and performance play in the revolution on college campuses? Some black student theatre groups, including Kansas State University's Ebony Theatre, have looked to the revolutionary dramas of the 1960s and1970s for inspiration.[16] Student artist-activists at Ithaca College, with a strikingly similar tale as Mizzou, used theatre as a lens to understand racism and ignorance with their recent production of a new play, "Student V." While commendable, these individual efforts are not enough. If educators truly believe theatre can invoke social change, then we must galvanize students to create meaningful art that exposes and dismantles institutional racism.

Artists, scholars, and educators must acknowledge that our institutions of higher education are in a state of emergency. Many of the gains made by black student activists of the 1960s have been lost in our so-called postracial society. Institutional racism and ineffective responses to racially motivated assaults on college campuses are not a regional issue but a national epidemic. Article V of the Legion of Black Collegians' demands includes a call to increase black faculty and staff at Mizzou by 10 percent between 2015 and 2017. This demand demonstrates that supportive faculty are not only needed but also vital to implementing long-term institutional change. Indeed, how can we nurture the next generation of black activists if we, the black faculty, are not visible? Lack of a diverse faculty, however, is not a Mizzou-specific problem. I taught at a highly ranked research university with more than two thousand academic staff and only two women of color serving as full professors. Two. How can we even begin to dismantle institutional racism if we are not present at the table?

Notes

Epigraph. Jennifer Wilson, "How Black Lives Matter Saved Higher Education," last modified December 31, 2015, http://www.america.alijazeera.com/opinions/2015/12/how-black-lives-matter-saved-higher-education.html.

1. Martha Biondi, *The Black Revolution on Campus* (Berkeley: University of California Press, 2012), 2.

2. Ibid., 1.

3. This company rendered its own name as both "Black Folk's Theatre" and "Black Folks's Theatre" (instead of Folks'). In accordance with their publications and for consistency while putting value on the plural, I have used "Black Folks's Theatre" throughout this chapter.

4. In the fall of 1965 only twenty-five black undergraduate students out of a student body of 6,500 were enrolled at Northwestern University. During the fall and winter of 1965–66 Northwestern officials began to actively recruit black students from seventeen Chicago public schools. With the financial assistance of the Wieboldt Foundation, Northwestern officials visited local high schools, interviewed qualified candidates, and guaranteed their college admission with generous financial aid packets. Northwestern's recruitment efforts contributed to the enrollment of fifty-four black freshmen in 1966. By the fall of 1967, Northwestern had reached an enrollment of 120 black students.

5. "Black Student Handbook," 1973–1974, Northwestern University Archives, Evanston, Illinois.

6. Ibid.

7. Ibid.

8. "We Hardly Heard You," program, 1974–1975, Northwestern University Archives, Evanston, Illinois.

9. Sonia Sanchez, interview with the author, June 30, 2010.

10. LeRoi Jones, "The Revolutionary Theatre," *Liberator* (July 1965): 4–5.

11. Wilson, "How Black," 2015.

12. 1950 marks the first year the University of Missouri admitted black students. The name

"Concerned Student 1950" honors the desegregation efforts of the previous generation of black student activists.

13. "Clear and Concrete Requests from a very Focused Protest Effort," last modified November 9, 2015, http://www.alternet.org/news-amp-politics/read-university-missouri-protesters-list-impressive-demands-led-presidents.
14. Ibid.
15. "Campus Racism Protests Didn't Come Out of Nowhere," last modified November 16, 2015, http://www.huffingtonpost.com/entry/campus-racism-protests-didnt-come-out-of-nowhere.html.
16. Kansas State University's Ebony Theatre was founded in 1977 as an artistic outlet for underrepresented black theatre students. The 2016 production of Amiri Baraka's *Dutchman* honors Ebony Theatre's tradition of creating politically minded art for the black community of Manhattan, Kansas.

Part IV

BOOK REVIEWS

Theatre and Evolution from Ibsen to Beckett. By Kirsten E. Shepherd-Barr. New York: Columbia University Press, 2015. xiii + 380 pp. $60.00 cloth.

Theatre and Evolution is a significant contribution to modern theatre and performance scholarship because of its science-oriented intervention into the familiar narrative of the history of modern European and American theatre and performance. Shepherd-Barr focuses on questions pertaining to evolution as she makes the case that modern drama, studied in relationship with other cultural performances, is not just about the rise of the individual but rather is deeply invested in the (very) long-term stakes of humanity. She deftly curates a vast quantity of archival sources to situate theatre and performance as integral to evolutionary discourse throughout the nineteenth and twentieth centuries. Shepherd-Barr unites the ostensibly separate spheres of art and science through her argument that modern dramatists "actively engaged with science and often transformed the ideas they encountered in the process" (3). Theatre did not merely interpret scientific concepts onstage but participated in a cultural conversation that in turn impacted the progress of evolutionary theory in the Western popular imagination.

Shepherd-Barr's interdisciplinary method keeps scientific and theatrical questions in equal view. She introduces competing nineteenth- and twentieth-century evolutionary theorists as she distills the socioscientific themes—natural selection, maternal instinct, adaptation, mutation, heredity, extinction, cooperation, eugenics—of the plays at the heart of her criticism. She also meets the great challenge to interdisciplinary scholarship (i.e., to demonstrate a balanced intellectual exchange among diverse practices and practitioners) by depicting scientists as cultural performers and by articulating clear paths of scientific inquiry on behalf of science-oriented playwrights. She describes the 1827 procession of a live baby giraffe that was gifted to the king of France, highlighting the involvement of the "celebrity scientist . . . esteemed zoologist and founder of ethology," Étienne Geoffroy Saint Hilaire, as a public performance of science that inspired spin-off zoological performances that were popular throughout the nineteenth century (27). Her case study of August Strindberg in chapter 5, "Edwardians and Eugenicists," reassesses the playwright's often-dismissed "inferno" phase, during which he wrote scientific essays and performed "alchemical" experiments, as demonstrative of "how central this phase was to his work" (128). In chapter 2, "Confronting the Serious Side," Shepherd-Barr articulates Eleanora Duse's capacity to blush and pale on command as theatrically defiant of Darwin's claim that the blush of shame is an involuntary reflex. Her final chapter, "Beckett's 'Old Muckball,'" addresses the shift from modernism to postmodernism through Beckett's deliberate "interplay between the organism and its environment" and contextualizes Beckett's oeuvre as a theatre of "ecocide," using *Happy Days* (1961) as a primary theatrical example and the playwright's "Whoroscope" notebook as a key indicator of Beckett's explicit interest in science (240).

"Two aspects of evolution have particular relevance for theatre," she claims: a fear of evolutionary degeneration and of women's roles as essential to the process of evolution as well as to the progress of evolutionary theory. She suggests that modern dramatic thinkers rejected Darwin, in part, because he did not take into account philosophies of individual will. Shepherd-Barr describes an anthropomorphic interpretation of Darwinian evolutionary theory by which "the mechanism of natural selection was understood as *purposefully* cruel, not just blindly and randomly so" (37). She marks Shaw's *Back to Methuselah: A Metabiological Pentateuch* (1921) as a modern dramatic work that synthesizes "Schopenhauer and Lamarck" in a "belief in the role of the will in human evolution" that resulted in an anthrocentric evolutionary dramaturgy (134). Shaw admired Schopenhauer's philosophy of human will, and he preferred Lamarck's pre-Darwinian theory of evolution that promoted the idea that behavioral and physical characteristics acquired during an organism's lifetime could be inherited by future generations. (Lamarckism is largely discredited, although Shepherd-Barr allows that "it is enjoying something of a return through epigenetics" [14].) A preference for an evolutionary philosophy that allowed intentional improvement of human physiology often led modern dramatists such as Shaw and Ibsen to adopt Sir Francis Galton's eugenics. Shepherd-Barr points out that Shaw often "gets the science wrong" and that "the eugenicist undertones can make his plays not only uncomfortable but also deeply problematic" (140). She mines this disturbing philosophical intersection exceptionally well. After a thorough interrogation of evolutionary themes expressed in Ibsen's plays (spanning the gamut from extinction to alternative women's roles), she ultimately asks that the reader "accept [Ibsen's] temporary embrace of eugenics as part of his response to the intellectual package of evolution as it was then understood . . . just as Darwin disappointingly rehearses the dominant Victorian views on the inferiority of women in the final section of *The Descent of Man*" (89).

Shepherd-Barr weaves the history of feminism and women's suffrage explicitly into two chapters, "'Ugly . . . but Irresistible': Maternal Instinct on Stage" and "Reproductive Issues," in which she describes theories regarding women's evolutionary roles and identifies contributions made by women to the development of modern Western evolutionary discourse. The examples in these chapters and others explicate contemporary arguments with Darwinian androcentrism made by playwrights, male and female, of the time. Shepherd-Barr considers breastfeeding in James A. Herne's *Margaret Fleming* (1890) and Eugene Brieux's *Les Remplaçantes* (1901), examples that respectively dramatize aspects of evolutionary altruism and the adverse socioevolutionary impact of wet-nursing. She incorporates philosophies of female science lecturers such as Helen Hamilton Gardener to illustrate women's activity within public evolutionary discourse. She critiques plays, written by female playwrights, which do not restrict female characters to acts of mothering. An excellent example of this is her analysis of Susan Glaspell's *The Verge* (1921), a play that features a female botanist and her experiments. Shepherd-Barr depicts Glaspell as a scientifically minded feminist by pointing to the playwright's overt references to Darwin within plots that dramatize women's will.

Shepherd-Barr's emphasis on the development of feminist ideals through evolutionarily oriented theatre is as compelling as her outline of those ideals within a eugenic context is disturbing. The breadth of her archival research reveals that there is much more work to be done at the intersection of evolution and performance. For instance, a related study about progress toward civil rights and resolving global racial and ethnic conflicts might be made within the evolutionary context that she advances with respect to the struggle for women's rights. She does address the racism that permeated Victorian and Edwardian anthropological displays, freak shows, and threads of evolutionary thought. She discusses Eugene O'Neill's *The Hairy Ape* (1922) as politically progressive through its "foregrounding and enacting [evolutionary] ideas of regression, degeneration, heredity, and savagery" while placing the play on a historical trajectory that reaches back to nineteenth-century "missing link" performances (232). A ground-up approach to plays that deal with conflict, race, and ethnicity from a broadly construed evolutionary perspective might be of interest to theatre historiographers also concerned with socially problematic junctures of science and theatre.

—VIVIAN APPLER
College of Charleston

American Traveling Tent Theatre, 1900–1940: Rural and Small Town Tent Show Plays Performed in the Midwest (Including Scripts of Popular Tent Theatricals).

By L. Dawn Larsen and Richard L. Poole. Lewiston, NY: Edwin Mellen Press, 2014. 668 pp. $350.00 paper.

As this volume's introduction states, histories of American theatre "focus almost exclusively on urban theatre" (1), which appears obvious at first glance. After all, one of the primary ingredients for a vibrant theatre culture is a large enough, informed populace who are at least somewhat economically well-off and who possess the leisure time necessary to indulge in theatregoing. This is also true of other national Western theatre cultures, which rate and support their theatres based on successful productions in taste-making urban centers like London, Paris, and Berlin. Likewise, American theatre is primarily aware of shows emanating from New York, Chicago, or Los Angeles. Little attention has been paid throughout the years to the underside of American theatre (i.e., traveling tent theatres along with community theatres), even though such a focus reveals much about American culture.

For the first half of the twentieth century, traveling shows were found in tents, local opera houses, and at county and state fairs, along with further varieties of live entertainment, such as circuses, religious revival services, carnival shows, musicals, and one-night stands at railroad stops. Their history in America goes back to the seventeenth century, though it truly flourished throughout the first decades of the twentieth century, until such performances were undermined by Hollywood, radio, and the Great Depression. Until then, the Midwest circuit demanded and reinforced the "specific rural American identity [that] combined fundamental Protestantism, individual responsibility and suspicion of urban life" (2). The authors contend—and the playscripts selected for this anthology certainly bear this out—that for "theatre to be acceptable in small town/rural America, it had to reflect rural/small town values [and] its plays, its personnel, the physical structure of its temporary auditoria had to be acceptable and accessible to the rural community" (3).

For the history of this particular brand of American theatre, the authors acknowledge a large debt to William Slout's classic *Theatre in a Tent: The Development of a Provincial Entertainment* (1972) and also provide a bibliography of the frankly slim studies previously available. What Professors Larsen and Poole provide in this entertaining study is an anthology of eight playscripts from the tent theatre repertoire, along with an analysis of key stock characters, genres, and themes, especially focusing on the nativist elements that audiences responded to.

The anthology proper begins with an 1858 temperance chestnut, *Ten Nights in a Barroom* by William W. Pratt, used in its day primarily for moral instruction regarding the harmful effects of drink on families and the community. That play is followed by the first of three scripts by Charles Harrison, a ubiquitous presence in the tent theatre during the early twentieth century. *The Awakening of John Slater* (1914) was a rustic play that identified the citified wife Adele as a malevolent and manipulative con artist whose relationship to the titular John is poisonous until her con is discovered and she is carted off to jail (and the marriage dissolved). It also contains a character, Lun, who functions as a "Toby" character, a "rube" with whom the agrarian audiences of this theatre generally identified. The Toby type became the "standard for all the silly kid roles" (81) as well as the standard name for this particular subgenre.

The next play in the anthology, *Clouds and Sunshine* (ca. 1909), is a Toby show by Cal Herman. At times, the term "Toby show" was used as a generic term for all tent shows, described by Larsen and Poole as a "traveling vaudeville-type melodramatic tent show featuring a character called Toby . . . a bucolic comedy juvenile leading man . . . [a] red-headed, freckled-face, silly kid rube character" whose makeup also included a blacked-out tooth and baggy, tattered clothing that made him instantly recognizable to audiences (178). *Clouds and Sunshine* is a morality melodrama involving a pious parson, his wicked brother, his straightlaced housekeeper, the schoolteacher with a secret whom the parson loves (and whom the wicked brother intends to lure to New York City to sell her to a brothel), and a Toby, whose presence identified for the audience the type of play they were viewing.

Saintly Hypocrites and Honest Sinners, by Harrison (ca. 1910–1920), is a "preacher play," a popular genre used by many tent companies that reinforced "the rural audience's belief that good does triumph over evil and true Christian charity will save the day" (263). Harrison presents his audience with a good parson, his neurotic wife, a prodigal brother returning after ten years, a life-loving, uninhibited younger sister-in-law, and a pair of corrupt church deacons not above making sexual threats against a poor young woman. Unlike some of the plays in this anthology, *Saintly Hypocrites and Honest Sinners* is still an effective melodrama that might hold some appeal for today's audiences.

Larsen and Poole then provide the reader with a pair of Jekyll and Hyde plays from the 1920s, the first one by Robert J. Sherman and the second an anonymous adaptation; both appeared to be pirated editions from a time when protections for authors were loosely enforced. The story in each is highly condensed from the novella, with religious themes permeating the good doctor's fall. *The Push, or Tamed and How*, also by Harrison, is a variation on the *Taming of the Shrew* set in small-town America with men threatening unruly women with spankings; a case in point is the chauffeur, who marries an heiress and "tames" her willful manner through force and its threat. If it sounds cringe-inducing, it is. Perhaps even more repulsive to the modern reader is the final play, *The Girl of the Flying X or Sputters*, by George Crawley, labeled a "western play." Sputters, a stuttering cowboy, was one of the most famous and popular of the Toby roles. Highly problematic is the anti-Hispanic racism that curdles throughout the play, directed entirely at one character by all the others.

In spite of the book's absurd cost, this is a worthy addition to our shelves, alongside Slout's classic *Theatre in a Tent* and Jere Mickel's *Footlights on the Prairie*, for its insights into the form and its history. Along with its anthologizing of these tent dramas—the first of its kind published—Larsen and Poole's play selections shed much light on our still embryonic culture of a century ago, a culture that reached a trio of peaks between the 1920s and the 1960s with the advent of radio, film, and television narratives. As these new media developed, modified forms of the characters and tropes found in these early plays would soon be broadcast hourly into American homes.

—STEVEN DEDALUS BURCH
University of Alabama

Rooms in Dramatic Realism. By Fred Miller Robinson. London: Routledge, 2015. xii + 113 pp. $29.95 paper.

Realism, asserts Fred Miller Robinson, needs to be revisited as "the revolution that Ibsen wrought onstage"; it needs to be probed for its theoretical and theatrical possibilities, moving the needle away from and beyond the usual "social issues reliant on text" setting on the critical dial (ix). In 106 readable pages comprising fifty-two trenchant, self-contained essays on individual plays—most of them well known—Robinson makes abundant good on the challenge he has issued. His interest is not anything so banal as the recognizable everyday in settings, much less mere environmental determinism. Rather, he looks to intersections of the psychological and the social, telescoped and distilled into high stakes dialectics that include the spatial and somatic.

The book's first section, called simply "Rooms," makes two things clear. First, realist plays, usually set in the rooms of homes, are nearly always about money. Second, they rarely resolve issues. Lest this seem obvious and simplistic, Robinson reminds us via the chapter's (and to some extent the whole book's) touchstone play—*A Doll's House*—that rooms are "*phenomenal* . . . reflect[ing] two levels of a character's experience of them: the unreflective and the reflective" (12). In this case, Nora "comes to recognize the room as an imaginary of the culture at large" via her "somatic awareness" (13). Rooms are not merely decorative and so-called historically accurate backdrops for discursive arguments. They are agents and, perhaps for the audience at least, messengers. Robinson notes that, even as the scenographic methods of depicting realist rooms morphed, Ibsen's realism, with legatees Shaw, O'Neill, Hansberry, and August Wilson, among others, maintained "the connection between characters and rooms . . . that keep them from whatever is outside the walls and trap them from whatever is outside that they need" (22).

Chapter 2, "Specimens," focuses on plays with a box set—something that points with a vengeance to what lies outside the room precisely by impeding access to it. Robinson repeatedly returns in this section to the delicate balance (Albee's 1966 play of that name indeed makes an appearance here) between the comforts of "indwelling" (42), a word he uses in his examination of Harold Pinter's 1957 *The Room*, and the outside powers that surround, underwrite, and threaten the characters' precarious situations. As an example of the suppleness of Robinson's thinking, the tavern in O'Neill's 1948 *The Iceman Cometh* is a public establishment offering safe haven (home, as it were) to its "inmates" (49), while the putatively private domestic interior of Marsha Norman's 1983 *'night, Mother* is "too public to *be* a refuge. The world that is being kept at bay is already inside, making Jessie leave the room when others visit" (58).

In chapter 3, "Variations," individual plays are either wholly set or contain individual scenes set outdoors, yet the experience of the outside does little to assuage "the two-faced phenomenon of comfort and entrapment" (61). Pride of place here goes to Chekhov, and Robinson notes that the aristocratic characters in *Uncle Vanya*, *Three Sisters*, and *The Seagull* are not really interested in "the ideals and obsessive pressures of the domestic" (63). Outdoor scenes deflect their immediate attention away from what really troubles them: money. Chekhov's legacy is not monolithic, however; consider Lanford Wilson's 1978 *Fifth of July*, which Robinson calls a "version of *The Cherry Orchard*" (70). Here the characters are gathered on the front porch of the family homestead, the porch being "a liminal space between inside and outside" (70). Rather than dreaming of the beyond or of sexual, professional, or political discovery elsewhere, however, the walking wounded of the extended Talley family present the audience with a situation engineered in reverse, as the desire for change—the "whatever they need"—leads to the inside of the house.

The final chapter, "Interventions," considers plays written between 1947 and 1997, two-thirds of these American, that have "elements of the extra-real heard or brought onstage" (81). In the earliest, and certainly one of the clearest, instances of the extra-real, the 1947 *A Streetcar Named Desire*, Tennessee Williams "wants Blanche's psyche to be *made real* onstage, not just to be part of her makeup" (89). Indeed, characterological interiority is of paramount importance in this chapter. Maria Irene Fornes's *Fefu and Her Friends* (1977) "subjects a structure of dramatic realism to visionary forces" (99). Here "the smooth surface of the house has been lifted to reveal a nightmare vision of what women introject to the point where they dare not recognize each other lest the insular world they inhabit with men will explode" (100). I wish Robinson had addressed the irony and challenge of needing actual discrete rooms for audiences to traverse in productions of *Fefu*, as the materiality and somatic he so powerfully foregrounds can surely function in performance on both sides of the footlights.

A few of Robinson's conclusions strike me as abstruse or attempts to be clever (e.g., his intermittent invocations of Walter Benjamin's *Arcades Project* and his not always clear use of the idea of dialectical reversal to play with awareness of dreaming and of having awakened from a dream). These stand out as too precious in the midst of the otherwise sure-handed, insightful essays of which the bulk of this book consists. This is, however, a minor complaint.

Because of the clarity of each chapter's introduction and the brevity of the individual case studies, this book should be immediately adoptable for graduate and undergraduate classes in modern drama, not to mention for reading pleasure.

—DOROTHY CHANSKY
Texas Tech University

Offstage Voices: Life in Twin Cities Theater. By Peg Guilfoyle. Saint Paul: Minnesota Historical Society Press, 2015. 224 pp. $22.95 paperback, e-book.

From major regional equity houses playing classics of Western theatre to small itinerant groups performing pop-up projects in unexpected locales, the Twin Cities is home to a dynamic and diverse range of theatre and performance. In recent years, it is experiencing many of the same issues facing communities of similar size across the country: an aging audience base with a complex philanthropic system that is aging with it, political hierarchies that determine who gets access to funding and space, a shifting real estate market that has forced the closure of a number of performance venues, and so on. The community is home to three regional Tony Award–winning companies but also is an environment where one of them—the internationally lauded Theatre de la Jeune Lune—closed in 2008, only three years following its Tony win, due to financial insolvency. Penumbra Theatre, one of the oldest African American theatre companies in the country and the company that helped launch the careers of notable figures like August Wilson, nearly closed in 2012 before announcing an ultimately successful campaign to raise $340,000 to cover a budgetary shortfall.

Yet all is not doom and gloom in the Land of 10,000 Lakes. A constant influx of fresh talent from local colleges and universities supports established companies, inspires the founding of new companies, and feeds creative new works on the ever-growing fringe. Several companies commission and produce new plays from emerging and established playwrights. Nonprofits like Springboard for the Arts assist fledgling companies in developing long-term strategic plans, raising funds, organizing advisory boards, and obtaining 501(c)(3) status. And in recent years, a new generation of artistic directors have taken over several landmark institutions that haven't seen leadership changes in decades, including Penumbra, the Guthrie, and the Jungle.

In short, there are many stories that need to be told about Twin Cities theatre, stories that not only illuminate the challenges and successes of this particular community but also shed light on growing trends in major metropolitan cities across the country.

Offstage Voices: Life in Twin Cities Theatre, by local stage manager and production manager Peg Guilfoyle, is a broad snapshot of this community at this particular moment. Geared toward subscription ticket holders who enjoy attending local theatre and want to know more about what it takes to put a show together, Guilfoyle offers a loving ode to the cities and the people who toil onstage and off. The structure of the book is largely broken down by the process of getting a show on stage: writing the play, making the decisions that go into producing them, assembling the team, casting the show, finding the audience, rehearsing a play, conducting technical and dress rehearsals, and managing opening nights. For introductory theatre students, the book offers what one might expect from a theatre appreciation text: a behind-the-scenes look at how theatre is made, peppered with the expected generalities on what Guilfoyle refers to as "the nature of theatre work" (i.e., the collaborative practice of making theatre, the transformative power of the empty stage, the ephemerality of performance, the magic and talent that brings it all together, etc.).

Each stage in the process of putting up a play is supported with anecdotes from more than forty local theatre practitioners, running the gamut from artistic directors and producers to actors and designers. Guilfoyle captures a broad range of voices from across the community, representing a diversity of theatre sizes and styles. By and large, the interviews focus on theatre broadly—for example, the artistic director of Theater Latté Da Peter Rothstein's observation under the heading "on making and keeping relationships that overlap workplace and life" that "in the theater, you build the lasting relationships by working together. That's the key. Until you work together you're just acquaintances, and when you work together, you really become colleagues and friends in so many ways" (82).

The moments where Guilfoyle and her interviewees speak specifically about the local community are the most illuminating. Scattered throughout the book are descriptions of the founding and operating of a number of local mainstays, such as Ten Thousand Things, a company "that performs without a stage or stage lights, in a rectangle of chairs; performance runs begin in homeless shelters, prisons, low-income housing, and community centers and finish with ticketed public events. Artistic director Michelle Hensley often welcomes the audience and reminds them of the obvious: the actors can see them and they can see each other. . . . The houselights do not go down; the sight of each other can be profound and revealing" (31). Such specific descriptions offer valuable insights into local companies that may be unfamiliar to non–Twin Cities audiences. Important historical context relating to the community or to specific companies appears only occasionally, such as Lou Bellamy's description of how the founding of Penumbra coincided with the regeneration projects in the wake of the destruction of the historic Rondo neighborhood in Saint Paul. Such brief contextual allusions only underscore the need for a more thorough, complex historical study of Twin Cities theatre.

Scholars and others interested in exploring the deeper dynamics of Twin Cities theatre will have to read between the lines of *Offstage Voices* or look elsewhere, but for those seeking a theatre appreciation text grounded in the voices and experiences of a specific community, they will find it here. Visitors or recent transplants to the Twin Cities may appreciate the suggestions in the back of the book for navigating the theatre scene—for example, choose a company, a director, a playwright, or a performer to follow and try to see everything they do—as well as the index to fifty-five theatres in the Twin Cities metro area. Instructors of Introduction to Theatre classes may also find it a useful tool for exploring the basics in concrete ways, particularly if these classes encourage students to make connections with their local communities.

—ERIC J. COLLEARY
University of Texas at Austin

Working in the Wings: New Perspectives on Theatre History and Labor. Edited by Elizabeth A. Osborne and Christine Woodworth. Carbondale: Southern Illinois University Press, 2015. vii + 246 pp. $40.00 paper.

Editors Elizabeth Osborne and Christine Woodworth, much like archeologists, discover artifacts, treasure, and the spooky remains of forgotten theatrical traditions in *Working in the Wings: New Perspectives on Theatre History and Labor.* In this collection of essays dedicated to the sweat and toil that make a theatrical performance seem cool and effortless, Osborne and Woodworth, along with twelve other historians of American theatre, recover work of all kinds—from the most manual and menial labors to the most intuitive and inspired creative acts—that often goes unacknowledged in the theatre, because it is either obscured, unpleasant, undervalued, or simply unfathomable.

In the introduction to their subject of invisible work, Osborne and Woodworth articulate the paradox of trying to capture and study work that is meant to remain hidden: "The legacy of shrouding the work of artists and craftsmen in order to foster a deceptively seamless or even intentionally ruptured night at the theatre has created enormous challenges for theatre and performance scholars hoping to document the creative process—the specific people and acts required to realize a work of theatrical art" (2). But the editors and their fellow scholars accept that challenge with essays spanning the eighteenth century to the present, covering a range of topics, from cake walks to comic operas, from domestic labor to domestic partnerships, from massive make-work programs like the FTP's Caravan Theatre to the obsessive, lonely labor of the tortured creative artist. What unites them all, however, is an intense focus on the hidden and sometimes grueling labor from which a finely crafted product or performance emerges. Mindful of the intrinsic connection between theatrical work and imaginative play, Osborne and Woodworth guide readers through what might seem like an eclectic exhibit of unrelated curiosities. Their coauthored essay, "The Work of Play in Performance," ties together this scholarly collection through logical groupings, persistent themes, and important questions: "How do we theorize the work of play when it has intentionally or unintentionally been hidden from view? What is missing from the current conversation about theatrical work? In short, what does it mean to work, and to create work, in the theatre?" (2). Moreover, these questions are situated within the larger context of recent events and conversations surrounding economics, employment, labor unions, wages, and work-life balance. No matter how far afield some of the essays might seem from contemporary notions of theatrical work, the authors draw striking parallels between their subjects and the current discourse surrounding workers' rights and the dignity of labor.

The first group of essays unites under the rubric "Working Conditions" and reveals the decidedly unglamorous day-to-day of work in or around the theatre: from labor unions and commercial scenic studios to underemployed actors trying to pay the bills. Sara Freeman discusses the working/life partnership of director Les Waters and designer Annie Smart, and Chrystyna Dail pulls back the curtain on the remarkably progressive UAW workers' theatre and its groundbreaking satire *Discrimination for Everybody!* Tom Robson's analysis of nineteenth-century scenic studio catalogs challenges prevailing assumptions about New York as the center for this highly competitive industry, and Christine Woodworth's "Don't Quit Your Day Job: Situating Extratheatrical Employment in the Performance Archive" weaves a fascinating tale of two actresses, Neysa McMein, a brilliant painter, and Kitty Marion, a housemaid, teacher, and union organizer, who made their names not in theatre but from their important work as artists and activists who drew inspiration from their theatrical milieus.

Part 2, "Inscription, Erasure, and Recovery: Palimpsests of Labor," presents essays about faded traditions and forgotten workers, including Dorothy Chansky's "Retooling the Kitchen Sink: Representing Domestic Labor in American Performance after 1963" and Jerry Dickey's illuminating analysis of the cakewalk contests of the Gilded Age, as performed by African American waiters. In "Beaten, Battered, and Brawny: American Variety Entertainers and the Working-Class Body," Max Schulman demonstrates how the maimed and tragic Leonard Trask, Eugen Sandow's act as a virile strongman, and Nat Wills's insouciant tramp character embodied American myths of persistence, strength, and rebellion. The standout essay in this group, Elizabeth A. Osborne's "Hidden in Plain Sight: Recovering the Federal Theatre Project's Caravan Theatre," offers a carefully documented study of one of the Federal Theatre's most popular programs and its sad dissolution in the wake of the maddening controversy surrounding the FTP's higher-profile, more politically charged works.

Essays under the heading "Myth, Memory, and Manifestation: The Work of the Public Mind" make up part 3, including AnnMarie T. Saunders's look at the mythology and mishaps informing the design and construction of the first theatre in Washington, DC, in 1803. Elizabeth Reitz Mullenix explores the power of memory in an essay on Dion Boucicault's *The Octoroon* by drawing intriguing parallels between the infamous John Brown and Boucicault's stage Yankee, Salem Scudder, particularly their espousal of "higher law theory"—the belief that American law could not be just if it sanctioned slavery. In situating "Labor, Theatre, and the Dream of the White City" between two decisive and bloody strikes that branded workers as "savages," Rosemarie K. Bank persuasively argues that the Columbian Exposition of 1893 forever shifted the focus from the labor of workers to the profits of big business as the pinnacle of American achievement.

Part 4, "The Creative Work/The Work of Creation," ventures into the labor of creation and how we think about work through the rhetoric of labor itself, as shown in Melissa Porterfield's delightful account of Pittsburgh's Three Rivers Shakespeare Festival and its ingenious "blue-collar Bard" marketing campaign. Tracey Elaine Chessum employs a similar methodology to investigate how John Philip Sousa used the rhetoric of labor and the American self-made man to advocate for the copyright laws that enabled composers to earn royalties for recordings. Finally, Jonathan Chambers provides the most lyrical evocation of work in his examination of Rinde Eckert's *And God Created Great Whales*, a searing look at the artistic process through the decaying mind of a composer, Nathan, trying to finish an opera based on *Moby Dick*: "Just as Melville characterizes Ahab's chase of his quarry as an act that is both transcendent and tortured, Eckert represents Nathan's artistic labor as simultaneously sublime and grueling. In both pieces, then, human beings use work to rise above the mundane in an effort to glimpse the divine" (212).

No words could better characterize the tremendous effort and ardent love of theatre that drove the subjects of all these essays to such remarkable, though often unremarked, achievements. *Working in the Wings* seeks to remedy that oversight and invites other scholars to continue this important work.

—STACEY CONNELLY
Trinity University

Child Labor in the British Victorian Entertainment Industry, 1875–1914. By Dyan Colclough. New York: Palgrave Macmillan, 2016. xiv + 227 pp. $88.00 hardcover.

Dyan Colclough's monograph is a well-structured, comprehensive assessment of child labor in the theatrical industry in Victorian England. Colclough draws extensively from primary sources, written by performers, managers, producers, reformers, audiences, the government, and proprietors of related industries, and uses them to create an interwoven assessment of these complex competing interests. On top of these sources, Colclough layers secondary scholarship, including studies on the history of children, educational reform movements, and labor legislation. The period under consideration is one wherein "child laws were believed to be addressing the issue of child labor, [and yet] the recruitment of child performers not only gained momentum but also became more rigorous and extensive" (44). The result is a detailed, layered, and nuanced discussion of complex social and market forces impacting child theatrical labor in this period.

The book is structured so as to present evidence of the broader issues that educational and employment reform legislation of the era sought to combat; thus, the early chapters address the economic and material conditions of theatrical employment for children and the relationships between the children and their audiences that led to their increased employment in this period. The sheer volume of child employees, stemming from the interplay of theatrical fads such as pantomime, fantasy, and crowd scenes, is explored amid a burgeoning Victorian fascination with childhood and children. Profit-seeking managers, employers, family members, and children are placed in conversation with each other and with educational and workplace reform movements that sought to protect valued Victorian children from exploitation. Children were becoming revered in part for their vulnerability, and yet that reverence also made them candidates for public consumption, enabling employers to exploit them in the workplace and sparking decades of conflict between reformers, employers, and parents. "The worth of the child as a family resource was matched by its importance as a source of profit for the industry and its value to the audience as a source of pleasure. Satisfying all those needs could not help but compromise a young entertainer's experience of childhood because despite all the rhetoric, those deriving some sort of return from the children's work were unwilling to acknowledge their vulnerability" (57).

After establishing that changing Victorian notions of childhood constituted a time for learning rather than labor and after clearly arguing that theatrical workplaces were simultaneously stark and yet economically beneficial for children and their families, managers, and producers, Colclough proceeds to analyze the various competing attempts to reform theatrical labor conditions and laws at the turn of the twentieth century. Managers, parents, and producers exploited various loopholes, including the lack of labor laws for under-five-year-olds, the legality of employing certain children outside school hours, the requirement of having classrooms to educate their school-age workforce, and the legal standing of private schools that removed child actors from certain legal protections. In response, reformers sought to limit the employment of children in theatres through numerous failed and partially successful legislative volleys made throughout the end of the nineteenth and beginning of the twentieth centuries. Reform was incremental, with the introduction of licenses and the gradual raising of the licensing age paralleling shifts in aesthetic trends away from huge crowd scenes and pantomimes overflowing with child actors. Colclough addresses the economic and political forces driving these developments through the final chapters.

The book's strengths reside in the interplay of sources and interrogation of motives. For example, the latter chapters position various reformers against each other, underscoring the at-times selfish motivations of the various industry and missionary forces that sought to control childhood experiences. Ellen Barlee, from whose writings Colclough draws throughout the volume, is indicative of this complex interplay. As Colclough notes, Barlee is both an advocate for child theatrical laborers and a potential exploiter of them as well. Her work took her backstage in many theatres and permitted her to detail working conditions, yet she also worked as a recruiter of domestic servants for Australia. The extensive source materials that provide the evidence for Colclough's arguments are well analyzed and contextualized throughout.

Also illuminating is the exploration of the backstage world of the child performer and the discrepancies between it and the idealized view of childhood presented onstage, an argument that Colclough traces throughout the chapters. The ramifications of the workplace on children's health and education are illustrative of the problems that reformers such as Barlee saw and are used to emphasize the disconnect between the world that the audiences saw onstage and the realities these children were living backstage, freezing in their fairy costumes. While managers and producers created purported schoolrooms as facades to feign compliance with laws, audiences willingly consumed the contradictorily messaged products onstage, at times with nefarious motives. As Colclough notes: "For stage-children, however, commerce and, frequently adult sexuality, lay at the heart of the product they were paid to produce. Thus, in delivering the imagery of romanticized childhood, their own innocence and quality of life was compromised" (93). The lives of child performers are explored through extensive primary source materials, as is the conflicted relationship between viewers and performers. Throughout, too, marketability and profit are highlighted as motivating forces behind the proliferation of child actors and the working conditions they faced.

Throughout, Colclough critiques rhetorical strategies employed in her source materials to highlight the conflicted position of child artists within worlds of leisure and work and to underscore the complex motivations of those invested in child theatrical labor. While the text would have benefited from more rigorous copyediting, the overall argument is well presented and draws responsibly and intelligently from extensive primary source materials. As such, the book presents a nuanced exploration of the numerous factors that led to the expansion and reduction of child laborers and the conditions in which they worked from 1875 to 1914.

—EILEEN CURLEY
Marist College

A Taste for Brown Bodies: Gay Modernity and Cosmopolitan Desire. By Hiram Pérez. New York: New York University Press, 2015. xii + 180 pp. $26.00 paper.

Hiram Pérez's *A Taste for Brown Bodies*, a recent addition to the Sexual Cultures series from New York University Press, has at its heart a provocative thesis that invites further development by future scholars. In his work, Pérez draws on queer theory and critical race theory to examine the inflection(s) of gay identity in a variety of texts. Through such representative (and historicized) exemplars of masculinity as the sailor, the soldier, and the cowboy, Pérez argues for their "queer cosmopolitanism" as the basis for a gay modernity uniquely suited to deployment by the forces of American imperialism.

In his lucid introduction, Pérez rightfully takes queer studies to task for its failure to sufficiently incorporate race into its critiques. The role of whiteness in relationship to an erotic politics of gay modernity provides a lever by which to destabilize naturalized and institutionalized accounts of the development of homosexual identities. Structurally, Pérez's text consists of five chapters, each a close reading carefully attuned to the complexities of the intersection(s) of sexual, racial, and political economies.

Chapter 1, a close reading of Melville's novella *Billy Budd, Sailor: An Inside Narrative*, centrally positions nostalgia as part of that which "defines the gay cosmopolitan imagination, staging exotic mise-en-scènes vital to the emergence and perpetuity of gay modernity and its collusions with U.S. empire" (25). To this end, the "brown bodies" of Pérez's title often manifest as representative(s) of an idyllic primitive state, sometimes literally "brown," sometimes only figuratively so. In this reading, even Billy's blondness serves as a stand-in for the primitivism that serves as an object of desire for gay cosmopolitanism. Understandably, this occasionally makes the complex parsing of racialized identities in Perez's argument somewhat challenging, though this challenge doesn't blunt the edge of his argument.

Chapter 2 focuses on the juxtaposition of James Baldwin's short story "Going to Meet the Man" with the (in)famous photos of prisoners at Abu Ghraib. Here Pérez provides a compelling examination of "the relation between the homoerotics of racist violence and modern gay identity" (51). His reading of the Baldwin text convincingly argues for a triangulation of "homoerotic interracialism" as foundational to modern male identities, both heterosexual and homosexual (66). This insight provides the basis for a reading of the Abu Ghraib photos that argues their homoerotic content as indicative of the instrumentalization, rather than the marginalization, of modern gay identity.

Although at nineteen pages it stands as the shortest chapter, chapter 3's close reading of the film *Strawberry and Chocolate* provides a clear example of the importance of critically situating works within their historical and local contexts. Indeed, Pérez argues that to fail to do so occludes an understanding of "how . . . local sexualities already form part of a more historically dynamic erotic circuitry" (80). Here Pérez's approach serves as an effective rejoinder to dominant critical voices that efface the local in favor of the global.

Chapter 4 is perhaps the most tantalizing and the most frustrating for those interested in performance. Pérez offers an account of his experience as a panelist at 2003's Gay Shame conference at the University of Michigan. As the only invited queer panelist of color present at the conference, Pérez offered a critique of the conference's "unacknowledged centering of white gay male experience" that met with resistance from some of the conference's participants. While his account of the conference clearly centers on his own experience, and while that experience makes for some troubling reading, particularly in his relating of how "brown" bodies were performatively deployed through visual and verbal constructions related to the conference presentations, I found myself longing for a more thorough accounting of how Pérez's challenge to the conference presenters, and their resistance to that challenge, manifested physically. Despite this, however, the chapter stands as an important and sobering account of how queer people of color often serve as a spectacle designed to reinstantiate existing racial hierarchies.

The book concludes with a chapter on the "gay cowboys" both in E. Annie Proulx's short story "Brokeback Mountain" and in Ang Lee's film adaptation, *Brokeback Mountain*. Here some of the larger concerns of Pérez's argument seem finessed to merit the chapter's inclusion (it previously appeared in a collection of essays devoted to the story and film), though he concludes the chapter with a callback to the introduction's appeal for a reexamination of the boundaries of queer political engagement.

While none of the texts providing the basis for the book's close readings are theatrical texts, Pérez's argument deserves to be taken into account and reckoned with by those theatre historians and scholars whose work might be informed by queer theory and critical race theory. Throughout the book the prose is lively and engaging. While Pérez is particularly attuned to verbal and linguistic nuance, the text's engagement with the visual might have been more fully served by the inclusion of some of the images referenced. Their absence, however, doesn't hamper an understanding of the issues in question.

—DARIN KERR
University of North Dakota

Kitchen Sink Realisms: Domestic Labor, Dining, and Drama in American Theatre. By Dorothy Chansky. Iowa City: University of Iowa Press, 2015. pp. ix + 291. $55.00 paper.

In their introduction to *Food and Theatre on the World Stage* (2015), part of the Routledge Advances in Theatre and Performance Studies series, Dorothy Chansky and coeditor Ann Folino White note that the late-twentieth-century growth in food studies demonstrates that food and the labor used to produce and consume it are enmeshed with cultural identity; for example, the time and energy spent rolling pasta and sautéing garlic are as integral to the traditional Italian American Sunday dinner as are the oral and physical interactions between family members creating and consuming the meal. While the articles included in *Food and Theatre* treat the mingling of food and performance throughout world history, *Kitchen Sink Realisms* affords Chansky the space to focus, in part, on "exposing causalities and ironies in the behaviors and assumptions that go with domestic labor and dining" (5), especially as they are influenced by *and* influence gender, as presented in American plays between 1918 and 2005. Through investigating how audiences' assumptions throughout these decades might have informed representations of cleaning, cooking, food preparation, and childcare in their theatres, Chansky provides a unique method for demonstrating the importance of plays to our understanding of cultural history.

In the latter part of the twentieth century, any play or production labeled, often derisively, as "kitchen sink realism" typically conjured images of a gritty, mimetic representation of "real" life, complete with a Belascoesque stage full of furniture, decorations, and appliances. Chansky's project offers a refreshing understanding of the form not as a single genre or style, too often limited by representations of middle-class white characters, but as a multiplicity of genres—*realisms*—that treat "material actuality" (5) in a variety of ways "across cultural space" (5) and that extend beyond the well-made-play structure. Here "kitchen sink realisms" also resemble advertisements for the "American Dream" and the longing of the intended audience member/consumer for material betterment (21). As a feminist critique of American drama, *Kitchen Sink Realisms* explores how domestic labor as it is visible (staged) and invisible (not staged) identifies a truthful way of life, especially for women who, Chansky notes, have historically been saved from the drudgery of difficult housework "only as it was directly legible to men and made sense to them" (14); the stove, for example, which saved men from chopping and hauling wood for fires, entered homes before washing machines or dishwashers did, which eventually made the mainly female job of laundry far easier. Chansky notes that it is the sink, even if time-saving appliances are present, in any home (real or fictional) that is the "ugly duckling" of the kitchen and is used to complete the "grubbiest" tasks (18). Although not all such plays include an actual sink onstage, Chansky reminds readers that the daily functioning of the house necessarily includes the use of a sink and that someone is involved in that labor. Another fascinating aspect of Chansky's text is her use of not only Burns Mantle's commentary over twenty-eight years in *Best American Plays* but also several household advice manuals (the result of the domestic science movement beginning in the nineteenth century) and cookbooks to provide context for the myriad domestic labors, including dining, in the almost fifty plays she examines.

Although Chansky briefly examines domestic labor in America before the twentieth century in her introductory chapter, she begins her chronological exploration with the year marking the end of World War I, in part because 1918 is the first year a drama was awarded a Pulitzer Prize and because it marks the end of "corny, joke-driven dramaturgy" (2) and the beginning of the more serious style of writers like O'Neill and Glaspell. The first two chapters consider changes to domestic labor, such as the shift from live-in servants to hourly workers, in primarily middle-class American homes, as depicted in plays like Glaspell and Cook's *Tickless Time* (1918), Gale's *Miss Lulu Bett* (1921), and Treadwell's *Machinal* (1928). For example, following a brief summary of *Tickless Time*, Chansky analyzes how the main couple's intent to bury their mechanical clock and use the more bohemian and progressive idea of a sundial threatens the departure of their live-in cook, who is now challenged to time out her food preparations, as well as the status and homemaking skills of the wife, who may be unprepared to handle the added burden if the cook departs. Also addressed in these chapters is the reality that throughout the 1910s and 1920s the number of women attending college increased, while the expectation that they would settle into wifedom and homemaking remained. Their newfound education, they were told, should be used not for outside work but to apply scientific knowledge to childcare, cooking, and cleaning. Thus, when Lulu Bett escapes, through marriage, the drudgery of laboring for her extended family, as depicted in the first two acts of the play, she in reality trades one life of domestic labor for another, since any Midwestern housewife of the 1920s would necessarily have lived "out her post-triumph days in a world of housekeeping" (58). Marketing, in newspapers as well as in the theatre of the time, also carefully targeted the female consumer. *Machinal*'s Young Woman's rubber gloves, Chansky observes, are not only a dramaturgical tool for protecting one of the few things over which the Young Woman has control but also material items that were heavily marketed to women in the 1920s "as a means of keeping their hands soft and, thereby, themselves sexually desirable" (62) and that would have meant something particular to audiences watching the 1928 production.

Subsequent chapters cover the Depression years (1930–39); World War II and the years immediately following (1940–47); the Cold War years (1949–62); three decades (1963–93) comprising the era of second-wave feminism, off-off-Broadway and not-for-profit theatres; and, finally, the era of Martha Stewart, the Food Network, third-wave feminism, and increased divorce rates (1993–2005). Chansky's detailed analysis of canonical plays in these chapters, such as *Awake and Sing* (1935), *Death of a Salesman* (1949), *Streetcar* (1947), and *Come Back, Little Sheba* (1950), refreshingly observes how, for example, "food and food-related activities" are used by Inge in *Come Back* to "signal the characters' disordered desire and frustration"(149). The Loman family in Miller's *Death of a Salesman* refer to food, yet none of the characters actually prepare or consume any; their plans "are disrupted by psychological crises and needs that refuse to be gridded onto normative food axes" (145). Appliances, like those in the Loman home, that were originally intended to make housework less taxing create tension and contribute to the crises, since they create the new chore of fixing the perpetually breaking machines. In ending her examination with a reading of Sara Ruhl's *The Clean House* (2005), Chansky demonstrates how our implacable stance on "waged labor as the *only* legitimate means of achieving" (225) any amount of income, status, and respect continues to the present. Thus, in Ruhl's play, the all-female cast, in a stylistically nonrealistic setting, contends with their assumptions about the action or refusal of domestic labor, as well as caregiving, and leaves the reader with questions rather than answers regarding how to ameliorate the conflict between domestic labor and capitalism's disregard for unpaid labor.

Included in each chapter of *Kitchen Sink Realisms* is a section on the drama written (mostly) by and about people of color, primarily African Americans. Titled "Domestic Labor in Black and White," these sections examine the significant differences that exist in the realm of domestic work for people of color such as Lena Younger in Lorraine Hansberry's *A Raisin in the Sun* (1959), whose "bifurcated and pragmatic" (166) view of her paid work leads her to see cleaning in her own home, for her family, as "a labor of life and source of pride," while "domestic labor for others" (i.e., for her *white* bosses) "is an oppressive necessity" (167). Even in more recent plays, such as Lisa Loomer's *Living Out* (2003), balancing private/home life with necessary public/work life affects characters of color uniquely. The Latina nanny, Ana, is conditioned to appear always available to care for her charge "at the expense of her own" (217) child, while the white, yuppie mother spends more time discussing her childcare than performing the hands-on necessary care.

Kitchen Sink Realisms: Domestic Labor, Dining, and Drama in American Theatre will prove useful to both theatre scholars and practitioners, especially stage directors for its meticulous examination of how a given character's use of stage properties, or how the stage directions involving food preparation and other housework inform a play's action. Chansky's research and writing is to be commended, and the detailed endnotes are a terrific resource for a general readership of American theatre scholarship.

—KARIN MARESH
Washington & Jefferson College

Playing God: The Bible on the Broadway Stage. By Henry Bial. Ann Arbor: University of Michigan Press, 2015. xii + 247 pp. $29.95 paper.

Henry Bial's impressive scholarship has contributed extensively to the broader historiography of theatre and performance, not to mention his research on two topics: (1) Bertolt Brecht and (2) Jewish history in American film and drama. Bial's most recent work falls under the latter category, an inquiry into adaptations of the Bible on Broadway. Like the rest of Bial's oeuvre, *Playing God* is remarkable for both the breadth and the depth of its analyses. As the introduction points out, from Broadway's unofficial modern beginnings (around the 1890s) to the present, the Great White Way has staged no fewer than 121 biblical adaptations. Beginning with Wilson Barrett's *The Sign of the Cross* (1896) in chapter 1 and concluding with an epilogue on Trey Parker and Matt Stone's *Book of Mormon* (2011), *Playing God* considers more than a century of Broadway productions, from the spectacularly successful (e.g., Lew Wallace's 1899 *Ben-Hur*, Archibald MacLeish's 1958 *J.B.*) to the dismally disappointing (e.g., Salmi Morse's 1879 *The Passion*, Neil Simon's 1974 *God's Favorite*).

Looking at eleven works that received commercial and/or critical recognition, as well as "a handful of flops" (10), the text considers the tenuous relationship between the (potentially sinful) theatre and the (holy) Bible. Bial maintains that among the "most urgent question[s]" productions face is "whether the biblical drama is understood to be primarily a religious exercise or a theatrical one" (11), and further, how a production might stage the latter without offending the former. He articulates four "performance strategies" (27) that Broadway has employed to respond to those questions. As each of the book's seven chapters explains, affiliation between the Bible and theatrical performance can portend anything from violation of the second commandment to blasphemous profligates taking too many liberties with a sacred text. These unique and often complex problems, arising when the sacred and the theatrical meet, are best addressed, Bial writes, with the right combination of said "performance strategies"—*Playing God*'s fundamental critical paradigm consisting of spectacle, irony, authenticity, and sincerity.

This paradigm of four mutually influential forces enables a productive unpacking of the tensions that exist between religion and performance, or as Bial writes, the conflicts that emerge from the "encounter between good and evil, or between the Word and the Infidel" (14). To be sure, staging the sacred presents what might seem like unwinnable difficulties: if the playwright comes too close to the original (yet unstable) text, the production potentially engages blasphemy ("giving offense to God"), while moving too far from the Bible comes with its own potential for offense, not the least of which includes heresy ("contradicting" religious dogma and text) (24). Chief in the arsenal of such artists and practitioners is what Bial describes as "reverence," a not completely definable, but you-know-it-when-you-see-it quality that can save a production from box-office or review-poisoning censure, whether it be from religiously or aesthetically based objections. With chapters on what Bial describes as the spectacle-infused "fan fiction" approach in juggernauts like *Ben-Hur* or the authenticity generated by the "infantilizing," "romanticized," and "imaginary" construct of black life and black religion for white audiences in *The Green Pastures* (75), each of the four performance strategies have been used in some combination to produce a "reverence" that prevents audience and/or religious sanction.

Among Bial's more provocative deliberations is his discussion of the performance strategy of irony. For example, chapter 3's consideration of Arthur Miller's commercially and critically disappointing Genesis adaption, *The Creation of the World and Other Business*, alludes first to the discrepancy in tone that marked neither a wry nor a comic retelling of creation. And while the production arguably relied on "dark irony" (82) rather than spectacle, sincerity, or authenticity to distance itself from claims of textual inaccuracy or disrespect, the inconsistent tone of the play's irony was accompanied by a problematic production history that helped it close after sixteen performances. Bial points out that *Creation*'s unpleasant casting history, which did not escape the press, soured the production after the African American actor Susan Batson (who had already received positive reviews) was replaced as Eve by producer Robert Whitehead's wife, Zoe Caldwell (84). Paradoxically, however, *Godspell*'s use of irony, vis-à-vis its status as a musical whose actors metatheatrically dress as clowns onstage mid-performance and later invite the audiences into the production, succeeds. In other words, for *Godspell*, the requisite reverence is achieved through the musical's irony, which, as Bial argues, itself generates sincerity (160–63).

In addition to a consistently engaging readability, much of what makes Bial's text successful is the span of its critical scope—a historiography that he, along with Charlotte Canning, Thomas Postlewait, David Savran, and Scott Magelssen, has helped articulate for present-day theatre studies. In addition to considering factors such as production histories and the play/musical text itself, *Playing God* incorporates playwright/composer biography, the playwright's/composer's larger body of work as context, stagecraft and dramaturgical interventions, close readings of the Bible as a literary text, the sociopolitical and historical moment from which the play/musical emerged, gender- and ethnically based casting decisions, performer biographies, commercial versus critical success and failure, spectator and scholarly reception, venue, and even a production's (positive and negative) influence on future biblical adaptations on Broadway. Indeed, *Playing God* is often as much a "good read" as it is a rich source of Broadway history. For example, in chapter 5, along with intertextual analyses of the Book of Job and three of its Broadway incarnations, readers also explore the extratextual relationship between (1) America's existential angst in the wake of World War I and the global influenza epidemic in 1918's *The Book of Job*, (2) subtextual Cold War anxieties and Hiroshima guilt in 1958's *J.B.*, and (3) Neil Simon's personal black comedy therapy after the loss of his young wife to cancer in 1971's *God's Favorite*. Blending a rigorous exploration of personal, political, theatrical, and sociohistorical contexts, Bial reveals how Broadway's treatment of the lamentable Job engages broader cultural apprehensions over the question, "Why do bad things happen to good people?" (122, 130, 133).

Because *Playing God* is as thorough as it is engaging, readers will find no shortage of passages useful in future research or just plain fun to read. Unlike a handful of other theatre scholars whose valuable offerings are sometimes mired in jargon or dense semantics, Bial's language and analyses are consistently accessible and absorbing, despite their academic rigor. *Playing God* is a valuable addition to the canon of theatre research as well as to scholars of religious, cultural, and performance studies.

—L. BAILEY MCDANIEL
Oakland University

Performance and Temporalisation: Time Happens. Edited by Stuart Grant, Jodie McNeilly, and Maeva Veerapen. New York: Palgrave MacMillan, 2015. ix + 247 pp. $95.00 cloth.

Performance and Temporalisation: Time Happens is a new addition to Palgrave MacMillan's Performance Philosophy series, edited by Laura Cull, Alice Lagaay, and Freddie Rokem. The series includes monographs and collections of essays that explore the relationship between performance and philosophy, allowing for a wide range of understanding within each of those terms. Its expansion of performative modes and philosophical studies allows the series to address not only the philosophy of performance but also performance-as-philosophy and philosophy-as-performance. This collection of essays is divided into four parts, and in this way, the collection is able to explore comprehensively its central argument: that time is "not a given, natural, objective phenomenon, but a condition and product of processes of human activity" (1). The book takes a necessarily interdisciplinary approach, including writings from not just the expected theatrical artists, dancers, and visual artists but also a variety of performance-makers (broadly construed), including architects, poets, and critics. The collection is intentionally wide in scope, allowing it to become a work of "performance philosophy" that addresses the many iterations of and approaches to both performance and philosophy, plus the many combinations thereof.

Part I: World, Space, Place contains five essays that look at the ability of a physical place to affect the understanding of time. Jeff Malpas kicks the book off with a deconstruction of the positionality of time and space in "Timing Space-Spacing Time." He breaks the philosophical argument into five major subarguments that peruse the points of layering and differentiation between temporality and spatiality and roots these explorations in philosophy and practical examples. "Situated Structures," by Amanda Yates and Gemma Loving-Hutchins, examines the performativity and temporality of architecture through the presentation of microarchitecture, as well as site- and time-specific pieces of architecture, as examples of how architecture can engage time and space. "Suspended Moments," by John Di Stefano and Dorita Hannah, works from Antonin Artaud's demand that theatre be a space of immediacy to investigate how real-life events can take the theatre from a place of artifice to a liminal space of change for the audience. In Ian Maxwell's "My Big Fat Greek Baptism," the reader is taken on an autoanthropological study of the transcendent quality of ritual in the Greek orthodox tradition, as different rituals lie on top of each other, creating a cultural palimpsest of community and meaning. And finally, "A Shared Meal," by Jeff Stewart, looks at meals as cross-sections of divinity within the everyday mundane.

Part II: Self, Movement, Body includes five essays that evaluate the role of movement and body in the performance of time. "The Crannies of the Present," by Brian Massumi, plumbs the murky depths of the cognitive gap between sensation and action, finding that the potentiality of action is directly tied to time and the subjectivity of experience. Jack Reynolds's "Time Out of Joint" presents the converse argument to Massumi's chapter; Reynolds engages Heidegger's triple layering of the temporal to argue that a poststructuralist understanding of the cognitive gap is an insufficient means of viewing that phenomena. Erin Manning ping-pongs the argument back to the poststructuralist side in "Three Propositions for a Movement of Thought" by proposing that the body is not a subject that moves but a movement in itself: The body begins in movement, is more than itself, and does not depend on an a priori intentional subject. Conversely, Lanei Rodemeyer, in "The Body in Time/Time in the Body," uses nonvisual bodily activities to consciously situate and gender bodies in a fundamental structure. Maeva Veerapen's "A Moment of Creation" lives in the "moment of waiting" between two dance partners in an improvised social dance, reflecting that dance reveals the performance of time.

Part III: Image, Performance, Technology presents another five essays but moves more firmly into the realm of performance. Jodie McNeilly constructs her own method of analyzing the temporal in "Temporalising Digital Performance" by considering the limits and potential of phenomenological description in performance philosophy. "Entanglement Theory," by Karen Pearlman and Richard James Allen, dives into the spiritual literature of the Vedas to study the transcendence of mixed-reality artworks that awaken "questions of entanglement, of common time in different spaces and realities" (177). Adrian Martin's "A Certain Dark Corner of Modern Cinema" looks at the works of Japanese filmmaker Naomi Kawase as literary expressions of identity that convey "story time," "plot time," and "emotional time" (18). "Cyclic Repetition and Transferred Temporalities," by Yuji Sone, suggests that mediated images can reveal both past and present through the complexities of repetition and rhythm. Barry Laing's "Labours of Love" studies the work of UK artists Lone Twin in conversation with Levinasian theories to expose how the work "assembles and re-assembles, re-members and re-makes time and place in unpredictable ways" (207).

Finally, Part IV: Apotheosis brings together the many arguments presented in the book through two chapters. Stuart Grant presents "Heidegger's *Augenblick* as the Moment of Performance" through a study of the development of the term and places it in context with his concept of the moment. Grant uses Heidegger as a jumping-off point for new understandings of stubborn problems in performance studies and performance as research. Alphonso Lingis's "Caves" rebuts the simplification of time to a linear model by positioning human performances on horizontal and vertical axes of temporality, thereby expanding our understanding of how temporality works and is at work in our human experiences.

Performance and Temporalization: Time Happens is a comprehensive collection of methodologies and theories of time and space, allowing the reader to explore the field through the filter of performance. A basic understanding of philosophy is imperative, as many essays dive right into the finer points of Heidegger, Kant, Foucault, Derrida, and their counterparts, and the theories are utilized in innovative and compelling ways. As noted in the introduction of this collection, there is surprisingly little "authoritative work" on the question of time, so the book suffers a bit for trying to be comprehensive. Part II in particular vacillates between theories so rapidly that it is difficult to find a comprehensive resolution of theory or position. However, that dearth of material makes this anthology a valuable addition to the scholastic canon and provides many intriguing, innovative, and exciting examples to shake up the way temporality is viewed in performance and philosophy.

—JULIA MORIARTY
Wayne State University

Seeing Sarah Bernhardt: Performance and Silent Film. By Victoria Duckett. Urbana: University of Illinois Press, 2015. xii + 248 pp. $30.00 paper.

Sarah Bernhardt, an internationally known actress who toured the world to great acclaim in the late nineteenth century, was perhaps best known for her golden voice. In the early twentieth century she embarked on a journey into the world of film—more importantly, silent film. How did an actress known specifically for her voice fare in a silent medium? How would her reputation for overseeing every aspect of a production, from management and performance to the mise-en-scène, translate to the burgeoning film industry? How would her film endeavors impact her celebrity and status? These are the questions that Victoria Duckett examines in *Seeing Sarah Bernhardt: Performance and Silent Film.* In Duckett's own words: "My work is driven by the practical need to contextualize and explain Bernhardt's popular success on film even (or particularly) given the fact that no film or theater theorist, historian, or critic has ever applauded this work" (2). Duckett chose five films for her analysis: *Hamlet*, *Camille*, *Queen Elizabeth*, *Sarah Bernhardt at Home*, and *Mothers of France*. Duckett carefully unpacks each film, analyzing the production, marketing, and audience response along with the larger repercussions to the arts and society.

Chapter 1 focuses on the mechanics of the silent film process. As I mentioned earlier, Bernhardt was known for her voice, but she also was a master of stage gesture. Duckett argues that Bernhardt's gestural presence was equally important to audiences and translated beautifully to film. Bernhardt embodied the influence of art nouveau in the late nineteenth century, as Duckett states: "Bernhardt's early films join her distinctive theatrical style of acting to a wider art movement that saw artists newly mobilize materials and audiences through novel uses of modern industry" (28). Another key aspect of silent film was the music chosen for the performance. Unfortunately, we don't have any way of knowing what music was played at each venue, as it wasn't standardized. Throughout the remainder of the book, Duckett returns to the artistic and cultural influences discussed in this chapter.

Hamlet, a short film first presented at the Paris Exhibition of 1900, is the subject of chapter 2. Just a few minutes in length, it featured a dueling scene with Bernhardt as the title character. While there is a discussion of the performance itself—Bernhardt costumed as a man with her legs visible and on display caused a bit of a stir—this chapter's primary concern is the marketing of new technology and the use of Bernhardt's celebrity to ensure its success. Although Bernhardt's presence lured the masses into the exhibit, it is important to note that the film also demonstrated her willingness to embrace new technology as a means to reach new audiences.

In chapter 3, Duckett examines the concept of cinematizing theatre. *Camille*, adapted from the novel *La Dame aux Camélias* by Alexandre Dumas fils, was not only a familiar story to most people in the early twentieth century but also one of Bernhardt's signature stage roles. She played Marguerite repeatedly throughout her career in various adaptations, most recently in 1910, just two years before the film was released. Bernhardt was a savvy businesswoman who certainly knew that filming her most famous role would introduce her to new audiences all over the world, perhaps even encouraging them to see the stage version as well.

Queen Elizabeth, the topic of chapter 4, was released in 1912 and is another example of cinematized theatre. Another well-known Bernhardt role, the film is noteworthy for its historical accuracy and pageantry. Duckett also introduces the concept of connecting famous artworks to the visual images seen on screen, particularly the works of Paul Delaroche. While Bernhardt never mentioned the connection publicly, it is evident that certain tableaus in the film are reminiscent of Delaroche's artworks. It is another example of the integration of the "high" arts into film, perhaps in an attempt to distinguish film as an art form rather than a novelty.

Sarah Bernhardt at Home, released in 1915, differs dramatically from the other films discussed in that it is a documentary. Filmed during a trip to her home on Belle Isle off the Brittany coast, it is an intimate portrait of the actress at home. She writes, sculpts, and interacts with the locals in a series of quiet, introspective scenes that show another side of the actress. Here, in chapter 5, the connections to various art works are much more obvious. Part travelogue, part slice of life, the documentary shows a more personal side of Sarah Bernhardt.

Chapter 6 analyzes *Mothers of France*, a propaganda film expressly created for American audiences to convince them to engage in World War I. While the film was scripted and featured fictional characters, it included actual footage of the horrors of war. Released in February 1917, it showed Bernhardt after her 1915 surgery to amputate her leg. Her immobility was hidden during the movie itself, but the publicity tour featured Bernhardt not only as a mother and a patriotic Frenchwoman but also as someone with intimate knowledge of the difficulties faced by soldiers returning from the front.

In her conclusion, Duckett admits that there are many more questions to answer when it comes to the early years of film and the interaction between the stage and screen. Her analysis is narrow in focus and does not include any in-depth biographical information about Sarah Bernhardt. Readers with limited knowledge of Bernhardt may want to begin with a more general biography, but Duckett's work provides an intimate portrait of an exciting period in Bernhardt's career and the early years of film. As an entry in the Women and Film History International series, I would highly recommend this book to any reader with an interest in Sarah Bernhardt, film history, women in early film, or women's studies in general.

—LAURA M. NELSON
University of Missouri

American Tragedian: The Life of Edwin Booth. By Daniel J. Watermeier. Columbia: University of Missouri Press, 2015. ix + 464 pp. $55.00 hardcover.

A labor of love and a work of careful scholarship, Daniel J. Watermeier's *American Tragedian* chronicles the life and career of Edwin Booth from his humble beginnings in the shadow of his famous actor father through his growth and maturation as a theatre artist and manager. Of course, much has previously been written about Edwin Booth, and at the outset of his book Watermeier openly acknowledges this fact. Yet the author clearly justifies his work, making the case that previous writings on Booth either lack sufficient documentation or tend to be skewed toward his connection to his infamous brother, John Wilkes Booth. Watermeier seeks to present a more measured and methodical look at Edwin Booth's biography. This approach proves to be both the book's strength and a potential weakness.

In eleven chapters culled from correspondence, diaries, articles, reviews, and previous scholarship, Watermeier maps out the major events of Booth's life divided into segments ranging from one to nineteen years. In chapter 1, "Father and Son, 1833–1852," we learn of the complicated Booth family tree, with family members on two continents. We also learn of Booth's upbringing and his apprenticeship to Junius Brutus Booth. In chapter 2, "From Stock Actor to California Star, 1852–1856," we follow Booth's early years as a journeyman actor playing the East Coast, traveling west to California, and then following the gold rush to Australia. We learn of his early professional associations with the likes of Keene, Jefferson, and Forrest. Yet, if there is fault to be found with Watermeier's work, it is in these early chapters, which, at times, read more like a reference source on Booth than a biography. Seasons of Booth's performances are sometimes presented as a simple narrative litany of roles, plays, and venues. Despite (or perhaps because of) Watermeier's previous work on Booth's performances, little attention is paid to how these early roles (i.e., the choice of part, the characterization, the interpretation, etc.) might have influenced or reflected Booth as a developing artist. It feels like a missed opportunity. As mere facts, painstakingly researched as they are, these pieces of information might best be presented as a table of Booth's roles in a given season. By folding so much of this information into the narrative, however, we temporarily lose sight of Booth the man, in essence missing the forest for the trees.

By chapter 3, "The Mantle of the Father, 1856–1862," however, Watermeier seems to work out the formula. His discussion of Booth's portrayal of Richelieu, for example, demonstrates what we can glean about Booth from the role he chooses and the way it is crafted. In subsequent chapters, his analyses of Booth's portrayals of Hamlet and Brutus likewise use the art to illuminate the man. In chapter 4, "Triumph and Tragedy, 1862–1865," Watermeier truly hits his narrative stride, expertly merging research with an informed analysis. We get not just the events of Booth's life but a sense of their impact. We become intrigued by Booth's ongoing struggles with alcohol, the somewhat open question of his sexuality, his marriage to Mary Devlin, and the birth of his daughter, Edwina. We see Booth grieve over the loss of his wife and the experiments with mysticism that grief leads to. We feel his shock and sadness dealing with the assassination of President Lincoln at the hands of his brother, and we marvel at the courage required to take the stage in the aftermath of such a personal yet public tragedy.

Chapter 5, "Producer and Theatre Builder, 1866–1875," tells the cautionary tale of Booth's attempt at building and managing his own theatre in New York. We see the actor struggle to balance art and commerce, eventually being left bankrupt with no choice but to tour to pay debts and suffering the ignominy of being a visiting actor in the theatre that bore his name. These tours, however, cement Booth's status as America's foremost tragedian. At the same time, Edwin and his second wife, Mary McVicker, experience personal triumph and tragedy with the birth and untimely death of their son, Edgar. In chapter 6, "National Star, 1875–1880," Watermeier again takes us on tour with Booth. However, unlike in earlier chapters, the author relies less on recitation of productions and roles and more on accounts from Booth himself and those around him. The story of Booth performing Hamlet using a large turnip carved to resemble Yorick's skull, for example, is as hilarious as the account of the assassination attempt by Walter

Lyon is shocking. Such firsthand accounts provide an invaluable look at the theatre and the life of a touring actor in nineteenth-century America.

In later chapters, the author traces Booth's 1880–81 season acting with Irving and Terry in London, the acrimonious separation from and eventual death of Mary McVicker, and Booth's successful tour of Germany and Austria. Watermeier next moves to summaries of Booth's tours later in the 1880s, including the Joint-Star Tours with Barrett and later Modjeska. Given the sheer volume of Booth's work, here Watermeier does an admirable job of addressing the sometimes dizzying array of cities, theatres, plays, roles, and receipts. He does so, again, by balancing data with context, mostly from newspaper accounts and correspondence. Chapter 11, "The Curtain Descends, 1890–1893" finds Booth retiring from the stage before succumbing to his own health problems. The author concludes with a description of Booth's burial and an excellent summation of the effect Booth's work had on the theatre of the day.

Daniel J. Watermeier's *American Tragedian: The Life of Edwin Booth* is the most authoritative account of Booth's career we are likely to see for some time. It is an achievement and one that should be a part of the library of any historian interested in Booth specifically or nineteenth-century American theatre in general.

—MICHAEL A. ROTHMAYER
Drake University

Lincoln and Shakespeare. By Michael Anderegg. Lawrence: University Press of Kansas, 2015. xvi + 222 pp. $29.95 hardcover.

Fortune's Fool: The Life of John Wilkes Booth. By Terry Alford. New York: Oxford University Press, 2015. 464 pp. $29.95 hardcover.

The location of Abraham Lincoln's assassination has made this infamous event a continued point of inquiry not just for historians generally but for theatre researchers. Two recent books focus on the principal actors in that drama, and, while admirable works of scholarship, each would have been better served had the author had a firmer grounding in the theatre world of the mid-nineteenth century.

Abraham Lincoln's fondness for Shakespeare has become something of a commonplace. In *Lincoln and Shakespeare*, Michael Anderegg examines the depth of the president's relationship to the Bard. Sensibly organized, this work analyzes the evidence of Lincoln as a reader and audience member while also examining Shakespeare's place in the popular culture of the time. Anderegg then turns his attention to the actors themselves, noting that many of the prominent Shakespeareans whose performances Lincoln attended also had personal contact with him. Throughout, the author does an excellent job of examining the available material and adjudicating its trustworthiness. He clearly states where he is operating on a basis of supposition and supports his conclusions commendably.

The image of Lincoln that emerges is one of a highly selective reader and an analytical, and often less than enthusiastic, spectator. While providing valuable insight into Lincoln's character, Anderegg cannot escape the fact that so little evidence exists on his subject. Only a small percentage of Lincoln's documented theatre attendance was for productions of Shakespeare, and his pronouncements on Shakespearean topics are few in number. As a result, Anderegg needs to cast a wide net to pull in enough material for a book-length study. For example, he dedicates considerable space to actor Charles W. Couldock's 1857 performances in Springfield while admitting that we cannot know whether Lincoln attended them. Elsewhere, Anderegg looks at Shakespearean allusions in Lincoln-era political cartoons. Fine so far, but it seems strange that in a chapter titled "Abraham Lincoln and America's Shakespeare," he is obliged to pull half the images from the British periodical *Punch*.

More crucially, Anderegg reveals a marked unfamiliarity with nineteenth-century theatre reviews. He mentions that critics both lauded and lambasted Couldock, adding, "neither of which tells us what kind of performer he was." (60) However, he then quotes several reviews that create a definite impression of Couldock's acting style. The same sensible approach Anderegg uses for other topics, such as how the young Lincoln may have been introduced to Shakespeare, he seems unable to apply to live performance. This is particularly unfortunate, given that the second half of the book focuses largely on that very topic. In the end, the reader is left with the impression that an interesting in-depth article (or two) has been stretched beyond its natural length.

Meanwhile, as Terry Alford states in the introduction to his new book, "*Fortune's Fool* is the first full-length biography of John Wilkes Booth ever written" (3). Other installments in the Booth canon focus, understandably, on his role as assassin. Scholarly, well-rounded accounts of Booth's whole life have been lacking, and Alford admirably fills this gap.

The book is exhaustively and expertly researched. Alford seems to have gone through every statement on Booth in the public record and in diaries and letters of the actor's intimates. What he provides, in clear and animated prose, is the story of a deeply contradictory, though seldom conflicted, individual. Booth was remembered by some associates as a model of chivalry and professionalism, by others as the picture of shiftlessness and instability. Alford does honor to the historic record by presenting both sides of the voluminous testimony regarding Booth's character, though in places he could have made stronger efforts to reconcile them.

He is similarly evenhanded when it comes to examining Booth's stage career. What is too often forgotten in the attempt to assign a pathology to Booth's life trajectory is the fact that he was, for much of his career, highly successful. He did, as Sondheim stresses in *Assassins*, suffer many bad reviews. At the same time, he received just as many raves, and numerous ones in between. Alford has read them all and does an excellent job of balancing the varied responses to Booth's acting. Indeed, he brings a laudable judiciousness to all matters regarding Booth's career. Wherever conflicting or questionable evidence appears, he applies not only his voluminous research but also a fair measure of common sense to the matter. For years, many have taken at face value a story of sibling rivalry that had Edwin dividing the map of the United States in two, claiming the Northern states for himself and restricting J. Wilkes's activities to the South. Alford is more circumspect: "But if there ever was such a plan, which is doubtful, the arrangement was untenable by 1862. The war forced actors, like other citizens, to make critical choices. Since his family lived in Philadelphia, John came north" (129).

If fault can be found, it is with the way that Alford, while trying to tell the story of Booth's entire life, misses numerous chances to flesh it out by providing greater context. This tendency is most apparent in his treatment of Booth's professional life. Alford provides lively descriptions of some of the theatrical figures who worked directly with Booth, like William Wheatley, E. L. Davenport, and Louisa Drew; however, he neglects almost all others. Only a few passing references are made to Edwin Forrest, for example, while Charlotte Cushman, Dion Boucicault, and Adah Isaacs Mencken, all of whom actively shaped the theatre world of Booth's time, do not get a mention.

In addition, Alford misses many opportunities to better illustrate his points. He drops the titles of plays that were Booth's stock-in-trade, such as *The Corsican Brothers* or *The Marble Heart*, without giving even so much as a plot summary to explain why Booth was a good match for such works. He rightly points out that Booth's performance of Richard III became his biggest success but does nothing to establish why that performance in particular could ensure a full house. With such minor additions, Alford could significantly deepen the reader's sense of Booth's artistry. Since that, not murder, was the primary activity of his adult life, such matters deserve attention. Their inclusion would transform an already remarkable work of biography into an even more impressive work of history.

—RICHARD SAUTTER
Gettysburg College

Childhood and Nineteenth-Century American Theatre: The Work of the Marsh Troupe of Juvenile Actors. By Shauna Vey. Carbondale: Southern Illinois University Press, 2015. xi + 217 pp. $40.00 paper.

Shauna Vey's microhistory of the Marsh Troupe of Juvenile Comedians—an antebellum company of child actors performing in popular melodramas, fantasies, and farces written for adults—functions as an act of recuperation, narrowing in on a successful yet unheralded theatre company working in America and abroad while also exploring larger interests around child labor, the commodification of idealized childhood, and the changing nature of entrepreneurship. This slim volume narrows its focus onto five members of the troupe: manager Robert Marsh, his children, Mary and Georgie, and two additional child performers, Louise Arnot and Alfred Stewart. "As members of a stock company led by an impresario," Vey writes, "these children were involved on a daily basis with the antebellum theatre's bid for respectability, shifting business practices, and cross-dressed and mixed-bill performances. They encountered the deep influence of melodrama, the shift to a wage-based economy, and the need for workplace reform. Their particular experiences illuminate the lives of nineteenth-century players" (3). Of great interest to Vey is the ever-shifting concept of childhood, and the Marsh Troupe serves as an allegorical site of investigation into the ideology of protected childhood and the paradox of the child performer who has "always occupied a liminal space between child and adult" (9). Here the child actor is rendered as a successful laborer and professional child while also remaining legally and financially dependent upon adult supervision and control. Both knowing and innocent, the child performer "exercises expressive agency, acts in a public sphere, and moves among adults. She is exposed rather than protected, free rather than confined" (9).

For Vey, the Marsh Troupe operated at the intersection between emerging narratives of Romantic childhood and the illusory fiction of placing the mask of innocence onto the faces of laboring professionals. The book thus engages issues around agency and action. How competent were these young performers? Were they precocious savants, unwilling participants, or simply young people developing skills and techniques for long-term careers on the stage? Of course, Vey's study offers up scholarly challenges. None of her child subjects left behind memoirs, letters, or diaries. Denied access to their inner lives, the book is based solely on adult records and observations. Additionally, though the book is exhaustingly researched, Vey is required to utilize guesswork and conjecture to fill in historical gaps. Relying on trace elements, however, Vey teases out useful historical insights based on close readings of letters, gravesites, business records, law cases, contract disputes, playbills, performance esoterica, photographs, and other promotional materials.

The first chapter documents the early career of Robert Marsh and the origins of his juvenile troupe, which began performing in 1855 and grew in popularity over the course of the next three years. In the second chapter Vey turns to two episodes in the troupe's history during their 1857–58 season. The first focuses on how financial difficulties with business partners led to a showdown between Marsh and the mother of juvenile lead Louise Arnot that can only be described as a kidnapping. Although Vey cannot access firsthand accounts of the alleged crime, three separate newspaper articles paint the event in a narrative style that borrowed heavily from the dramaturgical conventions of melodrama. Casting the thirteen-year-old Louise as a damsel in distress rescued from her mother's amoral clutches by a heroic Robert Marsh, Vey cannot help but wonder how much of a role Louise actually played in her own drama. As an object of economic exchange between fighting business partners and parents, Louise remains the one figure who seemingly has minimal agency over her destiny.

Similarly, fourteen-year-old Alfred Stewart, who joined the troupe in 1857, quickly found himself involved in a controversy over a contract dispute that put into conflict outdated forms of apprenticeship and newly emerging realities of child labor driven by cash-wage jobs. Vey writes: "The substitution of cash for cohabitation broke down the paternalistic conditions on both sides. Masters frequently became less caring and lost their moral authority" (49).

The centerpiece of the study covers the stage burning of eleven-year-old Mary Marsh in 1859 and the events that followed the aftermath of this horrific accident. Arguing that Mary Marsh "exemplified the paradox of coexisting innocence and eroticism common to many child performers" (62), Vey reads Marsh as a persona closely aligned with the sentimental ideal of childhood best represented by Little Eva in *Uncle Tom's Cabin*—a character Marsh began playing at the beginning of her short career and one whose tragic death as a child would mirror Marsh's own demise. Like Little Eva, Marsh never had to grow up and out of her innocence. Their deaths, real and fictional, solidified their angelic appeal and status as purity personified.

To strengthen her argument, Vey conducts three compelling close readings of the trace elements left behind in the wake of the young girl's death. In the first, Vey makes visible the angelic and the erotic in a promotional image modeled after a popular illustration that appeared in the first edition of Harriet Beecher Stowe's 1852 novel. The second focuses on a letter Robert Marsh shared with the public following the death of his daughter as critics questioned how the show could possibly go on. Again, Vey acknowledges the allure of melodramatic tropes and how they shaped public and private discourse, arguing that Marsh's letter worked to position his deceased daughter as "the epitome of ideal girlhood" untarnished by maturation (74). A third close reading cleverly deconstructs the rural cemetery in Georgia where Mary was buried and the pedestal monument that would become her final resting place.

Vey's study is not without faults. The book feels less like a whole than a collection of essays, and Vey often repeats herself unnecessarily. This results in a confusing narrative structure, as the reader is frustratingly pulled back and forth in time. Still, while Vey doesn't break new ground, her book is a nice addition to the growing literature on childhood studies, and though histories of nineteenth-century American theatre are plentiful, Vey's study of the Marsh Troupe of Juvenile Comedians provides a fresh perspective on well-trodden territory.

—JEFF TURNER
Hamline University

Early Modern Drama in Performance: Essays in Honor of Lois Potter. Edited by Darlene Farabee, Mark Netzloff, and Bradley D. Ryner. Newark: University of Delaware Press, 2015. vi + 196 pp. $74.00 cloth.

Early Modern Drama in Performance, a Festschrift in honor of Lois Potter, a professor emerita of English at the University of Delaware, is an excellent collection of thirteen short essays that explore the connections between early modern texts and theatrical performance. The topics of the essays are, by design, eclectic, reflecting Potter's varied work as a textual editor, theatre critic, biographer, and curator of "playreadings that she has hosted throughout her teaching career . . . [that] breathed life into many old plays and made participants aware of the dramatic possibilities of (mostly) non-Shakespearean drama (3)." The essays—all of which are by tenured, senior, or emeritus scholars—are arranged chronologically by topic, ranging from an examination of how English-language playgoers received the verse of Marlowe's contemporaries to a meditation on theatrical temporality revealed through the failings of the Royal Shakespeare Company video archive. Seven are primarily on Shakespeare's plays, but the other six are on lesser-known (or at least less-frequently staged) early modern dramas in performance.

In the first essay in the book, Roslyn L. Knutson questions the primacy of Marlowe's blank verse among his contemporaries. She troubles the twentieth-century truism that "good verse" before Shakespeare meant a successful imitation of Marlowe's bombastic style, effectively arguing that playgoers and readers of the day had more subtle and varied tastes. In the next essay, Bradley D. Ryner takes as a jumping-off point performances in 2009 of Marlowe's *The Jew of Malta* and George Chapman's *The Blind Beggar of Alexandria* at the American Shakespeare Center. Questioning the assumption that Chapman's play is a "radically incomplete . . . serious romantic story" (25) of which only the comic scenes survive, and instead reading it as a mostly complete comedy, Ryner argues that "*The Blind Beggar* not only shares structural and stylistic features with *The Jew of Malta* but, moreover, constitutes both an implicit reading and a conceptual extension of the economic ideas at work in it . . . and goes further to suggest theatrical virtuosity itself as a correlative for the capitalist generation of profit" (26). In the third essay, "Theater of Anatomy," Peter Hyland also uses as a starting point a modern performance of a lesser-known play, Henry Chettle's *The Tragedy of Hoffman*, a revenge tragedy in which the revenger is an overt villain. The play features a skeleton onstage, and Hyland teases out the theatrical implications of using a real skeleton as opposed to a reconstruction as a prop.

The next two essays are some of the strongest in the book. Ann Thompson and John O. Thompson create a semiology of rings utilized in Shakespeare's plays. They note how rings, which can be difficult to see from a distance onstage, are crucial rhetorically and theatrically to the plots of many plays. They argue that such a close-reading "study of how rhetorical figures work at the micro-level of the text helps the reader or audience-member to hear what this rich and complicated language is doing, and how it is doing it" (59). In "Editing and Staging *The Revenger's Tragedy*: Three Problems," Alan C. Dessen examines three scenes, each of which "poses a challenge to an editor, director, or reader trying to reconstruct the original staging" (64). Examining spaces for interpretation left open by early modern stage directions, or the lack thereof, he demonstrates through a close reading of six editions and three performances the fascinating multiplicity of theatrical interpretations available.

Arthur F. Kinney's contribution, "Shakespeare and Cognitive Vision," is the most ambitious (and longest) in the volume, using scientific studies of vision to recast scenes of seeing in Shakespeare's plays as scenes of cognitive interpretation: he argues that "Shakespeare saw even eyewitnessing as always cognitive and therefore always interpretive and partial, often *designed*" (99). Jay L. Halio similarly takes a theoretical approach, arguing that Shakespeare's conception of tragedy goes beyond the medieval idea of a violent fall from high to low status to depict what Aristotle called *anagnorisis*, the hero's "recognition or insight" (110) that the tragic mistake and its deadly outcome might have been avoided.

The remaining five essays are fascinating explorations of archives of performances and adaptations of Shakespeare's plays after his time. Michèle Willems discusses Jean-François Ducis's extremely influential and popular "imitations" of Shakespeare, created thirdhand without a reading knowledge of English. This very valuable essay will hopefully be expanded into a larger project, investigating "Ducis's role in the [international] transmission of Shakespeare's text[s]" (124). In "Un/natural Perspectives," Virginia Mason Vaughan, examining Viola on the nineteenth-century stage, studies the Violas of Adelaide Neilson, Ellen Terry, Ada Rehan, and Viola Allen, investigating how these actresses, playing a woman passing as a man, conformed to or departed from Victorian standards of femininity. Evelyn Tribble analyzes staged readings as liminal activities—not quite performance but not *not* performance—through the records of the Dunedin Shakespeare Club in New Zealand. In an essay originally delivered as a lecture in 1993, Zdeněk Stříbrný demonstrates the social power of theatre through an examination of three *Hamlet*s performed in Prague "from behind the former Iron Curtain" (165) that audaciously demonstrated to Czech audiences "that the time was out of joint not only for Hamlet but also for themselves" (172). In the concluding essay Andrew James Hartley views productions of *Julius Caesar* from the RSC video archive and discusses how an archival tape "creates an afterlife for the performance albeit in generically different and imperfect terms" (180).

There are a few areas where the collection could have been improved. The editors, Darlene Farabee, Martk Netzloff, and Bradley D. Ryner, crafted an introduction that ably ties the essays together and honors Potter. But this introduction, when quoting from individual essays, refers not to page numbers in the published book but in each essay. Moreover, Farabee's own essay, "The 'Most

Unsavoury Similes' and *Henry IV, Part One*," a textual examination of naming and name-calling, has little to do with performance. All the essays are brief and easily digestible, but several omit plot synopses of non-Shakespearean dramas that might not be familiar to nonspecialists.

These minor issues do not prevent the collection from being an extremely valuable contribution to the fields of early modern drama and theatre history. As they explore ways to "recover the aesthetic milieu of non-Shakespearean [English Renaissance] plays in performance" (4), to examine "the reciprocal relationship between text and embodied stage practice" (5), and to "interrogate the histories of modern performances and interpretations of early modern texts" (7), the authors demonstrate their devotion to detailed research and the craft of scholarship. The book is an engaging and fitting tribute to Potter's notable career.

—DAN VENNING
New York University

Victorian Classical Burlesques: A Critical Anthology. By Laura Monrós-Gaspar. London: Bloomsbury, 2015. iv + 298 pp. $112 hardcover.

Laura Monrós-Gaspar's annotated text is a welcome addition to the few published collections on Victorian burlesque, including those compiled by Richard W. Schoch, W. D. Adams, and by the Historical Libretto Series. To date, it is also the only one of its kind focused exclusively on Victorian classical burlesques—that is, theatrical travesties rooted in classical Greek and Roman texts and Victorian sensibilities.

As Monrós-Gaspar argues in the first section, classical burlesques moved between classical and Victorian mythologies and are, therefore, best understood "en masse" rather than as "solitary cases, exemplify[ing] . . . the social correlation of collective imaginaries and articular cultural and social realities" (8). The frequent use of topical humor may have immediately assigned these texts an expiration date in the public imagination, but considered as a larger body of work, Victorian classical burlesques offer a complex picture of cultural anxieties and ideological warfare. The four plays in this collection cover a wide range of political and cultural topics under hot debate in Victorian England. The author's significant focus on gender, though resisting any overessentialized reading of these burlesques as overtly political or revolutionary, also demonstrates that "the ambivalence of the politics of burlesque with regard to women gives voice to transgressive moulds which remained concealed in other cultural representations" (12).

The book is divided into five parts. The first section, "Why Classical Burlesque?: Enacting the Past and Present," offers important historical context for the popularity of classical work on the Victorian burlesque stage and the inherent familiarity audiences had for classical mythology and themes. This section also outlines Monrós-Gaspar's major justifications for the particular burlesque selections included in this anthology. The texts chosen were first staged between 1845 and 1859, the time in which classical burlesques experienced their greatest level of popularity. These texts also exhibit the key conventions of Victorian classical burlesque, many of which characterize other burlesques in the same period, as well as twentieth-century burlesque practices, including the use of dance, physical comedy, metatheatricality, parodies of famous classical passages, heightened theatricality and spectacle, and, as the author quotes Schoch, "traffic . . . in topical allusions" (9).

The following four sections each include a play accompanied by detailed annotations of sociohistorical commentary, including performance history, topical references, and slang. Situating each script in conversation with its particular historical production history is, in some ways, this anthology's greatest contribution to the field. In Edward L. Blanchard's *Antigone Travestie*, Sophocles's *Antigone* is retold in a shortened, parodic form that, most significantly, juxtaposes the familiar mythology with ruminations on the "Woman Question" as it permeated Victorian culture. Blanchard's Antigone, for example, intones a rhyming couplet: "Oh, silly belle, your language is a fiction/The diction of our sex is Contra-diction" (66). The annotation of this playtext reminds us that, to further complicate a reading of gender politics in this production, Antigone was played by the male actor George Wild. The second play in this collection, *Alcestis, the Original Strong-Minded Woman*, by Francis Talfourd, builds upon Euripides's version of the myth. In the burlesque, Alcestis regrets having ever married Admetus, who is "such a milksop" and looks forward to her trip to the Underworld (112). As the annotation notes, "strong-minded" operated as a Victorian shorthand for a "type" of woman—spinsterly and professionally independent. The third play, Robert Brough's *Medea, or, the Best of Mothers, with a Brute of a Husband*, is of particular note for the cross-gender casting in its premiere: Orpheus and Jason were played by two female actors and Medea by a male actor. The stage directions and allusions to circus entertainment in this script would also be especially interesting to scholars of popular entertainment stagecraft. The fourth and final play is Francis Talfourd's *Electra in a New Electric*

Light, which refashions Sophocles's Electra in the figurative glow of the newly minted electric light technology with which Victorians had become obsessed. Frequent puns about electricity, gas lighting, and other technology are sprinkled throughout the play, which lingers on women who are given the choice to follow or shun social conventions.

The value of this anthology is threefold. The book includes the first complete printing of Blanchard's *Antigone Travestie*. The other three plays, Talfourd's *Alcestis, the Original Strong-Minded Woman*, his *Electra in a New Electric Light*, and Brough's *Medea; or, the Best of Mothers, with a Brute of a Husband*, were published in Lacy's Acting Plays Collection but, more than a hundred years later, are somewhat difficult to access outside of library special collections. Second, the annotations of the plays themselves highlight Monrós-Gaspar's focus on the intertextual and anachronistic character of Victorian burlesque. Furthermore, for scholarly and pedagogical needs, the footnotes offer a greater accessibility to Victorian allusions. Without annotation, the tone of these plays would be largely lost to a modern reader. Finally, the presence of the critical anthology contributes significantly to our understanding of burlesque's lineage, from the impending emergence of Lydia Thompson and the British Blondes in the 1860s all the way to the beginnings of the twentieth century and the addition of the striptease to the art form. Though it is often marked as distinct from its more contemporary variety show cousin, Victorian classical burlesque's interrogation of gender and gender politics, the anachronistic nature of the genre, which pulls the past and present into theatrical conversation with one another, as well as the presence of the physical body in comedic parody are all trademarks of burlesque in its larger historical context.

—ELIZABETH WELLMAN
Ohio State University

BOOKS RECEIVED

Ammen, Sharon. *May Irwin: Singing, Shouting, and the Shadow of Minstrelsy*. Urbana: University of Illinois Press, 2017.

Anwar, Nadia. *Dynamics of Distancing in Nigerian Drama: A Functional Approach to Metatheatre*. Stuttgart: ibidem Press, 2016.

Barnett, Dennis, ed. *Dah Theatre: A Sourcebook*. Boulder, CO: Lexington Books, 2016.

Black, Cheryl, and Jonathan Shandell, eds. *Experiments in Democracy: Interracial and Cross-Cultural Exchange in American Theatre, 1912–1945*. Carbondale: Southern Illinois University Press, 2016.

Cardullo, R. J. *Dramatic Analysis: A Reader on Western Drama*. Boca Raton, FL: Brown Walker Press, 2016.

Carlyon, David. *The Education of a Circus Clown*. London: Palgrave Macmillan, 2016.

Coffey, Fiona Coleman. *Political Acts: Women in Northern Irish Theatre, 1921–2012*. Syracuse, NY: Syracuse University Press, 2016.

Dail, Chrystyna. *Stage for Action: U.S. Social Activist Theatre in the 1940s*. Carbondale: Southern Illinois University Press, 2016.

Davis, Carol Bunch. *Prefiguring Postblackness: Cultural Memory, Drama, and the African American Freedom Struggle of the 1960s*. Jackson: University Press of Mississippi, 2015.

Ibell, Paul. *Tennessee Williams*. London: Reaktion Books, 2016.

Isaka, Maki. Onnagata: *A Labyrinth of Gendering in Kabuki Theater*. Seattle: University of Washington Press, 2016.

Lake, Peter. *How Shakespeare Put Politics on the Stage: Power and Succession in the History Plays*. New Haven: Yale University Press, 2016.

Lindfors, Bernth. *Ira Aldridge: The Last Years, 1855–1867*. Rochester, NY: University of Rochester Press, 2015.

Paul, William. *When Movies Were Theatre: Architecture, Exhibition, and the Evolution of American Film*. New York: Columbia University Press, 2016.

Salz, Jonah, ed. *A History of Japanese Theatre*. Cambridge: Cambridge University Press, 2016.

Schoch, Richard. *Writing the History of the British Stage, 1660–1900*. Cambridge: Cambridge University Press, 2016.

Shimazaki, Satoko. *Edo Kabuki in Transition: From the Worlds of the Samurai to the Vengeful Female Ghost*. New York: Columbia University Press, 2016.

Sweet, Jeffrey. *What Playwrights Talk About When They Talk About Writing*. New Haven: Yale University Press, 2017.

Warren, Robin O. *Women on Southern Stages, 1800–1865: Performance, Gender and Identity in a Golden Age of American Theatre*. Jefferson, NC: McFarland, 2016.

CONTRIBUTORS

LEZLIE C. CROSS is an assistant professor at the University of Nevada, Las Vegas. Her articles and book reviews appear in *Shakespeare Bulletin*, *The Journal of American Drama and Theatre*, *Theatre Survey*, and *Theatre Annual* and the book projects *Shakespeare Expressed: Page, Stage, and Classroom in Shakespeare and His Contemporaries* and *Performing Objects and Theatrical Things*. She is also a professional dramaturg who works at regional theatres across America.

DAVID AFRIYIE DONKOR is an assistant professor at Texas A&M University. He earned his PhD in performance studies and doctoral certificate in African studies from Northwestern University, his MFA in directing and MS in multidisciplinary studies (ethnic studies, speech communication, educational foundations) from Minnesota State University, and a diploma in theatre from the University of Ghana. Donkor's publications include the book *Spiders of the Market: Ghanaian Trickster Performance in a Web of Neoliberalism* and entries in the volumes *Legacy of Efua Sutherland: Pan-African Cultural Activism*, by Ann Adams and Esi-Sutherland Addy, and *Cambridge Encyclopedia of Stage Actors and Acting*, by Simon Williams. Dr. Donkor has adapted and directed folktales, personal narratives, and literature for stage in productions like *Spiders and Spirits: Tale of Two Tricksters, Two Takes on Hurricane Katrina, Strange and Bitter Fruit* (a memorial of the 1906 Springfield Missouri lynching), and his own one-person show, *A Travelers Tale*, on migration and memory.

SHANNON EPPLETT is a PhD candidate in theatre history at the University of Illinois Urbana-Champaign. His dissertation, "The Steppenwolf Script: The Habitus of Chicago's Off-Loop Theatre," takes a sociological approach to examining how Chicago's off-Loop theatre community has been structured by the success of Steppenwolf Theatre. His article "The Press Release as Bully Pulpit: Stormfield Theatre Calls It A Day" appeared in the 2015 *New England Theatre Journal*. He has twice been awarded fellowships to the Newberry Library: in 2014, as part of the Newberry Consortium in American Indian Studies, and in 2015 he received the Susan Kelly Power and Helen Hornbeck Tanner Fellowship. He is a member of the Sault Ste. Marie Tribe of Chippewa Indians and in addition to his dissertation research is developing a performance piece based on the life and poetry of Anishinaabe poet Jane Johnston Schoolcraft.

LAURA FERDINAND FELDMEYER is a PhD student in the Interdisciplinary Theatre and Drama Program and a member of the British studies cluster, both at Northwestern University. She received her MA in theatre from Miami University in Ohio, where she also served as adjunct instructor in the College of Creative Arts. She has shared her research on constructions of childhood, wartime propaganda, and imaginative play at the American Society for Theatre Research conference.

LA DONNA L. FORSGREN received her PhD from the Interdisciplinary Theatre and Drama Program at Northwestern University. She has published her research in *Callaloo: A Journal of African Diaspora Arts and Letters, Frontiers: A Journal of Women Studies* and the *New England Theatre Journal*. She is an assistant professor of theatre at Notre Dame University, where she teaches courses in theatre history, dramaturgy, playwriting, and African American performance. Her book manuscript, *In Search of Our Warrior Mothers: Female Dramatists of the Black Arts Movement*, is forthcoming.

MARTINE KEI GREEN-ROGERS, PhD, is an assistant professor of theatre at the State University of New York at New Paltz. She is a freelance dramaturg who has worked at places such as the Oregon Shakespeare Festival, Pioneer Theatre Company, and the Court Theatre. Publications include the article "Talkbacks for 'Sensitive Subject Matter' Productions: The Theory and Practice" in the *Routledge Companion to Dramaturgy*.

NICHOLAS HOLDEN is an associate lecturer in drama within the School of Fine and Performing Arts at the University of Lincoln in the United Kingdom. His research is largely concerned with contemporary theatremaking, playwriting, and the work of the Royal Court Theatre. His PhD is titled "Building the Engine Room: A Study of the Royal Court Young Peoples' Theatre and Its

Development into the Young Writers' Programme" and looks to present a new history of the Royal Court Theatre from the perspective of its work with young people and playwrights.

GABRIELLE HOULE holds a PhD from the Centre for Study of Drama, Theatre and Performance Studies at the University of Toronto. Her primary research area is the recent staging history of the commedia dell'arte, as well as mask-making and masked performance. Houle trained in Canada, Italy, France, the United States, Costa Rica, and Denmark before working as an actor and a creator of masks. She has taught at several Canadian universities, including the University of Toronto, Dalhousie University, and Glendon College of York University.

JULIE JACKSON received her PhD from the theatre and drama program at the University of Wisconsin and an MFA from Chicago's Goodman School of Drama. She has been a member of United Scenic Artists Local 829 since 1985 and is currently a professor of theatre at Marshall University, where she teaches courses in theatre history, dramaturgy, and critical analysis of text in performance. Her book manuscript, *Show Me a Story: The Spectacular Storytelling of Director Frank Joseph Galati*, is forthcoming.

TODD LONDON is the executive director of and a professor at the University of Washington's School of Drama, holding the Floyd U. Jones Family Endowed Chair. He spent eighteen seasons as the artistic director of New York's New Dramatists, the nation's oldest center for the support and development of playwrights. He has published *15 Actors, 20 Years: Making Lives In and Out of the Theater*, *An Ideal Theater: Founding Visions for a New American Art*, *The Importance of Staying Earnest: Writings from Inside the American Theatre, 1988–2013*, *Outrageous Fortune: The Life and Times of the New American Play*, *The Artistic Home*, and *The World's Room*, a novel. "A Lover's Guide to American Playwrights," his column of tributes to contemporary playwrights, appears on howlround.com. He was the first recipient of a Visionary Leadership Award from the Theatre Communications Group and was given the George Jean Nathan Award for Dramatic Criticism. Under his leadership, New Dramatists received a special Tony honor. In June 2016 he received a doctor of humane letters (Hon.) from the Theatre School and School of Music at DePaul University.

MATTHEW MCMAHAN teaches theatre history, comedy, and acting at Boston-area schools, including Tufts University, Emerson College, and Merrimack College. He has a PhD in drama from Tufts University and an MFA in dramaturgy from Stony Brook University. His research has been printed by *The Journal of Dramatic Theory and Criticism*, *The New England Theatre Journal*, and the *Texas Theatre Journal*.

DEANA NICHOLS received her doctorate in theatre history, theory, and literature from Indiana University. Her dissertation, "Scottish Theatre in the Age of Devolution," explores the intersection between contemporary Scottish theatre and politics, from the 1997 devolution referendum to the 2014 independence referendum. Her article "'Only of Scottish Interest': 7:84's Devolution Trilogy" was published in the *International Journal of Scottish Theatre and Screen*.

ALEX N. VERMILLION is a genderqueer dramaturg, writer, and editor who graduated from the University of Utah with honors in English and a minor in theatre studies. Alex is the assistant dramaturg on *The Two Noble Kinsmen* for the Oregon Shakespeare Festival's *Play on!* project.

SARAH WYMAN holds a BA in English and American literature from Brown University, an MA in English and creative writing from Hollins University, and a PhD in comparative literature from the University of North Carolina at Chapel Hill. She also earned a certificate in French literature from L'Institut d'Études Françaises d'Avignon. She teaches comparative literature at SUNY New Paltz and has taught courses in twentieth-century US poetry, gender studies, and African American women's literature at the University of Konstanz in southern Germany.

www.ingramcontent.com/pod-product-compliance
Lightning Source LLC
LaVergne TN
LVHW050336120926
847717LV00020B/107